Global Democracy

Democracy is increasingly seen as the only legitimate form of government, but few people would regard international relations as governed
according to democratic principles. Can this lack of global democracy
be justified? Which models of global politics should contemporary
democrats endorse and which should they reject? What are the most
promising pathways to global democratic change? To what extent does
the extension of democracy from the national to the international level
require a radical rethinking of what democratic institutions should be?
This book answers these questions by providing a sustained dialogue
between scholars of political theory, international law and empirical
social science. By presenting a broad range of views by prominent
scholars, it offers an in-depth analysis of one of the key challenges of
our century: globalizing democracy and democratizing globalization.

DANIELE ARCHIBUGI is Research Director at the Italian National
Research Council and Professor of Innovation, Governance and Public
Policy at Birkbeck, University of London.

MATHIAS KOENIG-ARCHIBUGI is Senior Lecturer in Global Politics
in the Department of Government and the Department of International Relations at the London School of Economics and Political
Science.

RAFFAELE MARCHETTI is Assistant Professor in International
Relations in the Faculty of Political Science and School of Government
at LUISS Guido Carli University, Rome.

T0384779

Global Democracy

Normative and Empirical Perspectives

Edited by

Daniele Archibugi, Mathias Koenig-Archibugi
and Raffaele Marchetti

CAMBRIDGE
UNIVERSITY PRESS

CAMBRIDGE UNIVERSITY PRESS
Cambridge, New York, Melbourne, Madrid, Cape Town,
Singapore, São Paulo, Delhi, Tokyo, Mexico City

Cambridge University Press
The Edinburgh Building, Cambridge CB2 8RU, UK

Published in the United States of America by
Cambridge University Press, New York

www.cambridge.org
Information on this title: www.cambridge.org/9780521174985

© Cambridge University Press 2012

First published 2012

Printed in the United Kingdom at the University Press, Cambridge

A catalogue record for this publication is available from the British Library

Library of Congress Cataloging-in-Publication Data

Global democracy : normative and empirical perspectives / edited by Daniele
Archibugi, Mathias Koenig-Archibugi, Raffaele Marchetti.
    p.   cm.
  ISBN 978-0-521-19784-7 (Hardback) – ISBN 978-0-521-17498-5
(Paperback)
  1. Democracy. 2. Democratization. 3. Globalization. I. Archibugi,
Daniele. II. Koenig-Archibugi, Mathias. III. Marchetti, Raffaele.
  JC423.G585 2011
  321.8–dc23

                                                              2011018895

ISBN 978-0-521-19784-7 Hardback
ISBN 978-0-521-17498-5 Paperback

Contents

Figures

Tables

Notes on contributors

DANIELE ARCHIBUGI is a Research Director at the Italian National Research Council in Rome, and Professor of Innovation, Governance and Public Policy at Birkbeck, University of London. He works on innovation and on the political theory of international relations. He has worked at the universities of Sussex, Rome, Cambridge, London School of Economics and Harvard. In June 2006 he was appointed Honorary Professor at the University of Sussex. He is an adviser to the European Union, the Council of Europe, the Organisation for Economic Co-operation and Development, several United Nations agencies and various national governments. He has led many research projects for the European Commission and other international organisations. He has co-edited *Cosmopolitan Democracy* (with David Held, 1995), *Re-imagining Political Community* (with David Held and Martin Koehler, 1998), *Filosofi per la pace* (with Franco Voltaggio, 1999), and has edited *Debating Cosmopolitics* (2003). His latest book, *A Global Commonwealth of Citizens: Toward Cosmopolitan Democracy* was published in 2008.

B.S. CHIMNI is a Professor of International Law, Centre for International Legal Studies, School of International Studies, Jawaharlal Nehru University, New Delhi. He is the former Vice Chancellor of W.B. National University of Juridical Sciences, Kolkata. He has held visiting positions at Brown, Harvard, Cambridge, York and Tokyo universities. He has delivered several prestigious lectures including the Eighth Grotius Lecture at the Centennial Meeting of the American Society of International Law in Washington and the First Barbara-Harrell Bond Lecture at the Refugee Studies Centre, Oxford University. His central research interest is to elaborate in association with a group of likeminded scholars a critical third world approach to international law (TWAIL). His areas of research interest are international economic law, international refugee law and international legal theory. Among his books are: *The Third World and International Legal Order: Law, Politics and Globalisation* (co-edited with Antony Anghie, Karen Mickelson and Obiora Okafor, 2003), *International Refugee Law: A Reader* (2000) and *International Law and World Order: A Critique of Contemporary Approaches* (1993).

THOMAS CHRISTIANO is Professor of Philosophy and Law, Department of Philosophy, University of Arizona. He is Associate Director of the Center for the Study of the Philosophy of Freedom at the University of Arizona. He has been a visiting fellow at the Princeton University Center for Human Values, the Australian National University, All Souls College, Oxford, and the National Humanities Center. He writes on issues in distributive justice, political authority, human rights and global justice. He has written about the philosophical foundations of democracy and democratic institutions in *The Constitution of Equality* (2008) and *The Rule of the Many: Fundamental Issues in Democratic Theory* (1996). He is currently working on a book about the foundations of egalitarianism and on projects on the legitimacy of international institutions and on the nature of the human right to democracy.

RICHARD A. FALK is Albert G. Milbank Professor of International Law and Practice, Emeritus, at Princeton University where he taught for forty years. He is currently Research Professor, Global Studies, University of California, Santa Barbara. He is also currently directing a project on 'Climate Change, Human Security, and Democracy' and serves as Chair of the Nuclear Age Peace Foundation. He has been a major contributor to the world order literature for several decades. His books include: *A Study of Future Worlds* (1975), *Predatory Globalization: A Critique* (1999), *Religion and Humane Global Governance* (2001), *The Costs of War: International Law, the UN, and World Order after Iraq* (2007) and *Achieving Human Rights* (2008).

ANDREAS FOLLESDAL is Professor of Political Philosophy at the Norwegian Centre for Human Rights, Faculty of Law, University of Oslo. He publishes in the field of political philosophy with a focus on issues of international political theory, federalism, multi-level governance and human rights, particularly as they arise in the wake of changes in Europe. He is Founding Series Editor of Themes in European Governance, of Contemporary European Politics and, with Geir Ulfstein, of Studies on Human Rights Conventions, all with Cambridge University Press. Among his books are: *Political Theory and the European Constitution* (edited with Lynn Dobson, 2005); *Real World Justice: Grounds, Principles, Human Rights Standards and Institutions* (edited with Thomas Pogge, 2005).

BRUNO S. FREY is Professor for Economics at the University of Zurich, Distinguished Professor of Behavioural Science at the Warwick Business School at the University of Warwick, UK, and Research Director of the Centre for Research in Economics, Management and the Arts, Switzerland. He received honorary doctorates in economics from the universities of St Gallen (Switzerland, 1998), Gothenburg (Sweden, 1998), the Free University of Brussels (Belgium, 2009) and the University of Aix-en-Provence/Marseille (France, 2010). Among his books are: *The New Democratic Federalism for Europe: Functional, Overlapping and Competing Jurisdictions* (with Reiner Eichenberger, 1999), *Happiness and Economics* (with Alois Stutzer, 2002), *Dealing with Terrorism: Stick or Carrot?* (2004), and *Happiness: A Revolution in Economics* (2008).

CAROL C. GOULD is Professor of Philosophy at Hunter College and Professor in the Doctoral Programs in Philosophy and Political Science at The Graduate Center, The City University of New York, where she also directs the Center for Global Ethics and Politics at the Ralph Bunche Institute. She is Editor of the *Journal of Social Philosophy* and Executive Director of the Society for Philosophy and Public Affairs. Gould is the author of *Marx's Social Ontology* (1978), *Rethinking Democracy* (Cambridge University Press, 1988) and *Globalizing Democracy and Human Rights* (Cambridge University Press, 2004), which won the David Easton Award from the Foundations of Political Theory Section of the American Political Science Association. She has edited or co-edited seven books, including *Women and Philosophy* (1976) and *Cultural Identity and the Nation-State* (2001), and has published numerous articles in social and political philosophy, feminist theory, philosophy of law and applied ethics.

MATHIAS KOENIG-ARCHIBUGI is Senior Lecturer in Global Politics in the Department of Government and the Department of International Relations at the London School of Economics and Political Science. His research is on global health governance, international labour standards and other areas of global policy making, and on the democratization of global politics. His articles have been published in the *European Journal of International Relations*, *International Organization*, *Philosophy and Public Affairs* and other journals. He is the co-editor of *Global Governance and Public Accountability* (with David Held, 2005) and *New Modes of Governance in the Global System* (with Michael Zürn, 2006).

KATE MACDONALD is a Lecturer in the School of Social and Political Sciences at the University of Melbourne, having held previous positions at the London School of Economics and Political Science, the Australian National University and Oxford University. Among her publications are: 'Non-Electoral Accountability in Global Politics: Strengthening Democratic Control within the Global Garment Industry' (with Terry Macdonald, *European Journal of International Law* 2006), 'Globalising Justice within Coffee Supply Chains? Fair Trade, Starbucks and the Transformation of Supply Chain Governance' (*Third World Quarterly* 2007), 'Democracy in a Pluralist Global Order: Corporate Power and Stakeholder Representation' (with Terry Macdonald, *Ethics and International Affairs* 2010) and *Fair Trade, Corporate Accountability and Beyond: Experiments in Globalizing Justice* (co-editor with Shelley Marshall, 2010).

TERRY MACDONALD is a Lecturer in the School of Political and Social Inquiry at Monash University. She has worked previously as a Research Fellow at the Centre for Applied Philosophy and Public Ethics at the Australian National University, and as a Junior Research Fellow and Lecturer in Politics at Merton College, Oxford University. Her publications on the topic of global democracy include the book *Global Stakeholder Democracy: Power and Representation Beyond Liberal States* (2008) and a few papers co-authored with Kate Macdonald.

RAFFAELE MARCHETTI is Assistant Professor in International Relations in the Faculty of Political Science and School of Government at LUISS Guido Carli University, Rome. His research interest concerns international political theory and global politics, especially global democracy and civil society. He was Scientific Coordinator of FP6 Strep project *SHUR. Human Rights in Conflicts: The Role of Civil Society.* He is the author of *Global Democracy: For and Against. Ethical Theory, Institutional Design, and Social Struggles* (2008) and *Manuale di politica internazionale* (with Franco Mazzei and Fabio Petito, 2010), and the co-editor of *European Union and Global Democracy* (with Davorka Vidovic, 2009), *Civil Society, Ethnic Conflicts, and the Politicization of Human Rights* (with Nathalie Tocci, 2011) and *Contemporary Political Agency: Theory and Practice* (with Bice Maiguashca, forthcoming). He is currently working on a manuscript on *Models and Scenarios of Global Politics.*

TIM MURITHI is Head of the Transitional Justice in Africa Programme at the Institute for Justice and Reconciliation, in Cape Town, South Africa. He has also held positions at the Institute for Security Studies in Addis Ababa; the Department of Peace Studies, University of Bradford, UK; the Centre for Conflict Resolution, University of Cape Town; and the United Nations Institute for Training and Research (UNITAR), in Geneva, Switzerland. He has also served as a consultant to the African Union. He is the author of *The Ethics of Peacebuilding* (2009) and *The African Union: Pan-Africanism, Peacebuilding and Development* (2005), and editor of *Towards a Union Government of Africa: Challenges and Opportunities* (2008) and co-editor of *The African Union and Its Institutions* (2008).

JONAS TALLBERG is Professor of Political Science at Stockholm University. His primary research interests are global and European governance, with a particular focus on institutional design, change and effects. He is the author of *European Governance and Supranational Institutions: Making States Comply* (2003) and *Leadership and Negotiation in the European Union* (Cambridge University Press, 2006), and co-editor of *Transnational Actors in Global Governance: Patterns, Explanations and Implications* (2010), as well as articles in journals such as *International Organization, International Studies Quarterly, European Journal of International Relations* and *Global Governance*. He currently leads a research project on transnational actor participation in global governance.

ANDERS UHLIN is Professor of Political Science at Lund University. His main research interests are in comparative and international politics, with a special focus on processes of democratization, civil society activism and transnational relations. He is the author of *Post-Soviet Civil Society* (2006) and *Indonesia and the 'Third Wave of Democratization'* (1997) and has co-edited *Legitimacy Beyond the State?* (with Eva Erman, 2010) and *Transnational Activism in Asia* (with Nicola Piper, 2004). His articles have appeared in journals such as *Cooperation and Conflict, Democratization, Europe-Asia Studies, Global Governance, International Political Science Review* and *Third World Quarterly*.

Acknowledgements

The editors would like to thank the reviewers for Cambridge University Press for helpful comments and suggestions, the editorial team at the Press – particularly John Haslam, Josephine Lane and Carrie Parkinson – for their supportive and efficient handling of the whole project, and Joanna Pyke for her impressively thoughtful and thorough copy-editing of the book.

1 Introduction
Mapping global democracy

Daniele Archibugi, Mathias Koenig-Archibugi and Raffaele Marchetti

Until twenty years ago, very few international relations (IR) textbooks paid any attention to the problem of democracy across borders. If the word 'democracy' was mentioned at all (and sometimes it was not), it referred to how domestic regimes could affect national foreign policy behaviour, rather than the possibility of shaping global society or even international organizations (IOs) in accordance with the values and rules of democracy. When IR scholars started to be interested in the European Community, they usually saw it as a peculiar IO and neglected its embryonic democratic aspects. With rare exceptions, treatises on democratic theory mirrored this lack of interest and largely ignored the international dimensions of democracy. It is notable that even David Held, who played such a key role in placing the relationship between globalization and democracy on the intellectual agenda of the 1990s, had not yet addressed the issue in the first edition (1987) of his widely read *Models of Democracy*. In sum, the possibility of globalizing democracy was debated among people involved in political advocacy, such as the world federalists, but it attracted little scholarly attention.

Over the past twenty years, the intellectual landscape has changed considerably. Of course, many remain unconvinced that democracy can be applied beyond states, and regard the idea of a global democracy as an unachievable dream (Dahl 1999) or, worse, think that its advocates are barking to the moon (Dahrendorf 2001). But in spite of harsh dismissals by some authoritative democratic theorists, the issue can no longer be ignored. The seeds planted by scholars such as Richard Falk, David Held, Jürgen Habermas and Ulrich Beck have grown. Many recent handbooks in international relations and democratic theory discuss the issue of democracy beyond borders, and a new generation of scholars has developed the theme of democracy beyond borders in imaginative and sophisticated ways.

There are several good historical reasons that explain why the intellectual mood has changed so much and in a relatively short period of time. On the one hand, democracy has become widely, albeit not universally, accepted as the only way to legitimize political power; on the other hand, people around the world have become increasingly sensitive to global interdependencies – 'globalization' has become a ubiquitous catchword. Many supporters of democracy are increasingly keen and often optimistic about the possibility of extending their preferred system of governance to the global level. As it has often been said, the completion of the decolonization process, the end of the Cold War, and democratization processes in central and eastern Europe and in many countries of the global South, have all been historical events that provided a new impetus to the search for new and more progressive political scenarios. The momentous changes of the 1990s boosted interest in global democracy not only among scholars but also in old institutions such as the Inter-Parliamentary Union, whose 'Universal Declaration on Democracy' of 1997 boldly states that '[d]emocracy must also be recognised as an international principle, applicable to international organisations and to States in their international relations' (Inter-Parliamentary Union 1997). On 8 June 2011, the European Parliament asked the Council of the European Union (EU) 'to advocate the establishment of a UNPA [United Nations Parliamentary Assembly] within the UN system in order to increase the democratic nature, the democratic accountability and the transparency of global governance and to allow for greater public participation in the activities of the UN' (European Parliament 2011).

The justification, form, possibility and limits of a democratically organized global order are now studied by scholars from a variety of disciplinary backgrounds, especially normative political theory, international law and empirical social sciences. Philosophers and political theorists focus on the justifiability of global democracy and on the institutional implications of fundamental values. Political scientists and international relations specialists, on the other hand, examine to what extent global politics is moving beyond the so-called Westphalian model and what forces may be promoting or hindering the emergence of more democratic forms of international and transnational governance. In principle, normative theorists may acknowledge that work on empirical conditions is relevant to their aims, and empirically oriented scholars may acknowledge that exploring the reasons for democratic transformations of current international structures is an important task. But, in practice, normative and empirical scholars are often unaware of each other's work.

This book presents new scholarship on the theme of global democracy. It aims to be a bridge between different research communities and a vehicle for advancing the research programme on global democracy through cross-disciplinary dialogue. It consists of chapters that focus on normative questions and institutional models related to global democracy as well as chapters that examine the conditions of, and paths to, global democracy, including the exploration of embryonic forms of global democratic governance. In this introduction we provide a general background to the debate, we map various forms of global democracy considered by a number of scholars, we give a brief overview of various political, legal and social processes that may, or already do, contribute to the development of democratic governance beyond individual states, and we provide an overview of the rest of the volume.

The relationship between supranational governance and democracy

Advocacy of global democracy is based on the premise that forms of supranational governance can be combined with forms of democracy.[1] However, the relationship between supranational governance and democracy has been tense in theory as well as in practice. Among political thinkers, support both for democracy and for some kind of supranational union experienced a marked increase from the seventeenth and eighteenth centuries, but the two political projects did not always co-exist harmoniously. Authors such as Emeric Crucé (1590–1648) and the abbé de Saint-Pierre (1658–1743), for instance, argued that the elimination of war required a supranational authority to which states could appeal and envisaged a union with coercive powers provided by an international army composed of forces supplied by the member states. According to Crucé and Saint-Pierre, such a union would not only have guaranteed peace between states, but also reinforced the power that sovereigns had on their subjects. It can be said that they proposed to achieve peace at the expense of democracy (Archibugi 1992, 299). On the other hand, many of the growing number of advocates of democracy were wary of forms of supranational political organization. This attitude was to a significant extent due to the belief that democracy could flourish only on a small scale. Jean-Jacques Rousseau (1762/2008) not only

---

[1] We define 'governance' broadly, as the creation and implementation of rule systems that facilitate the coordination and cooperation of social actors and determine the distribution of the costs and benefits of collective action. Governance may, but need not, be provided by a 'government'. See Koenig-Archibugi and Zürn (2006).

maintained that 'the larger the State, the less the liberty' (61), but he also argued that, from a democratic perspective, 'the union of several towns in a single city is always bad, and that, if we wish to make such a union, we should not expect to avoid its natural disadvantages. It is useless to bring up abuses that belong to great States against one who desires to see only small ones' (92). Riley (1973) points out that, even if Rousseau took seriously projects to establish national and international federations, 'his affection for the small and isolated republic always overcame his federalism' (11).[2] In a similar vein, many so-called anti-federalists objected to the proposed Constitution of the United States mainly on the grounds that a continental government would have threatened republican liberties and self-government.

Subsequent historical experiences provided some support to the view of a tension between democracy and IO. The German Bund, for instance, which lasted from 1815 to 1866, may have contributed to managing tensions among its member states; but its Diet's legal authority to restore order within member states, even without a request of the government concerned, was used to put down by armed force several democratic uprisings (Forsyth 1981, 51). Various political scientists argue that institutionalized cooperation among established *democratic* states impairs the quality of democracy. For instance, 40 years ago Karl Kaiser (1971) noted that '[t]he intermeshing of decision-making across national frontiers and the growing multinationalization of formerly domestic issues are inherently incompatible with the traditional framework of democratic control' (706). Klaus Dieter Wolf (1999) points out that autonomy-seeking governments may pursue a strategy of 'de-democratization by internationalization', which can be seen as a 'new *raison d'état*' in an era of globalization and democratic government. Empirically, it has been shown that at times governments use international institutions to gain influence in the domestic political arena and to overcome internal opposition to their preferred policies, although the democratic implications of such an outcome are open to debate (Koenig-Archibugi 2004).

The pessimistic view of the relationship between democracy and supranational governance has been countered in various ways. For instance, it has been argued that, while IOs may occasionally be used to suppress or circumvent democracy, more often than not they help

[2] Among modern authors, the topic of size and democracy has been discussed in most depth by Robert Dahl, whose work of the early 1970s included a very valuable analysis of the extension of democracy beyond nation-state and of 'world democracy' (Dahl 1970, Dahl and Tufte 1973).

countries to establish and preserve democratic institutions. For instance, it has been shown that a country's membership in a regional organization with mostly democratic member states increases significantly the likelihood of a successful transition to, and consolidation of, democracy in that country (Pevehouse 2005). Other authors maintain that, even in well-established democracies, multilateral institutions can enhance the quality of democratic politics, as they can help limit the power of special interests, protect individual rights and improve the quality of democratic deliberation (Keohane et al. 2009).

Another response to the pessimistic interpretation of the relationship between democracy and supranational governance, which is particularly relevant to the topic of this volume, is that pessimism may well be justified, but only in relation to those IOs where governments have a monopoly of representing their societies. In the pyramidal international unions advocated by authors such as Crucé and Saint-Pierre, membership is clearly limited to the sovereigns and does not include the subjects.[3] Even in IOs whose members are mainly or exclusively democratic states, often the model of representation still is what has been called 'executive multilateralism' (Zürn 2005): governments are the sole representatives of their societies in international negotiations and this gatekeeper role gives them very substantial informational and other advantages over other actors in shaping global policies. The democratic credentials of such organizations may be further weakened by the de facto or de jure ability of the more resourceful states to block the organization from taking decisions they do not like. But the key point of the 'optimists' is that these are not necessary consequences of supranational governance. Executive multilateralism is not the only viable model of IO, and other models are much better suited to reconcile governance beyond individual states with effective democratic control. Indeed, some cosmopolitan theorists go as far as asserting that the establishment of a democratic form of supranational governance may be the only way to realize democracy (Marchetti 2008).

---

[3] Claude-Henri Saint-Simon, who advocated a European-wide representative government, spelt out clearly the different implications of non-democratic and democratic forms of supranational governance: 'The first result of the constitution of the Abbé de Saint-Pierre (assuming that it were possible at all), would be to perpetuate the *status quo* in Europe at the moment of (sic) it was set up. Thenceforward the remnants of feudalism still in existence would become indestructible. Moreover, it would encourage the abuse of power by making the power of sovereigns more dangerous to their peoples, and depriving them of any resource against tyranny. In a word, this sham organization would be nothing but a mutual guarantee of princes to preserve their arbitrary power.' C.-H. Saint-Simon, 'The Reorganization of the European Community' (1814), cited by Archibugi (1992, 306).

This response has illustrious intellectual ancestors. On the problem of the size of the polity, for instance, James Madison famously turned the conventional wisdom on its head and argued that large republics were better equipped to resist the disintegrative effects of factions than smaller ones. Of course Madison did not suggest extending the union beyond the boundaries of the proposed United States. But several other authors developed proposals for polities that combine supranational authority structures with mechanisms of citizen representation that are not mediated by national governments, such as William Penn and John Bellers in the late seventeenth and early eighteenth centuries, and Claude-Henri Saint-Simon, James Lorimer and Johann Caspar Bluntschli in the nineteenth century (Suganami 1989, Archibugi 1992). While these projects certainly displayed a certain degree of Eurocentrism, their authors often saw them as stepping stones towards *global* peace and sometimes even as a way to prevent unjust wars waged by Christians against non-Christians (Aksu 2008).

In the twentieth century, various intellectual and political movements have advocated democratic forms of global governance from a cosmopolitan standpoint: the World Federalist Movement that was especially active in the United States during and after World War II (for a history see Wooley 1988), the work by Grenville Clark and Louis B. Sohn on *World Peace Through World Law* (1958), the *World Order Models Project* developed by Saul H. Mendlovitz, Richard Falk, Rajni Kothari and others, the International Network for a United Nations Second Assembly (INFUSA), the Conferences on A More Democratic United Nations (CAMDUN), the 'cosmopolitan democracy' project (Held 1995, Archibugi and Held 1995, Archibugi et al. 1998), recent calls for 'global stakeholder democracy' (Macdonald 2008), to mention only some of the most prominent.[4] To be sure, such intellectual and political projects were and are based on conceptions of global democracy that differed on very substantial grounds. Some of these differences are examined in the next section.

Forms of global democracy

What is common to all conceptions of global democracy is the vision of a system of global governance that is responsive and accountable to the preferences of the world's citizens and works to reduce political

---

[4] Also the growing interest in international ethics since the 1970s (Beitz 1979) has played an important role in stimulating debates about the extension of democracy beyond individual states. The relationship between global democracy and global distributive justice is examined by Caney (2004).

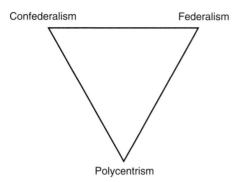

Figure 1.1 Ideal-typical forms of global democracy: confederalism, federalism and polycentrism

inequalities among them. This 'thin' understanding encompasses a wide range of more specific conceptions, blueprints and models. It is important to think systematically about the differences between these conceptions, as judgements of normative desirability, estimates of empirical feasibility and recommendations for political strategy may depend crucially on which conception is envisaged. Falk (1975), for instance, warned against the 'fallacy of premature specificity' with regard to the institutional features of new world order arrangements, and urged not to shift the focus from 'transitional processes' to the contemplation of a 'terminal model'. But he also noted that 'a proposed world order model requires a certain amount of concreteness to elicit support and facilitate understanding of what is being recommended' (152), and thus he presented a rather detailed plan for global institutions. Most discussions of global democracy either elaborate on the basic institutional features that are being envisaged or at least make implicit assumptions about them. Our mapping exercise is meant to facilitate the comparison of various conceptions, without any ambition to capture everything that is important about them.

We argue that most conceptions of global democracy differ principally in how close or distant they are from three ideal types, as shown in Figure 1.1.

The first ideal type is close to what authors have called 'confederation' (Archibugi 2008, 102–7), 'intergovernmental democratic multilateralism' (Marchetti 2008, 135), 'fair voluntary association among democratic states' (Christiano, this volume), or international democracy based on the communitarian principle (Bienen et al. 1998). Here we will call it democratic confederalism. Recently a variant of this type has gained political prominence in the form of calls for a 'league of democracies' or 'concert of democracies' (Carothers 2008). The key features of democratic confederalism are as follows: the constituent units are states that are democratically governed whose governments enjoy internal democratic legitimacy; these governments have exclusive rights to represent their citizens vis-à-vis other governments and the confederation as a whole, and citizens have no direct access to confederal institutions; member states participate in the confederation voluntarily and maintain the unilateral right to withdraw from it; decisions either require unanimity among all member states or, if votes are taken, they are based on the 'one state, one vote' principle (on 'state majoritarianism' see Buchanan 2004, 316–19); the confederation has no power of coercion of its own.

The second ideal type is what most authors would call a 'world government' or a 'world federation' (Archibugi 2008, 107–9; Marchetti 2008, 149–69). The key features of democratic federalism are as follows: there are several layers of state or state-like authority and citizens have a direct relationship of democratic authorization and accountability with each of them; elections to, and decisions in, federal institutions are guided by the principle 'one person, one vote', although this 'democratic' principle may be combined with 'federal' principles such as supermajority requirements and the overrepresentation of citizens from smaller constituent units; the federal level of authority (executive, legislative or judicial) usually has the final say on jurisdictional questions and has access to coercive power; secession from the federation is possible only in accordance with precise constitutional rules and is often subject to approval by federal institutions.

The third ideal type is more difficult to define. It is close to what has been variously identified as 'global governance' (Marchetti 2008, 139–42), 'global stakeholder democracy' (Macdonald 2008) and democracy under conditions of polycentric governance (Scholte 2008). We will call it democratic polycentrism.[5] The key features of democratic polycentrism are the following: in today's global space power is exercised not only by states but also by a myriad of non-state actors, such as companies, business associations, specialized IOs, non-governmental organizations (NGOs), social movements and networks of experts; these actors and sites of power can be democratized directly by linking them,

---

[5] The 'transnational discursive democracy' advocated by Dryzek (2006) may be considered an extreme variant of this type, as it unfolds in the communicative realm rather than in institutions and 'lacks formalized connection to binding collective decisions' (158).

through mechanisms of authorization and accountability, to those whose interests are more intensely affected by their activities; these mechanisms of authorization and accountability can be specific to particular non-state actors and sectoral networks rather than to overarching state-like political structures; these mechanisms do not need to take the form of electoral authorization and accountability, as long as effective control by the relevant stakeholder groups is ensured.

Apart from a general commitment to democratic principles, the commonalities between the proponents of different ideal types of global democracy are to a large extent based on what they tend to reject, on grounds of normative desirability or empirical feasibility. 'Confederalists' and 'federalists' tend to ignore or reject 'non-state' political authority. Confederalists and 'polycentrists' reject global concentration of power. Federalists and polycentrists reject traditional state sovereignty.

What we have presented are ideal types, and it should be emphasized that the forms of global democracy defended, criticized and/or empirically assessed by various authors working on these topics are usually more nuanced and complex. But confederalism, federalism and polycentrism delineate a conceptual space in which many of those more specific forms can be located. For instance, a prominent model of global democracy, 'cosmopolitan democracy' (Held 1995, Archibugi 2008), combines federal and confederal elements in an original synthesis. And Gould (2004 and this volume) emphasizes the role of regional supranational unions and non-territorial communities, which represents a combination of federal, confederal and polycentric dimensions.

Pathways to global democracy

Participants in the debate on global democracy are interested not only in its nature, its forms and its justification, but also in the question of how to get from here to there. This is not surprising, as many of the contributors to the intellectual debate on global democracy, including some of the contributors to this volume, also actively participate in various campaigns to promote its implementation in real life. But the question of which actors and processes do or may promote global democracy concerns not only its proponents. Critics of global democracy belong to various categories, such as those who think that it would be undesirable, those who think that trying to realize it would produce dangerous unintended consequences, and those who think that in all likelihood it would merely be a façade for the overwhelming power of the strongest states and groups. Unless they believe that no step towards global democracy is empirically possible,[6] such critics have no less reason to be aware of the forces and strategies that may promote it than its proponents.

In the following we discuss some of the processes that may increase the democratic quality of global politics. The first two sets of processes, social mobilization from below and the reform of IOs, have attracted much attention in recent years and are discussed in several chapters in this volume. The other two sets of processes are discussed less often in relation to global democratization, but deserve to be explored further: the expansion of supranational judiciary power, and 'cosmopolitan' changes *within* states.

Social mobilization from below

Global democracy involves greater political participation of individuals beyond the confines of their own states. The activities carried out by NGOs and other groups of activists are often independent from the agenda pursued by states (Keck and Sikkink 1998, Kaldor 2003). The participation of citizens can take different forms and motivations. Citizens may be mobilized because: (1) they have a sense of solidarity in relation to situations that are detached from their own lives, as happens in campaigns aimed at the protection of human rights in other parts of the world; (2) they feel that they have some common interests that are not faithfully represented by their governments and that transcend states' borders, as in the case of campaigns for environmental protection; (3) they perceive that there are specific problems that are better addressed by creating linkages across political communities; this may be the case when they organize specific interests that involve individuals on the basis of non-territorial affiliations (e.g., because they have common diseases, or because they are employed by the same multinational corporation, or because they are linked by a direct user–producer relationship). NGOs active in these three domains have grown in importance and have become more authoritative in global politics.

The participation of individuals in global politics may take a variety of forms. In principle, it may be fully organized and institutionalized, replicating at the world level the same channels of political representation existing in democratic states, in line with the federal view of global governance. In practice, it is usually voluntary and carried out by individuals without direct authorization or contact from their own states, in line with the polycentric view of global governance.

---

[6] This position is addressed by Koenig-Archibugi (2010).

According to proponents of global stakeholder democracy, NGOs and other non-state actors can be subject to mechanisms of democratic control and thus establish a polycentric system of global democracy (e.g., Macdonald 2008, and this volume; see also K. Macdonald and Frey, both this volume).

Reforming IOs

Several campaigns for the democratization of global politics target IOs and aim at triggering institutional reform. These campaigns have had some limited successes so far. IOs may be seen as promising starting points for global democracy because they incorporate in their own structure at least three core norms of democracy: the existence of formal treaties and charters, the publicity of acts, and formal equality among members. However, these norms do not allow us to regard existing IOs as democratic institutions, since they lack other fundamental features of democracy. This leads to two opposite views. On the one hand, there are those who argue that fundamental reasons prevent IOs from embodying basic norms of democracy (Dahl 1999, Christiano, this volume); on the other hand, there are those who argue that appropriate reforms may lead IOs to become democratic or, at least, more democratic (Held 1995, Archibugi 2008, Murithi, this volume). In what way would the reform of IOs contribute to the emergence of global democracy?

From the point of view of a confederal interpretation of global democracy, an IO can be democratic provided that its member countries are democratic. If there is a democratic deficit, this is not necessarily related to the structure of IOs, but rather to the nature of its members. Global democracy is therefore more an internal problem than a problem of IOs. This confederal perspective may suggest that there is a contradiction between inclusiveness and democracy: as long as IOs include despotic as well as democratic countries, they can never be fully democratic.

An alternative view suggests that an IO could become more democratic even if it has autocratic as well as democratic member states (Archibugi 2008). This argument is based on the view that the internal regime does not necessarily condition the foreign behaviour of countries: democracies have often opposed progressive reforms in the United Nations (UN) and in other IOs, while non-democratic governments are sometimes open to introducing into the UN the democratic accountability that they are denying their subjects at home. Proponents of this view maintain, for instance, that Cuba has often expressed its support for direct participation of individuals in UN institutions, while the United States has preferred to maintain the current confederal arrangements. Proponents of cosmopolitan democracy argue that allowing a direct representation to the citizens of the world inside IOs will contribute to democratization in two ways (see Archibugi 2008). On the one hand, it would make the operation of these IOs more transparent, more accountable and more responsive to the needs of citizens. On the other hand, it would act as a powerful incentive towards democratization in those member countries that still have despotic governments. The most active ongoing campaign in favour of global democracy aims to create a new directly elected world parliamentary assembly (Strauss 2007, Archibugi 2008, Marchetti 2008). Such an assembly would fit neither with confederalism (since it would be aimed at providing a voice to individuals independently from their own governments) nor with federalism (since it would lack sufficient powers to control executive and judicial powers in world politics).

While increased mobilization by activists and citizens and the reform of IOs are often discussed as routes towards global democratization, other processes may offer a significant contribution as well. We would like to mention only two of them.

Global judicial power

A new climate favourable to an active participation of citizens beyond their borders is also shaped by a rising global judicial power. Global judicial power is still in its infancy and it is far from uniform (Slaughter 2004). Two major components can be singled out. The first is the activity of *national* judges who are more active in terms of investigating cases beyond the boundaries of their own countries. Globalization is shaping crime, amongst many other things, and national judges investigate more frequently trans-border financial frauds and mafia organizations. But national judges have also become bolder in addressing issues that were traditionally the prerogatives of governments, such as genocide and major violations of human rights. While in several cases there is significant trans-border collaboration in investigation and prosecution, in other cases national judges act using legal procedures that interfere with national sovereignty.

The second component of the rising global judicial power is represented by *international* courts. The number of international courts is constantly increasing: according to some estimates, today there are more than forty active international courts (Cassese 2009). Some of these courts, such as the International Court of Justice (ICJ), are very old. A relatively recent one, the International Criminal Court (ICC), has already had a significant impact on world politics and public opinion. Others have much more modest aims and concentrate on international arbitration or administrative issues.

The combination of national courts acting beyond their borders and international courts may represent an increasingly important constraint on the power of governments. To the extent that the rule of law and the existence of effective checks and balances are important dimensions of democratic governance, the 'judicialization' of world affairs may be interpreted as a component of a broader trend towards its democratization. It should, however, be noted that the custodians of the rising global rule of law are not directly associated with a global *demos*. On the contrary, there is a growing distance between the development of a global rule of law on the one hand and of a global rule of the people on the other. There is a basic difference between the judicial institutions acting within state jurisdictions and the new global judicial power: within national borders, judicial power is always expected to come to terms with the legislative and executive powers and in the long term cannot evolve independently from them. In the global arena, on the contrary, judicial power cannot rely on an executive power that will enforce its decisions, nor can it rely on democratic legislative institutions.

What is happening today in the global arena has strong resemblances with the way in which the power of the people and independent judicial institutions have evolved within states:[7] we know that the two authorities developed in an uneven and combined way. But in the long run the evolution of the rule of law and of the rule of the people reinforced each other. The supporters of global democracy argue that a similar development is occurring today in the global arena. On the opposite side, the critics argue that giving too much power to judicial institutions detached from the power of the people risks creating a new judicial despotic rule.

The machinery of these new international judicial bodies is far from uniform. Competences and procedures are very dissimilar. This makes it difficult to associate them with any single ideal-typical form of global democracy that has been presented above. In a sense, the new judicial powers are promoting polycentrism since they are adding sites of authority and legitimacy and creating additional checks and balances vis-à-vis executive powers. But the existence of an independent judicial power is also an integral component of a federal system. Finally, most

[7] See Goodin (2010) for a similar argument with regard to the accountability of power-holders.

international judicial institutions, including the ICJ and the ICC, have been created by intergovernmental agreements that are a typical feature of confederalism.

Changes within states

Even the most fervent partisans of global democracy are aware that states are, and in all likelihood will continue to be, the most important players in the political arena. Although states act principally in defence of a territory and of their citizens, they may implement a variety of policies that may contribute to or obstruct global democracy. Some of these actions reflect states' foreign policy. The willingness to obey international law and to participate in the working of IOs contributes to a world climate that it is also conducive to expanding the values and norms of democracy.

But states may contribute to global democracy in two other key dimensions. The first is by facilitating the social mobilization process that we discussed above, and specifically by allowing their own citizens to participate more directly in world politics. They may promote polycentrism, simply by allowing their citizens to form associations and networks with other citizens abroad. Or they may strengthen the democratic quality of existing confederal arrangements – for instance, by allowing a greater control of parliaments over foreign policy, or through more innovative forms; some activists have, for example, suggested that one or two of the five ambassadors nominated by each state to the UN could be elected by the citizens (Strauss 2007).

Individual states may also contribute to global democracy by expanding the domestic franchise in line with cosmopolitan principles. The most straightforward reform consists in granting greater rights to immigrants. In all countries aliens have more duties (such as paying taxes) than rights (such as electoral franchise). There are already some significant experiments in which immigrants are granted political rights, such as voting for local governments (Cabrera 2010). These efforts could be expanded through the implementation of more friendly policies to accommodate immigrants and to enlarge their rights, generating a cosmopolitan atmosphere within their borders. A more ambitious and less likely expansion of the franchise would consist in granting to non-resident non-citizens the right to elect a number of representatives in national legislatures, on the basis that those non-resident non-citizens are affected by the decisions of the state and are entitled to some form of representation (Koenig-Archibugi forthcoming).

Overview of this book

The volume begins with a critical review of three dominant models of global democracy, as they emerge from current debates and from several contributions to this book. Raffaele Marchetti (this volume) argues that the delimitation of political agency – the so-called issue of the (global) *demos* – is crucial and preliminary to any discussion about global democracy. He shows that the three models differ in their answers to this fundamental question, adopting the principles of political community, stakeholdership and all-inclusion respectively, and that they differ with regard to the institutional designs that they envisage, supporting regional/universal multilateralism, hybrid networks and federal integration respectively. Marchetti concludes that the cosmo-federalist model of global democracy is the most consistent with the principle of political participation.

Chapter 3, by Terry Macdonald, addresses a criticism that Marchetti and others have raised against her vision of a global stakeholder democracy: that it violates the principle of political equality that is central to the democratic project, since it makes participatory entitlements dependent on being 'affected' by particular decisions rather than on membership in an inclusive political community. Macdonald counters such criticisms by changing the premise on which they are based: instead of asking which democratic framework is the most just one, she asks which democratic framework is the most legitimate one. In her approach to the question, what makes claims legitimate is not whether they conform to a philosophical theory, but whether they are made by actually-existing political actors against other actually-existing political actors. Macdonald argues that the political exclusions permitted by global stakeholder democracy qualify as legitimate in this sense, as exclusions do not violate egalitarian legitimacy when they do not result from denying actually-voiced political demands for inclusion.

Chapter 4, by Thomas Christiano, identifies some of the problems arising from the application of democratic standards to international institutions. Christiano examines two kinds of institutional system that might be thought to have democratic legitimacy: one based on the idea of a fair voluntary association of democratic states and the other based on global democratic institutions of the kind supported by Marchetti and other contributors to this volume. Christiano argues that neither system is attainable for the foreseeable future, and finds there is no reasonable solution yet to the normative impasse he has identified.

Andreas Follesdal, in Chapter 5, addresses some of these concerns in his criticism of arguments that the democratization of multi-level governance is impossible and/or unnecessary. Follesdal makes an argument in favour of democratic, majoritarian decision-making procedures, by drawing in part on the debate about the alleged need for a more democratic EU. He also considers some of the weaknesses of alternatives to majoritarian electoral democracy, namely 'networks' and 'participatory' democratic arrangements.

Like Follesdal, Carol C. Gould (Chapter 6) stresses the important role of the EU and other regional experiments. She highlights some problems with unitary conceptions of global democracy, such as the one proposed by Marchetti in Chapter 2, and shows why theorists of transnational democracy need to consider more carefully the regional dimension as well as the domains formed by transnational communities that crisscross territorial boundaries and by non-state actors such as transnational corporations.

The global implications of regional experiences play an important role also in Chapter 7. Drawing on the historical examples represented by the EU and the African Union, Tim Murithi suggests the application of a similar integration model to the UN. Noting the growing irrelevance of the UN in core issues of world politics, he proposes an ambitious set of reforms that go well beyond the proposals that are currently discussed by governments in diplomatic forums. Drawing on federalist blueprints for global reform, Murithi argues for a World Federation of Nations with a variety of reformed and new organs, and explores the possibility of introducing such reforms by changing the UN Charter.

Chapter 8, by Bruno S. Frey, examines the other domain stressed by Gould – that is, the web of transnational communities that criss-cross territorial boundaries. Frey argues that the development of such non-territorial communities should be promoted and accelerated. In his chapter he formulates two wide-ranging proposals. The first aims at creating flexible political units in which citizens can participate voluntarily and jointly finance the provision of public goods they care most about. In this vision, political units would no longer be constrained geographically. The second proposal aims to introduce and promote flexible forms of citizenship; this entails on the one hand the introduction of temporary, multiple and partial forms of national citizenship and on the other hand the creation and strengthening of citizenship in various types of organizations apart from states, such as the associations discussed by Kate Macdonald in Chapter 10.

The chapters mentioned so far present an array of institutional blueprints, which are variously inspired by federal, confederal or polycentric design principles. The next set of chapters focuses on the possibility that such institutional changes could be realized. Chapter 9, by Mathias

Koenig-Archibugi, is especially relevant to federal blueprints such as those defended by Marchetti and Murithi, but also the cases of regional integration considered by Gould and Follesdal, as it examines how experiences of democratization at the level of individual states can help us to understand the empirical conditions for, and possible paths towards, global democratization. He notes that scepticism about the possibility of global democracy may be based on the belief that the world as a whole lacks the conditions that have allowed democracy to emerge in some states, notably cultural heterogeneity, economic development, relatively low levels of inequality, small or moderate size of the polity, and established statehood. Koenig-Archibugi applies 'fuzzy-set qualitative comparative analysis' to 126 cases of democratic transition within states between 1945 and 2009, and finds that none of those conditions were necessary for democracy to emerge. He concludes by sketching some of the paths through which democracy could emerge at the transnational level.

One of the paths identified by Koenig-Archibugi is based on the mobilization of, and pressure by, civil society actors. Chapter 10, by Kate Macdonald, and Chapter 11, by Jonas Tallberg and Anders Uhlin, analyse the contribution of civil society actors to global democratization from two different and complementary perspectives: Macdonald examines how these actors can increase democratic accountability in 'pluralist' power structures and specifically global supply chains and transnational corporations, while Tallberg and Uhlin examine how they can increase democratic accountability and participation in international institutions. Macdonald argues that democracy should be defined in terms of principles of autonomy and equality and that there is a range of institutional arrangements at the global level that may be consistent with such principles. She examines how the global garment industry is organized, and finds that power structures have a 'pluralist' nature, as important aspects of the autonomy of workers are affected by a diffused, decentralized and heterogeneous set of actors and institutions. Her chapter shows how this pluralist power structure has generated a pluralist democratic response, which has had some success in constraining corporate power through democratic mechanisms. These mechanisms enhance transparency by identifying who holds power in global supply chains and publicly exposing abuses; they elicit and communicate the preferences of workers, mainly through intermediaries in developed countries in the context of so-called 'international solidarity campaigns'; and they enforce standards by threatening and applying sanctions against non-complying corporate actors, notably through consumer boycotts but also through broader reputational damage to company brands. Macdonald points to the achievement of such pluralistic democratizing mechanisms, but she also analyses their limitations.

Chapter 11, by Jonas Tallberg and Anders Uhlin, performs a similar task in relation to civil society involvement in international institutions and organizations. The normative criteria for assessing this involvement are accountability and participation, and the empirical analysis is conducted in two steps. First, Tallberg and Uhlin map the involvement of civil society organizations in international institutions and how they hold both those institutions and states accountable. They find that this involvement is 'unequal, select, circumscribed, and shallow'. Second, they examine the democratic credentials of civil society organizations themselves, and find that they are often weak. Despite these sobering findings, Tallberg and Uhlin also note that the expanded participation and strengthened accountability over the past two decades are steps in a process of democratization and thus provide some grounds for cautious optimism.

B.S. Chimni (Chapter 12) offers a more sceptical analysis of the relationship between democracy and global capitalism than Kate Macdonald, as his is based on a critique of liberal internationalism. If, as Marxists argue, democracy is a congenial political system for capitalism, will global democracy be the most appropriate political system for global capitalism? To prevent this, the global democracy programme should be substantially revised and made clearly anti-capitalist. Chimni calls for an insurgent cosmopolitanism that can take into account non-Western models of modernity. According to Chimni, progressive reforms should not diminish the role of the state which, on the contrary, will be needed to counterbalance the transnational capitalist class.

Chapter 13, by Daniele Archibugi, presents a critical perspective on another pillar of the liberal internationalist approach examined in Marchetti's chapter: the 'theory of democratic peace', according to which democracies do not fight each other. Much of the debate has somehow assumed that a more satisfactory international society could be achieved through an 'internal leverage': an increase in the number of democratic regimes, it is argued, generates a more peaceful world. But another important leverage, the 'external leverage', is often ignored, namely the effects of enhanced participation in IOs on internal regimes and on the prevention of violent conflicts. The chapter argues that a strengthened international society, in which individuals, collective players and stakeholders have access to decision making, may have an important role in fostering democratization and democratic consolidation. At the same time, this could also provide an effective method for preventing violent conflicts.

Richard Falk (Chapter 14), who is an undisputed pioneer in the study and advocacy of global democracy, concludes the volume by summing up the debate and issuing several warnings on the future of the global democracy idea. He points out the danger of creating 'a utopian disconnect' between models of global democracy and a world that is still ruled by power politics. There is a need to link the analysis carried out in this book with the historical conditions of the twenty-first century, which combine impressive scientific, technological, social and political opportunities with recurrent environmental, humanitarian and military emergencies. Falk's appeal to apply global-democratic thought to the everyday reality of our epoch is at the same time an apt conclusion for our book and a good starting point for future work on the theory and practice of global democracy.

REFERENCES

Aksu, Esref. 2008. '"Perpetual Peace": A Project by Europeans for Europeans?', *Peace & Change: A Journal of Peace Research* 33, 3: 368–87.

Archibugi, Daniele. 1992. 'Models of International Organization in Perpetual Peace Projects', *Review of International Studies* 18, 5: 295–317.

  2008. *The Global Commonwealth of Citizens: Toward Cosmopolitan Democracy.* Princeton University Press.

Archibugi, Daniele, and David Held (eds.). 1995. *Cosmopolitan Democracy: An Agenda for a New World Order.* Cambridge, UK: Polity Press.

Archibugi, Daniele, David Held and Martin Köhler (eds.). 1998. *Re-Imagining Political Community: Studies in Cosmopolitan Democracy.* Cambridge, UK: Polity Press.

Beitz, Charles R. 1979. *Political Theory and International Relations.* Princeton University Press.

Bienen, Derk, Volker Rittberger and Wolfang Wagner. 1998. 'Democracy in the United Nations System: Cosmopolitan and Communitarian Principles', in Daniele Archibugi, David Held and Martin Köhler (eds.), *Re-Imagining Political Community: Studies in Cosmopolitan Democracy* (pp. 287–308). Cambridge, UK: Polity Press.

Buchanan, Allen. 2004. *Justice, Legitimacy, and Self-Determination: Moral Foundations for International Law.* Oxford University Press.

Cabrera, Luis. 2010. *The Practice of Global Citizenship.* Cambridge University Press.

Caney, Simon. 2004. *Justice Beyond Borders: A Global Political Theory.* Oxford University Press.

Carothers, Thomas. 2008. *Is a League of Democracies a Good Idea?* Washington, DC: Carnegie Endowment for International Peace.

Cassese, Sabino. 2009. *Il diritto globale. Giustizia e democrazia oltre lo stato.* Torino, Italy: Einaudi.

Dahl, Robert A. 1970. *After the Revolution? Authority in a Good Society.* New Haven, CT: Yale University Press.

1999. 'Can International Organisations Be Democratic? A Sceptic's View', in Ian Shapiro and Casiano Hacker-Cordón (eds.), *Democracy's Edges* (pp. 19–36). Cambridge University Press.

Dahl, Robert A., and Edward R. Tufte. 1973. *Size and Democracy.* Stanford University Press.

Dahrendorf, Ralf. 2001. *Dopo la democrazia.* Interview edited by Antonio Polito. Roma-Bari, Italy: Laterza.

Dryzek, John S. 2006. *Deliberative Global Politics: Discourse and Democracy in a Divided World.* Cambridge, UK: Polity Press.

European Parliament. 2011 (8 June). 'Recommendation to the Council on the 66th Session of the United Nations General Assembly'. Available at: http://www.europarl.europa.eu

Falk, Richard. 1975. *A Study of Future Worlds.* New York: The Free Press.

Forsyth, Murray. 1981. *Unions of States: The Theory and Practice of Confederation.* Leicester University Press.

Goodin, Robert E. 2010. 'Global Democracy: In the Beginning', *International Theory* 2, 2: 175–209.

Gould, Carol C. 2004. *Globalizing Democracy and Human Rights.* Cambridge University Press.

Held, David. 1987. *Models of Democracy.* Cambridge, UK: Polity Press.
  1995. *Democracy and the Global Order.* Cambridge, UK: Polity Press.

Inter-Parliamentary Union. 1997. 'Universal Declaration on Democracy'. Adopted by the Inter-Parliamentary Council at its 161st session, Cairo, 16 September. Available at: www.ipu.org/cnl-e/161-dem.htm

Kaiser, Karl. 1971. 'Transnational Relations as a Threat to the Democratic Process', *International Organization* 25, 3: 706–20.

Kaldor, Mary. 2003. *Global Civil Society: An Answer to War.* Cambridge, UK: Polity Press.

Keck, Margaret, and Kathryn Sikkink. 1998. *Activists Beyond Borders: Advocacy Networks in International Politics.* Ithaca, NY: Cornell University Press.

Keohane, Robert, Stephen Macedo and Andrew Moravcsik. 2009. 'Democracy-Enhancing Multilateralism', *International Organization* 63, 1: 1–31.

Koenig-Archibugi, Mathias. 2004. 'International Governance as New Raison d'État? The Case of the EU Common Foreign and Security Policy', *European Journal of International Relations* 10, 2: 147–88.
  2010. 'Is Global Democracy Possible?' *European Journal of International Relations.* Published online before print, 16 June 2010: doi: 10.1177/1354066110366056.
  Forthcoming. 'Fuzzy Citizenship in Global Society', *Journal of Political Philosophy.*

Koenig-Archibugi, Mathias, and Michael Zürn (eds.). 2006. *New Modes of Governance in the Global System: Exploring Publicness, Delegation and Inclusiveness.* Basingstoke, UK: Palgrave Macmillan.

Macdonald, Terry. 2008. *Global Stakeholder Democracy: Power and Representation Beyond Liberal States.* Oxford University Press.

Marchetti, Raffaele. 2008. *Global Democracy: For and Against. Ethical Theory, Institutional Design, and Social Struggles.* New York: Routledge.

Pevehouse, Jon C. 2005. *Democracy from Above: Regional Organizations and Democratization.* Cambridge University Press.

Riley, Patrick. 1973. 'Rousseau as a Theorist of National and International Federalism', *Publius* 3, 1: 5–18.

Rousseau, Jean Jacques. 1762/2008. *The Social Contract.* New York: Cosimo.

Scholte, Jan Aart. 2008. 'Reconstructing Contemporary Democracy', *Indiana Journal of Global Legal Studies* 15, 1: 305–50.

Slaughter, Anne-Marie. 2004. *A New World Order.* Princeton University Press.

Strauss, Andrew (ed.). 2007. 'Symposium: Envisioning a More Democratic Global System', *Widener Law Review* 13, 2: 1–446.

Suganami, Hidemi. 1989. *The Domestic Analogy and World Order Proposal.* Cambridge University Press.

Wolf, Klaus Dieter. 1999. 'The New Raison d'État as a Problem for Democracy in World Society', *European Journal of International Relations* 5, 3: 333–63.

Wooley, Wesley T. 1988. *Alternatives to Anarchy: American Supranationalism since World War II.* Indiana University Press.

Zürn, Michael. 2005. 'Global Governance and Legitimacy Problems', in David Held and Mathias Koenig-Archibugi (eds.), *Global Governance and Public Accountability* (pp. 136–63). Oxford, UK: Blackwell.

2 Models of global democracy
In defence of cosmo-federalism

Raffaele Marchetti

Which *demos* for (global) democracy?

The proper scope of the democratic system represents a core, yet still under-explored issue in political science. Too often political debates on democracy concentrated on the handling of the *kratos* rather than on the subject constituting the *demos*. From Plato to Rawls, the typical assumption has been that of the political community as a self-contained social enterprise (which often entailed its correlate of power politics towards foreigners). This autarchic assumption is, however, unsustainable in the current world. Today we are forced to reconsider the traditional boundaries of our political communities because of the phenomenon of intensified interdependence. The boundaries and accountability of public power are increasingly under scrutiny. One of the merits of the debate on global democracy is precisely that of having provoked a reassessment of a number of fundamental tenets of the democratic ideal itself, among which the scope of the *demos* is key.

When the democratic ideal is extended at the global level, the question of which constituency has to be taken into account and prioritized is obviously crucial insofar as conflicts on jurisdictional boundaries generate continuous controversies in current international affairs. If many are suffering the consequences of actions that cross national boundaries, who is entitled to be included in the decision-making procedure on those cross-national actions? Who is entitled to demand accountability for those decisions? Citizenship, political participation and accountability are intermingled notions that are put under strain at the international level by increasing interdependence. Finding a consistent reconceptualization of these notions that is more adequate to the current international reality requires tackling the issue of the

In addition to the co-editors and the contributors of this volume, I wish to thank Andrew Rehfeld for challenging comments on an earlier version of this paper.

Table 2.1 *Summary of the models of global democracy*

	Demos's scope	Democratic principle	Institutional design
Intergovernmentalism	(Inter)national *demoi*	Association	(Regional or universal) multilateralism
Global governance	Transnational *demoi*	Stakeholdership	Hybrid networks
Global polity	Global *demos*	All-inclusiveness	Federal integration

proper scope of democracy, here taken to be the core issue of the general theory of democracy.

For those who defend the idea of global democracy, the dilemma on jurisdictional boundaries is particularly important. Different justifications in support of the idea of global democracy have recently been formulated both in teleological (increased provision of security or welfare) and deontological (increased guarantee of autonomy) terms (Cabrera 2010). I have formulated a defence of such a project in consequentialist, agent-centred terms as a way to maximize individual freedom of choice via multilayered enfranchisement (Marchetti 2008a). However, my contention here is that, independent of the question of which justification is preferable and of how objections can be rebutted (and this chapter does not deal with this topic, but see Follesdal (this volume), we first need to address the fundamental issue of political agency: the so-called issue of the (global) *demos. Who* are we talking about when we discuss democracy beyond borders? Are we talking of many national or transnational *demoi* or just a single global *demos*? How should jurisdictional boundaries be legitimately drawn in order to avoid both democratic underrepresentation and overrepresentation of the relevant actors? The question on the scope of the democratic *demos* is preliminary, and indeed crucial in political terms, to any other normative question related to the benefits delivered or the internal procedures adopted by the democratic system.

This chapter critically surveys the main models of global democracy in the light of their differing criteria for determining the relevant *demos*, and defends the case for a non-exclusionary theory of global democracy. As an introduction to help the reader capture the tripartition at stake, I have set out above a table summarizing the three models (see Table 2.1). They roughly correspond to the three models outlined in Chapter 1 (Archibugi et al., this volume): confederalism, polycentrism and federalism, though the models presented here address different aspects of the global democracy conundrum (i.e., the scope of the *demos*, democratic principles, and institutional design). For each model, the chapter looks at the principles used to delineate political jurisdictions and subsequently at the design of public institutions. So as to be clear from the outset, the models here scrutinized are not representations of current institutional arrangements, but serve as blueprints for reforming them. They constitute normative exercises, which thus should not be confused with empirical descriptions, though they may at times mirror a number of characteristics of existing institutions.

The models of intergovernmentalism, global governance and global polity are examined in relation to the issue of inclusion and accordingly ranked in a normative order. While the chapter provides a clear normative hierarchy of the three models, this ranking should not, however, be understood as entailing a total rejection of the suboptimal models. Rather, the three models have to be seen in a complex and dynamic perspective, according to which they serve distinct valuable political objectives for different political spaces and time frames. In brief, my argument holds that while the models of universal multilateralism and global governance are important because they provide bottom-up recognition to significant political communities (be they national or transnational), they are insufficient for framing a genuinely inclusive democratic system if they are not integrated with, and subordinated to, an overarching top-down model of global polity (see Figure 2.1). This is an exercise in ideal political theory. Its arguments are therefore to be considered as providing absolute political principles for long-term political change. The model which is presented as the most consistent in democratic terms aims at precisely such long-term objectives. However, if a more pragmatic or non-ideal perspective is assumed (as is the case in other chapters in this volume: see, for instance, T. MacDonald, Christiano, and Gould), then the other suboptimal models regain political relevance, as legitimate intermediate or short-term guiding principles for the democratization of international affairs.

To guide the reader through the chapter, I would like to begin with a working definition of democracy: a political system is more or less democratic to the extent that it is characterized by non-exclusion from an entitlement to an equal share of public power. With reference to the discussion in this chapter, it is noteworthy to mention that this entitlement significantly entails the right to partake the authority to delineate jurisdictional sub-units. This may ultimately be justified by a consequentialist appeal to the maximization of general welfare based on the enhancement of individual freedom of choice via political enfranchisement (Marchetti 2008a). While examining the principal alternatives at stake, this chapter demonstrates that the most consistent way to link

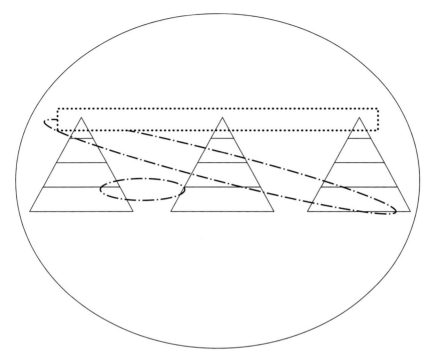

Figure 2.1 The ideal system of global democracy
Triangles: national *demoi*
Ellipses: transnational *demoi*
Rectangle: intergovernmental representation
Circle: global *demos*

ultimate principles to institutional design in democratic terms is
through an all-inclusive and cosmo-federalist model of global democracy. In sum, either democracy is global or it is not democracy.
Current democratic systems are only deficient approximations to such
an ideal.

As a response to the current state of international exclusion, the
radical project of stretching the paradigm of democratic inclusion to
the ultimate boundaries encompassing the whole of mankind as ultimately a single *demos* is thus presented. As opposed to this, the two
alternative models of the national and transnational *demoi* are rejected
on the basis of their lack of a non-discriminatory (in that it is all-
inclusive) authority capable of deciding on conflicts over jurisdictional
boundaries and political membership. If we stick to the idea of inclusion
as a key democratic requirement (Tinnevelt and De Schutter 2010),

we have to envisage a central all-inclusive authority charged with delineating distinct sub-units and accommodating their potential conflicts. An all-inclusive system is needed in order to solve disputes over the interpretation of jurisdictional boundaries, to deal with the '*Kompetenz-Kompetenz*' question. It is, in fact, only through an all-inclusive world system that the delineation of jurisdictional boundaries can be implemented democratically and the problem of political exclusion avoided. Exclusion is accordingly considered legitimate only when boundaries are collectively decided through an all-inclusive procedure. Hence, the delineation of the *demoi* at the different spheres of political action cannot but be generated in a procedural, participatory way. Any other substantive principle to discriminate between insiders and outsiders remains, from this perspective, just arbitrary. From a different angle, this also entails maintaining the position that pluralism without an overarching authority cannot but lead to a power-based system.

Intergovernmentalism

The first and most conventional model for considering democracy beyond borders is that of intergovernmentalism. This is indeed one of the classical models of organization of the international system and can be defined in its multilateral version as: 'an institutional form that coordinates relations among three or more states on the basis of generalized principles of conduct' (Ruggie 1993, 11). A number of scholars of mainly liberal internationalist persuasion hold that when multilateral intergovernmentalism is associated with democratic regimes we have the highest (or indeed only) opportunities to implement the democratic ideal at the international level. This is because the relevant *demoi* are here located decisively within the state borders, and can only indirectly take part in intergovernmental affairs. In particular, while from a non-ideal point of view, these scholars tend to prefer the restricted version of the model (e.g., the project for a League of Democracies), from an ideal and long-term perspective, their preference is for the universal version of multilateral intergovernmentalism (for a critical assessment see Archibugi, this volume). As explained below, this kind of 'global' democracy remains seriously deficient in terms of political inclusion, based as it is on the state-centric vision of international affairs.

Normative principle of intergovernmentalism: association

The traditional method for deciding on the membership of the *demos* and subsequently for drawing jurisdictional boundaries is based on the principle of national political autonomy (Charvet 1999, Nagel 2005, Agné 2006, Christiano 2006, Ypi 2008, Christiano, this volume). From this viewpoint, the jurisdictional boundaries of current democratic states are difficult to circumnavigate and any further step toward democracy beyond borders requires strict conditions to be met. In brief, despite the existence of some sort of global principle of justice, boundaries should remain as close as possible to the current ones, for individuals already enjoy a status of citizenship that guarantees them rights and duties within the national institutional framework. Thin moral cosmopolitanism, according to this view, does not thus entail institutional cosmopolitanism. Different reasons are advanced for this position known as associative democracy. Nagel, following Rawls, formulates a political conception according to which justice is understood as a specific associative virtue embedded in established social institutions that are able to both guarantee rights and impose obligations. Sovereignty and equality thus remain two intertwined notions that cannot be untied. Christiano argues in favour of the conservation principle, based on two sub-arguments: the state is the only current entity with a capacity to decide on the justice or injustice of a social and political order in an egalitarian way (the capacity for justice argument); and modern democratic states constitute a common world for their citizens – that is, a world in which most fundamental interests are intertwined (the common world argument). Finally, Ypi maintains that polities as associative contexts are needed in a non-ideal world for they provide two key elements: mechanisms that can impose mutual political constraints upon members (popular sovereignty); and a basis for mutual agreement which progressively educates citizens to a voluntary concern for cosmopolitan goals (civic education).

Overall, the associative principle constitutes the core exclusionary component of the democratic tradition. From this viewpoint, to protect the legitimate democratic aspirations of the insiders, the outsiders have to be excluded (Marchetti 2005). There is a structural discrimination in place between those who are in as citizens, and those who are out as foreigners and who consequently are treated as second-class political actors. The citizens of the political community feel no particular duty of political justice towards them. To be clear, the problem is not exclusion per se, but the arbitrary ground on which exclusion is determined. Since the boundaries of the political community are here determined through an endogenous process based on internal principles, those who happen to be outside and consider their state illegitimate cannot dispute this jurisdictional delimitation by appealing to a third, higher authority. Migrants living in the political community, foreigners living abroad and all those who claim to have a stake in the decisions taken inside the community are just ostracized. In brief, such a contextualistic approach has to be rebutted on the ground of its arbitrary method for delineating the community boundaries which in the ultimate analysis relies on mere historical contingencies. The scope of these communities has not been democratically decided and hence remains questionable.

Significantly, the associative democracy perspective underpins the traditional objection as to the global *demos*: any system of global democracy that radically transcends the state boundaries would be unacceptable not only because it would overlook state institutions as the locus of justice, but also because it would be missing its social component in the form of a global *demos* – allegedly a necessary social basis for any project of global democracy. The objection as to the lack of an international or even global *demos* may, however, be rebutted for at least three reasons. First, we need to observe the issue of the global *demos* from a historical perspective. The historical evolution in terms of the increase in social and political democratic interaction beyond borders and the subsequent increase in civil awareness from past times is evident. Not that today's interaction is by any means fully democratic, for the divide between individual political awareness and individual social and economical actions is still extremely evident, but there is growing recognition of injustices at the international level. As a result of this, the emergence of a global civil society and global public opinion is increasingly visible (Meyer et al. 1997, Anheier et al. 2001, Ruggie 2004). Second, without aiming to tackle the endless political-science debate on whether the individual comes before public institutions or vice versa, it is important to stress that participation in public political life crucially educates individuals to a civic attitude that recognizes public interests. The development and flourishing of a *demos* can, then, be understood most often to be a consequence rather than a cause of public institutions. The case of the European Parliament in which political stances are more and more defined in ideological rather than nationalistic terms provides evidence of the institutional capacity to forge new collective political identities (Kreppel 2002). Hence, the creation of international democratic institutions could have a notable 'pedagogic' and civic role to play in the maturation of a more consistent attitude of perceiving oneself as part of a politically heterogeneous, multilayered and global *demos* (Weinstock 2001). Third, we need to be clear about the fact that appealing to the global *demos* does not entail deleting the traditional bases of social and institutional political life at the domestic level. It only implies an addition of further levels of political interaction (i.e., enlarging the scope of responsibility and accountability) that need to be consistently combined with the lower, traditional levels. The state as a locus for political justice would remain an important component in the overall political system. Most public services, from the administration of legal justice to the provision of welfare support, would most likely still be managed through state infrastructures. And yet, some competencies would be moved up to the higher levels in response to the demands for global justice voiced by the excluded political actors beyond borders, as will be shown later. As a consequence, even in the best-case scenario where individual states were doing a reasonably good job in securing justice for their own people, we would still need a global authority that would allow the determination of sub-jurisdictional lines in a non-exclusionary way. To be clear, here the issue is not securing justice domestically, but rather delineating the *demos/demoi* legitimately. This suffices here to challenge the political method for drawing jurisdictional boundaries and the related objection as to the lack of a global *demos* that are developed along associative lines.

Institutional design of intergovernmentalism: universal/regional multilateralism

The traditional extension of the democratic ideal of political autonomy to the international level derives from the model of intergovernmental multilateralism in its regional or universal form. Originating in the normative principle of associative democracy, this model has been associated with the tradition of liberal internationalism (Doyle 1986, Russett and Oneal 2001, Franceschet 2002). Once a liberal democratic system is established domestically, its international correlate in terms of intergovernmental interaction will allegedly remain consistent with the democratic ideal. This is the core concept of liberal internationalism that underpins the theory of democratic peace. According to the classic view, democratic states are seen as politically independent bodies, in whose affairs other states should refrain from intervening. The theory of liberal internationalism holds that within states and in their international relations there are no real conflicts of interest, in that people ultimately want peace and commercial interaction only. According to this perspective, states are thus seen as management tools for problem-solving rather than collective holistic personalities. Were all political regimes a genuine product of national self-determination and liberal democratic values, there would be no war, and humanity would live in peace and ever-growing prosperity (Moravcsik 1993, Zacher and Matthew 1995).

While a fully consistent application of liberal universal multilateralism does not exist in the context of current international affairs, a couple of institutional instances can be identified as examples that come closer to this ideal for different reasons. On the one hand, the existing institutional example that most resembles the liberal internationalist model is the European Council of the European Union (EU) which is composed of democratic governments only. However, this is inadequate insofar as it has a regional scope and it is engrained in the more complex system of the EU. On the other hand, the existing institutional example that most resembles universal multilateralism is the United Nations General Assembly which is composed of almost of all recognized states. However, this is inadequate insofar as it also includes non-democratic members and is engrained in the more complex system of the United Nations (UN).

Recently, a number of intergovernmental reforms have been suggested that would strengthen the current application of this model to international affairs. The most obvious way to pursue this objective would be through strengthening international law. In opposition to realist interpretations of international law as a law of the great powers, a number of scholars have formulated interpretations and recommendations to increase its democratic character (Franck 1995, Crawford and Marks 1998, Benhabib 2005). A second way to increase the democratic nature of the intergovernmental system would be through increasing the scope and effectiveness of transgovernmental administrative networks based on a 'disaggregated' view of the state (Slaughter 2004, Cohen and Sabel 2005). Finally, a third option would consist in the recognition and expansion of the role of parliamentary assemblies within international organizations (Habegger 2008).

With regard to the intergovernmental multilateral model, a general set of criticisms relates to the issue of transnational exclusion and the democratic deficit of the liberal international system. While international liberalism proclaims faith in liberal democratic values and constitutional democracy at the domestic level, it has little to offer when the focus is moved to the transnational level. In essence, within the model of international liberalism, the entitlement of individuals to participate politically in the decision-making processes is preserved only at the local and national level, whereas at the transnational level individuals remain strictly excluded. Individual citizens are in fact deprived of the entitlement to directly elect their representatives to international institutions (with the outstanding exception of the European Parliament) and instead have to pass through a multiple chain of state-based delegation that simply dilutes their capacity to demand accountability. In this way, liberal intergovernmentalism remains flawed in democratic terms for it breaks the channels of reflexivity that constitute the basis of democratic congruence. Majorities are de facto excluded because of the multiple delegation mechanism, and to an even greater extent minorities and all those individuals who claim transnational interests are de jure excluded from relevant global decisions that affect their lives. National representatives are in fact elected/appointed by a national constituency, with a national mandate, and to an intergovernmental organization. Hence, they cannot reasonably adopt a full global or transnational perspective. As a consequence of these democratic limitations, the model of inter-governmentalism remains untenable due to its exclusionary character.

Global governance

The second and increasingly popular model for thinking about democracy beyond borders is that of global governance, which can be defined as a continuously growing net of authorities whose rule-making, political coordination and problem-solving transcends national frontiers (Czempiel and Rosenau 1992). This system is mostly constituted by mono-functional institutions which reflect the current process of redistribution of power at the transnational level. Since socio-economic power is transcending national borders and being expressed in new forms of governance, it is argued that political power should also expand its sphere of influence by appropriating and democratizing these new forms of governance. In this way, the emerging transnational *demos* that is consolidating along cross-national functional lines could be fairly incorporated into new democratic institutions. Rather than a comprehensive, single process, these authors tend to favour a gradual, brick-by-brick process of political construction of world society. As explained below, while such an approach offers a few advances in the public accountability of transnational affairs, it still remains inadequate in democratic terms for it preserves a degree of exclusion. By 'following' the current socio-economic patterns these proposals tend to be relatively feasible, but at the same time they remain constrained by these very same patterns, thus losing part of their critical democratic character in terms of inclusion.

Normative principle of global governance: stakeholdership

The principle for drawing jurisdictional boundaries that is most adhered to in the current debate on global democracy is the all-affected one (Pogge 2002, Keohane 2003, Held 2004, Goodin 2007). This principle is based on a notion of interaction-dependent justice according to which only those who are affected by a decision (the impactees) should be entitled to have a say in it. And, conversely, all affecting political actors should be accountable to the affected individuals. The standard understanding of this principle relies on direct causality – that is, while acts of omissions are usually not considered causally relevant, an act qualifies as causally relevant only if it solely causes injurious effects to a specific set of individuals. Regardless of territorial boundaries, this principle entails the application of the rule of political participation on different constituencies, be they local, national or transnational. Hence, while, on the one hand, this principle goes beyond the current state system by enlarging the sphere of political consideration, on the other, it remains exclusionary in that it is based on the idea that only those who are part of a determined interaction should have a voice, for where no interaction occurs, no duty of political justice applies (Marchetti 2005). And, importantly, no *super partes* judge may be invoked in order to assess the domains of the interaction at stake. As a consequence, despite its partly progressive features the all-affected principle remains insufficient and incomplete due to the fact that it does not allow for a fair hearing for the excluded actors.

Correlated to the all-affected principle is the model of stakeholder democracy, according to which all agents holding a relevant stake as members of a specific social interaction are entitled to participate in the political decision making (Pogge 2002, Gould 2004, Bauböck 2007, T. Macdonald 2008 and this volume). Accordingly, the relevant *demos* expands to cover the domain created by the socio-economic interaction, be it national, transnational or global. Pogge, for instance, holds that the duty of justice towards others, which can be discharged merely by not cooperating in the imposition of an unjust institutional scheme, is conditional on the contingent presence of social interaction and consequently does not exist with respect to the plurality of self-contained communities. Pogge admits that prior to any interaction there would still be fairly light duties of morality in terms of beneficence, but he is firm in maintaining that there would be no duties of justice. Another similar version of the stakeholder model is that based on human rights recently re-elaborated by Gould. According to this model 'people at a distance are to be regarded as affected by a decision if their human rights are affected, where these include economic and social, as well as civil and political, rights' (Gould 2004, 178). This would envisage a number of interlinked and possibly overlapping communities that would stretch across borders and be delimited by interactions related to human rights.

With regard to the stakeholder perspective, a number of specific objections (outlined in the next paragraph) and a general critical argument can be developed. According to the general argument, the notion of stakeholder is contrary to the received view of democracy, according to which democracy is interpreted as a system that allows for the participation of all its members on the grounds of the public component of political decisions. It is not only because I have a specific stake (mostly generated by a causal relation) that I am entitled to vote in a democracy, but it is also because the political system is in place to formulate and take decisions that have a public value. Political decisions may or may not directly affect me, and yet I should still be entitled to have a say on discussions and decisions that have general consequences that affect the public as such. In national democratic systems, citizens are enfranchised not only, as the stakeholder model would argue, because the parliament takes decisions that affect them, but also because the parliament takes decisions with a public dimension that may or may not personally affect them. Members of parliament, in fact, have a general mandate that allows them to vote on a number of non-specific issues. By contrast, a hypothetical stakeholder system would consistently envisage an almost infinite number of political bodies with a predetermined mandate to decide only on specific issues for which they have been delegated by those actors who are directly affected by the issue itself. Were this not the case, the system would be over-inclusive – that is, it would include also those who are not entitled to be included. However, all of these stakeholder characteristics remain far from being aligned with our more profound intuitions on the principles of political justice. The atomistic foundation of the stakeholder model should thus be rebutted for it relies on a self-regarding attitude that is unable to fully grasp the characteristics of impartiality that lie at the basis of political justice. Only by recognizing the public component of any political decision, beyond the trade-off between private interests, can the value of political entitlements be comprehensively understood and consequently associated with a consistent model of democracy.

Beyond those general considerations, three more specific objections impair the all-affected/stakeholder model: two are internal and one is external. First of all, it is highly difficult, if not entirely impossible, to specify who is affected by any kind of action. The principle risks running aground on indeterminacy. Chaos theory's description of the butterfly effects is an extreme, and illuminating, example of the indeterminacy of effect. Moreover, if possible effects of omitted decisions are also taken into consideration, any assessment becomes even more difficult. But also in the case in which a more moderate view is adopted and some kind of determinate relations can be assumed, two issues remain unresolved. On the one hand, the causal relation can only be established ex post: the decision on who is entitled to vote cannot be determined until after that very decision has been taken. On the other hand, the issue of interpretation remains open. Who has the authority to resolve conflicting interpretations on whether and what kind of interaction is taking place? Non-institutional, social contestation cannot be a viable criterion, for it too easily runs the risk of being influenced by social and economic power. If no specific and legitimate causal relation can be established, no political responsibility and accountability can be determined, and consequently no common jurisdiction can be defined. Second, actions provoke varying effects: there are people who are more affected than others. Since the extent of influence is different, in principle the more affected should be entitled to a stronger voice; perhaps fractional voting power or multiple votes. Common jurisdiction could be established, but the very principle of equality would be disputed and the democratic ideal would collapse. Third, and most importantly from the present perspective, the all-affected principle fails to deliver a non-exclusionary system in that the 'non-caused' and 'non-directly caused' victims would be excluded. Ultimately, this attitude equates to indifference to the injustices not immediately occasioned by the moral agent in question. To recall the famous example of the bystander unresponsive when faced with the child drowning in the pond: this attitude is the moral equivalent of the passive stance, the walking away with justification attitude.

Institutional design of global governance: hybrid networks

The common extension of the ideal of stakeholder democracy to the international level consists in the model of hybrid networks, typical of the mode of global governance. As already mentioned, the global governance system is multilayered, since it governs interaction wherever it is based, be it global, transnational, regional or national; and polyarchic, since it includes, often on an unequal formal standing, diverse actors involved in a given issue area, such as states, sub-national groups and transnational special interests and communities, including both private and public bodies. Institutional examples that come close to the model of governance via hybrid networks include all the recent developments in the so-called soft international law or contract-based law (e.g., the increase in private international arbitration and the development of the *lex mercatoria*), the hybrid standard setting transnational organizations (e.g., the International Accounting Standard Board [IASB], the Internet Corporation for Assigned Names and

Numbers [ICANN], the Society for Worldwide Interbank Financial Telecommunication [SWIFT], or the International Association of Insurance Supervisors [IAIS]), but also the United Nations Global Compact, the Global Environment Facility [GEF], and the Prototype Carbon Fund etc.

In this context, a number of scholars have formulated prescriptions to increase the degree of legitimacy of such network systems. The project of cosmopolitan governance aims at addressing the shortcomings of global governance (Held 1995) and purports to be a 'democratic' correction of the distorted 'executivism' of current forms of multilateralism. Other solutions look primarily (but not exclusively) to non-governmental actors, in that the overall challenge consists here in giving voice to global public opinion (Dryzek 2006, Bohman 2007) independently from the single national perspectives shaped by national interests. An institutional design consistent with the stakeholder perspective delineated earlier consists in envisaging different political forums (including the Internet) in which relevant interests can be transnationally and directly represented by the actors at stake (Macdonald and Macdonald 2006, Bauböck 2007, Johansen 2007, K. Macdonald, this volume). Proposals along these lines include the creation of new institutional mechanisms such as multinational civil and criminal juries (Gastil et al. 2010), global deliberation exercises (List and Koenig-Archibugi 2010) and publicly dispersed accountability (Steffek 2010). A different option is presented by the idea of random citizen participation according to which new bodies should be envisaged in which randomly selected citizens would have a voice to express their consent or dissent (Frey and Stutzer 2006). A third popular option consists in the alternative most incisively expressed by social movements and grass-roots organizations in terms of transnational networking from below (Scholte 2004, Smith 2007, Tallberg and Uhlin, this volume). In this alternative, democracy should first and foremost be enacted locally through a participatory process. Only at a subsequent stage can slender structures of transnational, people-to-people coordination be foreseen beyond the traditional intergovernmental organizations.

The hybrid networks' proposals for decision making deserve attention because they provide possibly the most feasible short-term reform of international decision making in terms of global democratization. Experiments in this direction have been already carried out in several international organizations with public hearings and consultations, which allow civil society actors to play an increasing role in global decision making (Pianta and Marchetti 2007, Smith 2007). And, yet, such proposals cannot be fully accepted as long-term political projects because of a lack of legitimate representation of all interests. While enlarging the political bases for transnational decision making, such models are still insufficiently inclusive in that only self-appointed, professional actors tend to be able to gain recognition and political visibility, and thus political leverage (Bob 2005).

When looking at the proposal for democratic revision of the system of global governance, our assessment cannot be but mixed. Without underestimating their relevance and effects as persuasive arguments for globalizing democracy, the democratic proposals for global governance warrant criticism precisely on the issue of the democratic deficit. While contributing to the overcoming of the purely intergovernmental system, democratic governance ultimately has to be rejected due to its inability to guarantee full inclusion to all world citizens in the global decision-making and frame-setting processes. Democratic global governance fails to guarantee inclusion in that it remains based on an uncoordinated system of independent jurisdictions relying on the principle of issue-oriented stakeholdership. Despite the appeal to some sort of global law, the lack of a truly global organization with effective and legitimate authority does not allow, in fact, for an adequate political control of world affairs in democratic terms. On the contrary, only a limited number of self-appointed actors may participate in the transnational jurisdictional decision-making processes of these would-be reformed models of governance. The 'others' – the victims, the vulnerable – have little chance to be included. In this sense, the project of cosmopolitan global governance based on ad hoc and limited functional bodies remains problematic, in that it lacks democratic centrality. In suggesting a net of delimited institutions, such proposals do not offer an opportunity to compare the effects of the uncoordinated decisions taken by different mono-functional agencies, which are considered equal in political authority (Thompson 1999). In multiplying specialized agencies (supposedly, one for each global issue), this democratic governance model fails to establish a central authority where a legitimate political discussion can take place to determine the allocation of competencies and responsibilities on any determined issue area. In brief, the project of democratic governance remains flawed as regards political inclusion for two reasons. On the one hand, it does not permit a proper coordination from above. On the other hand, it also precludes full participation from below. The current system of governance and the worldwide protests which have resulted from it amply prove that this is the most likely outcome of this kind of institutional arrangement.

Global polity

The third model for considering democracy beyond borders is that of global polity,[1] according to which the institutional framework at the international level is envisaged as all-inclusive and multilayered. Differing from the intergovernmental and global governance proposals previously examined, the global polity perspective considers the restructuring of the political system at the global level as a crucial democratic advance in comparison with the normative compartmentalization of state-centrism and mono-functionalism. From the global polity point of view, only by overturning the usual thinking about politics can the democratic ideal be genuinely and consistently implemented. Only by allocating public power to political authorities within which every single individual can be represented can the evil of political exclusion be avoided. Admittedly, in terms of feasibility, the proposals based on the global polity models are the worst positioned. This is due to their antithetic stance toward current institutional arrangements. However, this does not reduce their political significance. Accordingly, while the proposals based on this third model are of reduced worth for illuminating short-term reforms, they remain fully valid for formulating a critical stance for the political circumstances of our time and for guiding our political action for the long term.

Normative principle of global polity: all-inclusiveness

In contrast to the two previous models, the present proposal advocates a principle of inclusive democracy, granting political power within the decision-making and frame-setting processes of public rules to *all* citizens of the world, regardless of whether or not they are directly affected by a determined set of actions or are members of specific political associations. This arguably remains in line with the conventional model of domestic democracy, according to which citizens are included in the political structure as members of a *public* constituency, rather than as stakeholders of particular interests or members of specific communities, and consequently elect their representatives with a general or non-constrained mandate.

Individuals are entitled to take part in all public decisions via delegation because these choices first and foremost determine the boundaries

---

[1] The term 'global polity' has recently been used by other authors in relation to different organizational forms that are closer to what I refer to here as global governance (Ougaard and Higgott 2002, Ferguson and Mansbach 2004). In contrast to these, I see the notion of a single global polity as linked to a single (though not unitary) institutional framework.

of what is then to be considered legitimately private and hence left to individual self-determination in an exclusionary manner. From this perspective, it is the very same contractual logic of political societies that determines the boundary between what is public and what is private. Before the law, such a distinction does not make sense. With the law (an eminently all-inclusive, public framework), such a distinction is made. The private sphere exists therefore only because it is so determined by a public act. It would not otherwise come into existence. Thus, for example, property rights are only such because it has been collectively decided that a specific set of goods can be considered private property, if they comply with certain procedural requirements. Without such a public decision, private property would not be what it is. While the substantive input (the claim of ownership of a specific good) cannot but originate from below in a particularistic and exclusionary way, the ultimate authority that grants a legal status to that input cannot but come from above in an all-inclusive way. The same applies at the international level for what concerns national sovereignty. Without the recognition by international society, national sovereignty would not be what it is.

In contrast to stakeholdership, the all-inclusive principle holds that it is the collectivity in its entirety which has to decide and to draw jurisdictional boundaries and sub-units, for this is an exercise that can only be public if exclusion is to be avoided. Exclusion is considered legitimate here only when its boundaries are collectively decided through an all-inclusive procedure. Only self-exclusion is thus legitimate. In so much as an individual preserves his/her freedom while being at the same time ruler and ruled, so equally he/she preserves his/her political inclusion while being at the same time included and self-excluded. As a consequence, before any frame-setting decision is taken, every single individual has to be consulted or, alternatively and more feasibly, has to be granted the right to appeal. The general principle of universal inclusion should be firmly maintained as the fundamental basis of democratic practice.

In line with this, a fully inclusive principle has to be adopted also for the modelling of democracy beyond borders, one that grants to *all* citizens as members of the public constituency in each level of political action, including the global, a political voice and the power to make the choice-makers accountable. No discrimination or exclusion can be tolerated anymore, if we stick to the democratic ideal. All of humankind has to be considered as part of a single, global *demos*. With regard to the problem of jurisdictions, this stance entails on top of the jurisdictional scale an all-inclusive political authority empowered to draw the lower jurisdictional boundaries. An all-inclusive system, ultimately based on the acknowledegment of a single global *demos*, is in fact needed in order to solve in a legitimate way disputes about the interpretation of jurisdictional boundaries. National (association model) or transnational (stakeholder model) boundaries are, then, just to be considered as subsets that are included within, and legitimately determined by, the all-inclusive set of humanity. The all-inclusive authority here plays the role of a meta-level arbiter (or a court of appeal for those who feel unjustly excluded) that determines the contours of the actual decision making occurring in the sub-levels. In fact, while it is at the international or transnational level that the real action is, without a superior authority the question of who the actors are cannot be determined legitimately in a non-exclusionary way. As already recognized in the domestic sphere, only when an individual is entitled to participate in the delineation of jurisdictional boundaries can she or he feel unexcluded, for he/she has a valid and publicly recognized voice to claim inclusion in a relevant jurisdictional domain, within which the daily decision making then takes place. When this is not the case, any individual or group could be excluded by more powerful actors claiming they are the only relevant agents, namely the only relevant stakeholders, in the jurisdictional interaction at stake. Participation via direct voting in decision-making and frame-setting processes at the global level is thus the key mechanism to avoid transnational exclusion.[2]

Institutional design of global polity: federal integration

World integration is the most clear-cut alternative to both intergovernmental and hybrid networks' modes of decision making. Within this perspective, the most sophisticated institutional version is that of world federalism, or 'cosmo-federalism', in which a non-unitary world state would be constituted for joint action on a specific set of global issues. Rejecting the traditional model of double indirect representation

---

[2] The principle of all-inclusion may overlap with that of all-affected, if the latter is interpreted extensively, as recently suggested by Goodin (2007). However, a qualitative and procedural distinction remains in that the all-inclusion principle includes all in order to determine who is affected, while the all-affected principle (extensively interpreted) includes all because they are (self-appointedly) affected. Ultimately, a fundamental difference remains in that the principle of stakeholdership relies on an individualistic assessment of the causal relationship, while the all-inclusive principle relies on a collective procedure to assess the political relationships at stake. An intermediate position, proposed by Koenig-Archibugi (personal communication), suggests that the act of drawing jurisdictional boundaries should be interpreted as public because it is all-affecting.

through states' representatives, cosmo-federalism proposes a democratic rather than diplomatic union of states, according to which all political representatives would be directly elected to a law-making assembly by the people, and political decisions taken by the federal government would apply directly to citizens rather than states. In organizing political power on several levels, federalism benefits from the advantages of both centralization and decentralization, in that it allows for the application of the principle of self-government (thus preserving the identity of the units) to a plurality of centres of autonomous power, consistently and democratically coordinated. Every citizen would subsequently be subject to two powers (dual loyalty) without this implying the renunciation of the principle of 'uniqueness of decision', thanks to the mechanism of subsidiarity.

A new covenant would be signed among individuals, states and a world organization, according to which states would delegate power to a superior institution in charge of both addressing global issues and allocating competences on the sub-levels. This would lead to the transformation of interstate relations from an anarchic state to one of subjection to the rule of law. The institutional framework would comprise a world government, a world parliament, a world supreme court and a global constitution. These global institutions would then be associated with a number of other institutional sub-layers with relative autonomy. This institutional design would effectively give a voice to different actors – significantly, including all individuals, regardless of their nationality, thus effectively realizing the ideal of inclusive democracy (Baratta 2004, Delbrück 2004, Frankman 2004, Yunker 2007, Davenport 2008, Levi 2008, Marchetti 2008a, Murithi, this volume).

According to this latter perspective, a key international organization such as the UN should be transformed into a global federal organization in which individuals and states would share power for specific global purposes under a system of strengthened international law. Consequently, states would renounce a portion of their sovereignty and agree to a compulsory jurisdiction intended solely for a determined list of competences on global issues (typically, non-territorial or territorially intermingled issues),[3] while retaining those powers and specific institutional forms directed at domestic concerns. Rather than a loss, this delegation of power to the global government would be regarded as a

---

[3] Examples would include: global poverty; nuclear containment; transnational organized crime; demography, migration and trafficking in people; environmental degradation and the fate of future generations; spread of infectious diseases; wars to spread democracy; the global economy; and cyber crime.

gain in freedom and order, since states would be compelled only to accept decisions taken according to majority rule – General Assembly resolutions would have a legally binding status – and would be implemented through a subsidiary scheme of actions at both global and state levels. Transnational decisions would be authoritative insofar as they would not be determined by national governments but by a truly world assembly and accountable only to it. A multi-tiered system would be able to accommodate some of the institutions recently created along transnational hybrid lines, provided they remained consistently regulated by world legislation. Individuals would acquire a full cosmopolitan citizenship while remaining national citizens within a consistent scheme of multiple democratic allegiances. They would be enfranchised as voting constituents for an elected legislative world assembly with an authoritative mandate representing general as well as special interests restricted to global issues. National minorities could at last acquire their legitimate political weight in that their nationally marginal votes would be aggregated at the global level. Finally, since global agents would be recognized as having both rights and responsibilities, they would also be protected from, and punished for, global crimes, according to an appropriate multilayered and multi-agents scheme of sanctions.

A crucial point in an eventual federal reform of the UN would reside in the allocation of the diverse functions and powers between the central world government and the federal states. As with current forms of federalism, even in the case of the reformed UN a stable equilibrium would not be possible without a constitution whose authority is accorded primacy over all other powers. In the case of conflict between the different institutional layers, the supranational authority must prevail over the lower ones. A global constitution (and an ad hoc constituent assembly) would thus be required to delineate the distribution of legislative and executive authority regarding a number of functions among the different levels of political action. A clear demarcation of the issue of competence is crucial not only to allocate *ab initio* authority (and define its sphere), but also to solve conflicts that may arise about the power to judge. The authority to decide on who has to decide would reside neither with the central power (i.e., the unitary state) nor with the single states (i.e., the confederation), but only with the constitutional court (Kelsen 1945, Levi 2008). As a complement to the constitution, a global constitutional court should also be envisaged with the authority to settle any ultimate dispute concerning the so-called 'competence catalogue'. Among other benefits, this jurisdictional court would provide a further guarantee of lower (i.e., local, national or regional) prerogatives. By making the 'subsidiarity check' available, the court would offer a chance to lower parliaments to ask for reconsideration of any decision taken by an upper institutional level, in the event that they could reasonably claim the issue at stake could be decided more effectively at the lower level.[4] Moreover, the court, based as it would be on a global, all-inclusive authority, would also provide a robust alternative to the epistemic-deliberative quality of global governance institutions, as suggested by Buchanan and Keohane (2006, 425–32). Rather than relying on transnational civil society channels of accountability, which inevitably remain exclusionary for the reasons suggested earlier, the courts would legitimately offer an ultimate chance for political inclusion to all those who had been structurally excluded from international decision making so far.

Conclusions

Current global politics is characterized by a great instability due to the concomitant growing socio-economic integration and the emergence of new political actors who are claiming more political voice. A typical phenomenon of any democratization process is precisely the sense of instability generated by the emergence of new, un-institutionalized actors and innovative legitimacy claims previously unheard of in the public domain. These actors try to expand their limited political and institutional power in order to align it to their existing social and economic power. They try to reconfigure the *demos*. Within this context of new political representation, an unprecedented global public domain consolidates in which old, state-centred visions of international affairs mix with new transnational and global visions of world politics, producing a complex map of ideological positions (Marchetti 2009). This has been made possible through the partial erosion of the Westphalian international system, in which authority and legitimacy were circumscribed, to reciprocally exclude territorial jurisdictions. The global public domain remains a central place where new dimensions and new applications of global legitimacy are developed and advanced in contrast to current interpretations. This chapter has critically surveyed precisely the principal models of global democracy currently debated and has defended an all-inclusive political system. While this does not necessarily entail that a reformist or indeed revolutionary reading of legitimate global politics will influence concrete political action, the mere opportunity of initiating a change of norms in international politics makes this global

---

[4] I have discussed a number of objections to the model of cosmo-federalism elsewhere (Marchetti 2008a, Chapter 7; 2008b).

public arena and its ideal content extremely important for current global politics. It is to this global public discourse that we need to look in order to understand the future, long-term transformation of global politics.

REFERENCES

Agné, Hans. 2006. 'A Dogma of Democratic Theory and Globalization: Why Politics Need Not Include Everyone It Affects', *European Journal of International Relations* 12, 3: 433–58.

Anheier, Helmut, Marlies Glasius and Mary Kaldor. 2001. 'Introducing Global Civil Society', in Helmut Anheier, Marlies Glasius and Mary Kaldor (eds.), *Global Civil Society 2001* (pp. 3–22). Oxford University Press.

Baratta, Joseph Preston. 2004. *The Politics of World Federation*, 2 vols. Westport, CT: Praeger.

Bauböck, Rainer. 2007. 'Stakeholder Citizenship and Transnational Political Participation: A Normative Evaluation of External Voting', *Fordham Law Review* 75: 101–55.

Benhabib, Seyla. 2005. 'On the Alleged Conflict between Democracy and International Law', *Ethics and International Affairs* 19, 1: 85–100.

Bob, Clifford. 2005. *The Marketing of Rebellion: Insurgents, the Media and International Activism*. Cambridge University Press.

Bohman, James. 2007. *Democracy across Borders: From Demos to Demoi*. Cambridge, MA: MIT Press.

Buchanan, Allen, and Robert Keohane. 2006. 'The Legitimacy of Global Governance Institutions', *Ethics and International Affairs* 20, 4: 405–37.

Cabrera, Luis. 2010. 'World Government: Renewed Debate, Persistent Challenges', *European Journal of International Relations* 16, 3: 511–30.

Charvet, John. 1999. 'International Society from a Contractarian Perspective', in David Mapel and Terry Nardin (eds.), *International Society: Diverse Ethical Perspectives* (pp. 114–31). Princeton, NJ: Princeton University Press.

Christiano, Thomas. 2006. 'A Democratic Theory of Territory and Some Puzzles about Global Democracy', *Journal of Social Philosophy* 37, 1: 81–107.

Cohen, Joshua, and Charles F. Sabel. 2005. 'Global Democracy', *International Law and Politics* 37, 4: 763–97.

Crawford, James, and Susan Marks. 1998. 'The Global Democracy Deficit: An Essay in International Law and Its Limits', in Daniele Archibugi, David Held and Martin Köhler (eds.), *Re-Imagining Political Community: Studies in Cosmopolitan Democracy* (pp. 72–90). Cambridge, UK: Polity Press.

Czempiel, Ernst Otto, and James N. Rosenau. 1992. *Governance Without Government: Order and Change in World Politics*. Cambridge University Press.

Davenport, John J. 2008. 'A Global Federalist Paper: Consolidation Arguments and Transnational Government', *Journal of Value Inquiry* 42, 3: 353–75.

Delbrück, Jost. 2004. 'Transnational Federalism: Problems and Prospects of Allocating Public Authority Beyond the State', *Indiana Journal of Global Legal Studies* 11, 1: 31–57.

Doyle, Michael W. 1986. 'Liberalism and World Politics', *American Political Science Review* 80, December: 1151–69.

Dryzek, John S. 2006. *Deliberative Global Politics: Discourse and Democracy in a Divided World*. Cambridge, UK: Polity Press.

Ferguson, Yale H., and Richard W. Mansbach. 2004. *Remapping Global Politics: History's Revenge and Future Shock*. Cambridge University Press.

Franceschet, Antonio. 2002. *Kant and Liberal Internationalism: Sovereignty, Justice and Global Reform*. New York: Palgrave.

Franck, Thomas M. 1995. *Fairness in International Law and Institutions*. New York: Clarendon Press.

Frankman, Myron J. 2004. *World Democratic Federalism*. New York: Palgrave.

Frey, Bruno S., and Alois Stutzer. 2006. 'Strengthening the Citizens' Role in International Organizations', *Review of International Organization* 1, 1: 27–43.

Gastil, John, Colin J. Lingle, and Eugene P. Deess. 2010. 'Deliberation and Global Criminal Justice: Juries in the International Criminal Court', *Ethics and International Affairs* 24, 1: 69–90.

Goodin, Robert. 2007. 'Enfranchising All Affected Interests, and Its Alternatives', *Philosophy and Public Affairs* 35, 1: 40–68.

Gould, Carol C. 2004. *Globalizing Democracy and Human Rights*. Cambridge University Press.

Habegger, Beat. 2008. 'Democratic Accountability and Parliamentary Control of International Organizations: The Council of Europe, the OSCE, and Lessons for a Future United Nations Assembly'. Paper presented at the ISA Annual Convention, San Francisco, CA.

Held, David. 1995. *Democracy and the Global Order: From the Modern State to Cosmopolitan Governance*. Cambridge, UK: Polity Press.

2004. 'Democratic Accountability and Political Effectiveness from a Cosmopolitan Perspective', *Government and Opposition* 39, 2: 364–91.

Johansen, Robert C. 2007. 'The E-Parliament: Global Governance to Serve Human Interest', *Widener Law Review* 13: 319–45.

Kelsen, Hans. 1945. *General Theory of Law and State*. Cambridge, MA: Harvard University Press.

Keohane, Robert. 2003. 'Global Governance and Democratic Accountability', in David Held and Mathias Koenig-Archibugi (eds.), *Taming Globalization. Frontiers of Governance* (pp. 130–59). Cambridge, UK: Polity Press.

Kreppel, Amie. 2002. *The European Parliament and Supranational Party System*. Cambridge University Press.

Levi, Lucio. 2008. *Federalist Thinking*. Lanham, MD: University Press of America.

List, Christian, and Mathias Koenig-Archibugi. 2010. 'Can There Be a Global *Demos*? An Agency-Based Approach', *Philosophy and Public Affairs* 38, 1: 76–110.

Macdonald, Kate, and Terry Macdonald. 2006. 'Non-Electoral Accountability in Global Politics: Strengthening Democratic Control within the Global Garment Industry', *European Journal of International Law* 17, 1: 89–119.

Macdonald, Terry. 2008. *Global Stakeholder Democracy: Power and Representation Beyond Liberal States*. Oxford University Press.

Marchetti, Raffaele. 2005. 'Interaction-Dependent Justice and the Problem of International Exclusion', *Constellations* 12, 4: 487–501.

2008a. *Global Democracy: For and Against. Ethical Theory, Institutional Design, and Social Struggles*. New York: Routledge.

2008b. 'A Matter of Drawing Boundaries: Global Democracy and International Exclusion', *Review of International Studies* 34, 2: 207–24.

2009. 'Mapping Alternative Models of Global Politics', *International Studies Review* 11, 1: 133–56.

Meyer, John W., John Boli, George Thomas and Francisco Ramirez. 1997. 'World Society and the Nation State', *American Journal of Sociology* 103, 1: 144–81.

Moravcsik, Andrew. 1993. 'Liberalism and International Relations Theory'. Working paper 92–6, Harvard University, Center for International Affairs.

Nagel, Thomas. 2005. 'The Problem of Global Justice', *Philosophy and Public Affairs* 33, 2: 113–47.

Ougaard, Morten, and Richard A. Higgott (eds.). 2002. *Towards a Global Polity*. London: Routledge.

Pianta, Mario, and Raffaele Marchetti. 2007. 'The Global Justice Movements: The Transnational Dimension', in Donatella della Porta (ed.), *The Global Justice Movement: A Cross-National and Transnational Perspective* (pp. 29–51). Boulder, CO: Paradigm.

Pogge, Thomas. 2002. *World Poverty and Human Rights: Cosmopolitan Responsibilities and Reforms*. Cambridge, UK: Polity Press.

Ruggie, John G. 2004. 'Reconstituting the Global Public Domain – Issues, Actors, and Practices', *European Journal of International Relations* 10, 4: 499–531.

(ed.). 1993. *Multilateralism Matters: The Theory and Praxis of an Institutional Form*. New York: Columbia University Press.

Russett, Bruce, and J.R. Oneal. 2001. *Triangulating Peace: Democracy, Interdependence, and International Organizations*. New York: W.W. Norton.

Scholte, Jan Aart. 2004. 'Civil Society and Democratically Accountable Global Governance', *Government and Opposition* 39, 2: 211–33.

Slaughter, Anne-Marie. 2004. *A New World Order*. Princeton University Press.

Smith, Jackie. 2007. *Social Movements for Global Democracy*. Baltimore, MD: John Hopkins University Press.

Steffek, Jens. 2010. 'Public Accountability and the Public Sphere of International Governance', *Ethics and International Affairs* 24, 1: 45–68.

Thompson, Dennis F. 1999. 'Democratic Theory and Global Society', *Journal of Political Philosophy* 7, 2: 111–25.

Tinnevelt, Roland, and Helder De Schutter (eds.). 2010. *Global Democracy and Global Exclusion*. Oxford, UK: Blackwell.

Weinstock, Daniel M. 2001. 'Prospects for Transnational Citizenship and Democracy', *Ethics and International Affairs* 15, 2: 53–66.

Ypi, Lea. 2008. 'Statist Cosmopolitanism', *Journal of Political Philosophy* 16, 1: 47–81.

Yunker, James A. 2007. *Political Globalization: A New Vision of Federal World Government*. Lanham, MD: University Press of America.
Zacher, Mark, and Richard Matthew. 1995. 'Liberal International Theory: Common Threads, Divergent Strands', in Charles Kegley (ed.), *Controversies in International Relations Theory: Realism and the Neoliberal Challenge* (pp. 107–50). New York: St Martin's Press.

3   Citizens or stakeholders?
     Exclusion, equality and legitimacy in global
     stakeholder democracy

Terry Macdonald

Introduction

At the heart of the democratic project is the simple idea that individuals should have a say in all political decisions that significantly affect their lives. This idea is sometimes called the 'all-affected' principle (Goodin 2007, Koenig-Archibugi forthcoming) and is at other times associated with the concept of 'stakeholding'. In a recent book, I have developed in some depth a model of 'global stakeholder democracy', based on a liberal interpretation of such a principle (T. Macdonald 2008). My proposal is that in the era of globalization we should approach the task of democratization – at least in part – by making powerful global actors such as states, international organizations, non-governmental organizations (NGOs) and corporations directly democratically accountable to the individuals whose autonomy is prospectively constrained by their decisions. In other words, one of the things that democrats should try to do is place global institutions more firmly within the political control of their 'stakeholders'.

This approach to democratizing global politics faces many challenges at both practical and theoretical levels; in this chapter I focus on just one of these challenges. Specifically, I address the charge that placing the stakeholder principle at the heart of the democratic project has the effect of jettisoning another fundamental democratic value – *political equality*. This charge can be formulated roughly as follows. Stakeholder democracy allocates roles in collective decision making to individuals based on their political *affectedness* (by a particular decision or set of decisions), rather than their political *membership* – which in the global case entails membership within an overarching 'global society' with a shared global institutional scheme and associated

I would like to thank Laura Valentini and the editors of this volume for very insightful and constructive comments on an earlier version of this chapter.

political identities. On the stakeholder model, therefore, the *demos* defined as *the group empowered to participate in any given political decision-making process* will not necessarily or always be equivalent to the *demos* defined differently as *the population sharing a common scheme of political institutions, and political identities associated with these*. As a result, stakeholder democracy appears to some commentators to permit the *exclusion* of certain individuals and groups within global society – those who turn out not to be 'affected' in the relevant way by particular political decisions – from equal access to some important decision-making processes.

In what follows, I elaborate this egalitarian critique of stakeholder democracy, and explain how the stakeholder model can respond to, and withstand, it. I first consider three plausible variants of this egalitarian critique and identify which one poses the most serious egalitarian challenges to stakeholder democracy. I then argue that this egalitarian critique can be refuted by distinguishing two different views about how the value of political equality underpins the democratic project. The first of these views concerns the ideal of equal *citizenship*, and presupposes that the purpose of democracy is to deliver political institutions that are most conducive to the realization of a *just egalitarian society*, in which citizens have equal social status and political roles. (I call this the 'egalitarian citizenship' view of democratic equality.) On the second view, the more modest and less moralized goal of democracy is to ensure that the exercise of public political power achieves an egalitarian form of political *legitimacy*. To explain the different implications of these views for our thinking about the character and role of political equality within the democratic project, I briefly elaborate a view of political legitimacy associated with the 'political realism' of Bernard Williams (I call this the 'legitimacy' view of democratic equality), which provides an alternative way of understanding the normative purpose of democracy and political equality.

My core argument rests on this second 'legitimacy' view of the point of democracy, and the role of political equality within the democratic project. I agree with critics of stakeholder democracy that the forms of political exclusion it permits are in some respects unsatisfactory from the perspective of the *egalitarian citizenship* view of democratic equality. However, I maintain that stakeholder democracy is compatible with the alternative *legitimacy* view of democratic equality; moreover, there are good reasons for interpreting the purpose of democratic equality in this latter way in the context of contemporary global politics. On this basis, I conclude that the egalitarian credentials of the stakeholder model can be strongly vindicated in terms of basic democratic principle.

Stakeholder democracy and the egalitarian citizenship critique

At the root of the stakeholder model is a principle (the 'stakeholder principle') which delineates the *boundaries* of an institutional process for democratic political decision making – including the boundaries of both the 'public power' to be subjected to democratic control, and the group of decision makers (sometimes called the '*demos*') that is to control it.[1] According to the stakeholder principle, public power may be defined as any power that impacts systematically on people's lives in a potentially problematic way, giving rise to a demand for special political justification or legitimation through the democratic process.[2] This principle is underpinned by the idea that the delineation of democratic system boundaries should be based on some particular understanding of the *point* of a democratic system. On the liberal variant of the stakeholder principle that I have elaborated elsewhere, a political agency should count as 'public', and be subjected to democratic control, whenever its impact poses a systematic threat to the *autonomy* of some population of individuals (since on this liberal view the point of democracy is to protect and expand the scope of individuals' autonomy).[3] Traditionally, democrats have associated public power with the structures of sovereign states, or more recently with the 'constitutionalized' global political structures proposed by some cosmopolitan theorists. But the

---

[1] The theory of stakeholder democracy as set out in the book consists of much more than an account of democratic boundaries; it also explores some alternative institutional mechanisms for democratic social choice and political control which might be more capable of operating within the pluralist boundaries of a stakeholder system than traditional forms of electoral democracy. These institutional proposals generate an additional set of theoretical challenges, but I am bracketing these for the purposes of the present discussion, in order to remain focused on issues of political exclusion and equality.

[2] Exactly what kind of justification or legitimation is being sought through the democratic process is often left somewhat ambiguous in theoretical discussion of democracy; my purpose in this chapter is to show that how this is specified makes an important difference. But I take it that the general idea of public power as the category of power standing in need of some special political justification or legitimation is intelligible even before we have specified exactly what kind of justification or legitimation is being sought.

[3] For more discussion see T. Macdonald (2008, chapters 1 and 2). As noted there, a different interpretation of the basic point of democracy would yield a different operationalization of the general stakeholder principle and a different account of public power. For example, the view that the point of democracy is to promote some broader set of interests (beyond individual autonomy) would designate power as public – standing in need of democratic control – when it prospectively impacted on these other interests. I note also that I mean 'political agencies' to denote any social agencies that exercise power; I am intending to characterize 'public' power as a sub-category of 'power', and 'agents of public power' as a sub-category of 'political agents'.

stakeholder principle requires us to recognize that myriad non-state actors can also wield 'public' forms of power when they systematically affect people's lives in autonomy-threatening ways.[4]

Corresponding with this view of the scope of public power, the stakeholder principle has important implications for how the boundaries of democratic decision-making communities should be delineated. On the traditional theoretical image, a democratic *decision-making community* corresponds with a broader *political 'society'*, sharing a common scheme of political institutions and a collective political identity. These two groups are often referred to as the *'demos'* or 'public', reinforcing the widespread theoretical assumption that they must be equivalent. The stakeholder principle challenges this assumption. Within the contemporary *global* political domain – in which public power is distributed in a 'pluralist' structure across a range of states, international organizations and non-state actors such as NGOs and corporations – application of this principle shows how these groups can separate, because individuals within the overarching 'global society' can be members of multiple overlapping stakeholder communities, possessing participatory entitlements in relation to the various powerful political actors that impact significantly upon their lives.

One important criticism of the stakeholder model of global democracy is that its delineation of political boundaries in this manner violates the ideal of political equality that is central to the democratic project, by permitting the exclusion from political decision making of populations not 'affected' by particular decisions. As Raffaele Marchetti articulates this objection in his contribution to the present volume, the stakeholder principle misconstrues the proper grounds for according decision-making entitlements to individuals within a democratic system, by linking it to *affectedness* rather than *membership* in an inclusive and mutually responsible political community: 'the all-affected principle fails to deliver a non-exclusionary system in that the "non-caused" and "non-directly caused" victims would be excluded' (this volume, 34), As he explains the rationale for this verdict:

It is not only because I have a specific stake (mostly generated by a causal relation) that I am entitled to vote in a democracy, but it is also because the political system is in place to formulate and take decisions that have a public value. Political decisions may or may not directly affect me, and yet I should still be entitled to have a say on discussions and decisions that have general consequences that affect the public as such. (33)

---

[4] For a more in-depth discussion of this see T. Macdonald (2008, chapters 2 and 3). For further discussion of what I mean in this context by 'systematic' impacts, see also Macdonald and Macdonald (2010).

Philippe Schmitter (2009) has similarly criticized the stakeholder model for abandoning 'the notion that all adults have an equal right and inherent capacity to participate in politics' and instead 'restrict[ing] access only to those who are "constrained in their autonomy" by the impact of whatever is being decided' (484). He suggests that this shift from political equality among 'all adults' to the stakeholder principle involves performing 'radical surgery on democratic theory', presumably because he takes the principle of equal input for all adults to have a foundational status within the democratic project.[5]

As I understand it, the force of this critique emanates from a particular set of deeper assumptions about the nature of political equality and its role within the democratic project, anchored in a broader view of the purpose of democratic institutions, which I am here calling an *egalitarian citizenship* view of democratic equality. The bundle of normative ideas I have in mind here characterizes the democratic project as concerned at its core with building an egalitarian society, comprised of democratic 'citizens' whose equal entitlements within processes of political decision making facilitate (materially) and signify (symbolically) their broader social status as equals within a thickly shared social life. These ideas are pervasive within contemporary literatures in normative political theory – particularly those influenced by the Rawlsian project of political liberalism, which connects principles of egalitarian social justice at a constitutive level to the status of democratic citizens within an idealized 'closed society' (Rawls 1996). A highly influential account of democratic equality, so understood, has been articulated by Elizabeth Anderson (1999), whose well-known essay asks 'What is the Point of Equality?' and answers that the point is 'to create a community in which people stand in relations of equality to others' (289). As she elaborates:

In seeking the construction of a community of equals, democratic equality integrates principles of distribution with the expressive demands

---

[5] Schmitter's position on this issue is rather underspecified. He appears to reject the project of global democracy altogether (not only a stakeholder variant of this project), so it cannot be that when he talks about 'equal input for all adults' he means this to be interpreted on a cosmopolitan basis; when he says 'all adults' he doesn't literally mean *all*. Presumably (given his focus on 'real existing democracies' in the discussion cited) he prefers political exclusion based on traditional criteria of territoriality and/or nationality rather than political affectedness, although he does not supply any clear democratic rationale for preferring it. I take it that he is presupposing some version of the empirical claim that democratic institutions require societies with shared institutions and political identities of a depth and character that are not achieved at the level of global society, but his assumptions along these lines are not elaborated. Nevertheless, the challenge posed to the stakeholder model by the problem he highlights still stands on its own terms.

of equal respect. Democratic equality guarantees all law-abiding citizens effective access to the social conditions of their freedom at all times. It justifies the distributions of citizens in a democratic state. (Anderson, 1999, 289)

The egalitarian critique of the stakeholder model of democracy quite clearly rests on a view of democratic equality of this kind. The *cosmopolitan* version of the egalitarian critique defended by Marchetti is the most directly comparable to my stakeholder model, since both begin by assuming that the overarching political society within which democratic institutions should be established is global in scope. In what follows I therefore focus on Marchetti's formulation of the critique. Marchetti explicitly connects the rationale for this form of global egalitarianism to the egalitarian citizenship model of democratic equality I have sketched, drawing directly on both the idea of egalitarian social justice and the idea of egalitarian citizenship (in which political participation is a function of membership in the political community). In relation to justice, he claims that to justify global democracy, we need an argument touching the concept of global justice, and conversely that a viable solution to global justice can only be achieved through global democracy (this volume). In relation to citizenship, he argues that in place of the stakeholder principle we should endorse 'a principle of inclusive democracy granting political power within the decision-making and frame-setting processes of public rules to all citizens of the world, regardless of whether or not they are directly affected by a determined set of actions or are part of specific political associations' (37).

On Marchetti's formulation, this egalitarian critique of stakeholder democracy is quite broad, but building on this we can distinguish three more specific ways in which the stakeholder model might be thought to deviate from the requirements of democratic equality as seen from an egalitarian citizenship viewpoint.

First, stakeholder democracy might be thought to fall short of the requirement that all individuals should be accorded equal political standing in decision-making processes for the *symbolic* purpose of achieving equal 'status' as members of a global political society. This critique rests on the idea that individuals can only achieve equal status within global society if political institutions accord equal decision-making input to all, irrespective of their stake in these decisions – that is, the idea that equal social status is contingent on equal political participation. On this basis, it could be argued that stakeholder democracy permits the political marginalization of those who are already socially marginalized – in the sense of being less materially interconnected with wider global populations in domains that are the subject of political decisions, and therefore less 'affected' by political decisions – and in doing so fails to accord them public recognition as members of equal standing within global society.

This idea is a coherent one. It reflects a particular assessment of which social roles or activities attract respect or prestige and therefore generate the relevant kind of social 'status', and it might be further defended, for instance, by adopting the classical 'civic republican' view of political participation as a fundamental human interest in its own right, of intrinsic importance to an individual's access to the good life and therefore properly indicative of an individual's status within a society. Despite its coherence, however, I do not think that this idea is correct in its assessment of requirements for equal status *within global society*. In a small city-state or some other society where active political participation is valued as a basic precondition of a good life (arguably including many modern nation-states), it might make sense to regard as social inferiors those who cannot participate equally in all political decision making. However, I do not find it plausible, as a sociological matter, that one's level of active political participation has this kind of symbolic value as a marker of social status at the level of *global* society. I agree that equal social standing within global society requires political equality of a certain kind, but I think this requirement is satisfied by ensuring – in line with the stakeholder principle – that individuals should be accorded political input in proportion to their stake in the political decisions in question. It is beyond the scope of the present chapter to provide a more detailed argument in favour of this sociological judgement, but I have discussed it elsewhere (T. Macdonald 2008, 131–3).[6]

Second, the stakeholder model of global democracy fails to incorporate a new 'cosmopolitan' *framework of global public power* that can combat social inequalities (through global-level regulations, social policies, resource redistribution etc.) and provide means by which individuals can discharge civic responsibilities for contributing to this egalitarian social project. On the egalitarian citizenship view, political equality is not seen just as a mechanism providing equal opportunity for individuals to protect their own interests when these are implicated in political decisions; it is seen also as an institutional mechanism for enabling individuals to collaborate in discharging collective responsibilities for

---

[6] Other democrats have also offered theoretical defences (of varying kinds) of similar principles of proportional political input in some recent theoretical literature; for example, see Brighouse and Fleurbaey (2010). Robert Dahl (1967) has also highlighted the democratic value of factoring interest intensity into social choice procedures (though he does not consider it feasible to do so in practice).

securing the social conditions of an egalitarian society. Stakeholder democracy fails to institutionalize political equality of this kind, since it substitutes the stakeholder principle for global collective responsibility in delineating the public power that is to be democratically controlled, and the populations who are to control it. If we take the egalitarian citizenship view of democratic equality as our starting point, this critique of stakeholder democracy is a serious one.

Further, this failure of the stakeholder model to incorporate a 'cosmopolitan' framework of global public power points to a third possible egalitarian critique. Without an adequate shared institutional framework of global public power, not only will it be difficult for global citizens to collaborate effectively in creating an egalitarian global *social* order – it will also be difficult to ensure that social inequalities (in things that might affect one's capacity to participate politically, such as material resources, information, education, time and mobility) do not translate unjustly into *political* inequalities. Stakeholder democracy provides political institutions that are *formally* open to all participants on equal terms, but its lack of a strong cosmopolitan framework of global public power makes it poorly equipped to ensure equal input into political decision making *in reality* for all individuals – including those whose disadvantaged position within the broader global social order creates barriers to their capacity to understand, articulate and mobilize effectively in support of their interests at the level of global political institutions.

This feature of the stakeholder model is also problematic from an *egalitarian citizenship* perspective, since on that view democratic equality requires securing individuals' equal political opportunities against the effects of social disadvantage. A cosmopolitan democratic model based on Marchetti's 'all-inclusive' principle may well do better than a framework of stakeholder democracy in this respect, if it could be instituted effectively in practice, as it would incorporate formal provisions to foster active political participation of all global citizens, even against the background of social inequality. This apparent advantage of the all-inclusive cosmopolitan model over the stakeholder model is significantly weakened once we recognize that many of the political inequalities resulting from underlying social inequalities will persist even in a democratic system with formal mechanisms for ensuring equal input at the level of final political decision (such as those advocated by Marchetti), given the powerful effects of the *agenda-setting* processes (reflecting the dynamics of underlying social distributions and hierarchies) that shape the content of these final decisions (T. Macdonald 2008, 218–20). Nonetheless, this critique retains some real bite, and needs to be addressed in any robust defence of the egalitarian credentials of the stakeholder model.

Political legitimacy as the normative basis for global stakeholder democracy

There are several ways in which the stakeholder model of global democracy may be defended against the above egalitarian critique. One way would involve drawing upon a theory of *justice* different from the straightforwardly egalitarian theory that is associated with the egalitarian citizenship view of democratic equality. Beginning with the premise that the best form of democracy is the most just form, the aim of such an argument would be to explain how global justice can be achieved without global egalitarian citizenship, and to defend the model of global stakeholder democracy on that basis.[7] I find the prospect of such a justice-based defence of stakeholder democracy quite plausible, but here I do not try to develop such an argument. My point of departure from this line of argument is the first premise – that the best democratic framework is the most *just* one. In the remainder of this chapter I want to explore the kind of defence that might follow from a rather different premise: that the best democratic framework is the most *legitimate* one. In my conclusions here, I will present some reasons why thinking in terms of legitimacy rather than justice might be appropriate and helpful in assessing different institutional designs for global democracy; but before I can explain the advantages of a legitimacy approach, I first need to explain what this approach consists in and what its implications might be for our normative assessments of different democratic models. I therefore focus in this section on these theoretical tasks.

The notion of 'legitimacy' has been accorded a range of very different meanings within philosophical and social-scientific literatures. It is sometimes used as a generic term for the moral justifiability of political institutions – giving rise to a 'right to rule', but not in itself entailing any

---

[7] An argument of this kind might be developed with the resources of a certain kind of *liberal* theory of justice, taking individual autonomy rather than social equality as the most basic value, and arguing that the most just criterion for allocating participatory entitlements to individuals within global society is affectedness by autonomy-threatening power (in line with the stakeholder principle), rather than membership in global society (in line with the egalitarian citizenship ideal), since this better tracks the underlying point of justice, which is to justify autonomy-threatening power to those affected by it. I thank Laura Valentini for pressing the viability of this kind of defence in her comments on an earlier draft of this chapter. Her own liberal theory of justice might well provide the basis for a defence of this kind; for a statement and defence of her liberal view of justice, see Valentini (2011).

specific prescriptive norms or standards (such as some specific set of democratic standards), or any specific normative reasons for choosing some particular standards for institutions over others (Simmons 1999, Wellman 1996, Copp 1999, Buchanan 2002, Christiano, this volume). Accounts vary as to the type of moral justifiability required of institutions for them to have a right to rule; commonly 'legitimacy' is used to denote normative standards for moral acceptability – providing a kind of 'threshold' standard for institutions to possess the moral right to rule, rather than a higher moral standard for institutional aspiration, *within* a broader theory of justice (Rawls 1996). Within social scientific literatures, 'legitimacy' is widely characterized as an empirical property that institutions possess when subject populations *believe* them to be morally justified, and so have special motivational grounds for political compliance with institutional norms (Weber 1968, Lipset 1960, Habermas 1975).

The sense in which I am using the idea of legitimacy here is distinct from these more common usages. Instead I mean to denote a normative institutional quality or 'virtue' (not just an empirical or sociological property) that is independent from the institutional virtue of justice – neither a constituent element nor a consequence of it. In other words, legitimacy is a quality that it is good for institutions to have – and this implies that there is a distinctive set of reasons for designing institutions so that they possess this quality. Justice is an institutional virtue in this same general sense, but it is distinguished by the different set of reasons it provides as the basis for institutional design. Justice and legitimacy are therefore potentially *rival* institutional virtues; although the institutions required to realize each may converge under some social conditions, they will not necessarily always do so. Sometimes, then, the realization of justice and the realization of legitimacy might require competing institutional designs, in which case a choice must be made about which should be prioritized as the more important goal for political institutions to advance in that context.

The particular category of reasons (for favouring particular institutional designs) associated with justice is widely discussed. Broadly speaking, we can say that justice is a moral quality, consisting (at least) in the justifiability of institutions in terms of reasons that apply from some kind of *impartial point of view*, embodying equal concern for each member of the political community. Commitment to some kind of impartial moral justification is highly abstract, and under-determined with respect to the specific regulative principles for institutions it implies. Consequently, fully developed theories of justice construct broader arguments about the purposes and principles of justice – drawing in a range of additional normative and empirical premises along the way, depending on the particular theory, such as whether it is a more liberal or egalitarian theory, or a more 'ideal' or 'non-ideal' theory – to reach a wide range of conclusions about what institutions will count as just under a particular set of circumstances. But the idea of impartiality captures the underlying structure of the *special kind of justificatory reasoning* that is deployed (alongside other facts and assumptions) in arguments about the justice of institutions.

Legitimacy is a different kind of normative quality that is not (primarily or only) moral. Elsewhere, I have suggested that we can understand legitimacy as consisting (at least) in the justifiability of institutions in terms of reasons *embedded in the real social identities* of the existing political agents who are participants in the institutions in question – that is, who are governed in some way by the institutions and who are called upon to provide these institutions with political support (T. Macdonald 2010). Like the above claim that justice is a moral quality associated with impartial justificatory reasons, this statement does not amount to a fully developed normative theory of legitimacy,[8] and captures only the general structure of justificatory reasoning that is associated with the normative property of legitimacy. As is the case of theories of justice, additional claims of various kinds would need to be built into a theory of legitimacy before it could yield any specific set of regulatory principles for institutions.

The development of a full normative theory of legitimacy, and then the application of it to evaluate the legitimacy of the specific principles of stakeholder democracy, is clearly beyond the scope of this chapter.[9] In the absence of such a fully developed theory of global legitimacy, my goal here is more speculative. I aim to gain some traction on the question of the legitimacy of the stakeholder model of democracy by focusing on one particular feature of the general normative quality of legitimacy as I have characterized it, which I believe to be highly salient to analysis of the normative grounds of the democratic project. More specifically, I consider the congruence of stakeholder democracy with the following feature of legitimacy: *legitimacy is concerned not with the abstract moral justifiability of institutions as formulated in philosophical terms, but rather with their actual political acceptability, given some background set of sociological facts about the identities that political actors possess through their shared participation in these institutions.*

---

[8] Neither does the above claim that justice is a moral quality associated with impartial justificatory reasons.

[9] ... though I hope in due course to be able to supply one!

To make this general view of legitimacy operational, more needs to be said about the nature of 'political acceptability' and how this differs from the kind of moral justifiability associated with mainstream theories of justice. In explaining this here, I draw on the work of Bernard Williams. His is not a fully developed normative theory of legitimacy, and it opens up many questions on which much further theoretical work would be required before our understanding of the institutional virtue of legitimacy could approach the depth of our present understanding of justice; nonetheless, it provides a useful starting point for thinking about the subject. Williams's (2005) account of legitimacy is associated with a broader approach to political theory which he describes as 'political realism', as distinguished from the 'political moralism' underpinning most theories of justice. On this 'realist' approach to political theory, the goal is not to specify some morally ideal institutional arrangement; rather, the goal is to describe those institutional arrangements that provide the most acceptable available solution to the problem of political order. Williams calls this 'the first political problem', and characterizes it 'in Hobbesian terms as the securing of order, protection, safety, trust, and the conditions of cooperation' (3).

It is important to emphasize here that this 'realist' approach, on Williams's formulation of it,[10] does not entail abandonment of normative reasoning about institutions in favour of some kind of 'realpolitik' calculus or strategic bargain among political actors to achieve order via a short-term balance of power. Williams (2005) is clear that solving the first political problem 'is a necessary condition of legitimacy ... but it does not follow that it is a sufficient condition' (3). Rather, he argues that achieving legitimacy requires a public institution to 'offer a justification of its power to each subject' (4), on terms that will be politically 'acceptable' under the prevailing historical conditions – or, as he says, 'now and around here' (8) – such that those subject to the power will have reasons to accept that there is a morally significant distinction between the political power to which the political institution subjects them, and the forms of terror, coercion, suffering and so on that this institutional power is supposed to be preventing (5).

While this 'political realism' does not reduce to an amoral 'realpolitik', neither does it slide back into the 'moralism' characteristic of theories of

---

[10] To avoid misunderstanding, it is worth noting that there is a broader school of 'realist' political theory, often claiming Williams as a member, some proponents of which do want to employ more narrowly strategic forms of reasoning in the assessment of political institutions. For a good discussion of the tensions between Williams's work and these more strategic variants of realist political thought, see Sleat (2010).

justice, because the kind of 'justifying explanation or legitimation' Williams has in mind is one that is *sociologically grounded* in a special way. To count as a legitimation of a political institution, it is not enough for a justification to meet some abstract philosophical standards (such as some moral standards of impartiality); it must also 'make sense' to those who are subject to that institution as an account of what makes them acceptable. As Williams (2005) explains, this idea of 'making sense' is not strictly speaking a normative idea but rather a 'hermeneutical category', or a 'category of historical understanding' (11). As an example of this, he offers the case of liberalism, which he argues 'makes sense' as a legitimation only under the historical conditions of 'modernity'; liberalism should be understood not as an account of what is acceptable for institutions in some universalistic moral sense, but as what is required for acceptability under the historical conditions of modernity in which we presently live (7–11).

This view of legitimacy does not amount to some kind of normative relativism whereby anything that people happen to believe to be justified should for this reason alone be deemed acceptable. Rather, it highlights the fact that understandings of what should count as basic social interests (to be protected through political institutions), fundamental threats to those interests (which political institutions can be expected to address), and acceptable solutions to these threats (how much political institutions can be expected to be able to achieve) will vary in important ways under different historical conditions. They will vary because of differences in what kind of social agencies (individual and collective) exist and how they are constituted – more specifically, what needs and goals these social agencies possess, what they know, believe and understand, and what (materially) they are capable of doing and achieving through the exercise of their agency, given the resources, technologies and so on that they have at their disposal.

I want to highlight two implications of this account of the importance of political acceptability to the assessment of institutional legitimacy, which are especially salient to the assessment of global stakeholder democracy. The first of these is one that Williams (2005) himself articulates clearly: in order for some political claim to count in a process of legitimation, this claim must first be politically 'raised', as a matter of historical fact (7). This is because claims that have not in fact been raised in a given institutional context will not 'make sense' to participants in these institutions as justifications for the institutional power in question. This contrasts with justice-based arguments, which admit claims (for particular interests or reasons to be given weight in political decision making) based only on the fact of their being raised in philosophical argument, regardless of any sociological facts about the political standing of these claims in the particular institutional context.

Second, political claims will only count in a process of legitimation if they are *intelligible as claims made by actually-existing political actors, against other actually-existing political actors.* Legitimacy is a value that arises out of the clash of power and interests between existing actors: actors exist, some exercise power over others (and claim justifiability in doing so) and the others must assess the acceptability of these justifications, and consequently how cooperative (or recalcitrant) they should be. Legitimacy is the structure of justification that is offered and accepted in these political encounters, and its content is determined by the historical context of the encounter. This means that a justification cannot count as a basis for legitimacy if it entails allocation of responsibilities that no existing political agents have the capacity to discharge, as this would effectively require that existing political agents act to eradicate themselves, replacing themselves with some different kind of political agencies. It does not 'make sense', as a response to the problem of legitimacy, for a powerful institution to say to its subjects: 'I can justify my power to you by agreeing that I should cease to exist as an agent and be replaced by a different kind of institutional entity with some other set of capabilities and roles.'[11] At this second level also, we can see a contrast with moral justice-based arguments, which commonly justify institutions through hypothetical constructions representing the legitimate claims of idealized ('reasonable' or 'fully just') political actors, rather than the legitimate claims of actually existing political actors. As a result, they are able to produce arguments that prescribe radical *transformations of the identities of key actors within the social order,* as conditions for the justifiability of institutionalized power (Rawls 1999).

There is an important ambiguity in my account above of political acceptability, of the following kind. Given that a whole range of institutional models are 'raised' in some sense and 'acceptable' at least to a few philosophers (and in some cases to a group in the wider population), what is the criterion for determining *who* precisely needs to find it acceptable

---

[11] This observation allows for the possibility that the existence of certain political actors might not be *morally justifiable* – and that justice requires that they be dissolved. But as I have emphasized, moral justifiability and legitimacy are not equivalent; it is in principle possible (and in practice sometimes the case) that a given political actor can achieve legitimacy without achieving moral justifiability, and vice versa. My point here is that any political argument making claims and demands of this kind – that call for some fundamental change in the identity of key political agencies within a society – cannot be coherently supported with reasons of legitimacy (or at least not with reasons of legitimacy alone).

in order for it to count as legitimate? This is a central problem in the theory of legitimacy. I cannot give a fully developed answer here, but I will briefly indicate the *kind* of answer I think could be developed to this question. It cannot be adequate simply to *count* those individuals who find an institutional arrangement acceptable, versus those who do not. Although we know that such a procedure can produce a legitimate decision in circumstances where aggregative decision-making procedures possess legitimacy, this fact does not help us answer the deeper problem of how we can ascertain whether such an aggregative decision-making procedure is itself legitimate in a given social and institutional context. Nor can legitimacy be a straightforward function of what is raised by, or acceptable to, the most *powerful* political actors within a society. Powerful actors will often strongly influence social judgements of political acceptability, but they will not determine them – and the extent and means of their influence will be highly contextually variable.

Instead, I think the answer must involve a theoretical account of *collective or social* acceptability – at the level of a whole political society constituted through the institutional scheme under assessment. Such an account could be developed by drawing on the idea that there are normative reasons inherent in the *political identities surrounding participants' roles in the institutions through which a political 'society' is constituted* (in this case, the institutions constitutive of global society). It follows that what will count as acceptable in the relevant sense for assessments of global institutional legitimacy will be a function of the reasons inherent in the role – identities of participants in global institutions.[12]

Without presenting a more fully developed theory along these lines, along with some detailed sociological analysis of global institutions and the content of the role-identities of participants, I can make only speculative claims about which (if any) of the range of philosophically contested democratic alternatives for global institutions will count as legitimate. Accordingly, I cannot demonstrate robustly here that stakeholder democracy (or any other democratic model) is the most legitimate of the alternatives under discussion.[13] But despite the indeterminacy

---

[12] The idea that there can be such a thing as 'social' acceptability that is not reducible to acceptability to some number of individuals does not imply any problematic 'holist' social ontology; the facts about 'social' acceptability I am referring to here are facts about the content of the identities linked to participants' roles in social institutions, not facts about the existence of some mysterious metaphysical social entity.

[13] Even with a fully developed theory of legitimacy a significant degree of indeterminacy would remain; however, as Russell Hardin (2003) has powerfully argued, theories of justice are also highly indeterminate, in ways that their proponents do not always fully appreciate or acknowledge.

surrounding the idea of collective political acceptability, appreciation of the importance of political acceptability sheds light on how the political exclusions permitted by stakeholder democracy might well qualify as legitimate – regardless of whether we can make a successful moral argument that they qualify as just. If we assume that the deep purpose of democratic institutions is to make a society's institutions legitimate, then it follows from what I have just said that the forms of political equality associated with the egalitarian citizenship view will be required to sustain the legitimacy of a global democratic system only if these are deemed necessary – in the historical context of globalization – to achieve a politically acceptable solution (within global society as a whole) to the 'first political problem' of order. I judge that in the era of globalization – characterized by high levels of social and institutional pluralism – some kind of pluralist liberal institutional framework will give the most politically acceptable answer to the 'first political question', rather than a framework fostering global egalitarian citizenship.

This judgement is based on empirical assessments of two things. First, it is based on assessment of the kinds of interests that are widely valued and the kinds of threats that are widely feared within contemporary global society, as reflected in the role-identities of participants in global institutions; I take these to be captured by a liberal criterion of autonomy limitation. Second, it is based on assessment of what is institutionally achievable given present distributions of power and institutional capabilities, and thereby what will be considered politically 'acceptable' – in particular, given the existing lack of any cosmopolitan political institutions capable of discharging the highly demanding duties that would be entailed in a commitment to egalitarian citizenship within global society, and the enormous political obstacles to establishing such institutions in the near term.

From here it is a small step to stakeholder democracy: the stakeholder principle offers a liberal criterion for answering the question of which populations are subject to the kinds of threats that require legitimation as an acceptable solution to the 'first political problem' of order. Exclusion from political decision making of those populations whose 'autonomy-interests' are not threatened by political institutions is acceptable from the point of view of such liberal legitimacy, since on the liberal view it is only this category of interests that political institutions are expected to protect, and therefore it is only individuals with these interests who *require* the special forms of political justification associated with legitimacy. Moreover, the stakeholder strategy of subjecting existing political agencies (states, international organizations, corporations, NGOs and so on) to direct legitimation through democratic control is compatible with legitimacy being a normative quality concerned with political justifications offered among existing political agencies, rather than with political implementation of more deeply transformative moral projects. This shows how stakeholder democracy can withstand the second variant of the egalitarian critique discussed in the previous section, concerning its failure to provide a political framework for facilitating the collective discharge of egalitarian civic responsibilities.

Having explained how the stakeholder model's exclusions can be seen as legitimate, it remains for me to show how they can also satisfy sufficiently *egalitarian* standards of legitimacy, since standards of legitimacy need not always be egalitarian, but they need to be so if they are to count as *democratic*. While much has been written on the topic of egalitarian *justice*, this is not the same as egalitarian *legitimacy*. Further, there is no easy or established theoretical answer as to what would be entailed in attaching the qualifier 'egalitarian' to the distinct normative quality of legitimacy described above. Given the constraints of this chapter, I shall simply state my view of the implications for our thinking about political equality if we take legitimacy rather than justice to be the primary goal of political institutions, and highlight how this supports the egalitarian credentials of the stakeholder model of democracy.

The most fundamental implication of pursuing legitimacy rather than justice as the first virtue of democratic institutions is that the protections for political equality provided by a legitimate democratic system will be required *only to the extent that claims to equality are raised politically in the institutional context in question*. Exclusions (of some social actors, or representatives of some social interests) from political decision making will therefore be unacceptable on an egalitarian account of legitimacy *only if these exclusions result from the (unjustified) denial of political claims to inclusion*, and not if they consist merely in non-compliance with some moral ideal of justice to which no robust political claim has in fact been made in the relevant institutional context.

To count as egalitarian, a legitimate political institution must therefore make a *presumption* in favour of equality for all political actors in responding to political claims and demands. But unlike egalitarian justice, egalitarian legitimacy does not entail the provision of any institutional *guarantee* of equality, independently of the historical context in which political claims to inclusion may be raised. In other words, standards of legitimacy cannot (and do not aspire to) provide the basis for any deep structural critique of the egalitarian credentials of a social order itself, incorporating a critique of the egalitarian virtues embedded in the identities and goals of the social actors within it. Legitimate egalitarian institutions can ensure only that institutions are *open on equal terms* to input from existing social actors, however unequally these actors may be constituted under the prevailing historical circumstances. To count as egalitarian from the perspective of legitimacy, political institutions only need to be as egalitarian as the underlying social order permits – in other words, only as egalitarian as 'makes sense' to institutional participants given the prevailing historical conditions and associated facts about political values and relationships and institutional capacities.

Given that the stakeholder model of democracy satisfies the requirements of political equality understood in these terms (as should be clear from my discussion of the egalitarian credentials of the model in the previous section), it can be seen how the kinds of exclusions permitted within stakeholder democracy fall into the category of permissible exclusions within a framework of egalitarian legitimacy. This enables stakeholder democracy to withstand the third variant of the egalitarian critique I outlined previously, concerned with its failure to incorporate formal provisions to foster active political participation of all global citizens even against the background of social inequality.

Conclusions: is legitimacy an appropriate goal for democratic global institutions?

The stakeholder model does not provide a democratic theory that will fully satisfy those who see egalitarian citizenship, justified by a moral theory of egalitarian justice, as the underlying purpose of democratic institutions. However, it should satisfy those who instead identify this purpose with achievement of (an egalitarian form of) political *legitimacy*. To complete my defence of the egalitarian credentials of stakeholder democracy, I conclude by briefly explaining why democrats might think it appropriate to view the purpose of the democratic project in this latter way.

To begin, I take it that both justice and legitimacy are important goals for political institutions to advance, and if circumstances make it possible for institutions to achieve both simultaneously then they should strive to do so.[14] If the kind of liberal justice argument I flagged earlier

[14] I see the Rawlsian project of 'political liberalism' as built on the supposition that liberal democratic institutions operating within closed societies, under favourable conditions (such as within wealthy industrialized nation-states), should be able to achieve both with the same (liberal) institutions – or at least can come close enough that they should aspire to do so (see Rawls 1996). Rawls does not frame this project in terms of the idea of legitimacy as I have explained it here (he defines legitimacy differently), but I believe this

can provide a moral justification for stakeholder democracy, and if it can achieve a good deal of political legitimacy under present social conditions, as I have claimed, then it may be possible to achieve both justice and legitimacy via the stakeholder model. If not, then we may need to choose between these two underlying institutional virtues in evaluating competing democratic designs. In such an event, we would need to answer this question: why should a democrat choose legitimacy over justice as the primary goal to pursue?

The first answer to this question is a prudential one. We might choose a form of democracy that pursues legitimacy rather than justice because doing so would yield democratic institutions capable of sustaining stable political rule. Even if we aspire to achieve a fully just form of democracy, as a prudential matter it might only make sense to choose a just institutional design if it will also be legitimate – that is, if it will be acceptable to the actual political actors who exist and interact with the institutions, and whose support is required for their effective and stable operation. No institutional scheme can operate well in practice if it relies on the support of political actors that do not exist except in philosophical constructions, so it is arguably futile, and perhaps counterproductive, to use power to promote institutions that satisfy philosophical standards of justice but are unlikely to attract sufficient political support to enable them to function effectively or endure.[15] On this basis we might say that legitimacy, not justice, should be considered the 'first virtue' of social institutions;[16] justice should be pursued in addition, but only to the extent that it is compatible with legitimacy.

Even if we accept this position, there is a further challenge to be answered. A democrat might want to say: 'Fine, we should choose legitimacy and perhaps even a stakeholder model for achieving it, but let's not delude ourselves into thinking that we're choosing democracy. It's something else – a necessary choice perhaps, the right choice, but not a democratic one.' A number of democrats have already taken this kind of position in existing debates on global democracy – preferring to preserve the intellectual integrity of treasured historical ideals of

interpretation of the Rawlsian project can be defended – albeit with more detailed analysis than is possible here.

[15] I have in mind here the example of the philosophically constructed 'reasonable' cosmopolitan citizens, who are presupposed to constructivist justifications for standards of cosmopolitan justice and democracy but do not exist in political reality (at least not in a sufficiently critical mass to bring about stable cosmopolitan institutions). See, for example, Kuper (2000, 2004).

[16] Rawls (1999) has famously claimed that justice is the 'first virtue' of social institutions (3).

democratic citizenship at the price of abandoning the attempt to bring democratic insights and principles to bear, in a practical fashion, at the political level of global institutional design (Dahl 1999, Miller 2010).

In my view, such a position significantly underplays the potential contribution of the democratic tradition to practical institutional debates in the era of globalization. To appreciate the genuine democratic credentials of the stakeholder model, it helps to take a broader historical perspective, remembering that democracy has always been a practical institutional ideal which furnishes a set of prescriptive principles for the regulation of real political life, rather than an abstract moral standard detached from concrete empirical realities. As W.B. Gallie (1956) observed over half a century ago, democracy is a paradigmatically 'open' political concept, in the sense that ideals of democracy must inevitably change and adapt in keeping with the circumstances of particular historical eras: '[p]olitics being the art of the possible, democratic targets will be raised or lowered as circumstances alter, and democratic achievements are always judged in the light of such alterations' (186).

Throughout its history, democracy has incorporated political exclusions of many kinds that we now condemn as unjust: actually-existing democracies have at different times excluded slaves, non-landowners, women, members of particular ethnic, religious or national groups, and individuals born and/or resident outside their territorial jurisdictions. Indeed, still no democratic institution presently exists that does not incorporate at least one of these political exclusions (all of which are condemned as unjust on the cosmopolitan account).[17] While it is now uncontroversial to diagnose these exclusions as unjust, it would be downright eccentric to conclude that none of these existing or historical institutional schemes warrants the label of *democratic* – or to deny that any of them has achieved some reasonable degree of democratic legitimacy. In this light, it's not clear to me why democrats should suddenly come over all morally puritanical when they turn their attention to the case of global institutions, and withhold democratic endorsement to institutions (of stakeholder democracy) tailored to the historical circumstances of contemporary global politics.

In sum, stakeholder democracy does not offer a panacea for all social inequalities and injustices, but we should not expect any democratic model to deliver this – at least insofar as we are concerned with the really-existing democratic institutions that are the subject of practical projects of institutional design and reform. In political practice, it seems

---

[17] For an excellent recent analysis of the history of democracy, including a discussion of such political exclusions, see Keane (2009).

ambitious enough to hope that building democratic institutions will enhance the *legitimacy* of global governance. Viewed only as a vehicle for achieving political legitimacy, stakeholder democracy is able to meet a robust egalitarian standard.

REFERENCES

Anderson, Elizabeth S. 1999. 'What Is the Point of Equality?', *Ethics* 109, 2: 287–337.
Brighouse, Harry, and Marc Fleurbaey. 2010. 'Democracy and Proportionality', *Journal of Political Philosophy* 18, 2: 137–55.
Buchanan, Allen. 2002. 'Political Legitimacy and Democracy', *Ethics* 112, 4: 689–719.
Copp, David. 1999. 'The Idea of a Legitimate State', *Philosophy and Public Affairs* 28, 1: 3–45.
Dahl, Robert. 1967. *A Preface to Democratic Theory*. University of Chicago Press.
    1999. 'Can International Organizations Be Democratic? A Skeptic's View', in Ian Shapiro and Casiano Hacker-Cordón (eds.), *Democracy's Edges* (pp. 19–36). Cambridge University Press.
Gallie, W. B. 1956. 'Essentially Contested Concepts', *Proceedings of the Aristotelian Society* 56: 167–98.
Goodin, Robert E. 2007. 'Enfranchising All Affected Interests, and Its Alternatives', *Philosophy & Public Affairs* 35, 1: 40–68.
Habermas, Jürgen. 1975. *Legitimation Crisis*. Boston, MA: Beacon Press.
Hardin, Russell. 2003. *Indeterminacy and Society*. Princeton University Press.
Keane, John. 2009. *The Life and Death of Democracy*. New York: W.W. Norton.
Koenig-Archibugi, Mathias. Forthcoming. 'Fuzzy Citizenship in Global Society'. *Journal of Political Philosophy*.
Kuper, Andrew. 2000. 'Rawlsian Global Justice', *Political Theory* 28, 5: 640–74.
    2004. *Democracy Beyond Borders: Justice and Representation in Global Institutions*. Oxford University Press.
Lipset, Seymour Martin. 1960. *Political Man*. London: Heinemann.
Macdonald, Kate, and Terry Macdonald. 2010. 'Democracy in a Pluralist Global Order: Corporate Power and Stakeholder Representation', *Ethics & International Affairs* 24, 1: 19–43.
Macdonald, Terry. 2008. *Global Stakeholder Democracy: Power and Representation Beyond Liberal States*. New York: Oxford University Press.
    2010. 'Institutional Legitimacy and its Relationship to Justice'. Paper presented at the Workshop on Global Political Justice, Monash University Prato Centre, Italy, 22–3 June.
Miller, David. 2010. 'Against Global Democracy', in Keith O'Neill and Shane Breen (eds.), *After the Nation: Critical Reflections on Post-Nationalism* (pp. 141–61). Basingstoke, UK: Palgrave Macmillan.
Rawls, John. 1996. *Political Liberalism*. New York: Columbia University Press.
    1999. *A Theory of Justice*. Oxford University Press.
Schmitter, Philippe C. 2009. 'Re-Presenting Representation', *Government and Opposition* 44, 4: 476–90.

Simmons, A. John. 1999. 'Justification and Legitimacy', *Ethics* 109, 4: 739–71.

Sleat, Matt. 2010. 'Bernard Williams and the Possibility of a Realist Political Theory', *European Journal of Political Theory* 9, 4: 485–503.

Valentini, Laura. 2011. 'Coercion and (Global) Justice: A Conceptual Framework', *American Political Science Review* 105, 1: 205–20.

Weber, Max. 1968. *Economy and Society: An Outline of Interpretive Sociology* (ed. Guenther Roth and Claus Wittich). New York: Bedminster Press.

Wellman, Christopher H. 1996. 'Liberalism, Samaritanism, and Political Legitimacy', *Philosophy and Public Affairs* 25, 3: 211–37.

Williams, Bernard. 2005. 'Realism and Moralism in Political Theory', in Bernard Williams, *In the Beginning Was the Deed: Realism and Moralism in Political Argument* (ed.Geoffrey Hawthorn). Princeton University Press.

4 Is democratic legitimacy possible for international institutions?

Thomas Christiano

Humanity as a whole currently faces a number of fundamental challenges that can only be dealt with on a global scale. Global warming and other environmental problems, severe poverty and the need for a fair system of international trade all call for international solutions that are achieved by means of collective decisions. But these solutions will require sacrifices on the part of all persons and there is likely to be a great deal of disagreement about the optimal solution and the fairest distribution of the burdens imposed by any solution. We need to have means for making collective decisions that all persons and the states of which they are members have good reason to regard as binding upon them.

An institution has legitimacy when it has a right to rule over a certain set of issues. The moral function of the legitimacy of decision-making processes is to confer morally binding force on the decisions of the institution within a moral community even for those who disagree with them and who must sacrifice. This morally binding force is achieved for a decision-making institution when its directives create content-independent and very weighty duties to obey the decision maker. There are three main conceptions of the grounds of legitimacy in modern political thought. One says that the legitimacy of an authoritative decision process depends on the quality of the outcomes of the decision process. A second sees the legitimacy of an authoritative process as based on the consent of the members. And the third sees legitimacy as grounded in liberal democratic processes of decision making.[1] The latter two forms of legitimacy are particularly salient when there is considerable disagreement on how to assess the quality of outcomes.

My project is to explore the possibility of grounding the legitimacy of international institutions and law from a moral cosmopolitan standpoint

---

[1] See Raz (1986) and Estlund (2007) for mostly results-oriented conceptions of authority. Simmons (2001) and Singer (1974) have defended voluntarist conceptions of authority. Waldron (1999) has defended a purely democratic theory. Christiano (2008) and Klosko (2004) have defended more complex approaches.

devoted broadly to democratic principles. It is premised on the idea that when there is substantial disagreement among the parties who are deeply affected by international law and institutions, moral cosmopolitanism entails the requirement that persons have a say in the making of these entities. Furthermore, the persons must be enabled to participate as equals in the process of decision making. This implies that the legitimacy of international law and institutions is grounded in one of the following principles or a principle that combines and transcends three central notions of legitimacy available in modern political philosophy: the principle that decisions must conform to minimal standards of morality, the principle of fair voluntary association and the principle of democracy (Christiano 2008, chapters 3, 4 and 7).

But there is a further constraint on this exploration of the possibility of legitimate international law and institutions. The conception of legitimacy of international institutions must be properly attuned to the evolving nature of these institutions and the global political environment they operate in. Much of traditional political philosophy is mostly geared to figuring out the moral norms that apply to modern states. And some basic assumptions about how these political societies operate and what they are capable of are presupposed in most discussions. But our under-standing of international political institutions tells us that they are not at all like states. At the same time, they are not like the other kinds of institutions that get some legitimacy from their members: voluntary associations. And we must respect these differences when we explore questions of legitimacy and justification with regard to international institutions. But they do nevertheless have some political power and they will need more political power in order to solve some of the problems I described above.

To ascertain the peculiar situation political philosophy is in with regard to these institutions I lay out a puzzle about how legitimacy is possible for international institutions in a world where states are the main players and the main vehicles of accountability of political power to persons. According to the traditional legal doctrine, international institutions and international law seem to get their legitimacy from the consent of the states that create these institutions. The traditional account makes no reference to persons and eschews cosmopolitanism. But such an account of legitimacy can be grounded in cosmopolitan principles to the extent that the process of consent results from fair negotiation among states that represent the persons in their societies as equal citizens. Such a process of consent enables all persons to have a kind of say in a process of fair voluntary association among societies.

Immediately, two problems arise: first, fair negotiation implies that parties do not take unfair advantage of other parties in the process of negotiation; and, second, the states must all be highly democratic. As I understand it, taking unfair advantage involves two components. The terms give disproportionate advantages to one party over the other and this disproportion arises from the much greater bargaining power of the favoured party. Something like this may be at work in domestic society. The domestic legal systems of modern liberal democratic states attempt to limit unfair advantage-taking by providing a social minimum for each person, regulating pricing as well as contracts, and their courts tend to reject highly disproportionate agreements. The problem in international society is that these mitigating circumstances have no counterparts in the international sphere. Extremes of poverty are not mitigated, thereby enabling some to take unfair advantage of others and there are constant complaints about the disproportionate advantages drawn by powerful and wealthy states relative to developing societies, the negotiations among states in the World Trade Organization (WTO) in the 1990s being a prime example of this.[2]

The other difficulty is that not all states are democratic and certainly most states are not highly democratic. Democracy is a widespread ideal at the moment and the international community seems committed to its diffusion throughout the globe. Still, the question for an account of legitimacy based on fair voluntary association is what to do with societies that are not democratic? They do not represent their people very well so it would seem that their participation in the making of international law and institutions cannot satisfy the cosmopolitan idea behind the process of fair voluntary association. And yet their people are less well represented if these states do not participate at all. Either they should be left out of the process or they should be made more democratic. Yet both of these are unsatisfying results because either a substantial portion of the world's population is left out of the process of decision making or it commits us to a highly dubious process of forced democratization.

But these brief remarks suggest a deep puzzle. From the above considerations, it seems that powerful international institutions are needed to establish the background conditions for fair negotiations among states and to ensure that they are democratic. Only they can secure the background conditions for fair negotiation. Only they can resolve

---

[2] See Steinberg (2002) for an account of this bargaining.

controversies about when benefits are not grossly disproportionately distributed and enforce their judgements. And only they can effectively promote democracy. But in order to do this successfully they must be able to hold powerful states in check. International institutions are either strong enough to hold the most powerful states in check or they are likely to be disproportionately controlled by powerful states.[3] If international institutions have the kind of power to hold powerful states in check then the problem of legitimacy transfers to them and the ultimate standard by which they would be judged is a democratic standard. But the prospects for global democratic institutions are very low at the moment and for the medium-term future. If they are too weak to hold powerful states in check and those states have disproportionate control over them, they lack legitimacy at least by any remotely democratic standard. Hence, the two central standards of legitimacy, fair voluntary association and democracy, seem to be unattainable for international institutions for the foreseeable future, at least in the simple forms we know them. The realization of the first standard seems to depend on the realization of the second one but the second one is unattainable in part because the first one is unattainable on its own.

In the first part of this chapter, I will critique the idea of global democracy. In the next part, I will critique the voluntary association model of legitimacy. These critical discussions suggest an impasse in our thinking about how international institutions and law can be made legitimate. I will then address some critical remarks to an alternative conception of global democracy that has recently been defended.

I have no solution to this impasse at the moment. It may be that the best we can do currently is to ensure that minimal standards of morality or human rights are respected and promoted by international law and institutions and to try to make sure that these institutions satisfy some minimal standards of accountability.[4] I am not ready to adopt this conclusion as an account of legitimacy but I offer this chapter as a challenge to the thought that the application of more ambitious principles of legitimacy can be reasonably applied to international institutions.

---

[3] For some striking examples of this see Steinberg (2004) and Doyle (2009).

[4] See Buchanan and Keohane (2006) for this conception of legitimacy. The basic worry about this view is that though it does list some properties that it would be desirable for international institutions to have, it is hard to see how these properties can ground a right to rule for those institutions and associated content-independent duties (see also K. Macdonald, this volume).

Problems concerning the ground of transnational and global democracy

The reasoning with which I introduced this chapter suggests that powerful global institutions are necessary to treat persons as equals in the process of collective decision making about global issues. The main principle of legitimacy we have for centralized political decision making is democracy. Democratic decision making is a method of collective decision making that publicly treats persons as equals when there is substantial disagreement and conflict of interest over matters of common concern. Though all the outcomes of democratic decision making will inevitably be opposed by many, and a large proportion will be unjust, the method confers legitimacy on the results by publicly treating all the participants as equals, at least as long as the results satisfy some minimal standards of justice. Hence, many political theorists and philosophers have naturally turned to global democracy as a potential source of legitimacy for international institutions. By 'global democracy' in this section, I mean a centralized democratic decision-making process for solving global problems. These processes would involve a global legislature directly elected by the world's adult population.[5] It would operate in a roughly majoritarian way within certain limits grounded in basic human rights. I want to suggest three serious difficulties for the thesis that collective decision making ought to be done in this way at least for the near to medium-term future.

The problem of stakes

It is often argued that global democracy or transnational democracy can be grounded in the fact that people's activities all around the world have effects on people in other parts of the globe. Since people's activities in different parts of the globe have effects on those in other parts, each person should have a say in the overall organization of the globe. Each should have a say in what affects him or her. This argument has been put in different ways. Some have noted that actions of persons in one part of the world affect peoples in other parts of the world and so they all ought to have an equal say. This might be called the 'all affected' principle. Others note that actions of persons in one part of the world engage and direct the actions of persons elsewhere. Another criterion is that actions

---

[5] See Marchetti (this volume) for a discussion of this model and for references to the large literature on it. See also Murithi (this volume).

of persons in one part of the world affect at least some of the fundamental interests of those in other parts of the world.[6]

But these arguments fail to take into account one of the basic requirements for the desirability of democratic decision making. I have argued elsewhere that for democracy genuinely to treat people as equals, the combination of issues on which democracy decides must be one in which individuals have roughly equal stakes overall (Christiano (2008)). It is not enough that people are affected, or that some of their fundamental interests are affected, it must be that their fates are somehow mostly equally bound up with the package of issues they are dealing with. If two people have an equal say in a matter that affects one person's interests much more than the other's interests, and there are no other issues wherein the other's interests are more implicated, then it appears that there is some unfairness in them having an equal say. And the same holds for combinations of issues. If two people have fundamental interests in collective decisions over some combination of issues but the interests of one are much more bound up with that set of issues than the other's are, it does not seem fair to give each an equal voice. Indeed, it would seem that this would amount to not treating the people in question as equals. Normally, in those contexts in which people are likely to have very different stakes in issues to be decided, some kind of right of veto or exit is accorded each person, with which they can protect their interests. The matters are not decided by majority rule unless they are parts of larger combinations of issues in which the persons have equal stakes overall.

This is why democracy is particularly desirable at the modern state level in the modern world. At least in the normal case, individuals inhabit a world in common with others in which the fundamental interests of all are implicated. In such a political community there is a rough equality of stake for all the individuals. As a consequence, giving each person an equal voice is a fair way of distributing power among them.

But this cannot be said of individuals in different states. First, though their lives are mutually affected in a variety of ways they are not mutually affected to the same deep extent as the lives of members of a single modern state are. Overall, my interests are far more bound up with the interests of other persons in the United States than they are with persons in China or even in Canada even though there are clear ways in which we of different political societies influence each other's lives. We do

[6] See Gould (2004, 176–80, and this volume) for a review and critique of some different approaches and a defence of the approach that makes human rights central to determining who ought to have a say in collective decisions. See also Pogge (2002).

not inhabit common worlds with these other people. This is, at least in part, the implication of current institutionalist approaches to development economics, which assert that the main determinant of the economic well-being of a country is the set of domestic institutions that country has.[7]

But, second and more important, it is not clear that we have equal stakes in the decisions or the combinations of decisions that are made by transnational and global institutions. As a general rule there are inequalities of stakes in larger transnational institutions. For instance, in the WTO some member states have far greater stakes in external trade than other states, as can be seen from their very different export to gross domestic product ratios. But a democratic principle would appear to give them all equal voices. And thus the necessary condition for the intrinsic fairness of democratic decision making seems not to hold in the case of transnational institutions or global ones. The legitimacy of such institutions must always be called into question since it is unclear that equality of stakes is present.

These difficulties are magnified by the requirement that I have defended, which is that democracy publicly realizes equality among citizens. This demands that the equality be one that everyone can see to be in effect among them. I have argued that this is a key element in the argument for the intrinsic desirability of democracy. But if we have good reason to think that transnational institutions are unlikely to involve equality of stakes in the sets of decisions they make, there is a very strong reason for thinking that these collective decision-making areas cannot be egalitarian in a publicly clear way to all the members. Many will have good reasons for complaining that their interests are being given less than equal consideration on the grounds that others are given an equal say in matters that affect their interests more deeply than the interests of the others. Even if these complaints are not always justified, the appearance of inequity will not go away in these contexts. So we have here a general normative worry about the appropriateness of democratic decision making in the context of global collective decision making.

The problem of persistent minorities on a global scale

The second problem I want to discuss here is the problem of persistent minorities. In my view, the presence of persistent minorities in the

---

[7] See Rodrik (2007, 184): 'There is now widespread agreement among economists studying economic growth that institutional quality holds the key to prevailing patterns of prosperity around the world.'

modern democratic state undercuts the authority of the state with respect to those minorities. This is a significant problem in modern states as they are.[8] But it would appear to be an even greater problem in global and transnational institutions if they were fully democratized. The larger the constituency, the larger the chances are that particular minorities would simply get lost in the democratic decision making.

To be sure, not all minorities would be lost since some of them could make common cause with others on the larger global scale. And presumably global democratic institutions would have to be ruled by coalitions of different groups, each of which is a minority on its own. Still, in a world as diverse as the one we live in, it seems hard to imagine that there will not be large sections of humanity that will find themselves not part of any winning coalition for significant periods of time. We see this already in modern states where the level of diversity is generally considerably smaller than in the world overall.

But as I have argued elsewhere, the presence of persistent minorities undercuts the authority of the democratic assembly at least with regard to the persistent minority and it weakens the authority secondarily with regard to the rest of the population. The consequence of this is that we can infer that the authority of global democratic institutions will be severely weakened by this problem.

The way these problems are sometimes resolved in modern states is through the devices of political autonomy and consensual institutions. In the case of political autonomy, the most extreme measure available is secession, but less extreme methods are also available such as partial political autonomy for a particular region and a federal structure of governance. In these two kinds of institutional structures the problem of the persistent minority is partly resolved by allowing the minority to make decisions for itself either as an independent political unit or at least to make some broad class of decisions for itself.

Alternatively, these problems have sometimes been solved by methods of consensus politics including supermajority rules on some or all issues or some kind of consociational decision-making process. These kinds of rules ensure that the minority has some say by requiring that the supermajority be large enough so that it has to include the minority group in the final decisions.

As I see it, both of these kinds of devices are somewhat non-democratic. They involve departures from egalitarian ways of making decisions. The establishment of political autonomy involves cutting out a

---

[8] I argue this in some detail in Chapter 7 of Christiano (2008).

piece of the common world so that only a small group has a say over it, even though many persons' interests are deeply implicated. Over some issues only some of those whose fundamental interests are implicated in the decision have a say over those issues when political autonomy is established within a common world.

In the case of consensus decision-making rules, the rules are not democratic to the extent that they give minorities a kind of veto over the decisions. Instead of each having an equal say, a minority has a kind of veto power, though it may not be the minority whose interests we are trying to protect. The reason for majority rule is that it is the one rule for decision making that seems to treat each person as an equal in a variety of ways. The more we move towards supermajority rule, the more we endanger the equality in the decision making. Of course, it may be necessary to do this under certain circumstances, circumstances that the underlying principle of equality seems to pick out. But we should not be deceived into thinking that the consequent institutional structure is entirely democratic.

In addition, to the extent that we are talking about global governance institutions, it is not clear what the possibility of secession amounts to. It would appear that secession would simply imply that the institutions are not global after all. If we were to insist on global institutions, the possibility of secession would be ruled out. And thus one possible remedy for the problem of persistent minorities would be ruled out by global institutions even though the problem itself is likely to be far greater than it is at the national level.

The problem of persistent minorities, I have argued, cuts right at the heart of the legitimacy of democratic institutions and so democratic global institutions would start life with a very serious obstacle to estab-lishing their genuine legitimacy. Thus, we seem to be able to anticipate a very significant problem of persistent minorities on the global scale without some main devices, such as secession, that can be used to remedy this problem. Alternatively, the use of political autonomy and consociational decision making move us more in the direction of fair voluntary association among equals.

The problem of citizenship at the global level

There is one more difficulty that I want to raise for prospects of global or even transnational democracy. One difficulty concerning citizenship in large states is that citizens have little incentive to become informed about matters of politics because they have so little impact on the outcomes of decision making. Economists defend the idea that citizens are rationally ignorant on the grounds that a citizen cannot advance his or her interests through the political process.[9] But one need not agree with economists that citizens are exclusively concerned with narrow self-interest to think that there is a genuine problem here. First, it is well observed that citizens are not very well informed about politics in modern democratic states. Second, the sense of responsibility that is often necessary to engage the moral capacities is highly attenuated in the case of voting in large-scale democracies. Where one has little sense of responsibility for outcomes and the complexity of issues is very hard to grasp, it is hard to become interested in the moral issues that are involved in the decisions even if one is a moral person overall.

This problem is likely to be increased when it comes to decision making in transnational or global institutions. Here, the greater size of the constituencies combined with the even greater complexity of the issues at stake suggest that citizens are even less likely to vote in an informed way about matters connected to global institutions than they are in national democratic decisions. This worry is confirmed by the widespread observation that citizens of various countries tend to be far less informed about the foreign policies of their states than they are about the domestic policies.[10]

To some degree, citizens do seem to solve some of the problems relating to low levels of information in politics. They make decisions that help them advance their interests. But the way they solve them in part is by taking short cuts to information that are made available to them by established and settled political institutions such as interest groups and political parties. For instance, particular citizens tend to follow certain opinion leaders' judgements and the positions of their political parties.[11] The main point I wish to make here is that citizens overcome some of the problems of information in decision making with the help of settled institutions in civil society. These institutions are essential to making democracy possible even to the imperfect extent that it is in modern states.[12] And it is important that these are long-established and settled institutions precisely because it is only under

---

[9] See Downs (1957) for an account of this problem and for its implications for equality.
[10] See Dahl (1999) for a detailed discussion of this problem and the difficulties relating to citizens' knowledge of foreign policy. I agree in large part with his main conclusions.
[11] See Popkin (1990) for an excellent review of many cognitive shortcuts citizens take in making decisions about who to vote for in elections.
[12] See Christiano (1996, especially chapters 5–8) for a discussion of the question of what citizens ought to know if they are to participate as equals in a democratic process and of the institutional devices by which the problem of citizen information can be at least partly overcome.

these conditions that citizens can rationally come to trust these institutions so as to use them as shortcuts for important information. These institutional devices, imperfect as they are, are what stave off complete elite control of government.

The worry I wish to suggest here is that the danger of complete elite control of governmental institutions becomes very alarming when we consider global or transnational institutions, in the light of the problem of citizen information briefly sketched above. In addition, in the absence of established and settled institutions for debate and discussion, like political parties and interest groups that are connected to citizens, it is hard to see how the problem of information can be mitigated on the global scale. This is admittedly a problem that need not last forever but it is one that is likely to last for a very long time. This is because it is hard to see how non-governmental institutions of global reach such as political parties can establish the kind of trust that is necessary for citizens to be able to rely on them in the process of participation. Even in the case of the European Union, which has had European decision-making institutions for many years, strong European-wide institutions like political parties and interest groups have yet to arise. Therefore, the prospects for real democracy on the global level are not likely to be very good for many years to come.

It seems to me that the consequent dangers of elite control of transnational and global democratic institutions are likely to be with us for a long time. These dangers undercut the claim of such institutions to be in accord with the ideals that underpin democracy. And so we must be very sceptical about arguments that attempt to apply ideas of democracy on a global or transnational scale.

Fair voluntary association among democratic states

I have argued against global democracy as a way of addressing collective action problems in the world as a whole. Now I want to consider the problem of legitimacy from the standpoint of fair voluntary association. This is the natural alternative to global democracy as a way of thinking about the legitimacy of international institutions. It is one that I have defended elsewhere, but which I now worry about (Christiano (2010)). I will proceed by briefly describing this conception and its rationale. I will then discuss an issue which is normally at the root of this conception of legitimacy: conceiving of international law as composed of treaties that are thought of on the model of contracts among states. The contract model is highly problematic as a way of understanding treaties and it misrepresents the role treaties can play in the international arena.

First, I will briefly set out the idea of fair voluntary association among democratic states. The idea is rooted in the traditional doctrine of state consent as the basis of the legitimacy of international law and institutions. The traditional idea is that international law and institutions are made legitimate and have binding force as a result of the consent states give in the process of making treaties. The fundamental principle is '*pacta sunt servanda*'. There is something like a doctrine of tacit consent to customary international law. When a practice becomes regularized and a state does not express objections to participation in the practice, the state is then often thought of as bound to customary international law. For the most part the consent must be voluntary. The idea is that because states are bound to act in accordance with international law they must consent to it. There are some exceptions to the requirement of voluntary consent. *Jus cogens* norms bind states whether they consent or not and states may not abridge these norms in the making of treaties. These norms include norms against aggressive war, genocide, torture, piracy and slavery. And states may be coerced into accepting peace treaties if they have been the aggressors.

The traditional doctrine is based on the idea that states are the entities that are directed to act in international law. Individuals are not so directed in traditional international law. But as international law begins to intrude on national legal systems through requirements on the domestic economic system in trade law and environmental law as well as in human rights law, it is beginning to direct the actions of individuals. Hence, the traditional reason for state consent is being undermined to some extent.[13]

But we might think that we can preserve the doctrine of state consent as long as we introduce the requirement that the states represent their peoples as equals. This extends the binding character of consent through states to the individuals in those states whose actions are now being more and more constrained by international law. To be sure, this requires that the state be robustly democratic, that it give adequate protection and representation to minorities and that its foreign policy establishment be significantly more democratic than it currently is. Only then is there some reason to think that the consent of the state really does in some way reach all the way down to the individuals. The consent of highly representative states may be a kind of hybrid of consent and democratic legitimacy.

In addition to the requirement of democracy, the state consent model needs to be supplemented with an account of fair negotiation of treaties,

[13] See Bodansky (1999) for a discussion of this issue.

so that the consent of a state is not given under duress or other conditions that defeat the voluntariness of the agreements. Furthermore, since we are concerned here with the consent of states binding the equal individuals in the states, we must have a conception of fair negotiation that does not allow inequalities among states to play a large role in determining the distribution of advantages among persons in the different states. To be sure, the conception of equality required here does not require equality in welfare or material wealth; it requires something analogous to the equality in democratic decision making. The idea is that, broadly speaking, we can say that persons have an equal say in the determination of the treaties that bind them. Partly that is provided by the fact that the states are democratic, but partly we must develop principles that discern when states are taking unfair advantage of others. This conception of fair negotiation is the least well-worked-out part of the whole picture I am hoping to elaborate.

The hope with this conception of legitimacy is that it can build on something that is already partially in place in the modern international system. We have reasonably democratic states that accord significant protections to minorities and which make some effort to make the process of treaty making democratic, though not enough. Of course, the conception is quite demanding as well, since it requires that all states be democratic and it requires that there be some mechanism for assessing when states take unfair advantage of others and how this kind of exploitation should be rectified.

It is worth noting here how conceiving of the legitimacy of international law and institutions as based in state consent provides some relief from the problems we noted with global democracy. First, to the extent that it is liberal democratic states that engage in contract making for their advantage, the problem of citizenship that looms so large in the case of global democracy is diminished somewhat. Citizens can use all the devices of civil society within their own societies to inform themselves of the activities of their governments (assuming the foreign policy establishments are more democratic than they currently are). Second, the problem of persistent minorities is diminished because states can refuse to enter into negotiations and agreements. The system of fair voluntary association implements a standard way of solving the problem of persistent minorities. Third, to the extent that the people in states have different stakes in decisions, they can regulate their interactions with others to reflect that fact. States with high stakes in an agreement can invest a lot of time and energy in it, while states with lesser stakes presumably will invest less time and energy.

A natural way of thinking about the agreements states make with each other is to model interstate agreements on contracts. This gives us a way of thinking about the nature of interstate agreements and the conditions of their validity. But I will reject this model in what follows. The state consent model need not be essentially tied to contracts, though it usually is. Obviously consent can be based on things aside from the advantage of the consenting party and it can have its purpose in something other than mutual advantage. But once we separate state consent from the model of contract, we need to have a new way of thinking about state consent and its implications, as we will see.

The contract model of international treaties

The contract model thinks of treaties as if they were contracts between states. In doing this they suggest that the norms that govern the making of contracts ought to hold over the making of treaties as well. This fundamental idea is at the basis of many modern conceptions of the legitimacy of international law and institutions. The basic principle being that state consent is a necessary and sufficient condition of the legitimacy of international law and institutions.

One important qualification on the usual contract model is necessary if we are to take a cosmopolitan standpoint on the problem of the legitimacy of international institutions. From a cosmopolitan standpoint, the legitimacy of international institutions must ultimately be grounded in the interests of individuals, not of states. So for the contract model to serve as a model of legitimate institutions, it must be assumed that the state parties adequately represent the individuals who are members of the states. It seems to me that the only way that this can be done is if the states are democratic in a robust way. Not only do they have liberal democratic institutions for decision making, they adequately represent minorities and their foreign policy establishments are significantly more democratic than they have been in the past.

Here I want to discuss some considerations that have seemed to make the contract model plausible. First, the point of treaties has often been thought to be the mutual advantage of the state parties in the sense that they advance the interests of the states or their people understood in a non-moral sense. The thought is that states engage in an exchange with each other of rights. Once the state has made the treaty it is required to perform by right of the other state. Hence, we have the principle of *pacta sunt servanda*.

We might think, then, that the normative evaluation of the treaty making is the same as that of the evaluation of contracts. Contracts are often thought to have procedural and substantive dimensions that can be evaluated in terms of fairness. The procedural conditions on the fairness of contract making usually have to do with the voluntariness of the participant in the making of the contract. The two most frequent conditions are that the party be at least minimally informed or responsible for being informed and that the party has not been coerced or forced into the agreement. A third condition often asserted is that the bargaining powers of the parties are not wildly asymmetric.

The substantive conditions on the fairness of the exchange may include some notion of equality in the exchange between the participants. This notion is very hard to define clearly. But it is often invoked in the context of unconscionable contracts where both procedural and substantive elements combine to render contracts invalid. The standard philosophical description of such contracts involves taking unfair advantage of a person. The idea is that as long as neither of the parties thinks of the exchange as essentially one of gift giving, if one of the parties is highly vulnerable to failure to make the contract and the exchange is highly disproportionate in favour of the non-vulnerable party, then it is thought that the non-vulnerable party is taking unfair advantage of the vulnerable one.

The equality involved is not a distributive equality. It is equality in the things exchanged. An exchange is fair when what is received is equivalent in value to what is given. The usual way of measuring the value of the goods involved is in terms of their competitive market price. Here is a fairly straightforward application of this idea. Suppose p is the usual price a hospital charges for administering a kind of life-saving first aid to a person. Now, someone finds himself not far from a hospital bleeding to death but he is far enough away that he cannot get there before death sets in and a doctor comes upon him with the means to save him by standard first aid. The doctor demands a promise of payment that is $10 \times p$ and so massively greater than the standard price. And let us suppose that the doctor does not have any unusual costs of her own at stake. The contract between the bleeding person and the doctor for first aid in exchange for $10 \times p$ would not normally be thought to be a valid one. Most would think that this constitutes an exploitative offer and that the doctor is taking unfair advantage of the vulnerable person. Though there are some straightforward cases such as the one above, the evaluation of agreements in terms of whether each gives and receives in accordance with the competitive price is often going to be quite difficult. This will depend on the proper characterization of the circumstances in which the pricing takes place. How exactly to specify the conditions that are at least normally necessary and sufficient is quite difficult. To my knowledge, courts have tended to invalidate only the most seriously disproportionate contracts.

So the standard conditions under which contracts are thought to be problematic are some kind of absence of voluntariness and exploitation. And these considerations have dominated discussions of the legitimacy of international treaties. Thus, it looks as if the contract model is a good fit with international treaty making.

But there some important respects in which the model of contract does not apply well to international treaties and this is what we will discuss now.

Treaties and justice

Both Grotius and Vattel observe that many international treaties are concerned with establishing in treaty what the parties and individuals involved already have obligations to do (Grotius 1623/2005, Book II, 821; Vattel 1758/2008, 345). This is perhaps most obvious in the case of the modern law of human rights. But it is also evident in the case of peace treaties, treaties not to interfere with each other's commerce and other kinds of treaties. In this respect, treaty making resembles the normal activities of law making in a political society. Political societies legislate against murder, theft and rape not in order to create obligations where there were none before but in order to lay out more clearly the exact expectations that people are to have of one another so that the possibilities of misunderstanding are greatly diminished. And in the modern system of treaties some institutions of arbitration, deliberation and judgement usually accompany the treaties, such as the Committees on Human Rights established by the two major international covenants. And in some cases, enforcement mechanisms are set in place to rectify wrongdoing by states. This is still relatively rare. But one can see that treaties and the institutions that they establish play some of the roles that the political and legal institutions of domestic political societies play. Their object is to establish by known and settled law the terms of justice by which states are to interact with each other and with individuals.

This is distinct from the usual function of contracts, which are usually made against the background of purportedly just institutions. Contracts create obligations against a background of law. But treaties create law.

Another way in which treaties are connected with justice is in the structures of the agreements. Some treaties do not purport to establish justice between the parties; they purport to be mutually advantageous agreements between the parties. But even these are often structured in such as way as to acknowledge the importance of justice and fairness in the body of the treaty. They express commitments to fair terms among the parties. For example, the treaties making up the WTO make the principle of non-discrimination the centrepiece of the agreements. Partly this is to create more efficient treaties but partly it is to realize fairness in the treaties. The treaties creating the WTO and also those that have been agreed upon within the structure of the WTO are designed with an eye to fairness. Developing societies are given special trade preferences in many such treaties and the principles underlying these trade preferences have affected the structures of the treaties ever since. The idea is that developing countries are to be allowed special exemptions on grounds of their vulnerability to changing prices in international trade. All of this is accompanied by the language of fairness in the negotiations and outcomes.[14] To be sure, there is still much unfairness in the outcomes, and the protestations of fairness are often window dressing, but the point is that these are seen as necessary to a proper treaty. The same holds of international environmental treaties. They give special exemptions to developing countries so as not to retard their development. Again, these are normally defended in terms of fairness to the developing countries, and such a concern for fairness and justice in the terms of contracts is not a usual feature of contracts.

Voluntariness

Another feature of treaties that seems quite distinctive is that voluntariness is not required for some of them. The Vienna Convention on Treaties states that treaties may not result from non-lawful coercion. But it seems to leave open that treaties may result from lawful coercion. And presumably this is the case with treaties that impose peace on an unjust aggressor. These are often coercive but they are valid nevertheless. This is quite distinct from contracts where lack of voluntariness, as long as it is not due to negligence, standardly defeats the validity of a contract. In the case of coercively imposed peace treaties we are not looking at a standard case of mutual advantage in the sense that both parties regard the treaty as being to their mutual advantage.

Here again, it seems that the basic reason why some peace treaties can be coercively imposed is that they tend to promote and preserve international peace and justice. To be sure, they do this in a way that is quite different from the way states do this. They allow individual parties to realize justice through coercion in a way that is quite alien to political societies.

---

[14] See Franck (1996) for a discussion of trade preferences and Albin (2001) for a general discussion of fairness considerations in international negotiation.

Equality

The principle of equality in exchange is fairly central to contract law and the doctrine of unconscionable contracts.[15] Here the thought is that once we determine a reasonably competitive market price the value of a thing or service can be equated with that price. Exchanges that depart too far from that competitive market price are ruled invalid in many cases where no gift is intended. That the departure must be great is usually thought to be the result of the court's unwillingness to micromanage exchanges and a humility in its ability to estimate the prices of goods.

But this principle of contract law does not seem to be generally accepted in a lot of contemporary treaty making. It is usually accepted, for example, that developing societies may benefit from special exemptions to treaty provisions or that they may receive special treatment or 'preferences' in international trade treaties and environmental treaties. To be sure, these special treatments are granted only grudgingly and are often quite minimal, but they are there and they say something about treaties. Treaties are not expected to obey the principle of equality in exchange, which suggests that they may not be merely exchanges. They are not gifts either, which are the usual exceptions to equality in contract law.

What are these special treatment provisions gesturing towards? One natural interpretation is that they are gesturing towards a concern for distributive justice and fairness among peoples in the world.

In the case of contracts, the usual theory essentially involves setting the level of advantage of each party at zero for all the parties before the exchange. There is no concern for the differential starting points of the different parties. Distributive justice concerns are bracketed. Only equality between the things exchanged seems to matter.

But treaties do not attempt to abstract fully from the background distributive concerns. They seem to adjust for background disparities. They do not attempt to rectify the injustice of unequal distribution, but unequal starting points in terms of distribution of advantages are taken into account so that many treaties are decidedly asymmetrical. In this respect, they are quite different from equal contracts.

Important differences between treaties and contracts

So far I have noted that treaty making is much more concerned with issues of justice than we should expect if we conceive of treaties on the

---

[15] See Gordley (2001) for a defence of this principle.

model of contract. This argument has been an interpretative argument concerning contemporary practices in making treaties. But I think that there are good substantive reasons for the differences between treaties and contracts that we see.

First, there is a much greater difference between macro-justice considerations and micro-justice considerations in the case of contract law. In the case of contracts, it often seems unfair to impose the main burdens of redistribution on individual agents. They are usually only one of many millions of contributors to the actual distribution of advantages. The problems of distributive justice require many persons to chip in their fair share. Requiring redistribution through contract would seem to be excessively and unfairly demanding on particular persons. They are only one among many contributors to distributive inequity, but solving the problems through contracts would seem to impose the burden on them alone. To be clear here, I am referring to redistribution in the content of the contract. Many modern democratic states shape the law of contract so as to have some beneficial effect on the distribution of goods. Minimum wage legislation is an example. But this is not what I am referring to here. I am referring to the fact that the contracting parties do not use contracts to achieve distributive justice. They are usually concerned with more partial interests even though the state may attempt to effect the distribution of advantages by shaping the law of contracts. Second, attempting to achieve redistribution through contracts seems to be an inefficient way of doing it because it is a highly uncoordinated way of doing this and because it would seem to dampen the incentives to trade. The way distributive justice is best achieved in a political society is through some kind of unified tax and transfer system and through some kind of overall external regulation of markets.

Both of these points – the unfairness of imposing the burden of redistribution on contractors and the possibility of some general legal regulation and tax and transfer system – are inapplicable at the international level. At the international level the state is by far the most important player and will remain so for a while. There is no state at the global level that can achieve justice through tax and transfer or through large-scale regulation. Furthermore there are not many states and not very many large and wealthy states.

These two points suggest that while transactions among individuals are not a suitable place for redistribution in domestic economies, transactions among states may be more suitable for redistribution in the global environment. First, given the smaller number of states and the very small number of very wealthy states, it is not so clear that the type of collective action or coordination problems we would see at the individual contractor level in domestic societies occurs at the level of states. Each individual wealthy state can make a significant dent in the distributive inequalities we see today. And the wealthy states could fairly easily coordinate with each other to achieve much more sizeable redistribution. Though there is no global agency for creating redistribution, there is the possibility of coordinated redistribution.

Second, the idea of contracts as equal exchange can only have legitimacy against the background of a reasonably fair distribution of advantages. It makes little sense to require equal exchange between those who are impoverished and those who have a great deal. Equal exchange can only work justly when people at least have enough to participate. The idea in modern mixed economies is that markets can be legitimate to the extent to which everyone has enough to participate in them roughly as equals. And the state makes some attempt, however imperfectly, to achieve the wide distribution of wealth necessary for this.

At the global level the extent of poverty and inequality seem to me to vitiate the idea that all the peoples of the world ought to engage in equal exchange with each other even if they could. In addition, the extent of poverty and inequality also seem to me to imply that it is very difficult for many states to engage in equal exchange with other states. The poorest countries often are very vulnerable and are liable to be taken unfair advantage of in the current circumstances. There is significant evidence of this taking unfair advantage in the case of the WTO in the past 15 years. This again points to the fact that with such extremes of inequality and poverty, the background conditions that can ensure fair negotiations are not present.

One main way to express this substantive argument is via the idea of the moral division of labour between institutional and individual pursuits in society and its relative absence in international relations. That a contract is normally used in a society to advance the partial concerns of the contractors within the limits set by fairness is a function of the importance of the moral division of labour. The idea here is that the central concerns of justice are primarily assured by institutional arrangements. These arrangements established by property and contract law, regulation, public ownership and tax and transfer assure distributive justice and the basic political and civil rights. The institutions are designed so as to ensure that when people act on their partial concerns, the aims of distributive justice are secured. In contracting and associating with others, individuals are not required to take justice as their aim at least most of the time. They are permitted to act partially, again within limits set by fairness and the background institutions of society (framed with the purpose of achieving justice). This division of labour is justified by three main considerations. First, individuals' actions have very small effects on justice and there is great difficulty in organizing coordination and cooperation without state institutions. Second, this permits a reasonably fair distribution of burdens and benefits. It is important for the aim of justice that each pursues his or her interests in his or her own way. Third, there may also be some room for persons to pursue their own projects without always focusing on the impartial good.

So within limits individuals are permitted to pursue their own interests via contract to some significant degree. This characteristic structure of aims in the case of contract and voluntary association is distinct from the structure of aims of a person qua citizen or legislator. In the role of citizens, persons are expected to aim at justice and the common good in their actions of voting, organizing, negotiating and deliberating. Of course, they may look out for their own interests in the process but the dominant concern is normally justice and the common good. Here, the division of labour can be understood as a division between the roles of persons qua citizens and persons qua individual agents.

One way to express the difference between treaties and contracts is to say that while contracts take place within the moral division of labour that permits limited self-interest seeking, treaties do not take place in the context of a moral division of labour. The considerations that favour the role of contracts in the division of labour do not suggest such a role for treaties. First of all, treaty making does not take place against a background set of institutions that secure justice for all. Or if it does, those institutions are themselves established by treaty. In fact, they take place against the background of horrendous inequality and poverty. Second, treaties are made by states that are small in number and that are relatively easy to coordinate and organize for the common good (especially the small number of wealthy states). These can have a great impact on global justice. The burdens must be distributed fairly but this is much easier to do at the level of states. Finally, states per se do not have interests, individuals do, and so the kind of personal prerogative that a contract serves is not served by giving free rein to states. States already provide room for this prerogative within their political societies.

So, it seems to me that states must pursue the aims of justice in the context of treaty making. The structure of motivation here should be much like the situation or motivation of citizens or legislators.

This reasoning applies initially to ideal theorizing but I think it also holds in non-ideal situations to some degree as well. The moral division of labour holds to some degree in the non-ideal context.

To take stock here, I am arguing that international treaties ought not to be understood on the model of contracts because many treaties simply establish justice, they often depart from the principle of equality in exchange and treaties are a much more plausible site of distributive justice than contracts since they do not have the same role that contracts do in a moral division of labour.

In a way, all the points that I have been making about the centrality of justice to treaty making can be confirmed by the fact that international treaties are thought to create international law. And law, it seems to me, has the function of establishing justice among persons.

To be sure, not every treaty need implement justice in all respects. Just as only the system of domestic law and policy is supposed to realize justice so the system of treaties ought to be devoted to realizing justice on a cosmopolitan scale.

External effects

Another related worry is that the idea of legitimacy of treaties grounded in state consent may allow for large external effects on those states that do not consent (Bodansky 1999). This is an obvious concern for the contract model in which states agree to treaties based primarily on their interests. To the extent that the interests of non-participants are negatively affected and there is no larger set of institutions to rectify the illegitimate setbacks to interests, the scheme does not adequately take into account the interests of all affected.

But the worry remains even if we reject the contract model and expect states to act on the basis of an assessment of justice and the common good. The reason why is grounded in a fairly basic principle behind democracy. We expect people's judgements of justice and the common good to be biased towards their own interests, in ways that are hard to defeat even if they are acting conscientiously. So we can expect that when states make agreements amongst themselves, the external effects of those actions on others will not usually adequately take into account the interests of those negatively affected.

Democracy

A final worry is that most states are not democratic to the extent necessary to make it possible that they can be said to represent their people. Most states now are at least formally democratic, but many of these are not democratic in a way that assures serious representation. Many elections are undertaken in an atmosphere of severe intimidation of the opposition. Many elections are fixed in ways that it is hard for election monitors to detect. So many states that are formally democratic in the sense that they abide by majority rule with universal suffrage and few if any legal barriers to competition do not represent their people well at all.

How are these people to be accommodated within a process of negotiation among states? When states that are not democratic negotiate with states that are democratic with an eye towards creating international law that impinges on the domestic legal systems of the society, it seems that we may describe this as a kind of imposition of international law on the populations that are not participating in their political societies. They have little voice and their interests are only very partially registered by the elites in their society. It seems that the consent of these states can do very little by way of conferring legitimacy on the agreements in a cosmopolitan picture devoted to legitimacy grounded in persons.

In some circumstances the international institutions created by democratic and non-democratic states may be legitimate for the democratic states but not for the non-democratic ones. This may happen when the agreements require things of each state that are separable in the sense that one state's compliance does not require another state's compliance. Then members of the democratic state may be duty bound to comply with the agreement. But in those cases where there is no separability, and what the democratic state is required to do impinges on the interests of the non-consenting members of the non-democratic state, then there is a threat to the legitimacy of the system overall. The duties of the citizens of the democracy must normally be defeated when what they are required to do constitutes impositions on the subjects of the non-democratic states. They are in effect colluding with the elites of the non-democratic state to take advantage of the incapacities of the non-democratic subjects.[16]

In a way these last two problems of external effects and non-democratic states are analogues of the problems of persistent minorities and an absence of civil society in the case of global democracy. In the first case there is a failure of inclusion and in the second there is a failure of representation of the people by their rulers.

The puzzle of legitimacy

If we think of international law in this way, there is a great deal of significance in how to think of fairness in the processes of making

---

[16] This is a kind of general account of the danger Thomas Pogge (2002) points to in his discussion of the international resource and borrowing privileges.

international law. The most obvious one is that the fairness of negotiations cannot be evaluated in terms of the traditional norms of contract such as equality and voluntariness. More generally, we should not think of international negotiation on the model of bargaining and the standards of bargaining theory. The norms of justice are really the principal norms that apply to the outcomes of treaty making. Treaties have the function of establishing justice in the world as a whole. As a consequence, the process of making international law must become a deliberative process in part where alternative conceptions of justice and the common good are debated and discussed among societies and where negotiation and compromise are used when disagreement cannot be resolved. Though a concern to advance the interests of the society represented by the state is legitimate, it must always be within the context of a larger shared concern for the common good and justice.

To be sure, if international treaties are to be made in a way that treats persons as equals the conditions under which agreements among states can be made legitimate must be constrained by certain procedural norms. These norms must give rise to fair processes of negotiation and deliberation among societies about the common good and justice. Obviously they will have to protect societies from having to negotiate from positions of excessive vulnerability and they will have to ensure some kind of equality in the process of negotiation and deliberation among societies.

These points suggest that we need to develop a conception of fair deliberation and negotiation among groups that we currently don't have, at least for the case of decentralized voluntary association. They also suggest that there is some need for background global institutions to rectify excessive inequalities and to ensure that the conditions of deliberation and negotiation are reasonably fair as well as inclusive. This seems to drive us in the direction of global institutions, which in turn must be evaluated in terms of democratic principles.

But this leaves us at a kind of impasse. We find ourselves in a position that usually calls for democratic deliberation and decision making but without the possibility of global democratic institutions. We have individual states negotiating with each other but the usual standards of contract do not apply and there is little to ensure that the negotiations are fair or sufficiently inclusive. This means that the two central ways in which group decisions come to be legitimate in domestic societies are not in the offing in the case of international collective decision making. Democracy and voluntary association are both problematic from the standpoint of justice and legitimacy when in the context of international decision making.

Clearly, this menu of choices for grounds of legitimacy is too small but it is hard to know where to proceed from here. One possible avenue for further exploration might be to examine some different varieties of multilateral institutions in which many states must agree with each other on certain policies (Moellendorf 2008, Chapter 8). Some of the bargaining disadvantages of developing societies could be partly offset in this context by the fact that there are many developing societies and that they can form powerful coalitions to counter the bargaining power of the developed societies. I do not have the time to explore this option here in sufficient detail but this method suffers from the usual defects of consensus-based systems in which there is a very diverse set of parties who do not share common goals or values. When serious interests conflict, they fail to make decisions and tend to favour the status quo. And it is usually the most powerful and wealthy states who benefit most from the status quo, so they have significant bargaining advantages in multilateral institutions, particularly if the wealthy and powerful states can make common cause. And we have clear records of very great disparities in bargaining power playing a large role in determining how these multilateral institutions develop. We need only look at the formation of the United Nations in the San Francisco conference and the formation of the WTO in the Uruguay round to see how powerful states, when they can form coalitions, can determine how these go.[17] Perhaps there is some way to limit this kind of unfair advantage taking but it is hard to see how, given the distribution of wealth in the world as a whole.

The other approach that has been taken by a number of recent theorists is the idea of informal democracy. The idea here is that global society can be regulated in some way by a global civil society in which non-governmental organizations (NGOs) and other non-state groups, which are made accountable to people, engage in a decentralized global process of deliberation that is meant to exert pressure on states and corporations.[18] The study of global civil society and its potential contribution to a genuinely cosmopolitan approach to global decision making is essential, but there are a number of difficulties with this approach. One is that there is no real way of publicly realizing equality in this highly complex and fluid process of deliberation. One suspects that power could well be wielded by elites in this process. The suspicion is increased

---

[17] See Steinberg (2002) for the WTO. See Schlesinger (2003, 223) for a discussion of the hard bargaining behind the creation of the Security Council great power veto.

[18] See T. MacDonald (this volume) for this approach. For an empirical account see Tallberg and Uhlin and K. Macdonald (this volume).

when one notes that the NGOs that exist seem primarily to represent the standpoints of groups in wealthy Western democracies. Second, while NGOs are clearly a very important part of global decision making it is hard to see how they can be more than inputs into a more formal system of decision making. This kind of view has not given us an adequate account of how power is exercised and decisions are made (Bohman (2007)).

Conclusion

The arguments of this chapter are very sceptical. I have argued against global democracy. I have called into question the idea that fair voluntary association among democratic states, as I have understood it, gives us a complete picture of legitimate global institutions. It may be that the best we can do in constructing global institutions is to make sure that they respect and protect human rights and that they satisfy some basic standards of accountability such as transparency. I am not satisfied with this account partly because I don't think it gives us legitimacy. It may give us reason to think that the institutions will produce minimally desirable outcomes. We may often have reason, therefore, to go along with those outcomes. But it does not give us the kind of moral legitimacy that implies reasons to go along with them even when we disagree with the outcomes.

To the question, is legitimacy possible in the current global order for the foreseeable future, the answer is I don't know yet. I continue to think that fair voluntary association among democratic states is the most likely account to give us a plausible model of legitimacy in a contemporary global society characterized by states being the main powers, but it is not clear to me how to work out the difficulties I have discussed.

REFERENCES

Albin, Cecilia. 2001. *Justice and Fairness in International Negotiation*. Cambridge University Press.
Bodansky, Daniel. 1999. 'The Legitimacy of International Governance: A Coming Challenge for International Environmental Law?', *The American Journal of International Law* 93, 3: 596–624.
Bohman, James. 2007. *Democracy across Borders*. Cambridge, MA: MIT Press.
Buchanan, Allen, and Robert Keohane. 2006. 'The Legitimacy of Global Governance Institutions', *Ethics and International Affairs* 20, 4: 405–37.
Christiano, Thomas. 1996. *The Rule of the Many*. Boulder, CO: Westview Press.
    2008. *The Constitution of Equality: Democratic Authority and Its Limits*. Oxford University Press.

2010. 'Democratic Legitimacy and International Institutions', in Samantha Besson and John Tasioulas (eds.), *The Philosophy of International Law* (pp. 119–38). Oxford University Press.

Dahl, Robert. 1999. 'Can International Institutions Be Democratic? A Sceptic's View', in Ian Shapiro and Casiano Hacker-Cordón (eds.), *Democracy's Edges* (pp. 19–36). Cambridge University Press.

Downs, Anthony. 1957. *An Economic Theory of Democracy.* New York: Harper & Row.

Doyle, Michael. 2009. 'The UN Charter – A Global Constitution?' in Jeffery L. Dunoff and Joel P. Trachtam (eds.), *Ruling the World?: Constitutionalism, International Law, and Global Governance* (pp. 113–32). Cambridge University Press.

Estlund, David. 2007. *Democratic Authority: A Philosophical Framework.* Princeton University Press.

Franck, Thomas. 1996. *Fairness in International Law and Institutions.* Oxford University Press.

Gordley, James. 2001. 'Contract Law in the Aristotelian Tradition', in Peter Benson (ed.), *The Theory of Contract Law: New Essays* (pp. 265–334). Cambridge University Press.

Gould, Carol C. 2004. *Globalizing Democracy and Human Rights.* Cambridge University Press.

Grotius, Hugo. 1623/2005. *The Rights of War and Peace* (ed. and trans. Richard Tuck). Indianapolis, IN: Liberty Fund.

Klosko, George. 2004. *The Principle of Fairness and Political Obligation* (2nd ed.). Lanham, MD.: Rowman & Littlefield.

Moellendorf, Darrel. 2008. *Global Inequality Matters.* London: Palgrave-Macmillan.

Pogge, Thomas. 2002. *World Poverty and Human Rights.* Malden, MA: Polity Press.

Popkin, Samuel. 1990. *The Reasoning Voter: Communication and Persuasion in Presidential Elections.* University of Chicago Press.

Raz, Joseph. 1986. *The Morality of Freedom.* Oxford University Press.

Rodrik, Dani. 2007. *One Economics, Many Recipes: Globalization, Institutions and Economic Growth.* Princeton University Press.

Schlesinger, Stephen C. 2003. *Act of Creation: The Founding of the United Nations.* Boulder, CO: Westview Press.

Simmons, A. John. 2001. *Justification and Legitimacy: Essays on Rights and Obligations.* Cambridge University Press.

Singer, Peter. 1974. *Democracy and Disobedience.* New York: Oxford University Press.

Steinberg, Richard H. 2002. 'In the Shadow of Law or Power? Consensus-Based Bargaining and Outcomes in the GATT/WTO', *International Organization* 56, 2: 339–74.

2004. 'Judicial Lawmaking at the WTO: Discursive, Constitutional, and Political Constraints', *American Journal of International Law* 98: 247–75.

Vattel, Emir. 1758/2008. *The Law of Nations* (ed. Bela Kapossy and Richard Whatmore). Indianapolis, IN: Liberty Fund.

Waldron, Jeremy. 1999. *Law and Disagreement.* Oxford University Press.

5   Cosmopolitan democracy
Neither a category mistake nor a categorical imperative

Andreas Follesdal

Introduction

Under globalization, individuals' opportunities, life plans and choices
are influenced not only by the political decisions of their own national
governments, but also by various non-state actors. Regional and international organizations set up by states themselves, and powerful private
actors such as transnational corporations, affect the opportunity space
and choices of individuals directly. Other such actors have great indirect
effects, by influencing the scope of decisions available to national
governments, the expected results and thus the strategies that states
pursue – with important consequences for citizens.

Such globalization affects the value of even well-functioning democracies which can no longer buffer their own citizens from the effects of
actors outside their territorial borders – if they ever could (Ruggie 1982).
Thus, many are concerned about the global structures that frame the
opportunities and choices of individuals: the rules and practices that
specify the actors, the scope of decision they may take and that influence
their choices. Some actors such as states and interstate organizations
are legally authorized to make binding decisions, at various territorial
levels that often overlap, such as the European Union (EU) and United
Nations (UN) bodies. Other actors such as transnational organizations or
regulatory networks are evidence of more diffuse forms of 'governance':
they have de facto power to get things done, sometimes without legal
competence to command compliance (Czempiel 1992, Rosenau 1992).

'Multi-level governance' (MLG) is sometimes used to refer to this
complex of private and public actors at several territorial levels, who create,
implement and change systems of rules that facilitate or hinder coordination and cooperation. MLG thus affects the resultant distribution of costs

I am grateful for constructive comments from the editors, especially Raffaele Marchetti.

and benefits of interaction among these actors – including political actors such as states and their organizations, private corporations and civil society organizations (Koenig-Archibugi and Zürn 2006).

Many authors hold that since MLG wields such great influence, this complex of actors and the perplexing network of multi-level rules above the state must be assessed by standards of normative legitimacy. In particular, several authors – including many in this volume – argue for more specific requirements of democratic control. They hold that central decisions, either about how to set up and change such global structures of authority and/or decisions by several major actors within them, should be under more *democratic control*. In particular, some non-state actors with de facto decision-making authority should be subject to mechanisms of democratic accountability, either directly toward citizens or mediated via their national representatives. And at least some of these decisions may be made by (qualified) majority vote, rather than by unanimity. Call such claims 'more democratic multi-level governance' (MDMLG). For instance, defenders of 'cosmopolitan democracy' argue for more democratic relations among and beyond states (Archibugi and Held 1995). MDMLG may include one or more of the following:

1. calls to create an assembly of democratic states (Held 1993, 41) with a fair representative system of decision making, whose voting rights are limited to highly representative states. This institutional arrangement is intergovernmental, and is a 'confederal' element or feature of MLG (Archibugi et al. and Christiano, both this volume; Follesdal 2011).
2. a global parliament, directly elected by individuals globally. It might possibly have quite limited competences, with other responsibilities placed with regional and state-level organizations (Held 1993, 40; Marchetti 2008 and this volume).
3. empowerment of regional parliaments 'as legitimate independent sources of regional and international law' (Held 1993, 40). One example is the calls to strengthen the European Parliament to combat the 'democratic deficit' of the EU (Follesdal and Hix 2006, Gould, this volume).
4. democratic supervision and/or accountability mechanisms over international bodies such as the EU, the UN, World Health Organization (WHO) etc., as well as various other non-state actors (Held 1993, 40).

For the sake of the present discussions, I do not include some other proposals that may arguably also increase the legitimacy of MLG by means that are less clearly democratic in a fairly straightforward sense. For instance, some authors plausibly defend non-electoral accountability mechanisms, such as various consultation mechanisms (Macdonald and

Macdonald 2006; T. Macdonald 2008 and this volume; K. Macdonald, this volume; O'Brien et al. 2000). Others defend the 'judicialization' of world affairs through more effective legal and (quasi-)judicial constraints on governments and international organizations (see the discussion by Archibugi et al., this volume). Some such courts may in principle be legitimate, and possibly defended as part of justifiable democratic governance (Follesdal 2009, *pace* Waldron 2006). Yet for purposes of the arguments pursued in this chapter, such consultation arrangements and checks by 'non-accountable' judges over democratically accountable legislators and executives are not included as part of MDMLG.

Combinations of these are of course possible, thus a 'world federation' (Archibugi et al., this volume; Marchetti 2008 and this volume; Murithi, this volume) would consist of a multilayered political legal order where citizens elected representatives directly to several bodies at national, regional and possibly global levels. There might also be benefits to having democratically accountable governments or parliaments participate not only at a global assembly of democratic states, but also at regional levels, such as the Council of the European Union. In contrast, 'world government' might describe a political order where most political authority is centralized, under democratic control, but without significant national and regional democratic bodies.

This chapter mainly considers and rebuts some of the objections raised against MDMLG, namely those that regard MDMLG as a fundamentally mistaken requirement – close to a category mistake. Thus, Robert Dahl (1999) famously doubted the possibility of democracy beyond state borders – for instance, of international organizations – due to concerns about the size of the electorate and resultant weak chains of accountability.

The first section below lays out a brief defence of the legitimacy of democratic, majoritarian rule. Some of those who favour MDMLG might find such defences objectionable or at best unnecessary: majoritarian democratic decision making might be regarded by some as close to a categorical imperative, a necessary, perhaps analytically true requirement independent of empirical considerations about its instrumental value to secure basic needs and otherwise achieve social justice. Thus, some hold that legitimate modes of governance *must* be democratically decided. Symptomatically, 'in our Western view, only democratic systems, advocating the values of liberty, equality and community, deserve the loyalty of the citizens. Hence, the notions legitimacy and democratic legitimacy must be considered as interchangeable' (Lenaerts and Desomer 2002, 1220). Waldron (2000, 114) holds what might be regarded as a weaker version of this view, that majority rule among democratically elected representatives is one of the few principles for decision-making processes that is practically consistent with fairness and equal respect for all (cf. Dahl 1989, Held 1993, 26).

The central normative question of legitimacy of concern here is with what right the multifarious private and public authorities can expect subjects – states and individuals – to comply, even with decisions they have voted against as a minority against a majority. Answers rely on reflections about whether and under what conditions MLG can be justified to all subjects regarded as equal members of that complex legal, political and economic order they find themselves part of. The issue is thus whether such a system of MLG must include substantial democratic controls in order to be defensible to all, and if so why. I explain why such arguments within institutional political theory are essentially comparative: we must consider the likely effects of alternative institutional schemes – for example, with and without democratic accountability mechanisms.

The second section below then presents and challenges some claims that deny that the present global MLG structure can be judged by standards of justice at all. The third section responds to challenges that MDMLG is not necessary – that democratic accountability is not needed, since alternative, non-democratic modes suffice. This section illustrates the kinds of empirical comparative claims that are required. The discussions draw in part on relevant debates about the alleged need for a more democratic EU regarded as an exemplar of an international organization or (quasi-federal) political order, voiced by Moravcsik and Majone (cf. Follesdal and Hix 2006). I also consider some of the weaknesses of alternatives to majoritarian electoral democracy, namely 'networks' and 'participatory' democratic arrangements. I again draw on literature concerning experiences within the EU, since several of these general arguments have been brought to bear and discussed in detail based on the experiences and experiments of European integration.

Democracy

This section presents some key features and benefits of 'majoritarian democracy' as this term will be used here. This incomplete sketch only seeks to lay out some of the most salient features of relevance to the discussion at hand (cf. Follesdal and Hix 2006, Follesdal, 2011). In particular, it is apparent in what sense this is an *institutional* normative theory which has institutions as its prime subject matter, and that seeks to assess alternative institutional arrangements against various defended normative standards. I also explore some implications for how to assess proposals for more democratic MLG. In particular, I am wary of committing the 'monotonicity mistake'. It is not true that every increase in one component of democratic rule – transparency, deliberation or representation – also renders a decision-making system more *democratic*. The latter is a matter of how the institutions fit together and how transparency, deliberation, representation and so forth must all be present, in certain ways. We return below to consider how this approach challenges some claims that more inclusive networks etc. enhance democratic values *simpliciter*.

The literature on how to define democracy shows great variance. The editors of this volume identify certain common features that fit well with the concerns addressed in this chapter: a system of governance that is responsive and accountable to the preferences of citizens, majority rule and the direct participation of citizens in appointing the rulers (Archibugi et al., this volume).

For the purposes of assessing some criticisms against MDMLG, we must specify the term 'democracy' slightly more, to refer to a set of institutionally established procedures that regulate competition for control over political authority. Democratic arrangements permit all or most adult citizens who live their lives within certain social institutions to participate in an electoral mechanism whereby their expressed preferences over alternative candidates, established on the basis of public deliberation, determine the contents of these institutions. The mechanisms are such that the government is accountable to, and thereby responsive to, all those subject to it. Several contested issues in this brief description merit more attention, and receive it in other contributions to this volume. In particular, *who* are to be included: all those 'with a stake in them' – that is, causally affected by the institutions – or only those who in some sense share in upholding these institutions, and are cognizant of this shared political identity? And must these decisions about the boundaries of the *demos* themselves be made democratically? (Marchetti, this volume)[1]. For our limited purposes, central features of democratic rule are

- control by elected, party-based, democratically accountable representatives over governing functions; and
- public *debates in the public sphere*, involving civil society, that require policy makers to account for their decisions and the outcomes (Follesdal and Hix 2006).

---

[1] Note that this focus on formalized institutions is at odds with Dryzek's (2006) definition of 'transnational discursive democracy'. It is also stricter than K. Macdonald's (this volume), in that democratic institutions must not only be 'consistent with' principles of autonomy and equality, or ensure transparency.

I submit that a satisfactory argument for such democratic decision making is that – *under certain conditions* – democratic rule is over time more reliably responsive to the best interests of the members of the political order than any alternative institutional arrangements and more trustworthy in this regard.[2] Currently, these conditions are not sufficiently secured at levels above the state, and arguably not very well in all states.

All those who are subject to the use of public power should partake in its control, for at least two reasons: individuals have an interest in a share in such control to reduce the risk of domination; and dispersed control of this kind is instrumentally valuable to ensure informed policy choices that best secure the interests of all in a justifiably balanced way.[3] To ensure these objectives, and to assure citizens of this, several conditions must be in place – which is not yet the case for MLG.

Representation of those who are affected is a fundamental premise for why democratic rule is more legitimate than other arrangements: in the absence of voice and voting power, the interests of some affected subjects might well go unnoticed.

The decision structures must be sufficiently *transparent*, and it must be possible to place responsibility with sufficient clarity. In the EU – not to mention the multi-level global political, legal and economic structures – the governance arrangements are far too opaque.

Furthermore, *party contestation* is important for democratic processes to foster *deliberation* that is central to voters' opinion formation, and to ensure informed, efficacious and cost-effective policy choices. Contestation can provide credible monitoring, and helps voters determine the effectiveness of chosen policies compared to the alternatives. This is important to assure voters that the authorities reliably govern fairly and effectively. Such awareness in turn gives incentives to politicians, that they are responsive to voters over time, and to ensure that political parties search for topics that they may make salient for media and voters. Thus, competition is crucial to maintain elected officials' responsiveness to voters' preferences. At present, conditions for such valuable democratic contestation are not acceptable, in the EU or at the global level. There are few opposition parties and little in the way of civil society or media scrutiny to judge the authorities' agenda and performance, offering plausible alternatives and the like.

---

[2] See Beitz (1989), Shapiro (1996), Weale (1999) and Sen and Drèze (1990).

[3] Several authors offer additional arguments, such as the need to respect political autonomy. I bracket these arguments, partly to avoid criticism of reliance on comprehensively liberal conceptions of the good life. See Held (1987, 271).

Responsiveness to the best interests of citizens is ensured by democratic accountability only if the information flow is not controlled by the present power-holders. Critical media and independent research can alleviate the information asymmetry between the power-holders and voters (see K. Macdonald, this volume, on transparency in the exercise of public power). Without electoral competition and with little media scrutiny these mechanisms are unlikely to be fully effective at the European and global levels. The relative dearth of public arenas for political discussion makes it difficult to mobilize political opposition.

The upshot of these arguments is modest: I have only sketched argument strategies for a comparative claim to prefer democratic arrangements over alternatives, under certain circumstances. While we have good reason to value mechanisms of democratic accountability in general, the case seems weaker in the EU at present, and certainly even worse for other parts of MLG.

To summarize, we have good reasons to value transparency, accountability, representation, deliberation and good outcomes as features of democratic rule.

Transparency is *inter alia* necessary to enable subjects and opposition parties to determine whether public authorities actually act as promised, and whether any deviations are appropriate.

Accountability is valuable both in the sense of subjects being able to receive an account from the authorities about their decisions, and the ability of subjects to replace those who hold office if alternative candidates appear better. These features help align the incentives of the rulers with the considered preferences of citizens.

Representation in the decision-making bodies is important to ensure that decisions are as informed as possible and that they take into account fairly the impact on as many affected parties as possible.

Deliberation is important both for subjects' preference formation – about what they have reason to believe should be the objectives of the political order – and to discern what are the most plausible ways and means to achieve them with acceptable trade-offs.

Good outcomes are somewhat more likely from democratic institutions than from alternative institutional arrangements insofar as deliberation and the socializing functions of political parties affect the preferences of citizens, both toward a better understanding of their own best interests, and toward a more other-regarding and fair ranking of alternative policy options.

Two reminders are appropriate. First, it should be clear that increased 'transparency', 'deliberation' or 'participation' is not always conducive to reducing domination or increasing responsiveness to individuals' best interests, and their trust that this is the case – these being the main arguments in favour of democracy. Such assumptions are understandable, but I submit that this would be based on a 'monotonicity mistake'. To illustrate this, to include some more groups in the decision-making processes and proceed on the basis of mutual consent among them may certainly yield benefits, more responsiveness to their interests and enhance their trust. Yet such partial inclusion may also cause damages familiar from cartels and corporatist arrangements. Goods may well be created and shared among those around the table, while any negative 'externalities' may be ignored or wilfully imposed on those not invited in. Thus, any beneficial effects from increased participation, or democratic responsiveness to the best interests of subjects, depend crucially on how the mechanisms of democratic politics work in practice.

Second, the hesitation expressed on behalf of democratic rule under present sub-optimal circumstances does not entail that non-democratic modes of governance fare any better, under these or other conditions. Note that this comparative perspective is central to the normative arguments I entertain. The case in favour of democratic rule is only that it better secures these objectives, under certain circumstances, than *alternative* modes of decision making.

'More democratic multi-level governance is not possible'

We now turn to consider whether specifically democratic decision-making institutions *can* be included at levels above the state. Democratic rule of the kind worth promoting and obeying is sometimes said to not be possible. The conditions for securing transparency, accountability, representation, deliberation and good outcomes cannot be implemented (for a discussion on the conditions for democracy see also Koenig-Archibugi, this volume). Consider two separate arguments.

Some have ruled out the possibility of a sufficiently well-functioning European or global-level democracy because there is insufficient in the way of a common identity for substantial solidarity, and bleak prospects for public forums for the requisite transparency and deliberation to secure good outcomes. Thus, some lament the alleged present lack of a European or global '*demos*' in the sense of no shared political identity, or opportunities for it to develop (Grimm 1995). I submit that many authors have pointed out that such pessimism is unfounded, at least in the long run. First, there are already pockets of public debate about matters of global distributive justice (cf. Marchetti 2008, K. Macdonald, this volume). Second, the requisite public debates and forums need not occur *prior to* political contestation, but may develop – for instance, when media and then the greater public respond to increased competition among parties. Thus, central conditions for well-functioning democratic arrangements may well develop as a result of the workings of such (demo-cratic) institutions of governance. Consider the prospects of European-level democracy: there are signs of increased party organization and competition in the European Parliament, and some scholars observe policy contestation within the Council of Ministers (Hix 2008). Third, insofar as regional and global democratic decisions are limited to certain issues, the need for deliberation and arenas may be similarly limited. The more all-encompassing agenda of national parliaments of yore, and the wide ranging public debates surrounding them – at least in more nostalgic descriptions – is thus not even required as an ideal.

The second objection against the possibility of effective MDMLG may seem to follow from the arguments of several authors addressing MLG. Not only does the low impact of MLG institutions mitigate against any worry about them, but their low impact would also seem to imply that democratic decision making at levels above the state would have little, if any, effects. There are at least two versions of such arguments.

Samuel Freeman (2006) claims that a global basic structure, insofar as it exists, is secondary and supervenient upon sovereign states. The role of commercial treaties is mainly to determine which nation's laws apply. Trade agreements also largely take as given people's existing domestic 'property, economic, and political system' (18). Any global regulators and courts enjoy whatever power they have only as grants by the political acts of different peoples.[4] A global basic structure is thus 'nothing more than "the basic structure of the Society of Peoples"' (17):

> For example, the so-called "international property law" that exists is trivial in its extent, and it is simply the result of treaties, and is attuned to and builds on domestic property laws. It is not the product of an international legal body recognized as having original legislative powers and legal jurisdiction independent of treaties among peoples. (17n14)

According to this view, it is only states, rather than international regula-tions, that warrant normative assessment – not only for their domestic decisions, but also for the decisions they make about the rules of MLG. Against this view, I submit that Freeman's sense of 'supervenience' seems irrelevant for whether MLG should be the subject of normative standards. The fact that states are the main authors of international

---

[4] Much may be said against these claims – for example, about the creation of new international legal regimes which are hardly describable as trivial or a mere compilation or extension of domestic laws (Follesdal et al. 2008).

rules does not seem to affect the central concern, namely that insofar as the global basic structure *does* affect peoples' lives profoundly, these choices by domestic governments do structure and regulate the everyday lives of foreigners. Large components of these structures are created and maintained primarily by domestic authorities, but this does not reduce their impact on foreigners, nor does their origin in treaties exempt them from normative assessment. Rather, this situation suggests that the present MLG structures should be changed so as to ensure foreigners have a voice, and possibly a vote, in the domestic democratic decision-making structures. This might be secured by letting some legislators in each jurisdiction be elected by affected persons outside the jurisdiction itself (Koenig-Archibugi forthcoming).

Moreover, the actual design – both the procedures and the results – of international institutions is to a large extent *not* controlled by state governments. Many crucial details are instead the result of private parties engaged in 'private governance' that leave governments with neither choice, exit nor voice (e.g., Hall and Biersteker 2002, Ruggie 2004, Follesdal et al. 2008). Thus, the democratic control that there may be over (some) governments is insufficient to alleviate the normative concerns.

A second version of the claim that democratic institutions should not be expected to have any significant impact on the output of MLG, because international regulations have very small impact, might draw on arguments such as those of Christiano in this volume. Christiano compares international legal regulations to those of a state. About the former, he holds that 'they play a fairly small role in the lives of people throughout the world ... They do not enter into the systems of property and exchange in domestic societies except in very abstract ways' (Christiano 2008, 10). Indeed, 'the system of international trade does not reach nearly as deeply into people's lives as most domestic systems of trade and exchange. Furthermore, the capacity of international institutions to regulate the flow of trade is still quite small' (10). Christiano concludes that this differential impact of international and domestic institutions *weakens* normative claims to have the basic structure under democratic control. Other authors draw more extensive conclusions, partly because it is only states that can provide assurance of general compliance with institutions. Thus, Thomas Nagel (2005) holds that 'the kind of all-encompassing collective practice or institution that is capable of being just in the primary sense can exist only under sovereign government' (116). So, while there are global humanitarian duties to alleviate global poverty, this is not a matter of justice.

Against these claims, I submit several objections. First, many will agree with Amartya Sen (2001) and others that in our interconnected world, it is nearly impossible to disentangle the impact of domestic and international or global institutions – for example, concerning the economy. Witness, for instance, the current financial crisis that has hit almost all states – but with a different impact in Canada, Iceland and even among the different states of the EU, partly due to domestic decisions. Second, we should challenge the empirical assumption: the impact of the *existing* combination of domestic and international institutions is immense for some individuals, though not so for others – though this impact is certainly less *visible* for some than for others (Buchanan 2000, Pevnick 2008). The fact that even morally concerned citizens in many states do not *observe* the impact of the rules of MLG on 'distant' people, and especially the fact that citizens in countries who benefit disproportionately from such rules do not see this, certainly does not settle the issue. To the contrary, the opacity of this impact should counsel further transparency, wrought by monitoring – for instance, stimulated by democratic contestation. In domestic settings these functions are typically provided by media and opposition parties – which form yet another reason for democracy or some functional equivalent trust-building measures, also at the global level. Finally, the fact that governance mechanisms currently cannot do much to regulate and sanction the multi-level regulatory order does not yield the conclusion that institutions *cannot* be changed purposively, and hence cannot be assessed by normative standards (Abizadeh 2007). Arguably, this 'governance gap' (Ruggie 2003) should instead urge us to call for improvements to the decision-making structures for MLG.

'More democratic multi-level governance is not necessary'

This section considers three arguments to the effect that while it might be possible to establish and maintain more democratic forms of MLG, this is not normatively required. The discussions generalize somewhat from the alleged need for a more democratic EU regarded as an exemplar of an international organization or (quasi-federal) political order.

'Unnecessary due to little impact'

One extension of some of the arguments considered above is that while MDMLG might be possible, MLG has so little impact on individuals that democratic control is unnecessary. Some such arguments with regard to the EU illustrate the point and the weaknesses of such claims.

Andrew Moravcsik (2002) has argued on several occasions as to why the EU does not need to be democratic. The formal competences of the EU are limited in scope, and they are neither important enough for Europeans nor sufficiently salient for them to warrant democratic scrutiny.

In response, we should note that what matters is not only the limited legal authority of the EU – or, by extension, the limited authority of international organizations and the system of MLG in general. Instead, we must consider the impact of this allocation of decision-making authority on individuals, especially in the light of the effects of possible alternatives (Follesdal and Hix 2006).

Moravcsik and others are surely right that the impact of domestic, regional and international rules is *partly* an effect of the rules of international law. Important factors that affect the content of such rules are, of course, state consent, states' interests and the relative bargaining power of states. While some states can shape trade, patents and financial regimes to favour their interests, however they have defined them, many other states are often merely regime takers. And lax regimes – for international human rights protection, labour standards etc. – are as much a result of states' decisions as the quite strict regimes concerning patents and trade (Ruggie 2003). Thus, the claim that international institutions only affect a 'thin' set of issues does not seem plausible: we must also consider their indirect impact and the impact of the intended absence of demanding rules.

With regard to claims that such concerns are not salient among citizens, recall the role of democratic political contestation for bringing important issues to public attention. It thus seems ill-founded to dismiss calls for democracy at the European level on the basis that the EU only deals with issues that are not salient to the citizenry (Moravcsik 2002, 615). Salience of a policy issue is partly a result of democratic contestation. Without political parties seeking votes, there will be fewer incentives to articulate alternative policy choices, and therefore less public attention by the media. Thus, the implication of a lack of salience is not that democratic governance mechanisms are unnecessary. To the contrary, the present lack of salience concerning important policy choices within the structures of MLG is a further reason for democratic control thereof.

'Unnecessary because states consent'

A second line of argument as to why democratic arrangements for MLG may be thought unnecessary draws on the perceived strong role of states. Since sovereign states voluntarily agree to the various international regulations that constitute MLG, these regulations leave all signatories at least as well off as they were before. The treaties are thus 'Pareto improvements', and it is argued that these do not raise concerns about distributive justice and democratic rule. This is because contestation and decision making with majority rule largely concern how to distribute benefits and burdens among winners – and losers, of which there are none in the case of MLG, or so this argument goes.

Giandomenico Majone (1998b has made such claims in favour of allowing the 'democratic deficit' of the EU to continue (122–3)). This case is especially relevant since it brings out some of the complexities of the creation and effects of MLG, and the role of comparative assessments of institutions.

Majone holds that an EU dominated by elected representatives would hinder the objective of the EU, which he holds is precisely to secure such Pareto improvements. Democratic decision making threatens this objective, since the politicization and conflicts concerning regulatory policy making will turn the regulatory task into one of redistribution *rather than* staying with securing Pareto improvements (Majone 1998b, 2001). Against Majone's argument and, by extension, similar objections concerning MDMLG, I submit that such arguments fail to address the kinds of regulations that the EU and MLG provide.

The issues facing the EU – and MLG – are hardly ever how to identify and reach the one unique Pareto improving bargaining solution among the parties (Follesdal and Hix 2006). To the contrary, global regimes – as well as individual EU policies – very often cause benefits to some and burdens to others, compared to alternative regimes. After all, many of the signatory states are not democratic, and even in democratic states the majority can overrule individuals who may suffer from the interstate agreements. Very often, Pareto improvements also have distributive effects both within and between states, as to *who receives which benefits*. Finally, very often rule-makers face a choice between several rules, all of which are Pareto improvements. When this is the case, their choice has distributive effects.

The upshot is that even in the cases where rules of MLG are Pareto improvements, there are a host of distributive issues that must be decided – but which often go unnoticed. Indeed, this concern seems central to the agenda of the 'anti-globalist' movement: the aim is not to end globalization, but to ensure that the benefits and burdens of globalization are less unfairly distributed (Sen 2001, Ruggie 2003). An important issue is therefore to identify and implement decision-making procedures that can assess and decide the rules of MLG in terms of how best to serve the interests of all to a defensible extent, and to secure rules that engender a fair division of benefits of cooperation. Domestically, democratic rule has a better success rate on this count than other decision-making procedures that have been tried.

'Unnecessary because "participatory bodies" and "networks" suffice'

One argument against MDMLG holds that networks and other forms of participatory decision-making arenas suffice; indeed, some hold that these are exemplars of MDMLG (T. Macdonald and K. Macdonald, both this volume), because they exemplify some sort of deliberation among some parties 'represented' around the table – claims that I am inclined to deny. The experiences and discussions concerning such arrangements in the EU may again be helpful.

The EU has had extensive experience with what is called 'new modes of governance', including regulatory networks. These networks recommend the substantive contents of regulations, even though they are outside the ordinary legislative arenas. They typically involve both private and public actors for specific sectors and are not directly accountable, since the participants cannot be voted out of office. The literature offers several arguments as to why we might sometimes favour them over democratic arrangements (Majone 1996). Such networks are sometimes said to be legitimate since they secure 'output' effectively, and – if they are 'well balanced' – they are more likely to do so than democratic arrangements, even without 'input' from voters (Heretier 1999). This is because the networks command more expertise, can open up policy-making opportunities for more actors and may respond more speedily (Follesdal 2011).

Another favoured strategy to gain legitimacy for EU decision making is somewhat related: to include affected parties to allow their participation on issues that concern them. Thus, the European Commission (2001) issued a *White Paper on Governance* that argued for more participatory mechanisms. This appears laudable, especially given the general perception that the Commission is excessively favourable to business and organized interests (Streeck and Schmitter 1991). The central rationale for representation of various social groups seems to build on a conception of participatory governance, that policies are more responsive and will be seen as more legitimate by involving those affected.

What are we to make of these modes of multi-level governance? Networks and private actors often have more expertise and may respond more speedily than when public actors seek to act alone. But such decision-making arrangements have several weaknesses. In the absence of transparency and oversight, citizens may have little reason to trust that expertise and efficiency is in fact ensured. The networks and participatory arenas may certainly help socialize participants, and hence foster solidarity and mutual concern among them. This may be one desired effect of their deliberations. Yet, this may be less attractive insofar as the members of the MLG do not represent all affected parties, and insofar as the deliberations are not open to public scrutiny. This is therefore a possible monotonicity mistake. For instance, their opacity and non-representativeness increase the risk that externalities will at best be ignored and possibly callously planned and imposed – and the risk may fuel public mistrust even of well-functioning networks.

Equitable policies are only likely to emerge if the representation is equitable among those stakeholders whose needs are in conflict. And the representatives must understand their role as ensuring the common good, however understood, rather than only serving as delegates for their own constituency (Bellamy et al. 2010, Follesdal 2011). In the EU there are few, if any, mechanisms to ensure that the Commission or other EU bodies include representatives of all affected parties to the networks and 'participatory' arrangements; nor are there mechanisms in place that make their selection and decisions trustworthy. Similar concerns apply with even greater force to other parts of the global MLG structure.

With regard to *transparency* and *accountability*, we may note that all multi-level arrangements are complex. However, these networks and participatory arrangements are typically issue or sector specific, and this adds to the complexity – and creates several additional problems. Who should count as an affected party and be included as a stakeholder? Who should identify and adjudicate conflicts between the various regulations that emanate from partly overlapping regulatory networks in different issues (Hooge and Marks 2001)?

With regard to identifying the appropriate objectives and standards, it might be thought that they are likely to emerge on the basis of constructive debate among the participants within networks or participatory arrangements. So we return to the questions of who should have the authority to decide on membership, and how to guard against skewed bargaining power and co-optation, so that the agreements actually reflect and balance all affected interests. Moreover, it is unclear whether citizens can have reason to trust that these networks or deliberating bodies do in fact secure outcomes that are sufficiently responsive to their best interests. Empirical findings give reason to doubt whether the set of deliberators is sufficiently representative, and the quality of the debate sufficiently 'deliberative' (Smismans 2008).

One way to correct some of these flaws is to resort to familiar arrangements of democratic accountability that would take on responsibilities precisely for inclusion, transparency etc. Such 'nesting' of regulatory networks and arenas of consultation may render such non-democratic modes of governance much more acceptable. Indeed, such 'nested' networks or participatory arenas, within democratic procedures, might allow more creative and informed problem-solving by non-accountable bodies. The membership would then be decided by democratic author-ities concerned to have a 'balanced' set of participants. The proposals that emerge from these processes would in turn be ultimately decided by accountable authorities, who would also have to address conflicts, spillovers and any externalities. This way, networks and participatory arrangements would presumably also be subject to much more public scrutiny than at present, by media and by competing political parties. In short, the output from these nested networks and participatory arrange-ments would not replace and silence broader public debate, democratic deliberation and contestation, but rather enhance them. This would help render the multi-level structures of governance more trustworthy.

To conclude this discussion of objections that MDMLG is unneces-sary, I have responded in ways that should make clear that democratic arrangements need not be seen as a categorical imperative, independent of empirical arguments. Instead, we have reasons to believe that the decisions made in MLG are of the kind that require responsible trade-offs based on acute awareness of the impact on all affected parties. Alternatives to democratic rule may be even less trusted to be sufficiently responsive to the best interests of all those subject to these decisions.

Conclusion

The present reflections have sought to lay out the case for a modest claim, namely to rebut some of the objections raised against a more democratic multi-level system of governance. The conclusion is that we still seem to have good reason to argue that the constitutionalization of public international law and other forms of multi-level regulation should include, in some way or other, mechanisms of democratic accountability, directly toward citizens or mediated via their national representatives.

I have sought to defend this claim against two alternative views. Some authors regard this as an impossible requirement: the MLG structure cannot be so governed. Other authors agree that such democratic accountability might be established, at least in the medium range, but they object that it does not seem necessary, in the light of the small effects of MLG on individuals' lives. In response, I have laid out a brief account of a case for democratic institutions, based on comparative assessments with regard to decision making at the national level: that under some conditions, alternatives to democracy are less likely to reliably remain responsive to the best interests of affected persons over time. Whether democratic arrangements are preferable to the best institutional alternatives also at the global level is in part an empirical matter. It seems clear that such questions cannot simply be dismissed as category mistakes about the impact of, and possible control over, our global multi-level system of governance.

REFERENCES

Abizadeh, Arash. 2007. 'Cooperation, Pervasive Impact, and Coercion: On the Scope (Not Site) of Distributive Justice', *Philosophy and Public Affairs* 35, 4: 318–58.
Archibugi, Daniele, and David Held (eds.). 1995. *Cosmopolitan Democracy: An Agenda for a New World Order.* Cambridge, UK: Polity Press.
Beitz, Charles R. 1989. *Political Equality.* Princeton University Press.
Bellamy, Richard, Dario Castiglione, Andreas Follesdal and Albert Weale. 2010. 'Evaluating Trustworthiness, Representation and Political Accountability in New Modes of Governance', in Adrienne Heretier and Martin Rhodes (eds.), *New Modes of Governance in Europe* (pp. 135–62). Basingstoke, UK: Palgrave Macmillan.
Buchanan, Allen. 2000. 'Rawls's Law of Peoples: Rules for a Vanished Westphalian World', *Ethics* 110, 4: 697–721.
Christiano, Thomas. 2008. 'Democratic Legitimacy and International Institutions'. Paper presented at the ISA Convention, San Francisco, USA, March 26–9.
Czempiel, Ernst-Otto. 1992. 'Governance and Democratization', in James N. Rosenau and Ernst-Otto Czempiel (eds.), *Governance without Government: Order and Change in World Politics* (pp. 250–71). Cambridge University Press.
Dahl, Robert A. 1989. *Democracy and Its Critics.* New Haven, CT: Yale University Press.
  1999. 'Can International Organizations Be Democratic? A Skeptic's View', in Ian Shapiro and Casiano Hacker-Cordón (eds.), *Democracy's Edges* (pp. 19–36). Cambridge University Press.
Dryzek, John. 2006. *Deliberative Global Politics.* Cambridge, UK: Polity Press.
European Commission. 2001. European Governance: A White Paper, Com. (2001) 428. Brussels.
Follesdal, Andreas. 2009. 'The Legitimacy of International Human Rights Review: The Case of the European Court of Human Rights', *Journal of Social Philosophy* 40, 4: 595–607.
  2011. 'The Legitimacy Challenges for New Modes of Governance: Trustworthy Responsiveness', *Government and Opposition* 46: 81–100.
Follesdal, Andreas, and Simon Hix. 2006. 'Why There Is a Democratic Deficit in the EU: A Response to Majone and Moravcsik', *Journal of Common Market Studies* 44, 3: 533–62.

Follesdal, Andreas, Ramses Wessel and Jan Wouters (eds.). 2008. *Multilevel Regulation and the EU: The Interplay between Global, European and National Normative Processes*. Leiden, Netherlands: Martinus Nijhoff.

Freeman, Samuel. 2006. *Distributive Justice and the Law of Peoples*. Unpublished manuscript.

Grimm, Dieter. 1995. 'Does Europe Need a Constitution?' *European Law Journal* 1, 3: 282–302.

Hall, Rodney Bruce, and Thomas J. Biersteker (eds.). 2002. *The Emergence of Private Authority in Global Governance*. New York: Cambridge University Press.

Held, David. 1987. *Models of Democracy*. Cambridge, UK: Polity Press.
    1993. 'Democracy: From City-States to a Cosmopolitan Order?', in David Held (ed.), *Prospects for Democracy: North, South, East, West* (pp. 13–52). Oxford, UK: Polity Press.

Heretier, Adrienne. 1999. 'Elements of Democratic Legitimation in Europe: An Alternative Perspective', *Journal of European Public Policy* 6, 2: 269–82.

Hix, Simon. 2008. *What's Wrong with the EU and How to Fix It*. Oxford, UK: Polity Press.

Hooge, Liesbeth, and Gary Marks. 2001. 'Unravelling the Central State, but How? Types of Multi-Level Governance', *American Political Science Review* 97, 2: 233–43.

Koenig-Archibugi, Mathias. Forthcoming. 'Fuzzy Citizenship in Global Society', *Journal of Political Philosophy*.

Koenig-Archibugi, Mathias, and Michael Zürn (eds.). 2006. *New Modes of Governance in the Global System: Exploring Publicness, Delegation and Inclusiveness*. Basingstoke: Palgrave Macmillan.

Lenaerts, Koen, and Marlies Desomer. 2002. 'New Models of Constitution-Making in Europe: The Quest for Legitimacy', *Common Market Law Review* 39: 1217–53.

Macdonald, Terry. 2008. *Global Stakeholder Democracy: Power and Representation Beyond Liberal States*. Oxford University Press.

Macdonald, Terry, and Kate Macdonald. 2006. 'Non-Electoral Accountability in Global Politics: Strengthening Democratic Control within the Global Garment Industry', *European Journal of International Law* 17, 1: 89–119.

Majone, Giandomenico. 1996. 'A European Regulatory State?', in Jeremy J. Richardson (ed.), *European Union: Power and Policy-Making* (pp. 263–77). London: Routledge.
    1998a. 'Europe's "Democratic Deficit": The Question of Standards', *European Law Journal* 4, 1: 5–28.
    1998b. 'State, Market and Regulatory Competition: Lessons for the Integrating World Economy', in Andrew Moravcsik (ed.), *Centralization or Fragmentation? Europe Facing the Challenges of Deepening, Diversity, and Democracy* (pp. 94–123). New York: Council on Foreign Relations.
    2001. 'Regulatory Legitimacy in the United States and the European Union', in Kalypso Nicolaidis and Robert Howse (eds.), *The Federal Vision: Legitimacy and Levels of Governance in the US and the EU* (pp. 252–74). Oxford University Press.

Marchetti, Raffaele. 2008. *Global Democracy: For and Against. Ethical Theory, Institutional Design, and Social Struggles.* London: Routledge.

Moravcsik, Andrew. 2002. 'In Defence of the "Democratic Deficit": Reassessing Legitimacy in the European Union', *Journal of Common Market Studies* 40, 4: 603–24.

Nagel, Thomas. 2005. 'The Problem of Global Justice', *Philosophy and Public Affairs* 33, 2: 113–47.

O'Brien, Robert, Anne Marie Goetz, Jan Aart Scholte and Marc Williams. 2000. *Contesting Global Governance: Multilateral Economic Institutions and Global Social Movements.* Cambridge University Press.

Pevnick, Ryan. 2008. 'Political Coercion and the Scope of Distributive Justice', *Political Studies* 56, 2: 399–413.

Rosenau, James N. 1992. 'Governance, Order, and Change in World Politics', in James N. Rosenau and Ernst-Otto Czempiel (eds.), *Governance without Government: Order and Change in World Politics* (pp. 1–29). Cambridge University Press.

Ruggie, John G. 1982. 'International Regimes, Transactions and Change: Embedded Liberalism in the Postwar Economic Order', *International Organization* 36, 2: 379–415.

2003. 'Taking Embedded Liberalism Global: The Corporate Connection', in David Held and Mathias Koenig-Archibugi (eds.), *Taming Globalization* (pp. 93–129). Cambridge University Press.

2004. 'Reconstituting the Global Public Domain: Issues, Actors and Practices', *European Journal of International Relations* 10, 4: 499–531.

Sen, Amartya K. 2001 (17 July). 'A World of Extremes: Ten Theses on Globalization', *Los Angeles Times.*

Sen, Amartya K, and Jean Drèze. 1990. *Hunger and Public Action.* Oxford University Press.

Shapiro, Ian. 1996. *Democracy's Place.* Ithaca, NY: Cornell University Press.

Smismans, Stijn. 2008. 'New Modes of Governance and the Participatory Myth', *West European Politics* 31, 5: 874–95.

Streeck, Wolfgang, and Philippe C. Schmitter. 1991. 'From National Corporatism to Transnational Pluralism: Organized Interests in the Single European Market', *Politics and Society* 19, 2: 133–64.

Waldron, Jeremy. 2000. *Law and Disagreement.* Oxford University Press.

Waldron, Jeremy. 2006. 'The Core of the Case against Judicial Review', *The Yale Law Journal* 115: 1346–406.

Weale, Albert. 1999. *Democracy.* New York: St Martin's Press.

6 Regional versus global democracy
Advantages and limitations

Carol C. Gould

Introduction

Regionalism has come to the fore in recent economic and political developments and has been an important subject of attention in contemporary political science. Especially in view of the rise to prominence of the European Union (EU) over the past decades (despite the various setbacks), theorists have taken notice of the new forms of regional coordination and cooperation not only there but in other parts of the world (e.g., Latin America, southeast Asia etc.), where these particularly concern economic matters, though in some cases political organization as well. However, there has been considerably less attention to the normative implications of these developments, though some theorists (especially of international law) have pointed to the regional human rights agreements that are beginning to be taken seriously, while other theorists (especially of international relations) have commented on the democratic deficit in the EU. Further, while theorists of democracy and human rights have analysed the justifications and roles that these norms may play in *national* contexts and increasingly even in *global* contexts, scant attention has been given to their potential for guiding and constraining *regional* economic and political development. Instead, several cosmopolitan democratic theorists, as also cosmopolitan theorists of justice, seem to want to move the discussion directly from the level of the nation-state to that of the world as a whole, with little analysis of the emerging regionalism, increasingly recognized as important in practical affairs and in political science generally.

Earlier versions of this paper were presented at the Political Studies Association Annual Conference, Edinburgh, Scotland, March 31, 2010 and at the American Political Science Association, Washington, DC, September 5, 2010. I would like to thank the participants in those sessions, as well as my research assistant Joshua Keton, for helpful comments on the manuscript.

115

Where more cosmopolitan forms of democracy have been discussed, what many thinkers have in mind is either full global democracy or else simply more democratic accountability in the institutions of global governance, again without attention to the normative requirements for democracy in the new regional associations. And where regionalism is considered in its implications for democracy, the discussions have tended to concern only the case of the EU, with considerations directed to strengthening its parliament, implementing European political parties etc. Equally striking and important, perhaps, where regionalism is projected elsewhere and evaluated for its potential contributions for new forms of cooperation, it tends to be thought of exclusively in terms of the model provided by the EU. Yet, one of the main advantages of regionalization would seem to be the retention or enabling of a certain level of cultural diversity around the world, rather than supposing that all regions should simply follow the model of the EU.

There have been noteworthy exceptions to the lack of attention to regions among normative theorists. In particular, two political philosophers who have placed some weight on regionalism are Yael Tamir and Jürgen Habermas. While neither has especially emphasized regional human rights agreements, both have called attention to regions as important settings for increased transnational cooperation and regulation, particularly concerning economic and social justice matters. Expanding my own earlier account (Gould 2004), I will investigate whether the development of regional forms of democracy bounded by regional human rights agreements constitutes an important new focus for normative theory. But I also want to compare the arguments for such regional forms to those that have been given for more global institutions of democracy, presumably bounded by global human rights agreements and protections. In order to do so, I will attempt to lay out and assess some of the arguments that can be given for cosmopolitan democracy as well, and to briefly consider the relation between the regional and global arenas in this context, as well as to indicate some flaws that I believe have characterized the entire discussion of transnational democracy to date. These concern the validation that they continue to offer to old notions of sovereignty – by transposing them to the global level – and their omission of the numerous other domains in which democratic decision making is normatively required. These domains include new transnational communities and interactions that criss-cross these presumably orderly nested territorial frameworks, and also the quasi-public institutional contexts that make up corporations and other important social, economic and political non-state actors. I suggest that no forward-looking democratic theory can claim to be complete without considering these important new domains.

Moreover, the ways that have been proposed to increase democratic participation in the institutions of global governance also need to be taken into account and related to the regional and global spheres. While it will not be possible to lay out a complete and coherent picture of increased democratic participation at all these various levels in this chapter, I suggest that the omission of the consideration of regional and transnational forms of democratic participation, including how they pertain to the economy, render the global accounts of democracy incomplete if not wholly empty of content. Moreover, in all these interrelated inquiries concerning the scope of expanded democracy, we will need to evaluate again the relevance of the various criteria that have been promulgated – the 'all-affected principle', more communitarian ones, citizenship claims etc.

Extending regional democracy framed by human rights agreements

In this section, we may ask whether it is in fact desirable to prioritize new forms of regional democracy within human rights frameworks of regional scope. In the early 1990s, Yael Tamir offered a justification for an emphasis on regional cooperation that focuses on the need for economic, military and ecological coordination and planning beyond the level of nation-states. She argues that this sort of cooperation, as well as participation in decisions at that level, is required by what she calls *self-rule* rather than by considerations of *national self-determination*. The latter is best realized by autonomous national communities below the level of nation-states that are 'sheltered under a regional umbrella'. On her account, 'self-rule implies that individuals should affect all levels of the decision-making process', while 'national identity is best cultivated in a small, relatively closed, and homogeneous framework' (Tamir 1993, 151). Moreover, she goes on to argue that 'regional organizations will enable nations to cooperate as equal partners, rather than support one's nation (sic) domination over others' (153). Thus, in Tamir's view, the regional focus meets the need for the larger-scale coordination in modern economies that goes beyond the capacities of existing nation-states and at the same time is 'more likely to foster toleration and diversity than political arrangements based on oppression and domination' (153).

It may be observed that Tamir (1993) here aligns herself with the 'affected interests' justification of democratic participation. 'Self-rule', she writes, 'is meant to allow individuals to participate in the making of those decisions that have a major influence on their lives' (150). More important for our purposes, her notion of a regional alliance among nations suggests that the justification of a regional focus should not be framed directly in communitarian terms, where the region would simply be a larger or broader community. Rather, she suggests that regions support communal concerns, practices and traditions indirectly by potentially allowing nations more autonomy within them.

However, given that Tamir's understanding of a regional association is a revisionist and ideal one in its proposal for nations generally smaller than existing states, we should perhaps instead look at the de facto current regions of the world and consider whether democracy within them is a plausible and appropriate normative desideratum. Of course, one difficulty here is identifying what is to count as a region and, especially if it is geographically defined, whether it encompasses an entire continent or is better understood as having a smaller extent.

Habermas advances a view that gives an important place to regionalism conceived along continental lines – for example, in the EU – which he regards as *transnational* in distinction from *supranational*, where the latter applies to fully global institutions and, in particular, the United Nations (UN). In his discussion in *The Divided West* (2006), and as further developed in his more recent piece 'A Political Constitution for the Pluralist World Society?' (in Habermas 2008), he argues (like Tamir) for the enhanced role of regions in coordinating economic and ecological issues as required by globalization, instead of arguing for new forms of cosmopolitan democracy or world government to address these issues. Indeed, even the institutions of global governance seem to play a secondary role in Habermas's account, inasmuch as he regards them as not strong enough to address the financial, monetary, regulatory and redistributive requirements thrown up by economic globalization. Only strong continental regions can address these, and perhaps such regions can develop new democratic legitimacy over time. Nonetheless, Habermas seems to allow that a lot of the work of these regions can proceed by judicial and legal processes rather than strictly political means. This is even more strikingly the case for what he calls the supranational domain of the UN, which is to concern itself primarily with the maintenance of security and the protection of people against human rights abuses. Crucially, he limits the relevant human rights to the traditional civil and political ones, rather than economic and social ones. Moreover, he seems to think the former set of human rights can be protected through courts (especially a more effective International Criminal Court) as well as through a strengthened Security Council in the UN. In his view, less democracy and less politics are needed at this supranational level; thereby he thinks the criticism that democratic legitimacy is missing at this level is defused. Presumably, the situation is further aided by opening up the functioning of these institutions to deliberative input in a global public sphere.

Along these lines, in *The Divided West* Habermas (2006) explains:

On this conception, a suitably reformed world organization could perform the vital but clearly circumscribed functions of securing peace and promoting human rights at the supranational level in an effective and non-selective fashion without having to assume the state-like character of a world republic. At the intermediate, transnational level, the major powers would address the difficult problems of a global domestic politics which are no longer restricted to mere coordination but extend to promoting actively a rebalanced world order. They would have to cope with global economic and ecological problems within the framework of permanent conferences and negotiating forums. (138)

In his more recent piece 'A Political Constitution for the Pluralist World Society?' Habermas (2008) speaks more directly of a 'constitutionalized world society', but explains it as 'a multilevel system that can make possible a global domestic politics that has hitherto been lacking, especially in the fields of global economic and environmental policies, even without a world government' (322). As in the earlier account, its structure is held to consist in three levels or 'arenas'. The first, the supranational, is dominated by the UN and limited to the functions of 'securing peace and human rights on a global scale'. It remains composed of nation-states rather than world citizens. In order to deal with issues of global justice and even the less demanding Millenium Development Goals, Habermas calls for the elaboration, in what he terms the transnational arena, of 'regional or continental regimes equipped with a sufficiently representative mandate to negotiate for whole continents and to wield the necessary powers of implementation for large territories' (322). What he calls 'a manageable number of global players' (325) would be needed to negotiate effective economic and environmental regulations. He believes that conflict among them could be avoided by the enhanced UN security regime he envisions. The third level in this account remains that of nation-states, which, however, require supplementation by regional alliances, to better deal with the 'growing interdependencies of the global economy' that overtax 'the chains of legitimation' within nation-states. As Habermas notes (in an appeal to the affectedness principle), 'globalized networks in all dimensions have long since made nonsense of the normative assumption in democratic theory of a congruence between those responsible for political decision-making and those affected by political decisions' (325).

Habermas (2008) views current regional groupings (e.g., Association of Southeast Asian Nations [ASEAN], North American Free Trade

Agreement [NAFTA], Organization of American States [OAS] etc.)
as weak and he calls for strengthened alliances that could 'assume the
role of collective pillars of a global domestic politics at the transnational
level ... and confer the necessary democratic legitimacy on the outcomes of transnational political accords' (326). He regards the EU as
the only current example of this sort of major player. He calls for greater
political integration in the EU, with democratic legitimation, which
would also enable it to serve as a model for other regions. Yet the extent
of democratic decision making within these regions is not clearly
addressed here, and states (rather than the region's citizens) seem to
retain many of their traditional prerogatives. Certainly, as far as interactions among the regions are concerned, Habermas primarily envisions
forms of negotiation and compromise.

One of the advantages of the emphasis on regions that Habermas
points to is that their development is probably a relatively realistic
expectation in contemporary world affairs. While their precise borders
and scope remain an open question, it is nonetheless evident that some
degree of regionalization is taking place with regard to economic and
even political matters. Thus, I agree that it is plausible to argue for
enhanced regional scope for democratic decision making on the grounds
that it can be envisaged, as opposed to the more visionary introduction
of full global democracy.

Before considering some other possible advantages of a regional focus,
we can add an emphasis that is somewhat underplayed in Habermas's
account. This is the importance of regional human rights agreements
to frame increased regional democratization processes. Importantly, a
broader adoption of such human rights agreements would protect individuals operating in the new cross-border communities and provide a
basis for appeal in connection with cross-border democratic decisions
about their collective activities. Moreover, such agreements can serve
not only to protect human rights but to establish them as goals around
which social and economic development can be mobilized. Although
Habermas at various points recognizes the significance of the European
human rights courts, his focus on guaranteeing human rights at the
supranational level of the UN perhaps leads him to underplay this
emerging regional level of human rights agreements and jurisprudence.

Beyond its relative practicability, regional democracy has some other
possible advantages that can be noted here, which have to do with
notions of communities and with cultural issues and interpretations.
In distinction from Tamir, who thought that regions could primarily
provide a home for diverse nations – generally smaller than present
nation-states and relatively more homogeneous – it could also be said

that regionalization can itself permit greater expression of diversity in global mores and even human rights interpretations. Of course, this would be the case only to the degree that the regions themselves, though not homogeneous, represent forums for traditions that overlap with each other. Needless to say, this can only be strictly the case in an idealized representation because, like culture generally, the existing strands of traditions within regions are themselves very diverse. Yet, to the degree that there are overlapping shared histories and traditions, respecting these can enable some diversity not only in the forms of democratic decision making but in the human rights interpretations that may be offered or emphasized by these various regions.

The communitarian considerations have a similar bearing. Although quite disparate, some of the traditions and local mores are perhaps more similar to each other than they are to those in other regions. Instead of seeing the region as a single community, however, we can spell it out more sensibly in a way that is consonant with what I have called common activities (along with social networks), rather than community generically. That is, like the social connections model, such an approach looks to actually-existing interrelations that develop over time as serving to bring people together, not only in new collectives, but as sharing new sorts of goals and projects in relation to the economic, ecological and political problems that they face. Further, in my view, such spheres of common activity serve to justify new arenas for democratic decision making, without involving an appeal to inherently vague notions of affected interests.

Finally, we can note another point in favour of the regional emphasis and that is that it preserves a connection to localities and hence to territory. Despite the virtual character of much activity under globalization, a connection to place remains significant. Of course, this territorial interpretation of regions can also be a negative, inasmuch as many contemporary activities and interconnected communities are truly transnational in a way that transcends regions. Also, localities themselves can in this way be transnational, as I have argued elsewhere (Gould 2007). Indeed, a general drawback to a region-centred approach to democracy is that it can fail to deal with the many problems that are truly global, especially perhaps ecological ones such as climate change.

Other drawbacks of the regional emphasis are normative as well as practical. In particular, we can mention the potential that these new forms of association might have for engendering conflicts between or among regions (thereby replicating and perhaps intensifying the conflicts among nation-states at this new level). In addition, it is possible that an established regionalism could reify and perhaps intensify cultural differences in the interpretation of basic international norms, including possibly weakening the force of some human rights.

As for the regional human rights agreements themselves, we can cite several problems. Only the European ones are really effective, and even there the implementation of them varies considerably and is less consistent and more difficult in parts of the continent – for example, Turkey and Russia. The Inter-American agreement is even less efficacious, and the African one almost not at all. As James Cavallaro and Stephanie Brewer (2008) point out in their article 'Reevaluating Regional Human Rights Litigation in the Twenty-First Century: The Case of the Inter-American Court', in situations where deference to the rule of law is lacking, such agreements are not respected. Thus, there are two major problems with these agreements – they are lacking in most world regions and, where they exist, they are implemented in a rather spotty fashion.

Extending democracy globally (within global human rights agreements)

We can now turn to the alternative approach that emphasizes moving directly to global forms of democracy. Those who have recently advocated such an approach include Torbjörn Tännsjö (2008), Raffaele Marchetti (2006, 2008 and this volume) and Eric Cavallero (2009) (see also Murithi, this volume). I will briefly consider the approaches of Marchetti and Cavallero here. Although these global democrats may recognize principles of subsidiarity, those who call themselves cosmopolitan democrats tend to explicitly argue for views that incorporate both regional and global perspectives (e.g., Held 1995). I will briefly touch on the role of subsidiarity in a final section in which I summarize the core elements of my own constructive view.

Raffaele Marchetti in a 2006 article and in his 2008 book *Global Democracy: For and Against,* and Eric Cavallero, especially in a recent article 'Federative Global Democracy' in the journal *Metaphilosophy,* have proposed robust conceptions of global democracy, understood in terms of a strong federation at the global level, which takes charge of decision making about world affairs and operates through new global representative institutions or parliaments.

Without reviewing their positions in detail here, I want to focus on a few philosophical issues in their accounts and to defend and contrast the alternative view that I have presented on these matters. My own approach has stressed the relevance of two criteria, both of which justify extending democracy beyond (and beneath) nation-states, though each criterion has a distinctive application. The first is the 'common activities' criterion noted above. While this necessarily remains quite general, it proposes that democracy is called for in all institutional contexts where people are related in joint activities oriented to common goals. These may also be called 'systems of cooperation'. But that phrase may over-estimate the orderly, intentional and systematic character of these enter-prises, rather than seeing them as institutional contexts that have arisen historically or emerge in ongoing practical activities of production, social association and governance. I argue that in all these institutional frameworks, increasingly of a transnational sort, members of these associations have equal rights to participate in their direction. The argument for this, in short, is that inasmuch as participation in such shared activities is a condition for people's freedom or agency and since they are equally free in this positive sense of freedom, they have rights to co-determine these common or joint activities, which thus take the form of rights of democratic participation in deciding about their course or direction (Gould 1988, 80–8).

The second criterion recognizes that, especially with intensive globalization, the decisions of many institutions in economic, social and political life impact on people at a distance, which gives rise in turn to rights of input into the decisions in question rather than full and equal participation. I further specify the nature of the impact or effect on others here that leads it to rise to the level of a normative requirement in terms of people being *importantly affected* by the decision in question, understood *as affected in their possibilities of fulfilling basic human rights* (Gould 2004, 210–12; 2009b).

What lies behind the distinction between these criteria and also between the notions of input and full participation is in part the critique I and others have offered of the 'all-affected' principle as a general justification of democracy (Saward 2000, 37; Gould 2004, 175–8). That principle asserts that all affected by a decision should be able to partici-pate in making it. In fact, in his 2008 book, Marchetti relies on just such a principle to justify global democracy, which he claims follows from the idea that the choice-bearers and the choice-makers (as he puts it) should be one and the same. This therefore constitutes one interpret-ation of the principle of self-rule at the heart of many conceptions of democracy (cf. Tamir above). Marchetti adds the idea that this coinci-dence of choice-bearers and choice-makers applies to what he calls the public domain, or 'public constituencies'. Thus, he proposes that 'a political principle has to be adopted that grants to all choice-bearing citizens as members of the public constituency in each level of political action, including the global and trans-border, a political voice and the power to make the choice-makers accountable' (Marchetti 2006, 294).

However, two problems can be discerned with this sort of view. The first is the inherent vagueness involved in determining all affected by a given decision. Because of the widespread consequences of decisions and policies, particularly in the economic domain, it is difficult to contain the number of choice-bearers or affected people. This could well lead nearly all decisions to be moved up to the global level, contrary to the intention of such theories to maintain some account of levels of decision making. And if decisions all become truly global, clearly people's degree of input or influence on these decisions would become extraordinarily dilute. I suggest that some notion of *important effects* needs to be added. Even so, we may wonder whether that will work to ground democratic decision making, particularly if we want to retain some notion of equal rights of participation, which would be violated by people's being *differentially* affected by decisions as in fact they are (cf. Saward 2000).

The second problem is that the demarcation of a *public constituency* remains somewhat obscure in Marchetti's account, and would have a question-begging air if it were to be used as a criterion for determining who is to participate, since it is precisely how a public is to be constituted – that is, who is to be included in which 'public' decision-making process – that is in question. We cannot assume that we know what the relevant public constituency is in advance, and it would be circular to define it in terms of those affected by a decision. Clearly, people are affected by private and interpersonal decisions as well,[1] so it is natural that Marchetti would want to appeal to some notion of public issues or constituencies. But he would need an independent definition of these, which he does not seem yet to have provided.[2]

---

[1] An extreme example is offered by Pogge (1992) in which someone might claim 'I should be allowed a vote on the permissibility of homosexuality, in all parts of the world, because the knowledge that homosexual acts are performed anywhere causes me great distress' (64n28).

[2] Marchetti's most recent reformulation of his view in terms of an 'all-inclusive principle' (this volume) raises additional concerns. The idea that 'before any frame-setting decision is taken, every single individual has to be consulted or, alternatively and more feasibly, has to be granted the right to appeal' (38) seems deeply impractical or even impossible, especially since framework setting would be an endlessly evolving process (even leaving aside the cross-cultural barriers involved). It would also appear to be insufficiently protective of privacy, understood not only in terms of a sphere of individual autonomy, but also as a domain of our significant social relations. The proposed priority to decisions by a global public in the first instance seems to land us on a slippery slope in which it would be difficult to demarcate the private from the public sphere in any principled way and in which nearly all decisions could become subject to the global polity (with its coercive power).

It can be added that a notion of affected interests shares the problem of interest views generally, inasmuch as the notion of interest is highly individual and not altogether clear in any case. Indeed, we can ask whether an individual can be adequately construed as a bundle of interests; and also whether simple impact on individuals, without an account of their social relatedness, provides a sufficient basis for justifying democracy. The common activities view has the advantage here in being futural (defined by shared goals) and socially based, recognizing the diversity of arenas for collective actions and decision making. It shares with Marchetti's view an emphasis on people's equal freedom, but in my view this requires not only bare freedom of choice (which Marchetti highlights) but also a positive notion of the development of people over time, which presupposes their having access to material and social conditions for their activity, which moreover can take the form of both collective and individual agency. I suggest that a view of this sort can provide a better account of when co-determination of decisions – that is, democratic participation – is required. I will later consider the implications of this notion for decision making at the regional and global levels.

On the notion of impact on individuals which is central to 'affected interests' approaches to justifying democracy, I agree, then, that such impacts are important, particularly with regard to the exogenous effects of decisions on those not part of any given collectivity. But my suggestion is that this gives rise to the somewhat less demanding requirement of significant *input* into the decision in question, and to a notion of equal consideration of interests rather than strictly equal rights to participate. The latter remains a notion of equal rights to co-determine all spheres of common activities that are conditions for members' free activity, where these spheres characterize existing institutional contexts as well as historically arising communities. Such institutions and communities are intentionally understood to be the institutions and communities that they are. These contexts for decision making therefore do not have to be constituted each time anew by considering who is affected by a given decision, and this is indeed one of the strengths of this account, I suggest. Yet, the notion of being importantly affected with regard to human rights fulfilment remains relevant in innovating new institutional ways for people to have input into decisions, including distant ones, that significantly affect them, and this has consequences for enabling democratic input into the institutions of global governance (Gould 2009b). It is again an advantage of this account that the required input into a given decision can be gathered independently of a master plan that in advance would group everyone affected into established constituencies.

(The proposed account would, however, call for the introduction of new forms of deliberation across borders.)

In a way somewhat related to Marchetti, Eric Cavallero (2009) uses the all-affected principle to argue for a federative account of global democracy. He specifies the all-affected principle in terms of 'an analysis of relevant effects such that those relevantly affected by an activity should have a say in the democratic processes that ultimately regulate (or fail to regulate) it'. He explains: 'According to this interpretation, an individual is relevantly affected by the exercise of a sovereign competence if (1) its exercise imposes governance norms on her, or (2) its exercise could otherwise reasonably be expected to impose external costs on her' (56). He explains the first case by drawing on Andrew Kuper's *Democracy Beyond Borders* (2004) and on my *Globalizing Democracy and Human Rights* (2004), pointing to the importance of the decisions and policies of the institutions of global governance that have important impacts on people's lives but in which they have no say. It is in this context that I have proposed devising new forms of democratic deliberation that permit input into the epistemic communities of these institutions, as well as new forms of transnational representation into their working, initially through international non-governmental organizations (Gould 2004, 2009b).

The second part of Cavallero's (2009) interpretation of this principle, the one that emphasizes external costs, is somewhat more problematic. A strength of his analysis is the detailed breakdown he gives of the types of external costs that may be relevant. With this analysis, Cavallero opposes my own proposal to specify 'affectedness' in terms of importantly affected interests, in which the latter are explained by reference to impact on people's human rights, especially their basic human rights. He argues that my proposal is underinclusive. Cavallero gives the example of a river that two countries share, where, he argues, 'it seems reasonable that citizens of the country downstream should have some say in determining what kinds and levels of pollutants are permitted to be discharged into the river upstream – even if unregulated discharges will not actually impact anyone's basic needs or human rights' (56). But in response to this objection, we can offer a few comments. First, many pollutants will in fact impact health, an important human right. This impact would support input by the affected second country into the decisions of the first regarding pollutants. Second, it can be noted that the criterion of impact on basic human rights gives rise to the requirement for input by people at a distance, and is not designed to rule out the emergence of new transnational communities that share economic and ecological interests organized in the mode of 'common activities'. Instead, the principle of distant impact is supposed to supplement those communities, whether old or newly emerging (as may happen in this case of the shared river), national or transnational. Third, the required input for which I advocate is also designed to supplement the sorts of considerations that are provided by stakeholder theory, where even impacts on relevant stakeholders (e.g., the community) that do not rise to the level of affecting their human rights are normatively required to be considered in decision making, even if the requirement does not rise to the level of mandating direct input in the decisions or shared democratic participation. Consideration of the impact on stakeholders can take the form, for example, of environmental impact assessments, which the decision makers should be expected to take seriously as a guide to their policies. While it is nearly always desirable to hear from the relevant stakeholders (Gould 2002), a consideration of their interests can sometimes occur without this.

In Cavallero's view, where policy decisions foreseeably impose external costs on others outside the polity in question, what he calls the 'internalization condition' kicks in, which 'requires that certain otherwise external costs be internalized through the constitution of composite polities comprising all who bear those costs' (Cavallero 2009, 58). Again, my problem with this is that the external costs, especially of economic policies, are extremely wide-ranging and so might well drive us to fully global levels of 'composite polities' too readily. Cavallero discusses this briefly by ruling out the adverse effects of macroeconomic policies that are designed to produce public goods (61). But this exception is not adequately explained or fully justified in his account.

We can mention a few other difficulties with such global democracy views. One, present especially in Cavallero's (2009) account, concerns the generalization that it entails of the notion of sovereignty now raised to the global level. We can object that this would likely simply exacerbate the problems with sovereignty that were pointed out long ago by Harold Laski among others. As Jeanne Morefield (2005) points out, Laski argued that the notion of state sovereignty serves to obscure and maintain the underlying conflicts in society between capital and labour, and the role played by the state in upholding the power of large corporations by coercively maintaining institutions that protect unlimited private property. In addition, state sovereignty in its internal dimension often involves the exercise of excessive coercion. It is not clear that simply expanding sovereignty to the global level will counter these problematic features. (Of course, Cavallero and other global democrats do usually propose some constraints on sovereignty in terms of human rights regimes. But the way these would work to constrain sovereignty and protect individuals is not adequately elaborated.)

Further, global democrats like Marchetti and Tännsjö tend to give what I take to be an insufficiently developed response to the standard challenge posed by the problem of possible tyranny, if all means of coercion come under the control of a global government. This is what I refer to as the *Weimar problem*. To put it in crude terms, human error and other social factors can conceivably lead to electing dictators, particularly if democracy is understood to consist entirely of voting and majority rule. The response that these theorists give is that tyranny is less likely with a democratic global government than without it. But this isn't yet much of an argument, insofar as it simply posits that the global government will continue to function democratically indefinitely. Indeed, according to an alternative line of argument, while the concentration of the means of coercion that such a system entails may indeed work out well, it could also function to exacerbate any anti-democratic or authoritarian tendencies that may arise and could thus contribute to eliminating freedom from a substantial portion of the populace. It is not necessarily that such global democratic views are incorrect, then, but rather that they tend to be a bit too rosy in disregarding these system defects that can arise both from institutional design and human error (or from more malicious causes as well).

A multi-dimensional conception of transnational democracy

In closing, we can propose that an adequate conception of globalizing democracy should be attuned to the historical possibilities of the present situation and should accommodate a diversity of existing forms of social organization and a variety of transnational relationships while still advancing more cosmopolitan conceptions of democracy and human rights. The emphasis on beginning with the current situation suggests the desirability of focusing on democratizing the functioning of global governance institutions (e.g., by enabling public input and deliberation, including by distantly situated representatives, as contributions to the functioning of their 'epistemic communities'). An emphasis on what is foreseeable also supports a focus on regional forms of democracy as a possible eventual development of the contemporary trends towards (limited) regionalism, within new or strengthened human rights agreements. The forms of such regional democracy remain in large part to be constructed. Viewed from the present, forms of global democracy seem more far-fetched, though there is a significant current movement to

introduce a People's Assembly in the UN. The human rights framework
for the new forms of global democracy will also need considerable
expansion, in ways that can nonetheless preserve some openness for
local diversity in interpretation, compatible with an overall commitment
to the equality and universality of human rights norms.

Yet, it can be observed that neither regional nor global democracy, nor
even the democratization of the institutions of global governance, would
be sufficient for transnational democracy. Two additional features of an
adequate approach to such new modes of democracy would be needed.
One involves addressing the emerging cross-border or transnational
and transregional communities that cross national or even regional
boundaries but that fall short of full globality. Most emerging communities, whether economic, ecological or communicative (e.g., through
the Internet) are in fact transnational in this way and not fully global,
where the term transnational connotes a more partial notion than does
the global. If we emphasize, as I have proposed, the way that common
activities come to be organized as part of ongoing practices, we can
see the need for introducing democratic participation into each of
these emerging institutions or communities (see T. Macdonald and
K. Macdonald, both this volume), for additional normative and empirical argument on this). This, in turn, resonates well with what I regard
as a second requirement for an adequate account of enhanced democracy in a more globalized society. This is that democracy at the level of
government and governance cannot be adequately realized without a
complementary intensification of democratic participation in the range
of smaller-scale institutions in economic, social and cultural life and in
more local political forms as well (Gould 2007). As Pateman (1970)
(following Mill) has argued, the practice of participation is educative.
And in addition, as I have proposed, opportunities for democratic
participation are normatively required for all members active in these
various institutions.

In short, then, the criteria of common activities and impact on human
rights fulfilment for distant people support the need for a distinctively
multidimensional approach to transnational democracy. Such an approach advocates increasing democratic input into global governance
institutions, participation in economic and social institutions generally,
new forms of regional democracy, and the creation of new cross-border
and transnational communities, themselves organized democratically.
In addition, robust forms of global democracy have a place in this
picture to the degree that people recognize that they share important
goals with all others worldwide. It is also plausible to suppose that
principles of subsidiarity will be relevant in determining how decisions

should be allocated among many of these levels of institutions and communities, at least to the extent that notions of locality and territoriality continue to play a role. But it would be a mistake to limit our account of transnational democracy to nested territories (cf. Pogge, 1992, Held 1995), inasmuch as many communities cross territories while not being fully global. I have proposed dealing with that problem by advocating democratic participation in all those contexts. Of course, a necessary condition for successfully implementing such forms of transnational democracy is the existence of regional and global protections of human rights. However difficult, it seems to me that such frameworks are needed both to protect individual and minority rights in cross-border and transnational communities, and to frame a more egalitarian fulfilment of basic human rights worldwide (including economic rights to means of subsistence), which will hopefully be carried out by the newly democratized institutions at regional, transnational and global levels. But the difficult consideration of the relation of regional and global democracy to this requirement of global justice would require an extended treatment of its own.

REFERENCES

Cavallaro, James L., and Stephanie Erin Brewer. 2008. 'Reevaluating Regional Human Rights Litigation in the Twenty-First Century: The Case of the Inter-American Court', *The American Journal of International Law* 102: 768–827.

Cavallero, Eric. 2009. 'Federative Global Democracy', in Ronald Tinnevelt and Helder De Schutter (eds.), Special Issue, 'Global Democracy and Exclusion', *Metaphilosophy* 40, 1: 42–64.

Habermas, Jürgen. 2006. *The Divided West* (ed. and trans. Ciaran Cronin). Cambridge, UK: Polity Press.

2008. *Between Naturalism and Religion: Philosophical Essays* (trans. Ciaran Cronin). Cambridge, UK: Polity Press.

Gould, Carol C. 1988. *Rethinking Democracy: Freedom and Social Cooperation in Politics, Economy, and Society.* Cambridge University Press.

2002. 'Does Stakeholder Theory Require Democratic Management?', *Business & Professional Ethics Journal*, 21, 1: 3–20.

2004. *Globalizing Democracy and Human Rights.* Cambridge University Press.

2007. 'Negotiating the Global and the Local: Situating Transnational Democracy and Human Rights', in Deen K. Chatterjee (ed.), *Democracy in a Global World: Human Rights and Political Participation in the 21st Century* (pp. 71–87). Lanham, MD: Rowman & Littlefield.

2009a. 'Envisioning Transnational Democracy: Cross-Border Communities and Regional Human Rights Frameworks', in Omar Dahbour, Ashley

Dawson, Heather Gautney and Neil Smith (eds.), *Altered States: Politics after Democracy* (pp. 63–77). London: Routledge.

2009b. 'Structuring Global Democracy: Political Communities, Universal Human Rights, and Transnational Representation', in Ronald Tinnevelt and Helder De Schutter (eds.), Special Issue, 'Global Democracy and Exclusion', *Metaphilosophy* 40, 1: 24–41.

Held, David. 1995. *Democracy and the Global Order.* Stanford University Press.

Marchetti, Raffaele. 2006. 'Global Governance or World Federalism? A Cosmopolitan Dispute on Institutional Models', *Global Society* 20, 3: 287–305.

2008. *Global Democracy: For and Against.* London: Routledge.

Morefield, Jeanne. 2005. 'States Are Not People: Harold Laski on Unsettling Sovereignty, Rediscovering Democracy', *Political Research Quarterly* 58, 4: 659–69.

Pateman, Carole. 1970. *Participation and Democratic Theory.* Cambridge University Press.

Pogge, Thomas W. 1992. 'Cosmopolitanism and Sovereignty', *Ethics* 103, 1: 48–75.

Saward, Michael. 2002. 'A Critique of Held', in Barry Holden (ed.), *Global Democracy: A Debate* (pp. 32–46). London: Routledge.

Tamir, Yael. 1993. *Liberal Nationalism.* Princeton University Press.

Tännsjö, Torbjörn. 2008. *Global Democracy: The Case for a World Government.* Edinburgh University Press.

7 Towards the metamorphosis of the United Nations
A proposal for establishing global democracy

Tim Murithi

Introduction

On 14 July 2010 Inga-Britt Ahlenius, the outgoing United Nations (UN) Under-Secretary-General for Internal Oversight Services, issued a scathing end-of-assignment report in which she stated that the UN was 'in a process of decline and reduced relevance'. Ahlenius (2010) was even more damning when she concluded that the UN seems 'to be seen less and less as a relevant partner in the resolution of world problems ... [T]his is as sad as it is serious' (3). The continuing relevance of the UN is a lament that is often heard within the corridors of the organization. Yet the institution remains a forum of last resort when a particular global crisis threatens to overwhelm the international system. This chapter will assess whether the UN remains a viable institutional model for addressing the challenges of the twenty-first century. In particular, the chapter will assess the fallacy of UN reform and suggest that radical transformation is what is required given the never-ending nature of current models of institutional revival. The chapter will assess the recent debates on deepening global democracy and propose a radical transformation of the UN into a World Federation of Nations (WFN). It will assess the practical steps that would be necessary to initiate a radical overhaul of the international system in a manner that could lay the foundation for global democracy.

Global challenges to the UN system

Criticisms of the organization rarely come from within its ranks because the staff for the most part are constrained from openly articulating their views. It is therefore almost impossible to determine whether the views held by Ahlenius are widespread within the organization, or whether they should be regarded as the isolated views of a disgruntled former staff member.

132

We should not lose sight of the fact that the UN is the composite formation of its Secretariat, the member states and its numerous agencies. A number of member states have openly voiced their concerns about the continuing relevance of an institutional architecture that was established in 1945 to, in effect, constrain the excesses of global powers. These criticisms have precipitated the numerous UN reform initiatives that have plagued the organization for decades.

UN reform in its current formulation through the Open-ended Working Group is dominated by the discourse about Security Council restructuring and is unlikely to bring about the establishment of global democracy. The likely scenario is that the appearance of progress towards UN reform will continue to plod along for another few decades until some member states come to a realization about the abject futility of the exercise. If one takes the end of the Cold War as a turning point in history which could have served as a catalytic trigger for establishing global democracy, then after two decades the general lack of seriousness in bringing about genuine change is evident for all to see. The status quo is fully intact. The powerful members of the UN have demonstrated their ability to ratchet up geo-political pressure to achieve their desired self-interests. They have also demonstrated their willingness to utilize the UN as a prophylactic to achieve their nefarious ends. The illegal Iraq invasion was the clearest demonstration of this predilection to perverting the international rule of law. The US and UK governments deployed their considerable arsenal of legal opinion to make the case for a UN-sanctioned invasion of Iraq on the basis of humanitarian intervention. This is one situation in which the UN Charter came under direct threat from the dogmatic interests of powerful permanent members (P5) of the Security Council. Fortunately, the diplomatic winds did not favour the US–UK plans for military adventurism because other members of the Security Council could not be compelled or coerced to assent to the Iraq invasion. The US and UK nevertheless amassed a coalition of the coerced and mounted their invasion, in direct contravention of the UN Charter, specifically Article 39 and its injunction against interstate aggression.

This event was nevertheless a notable nail in the coffin of the UN Charter and a clear illustration of the undemocratic character of the international system. If powerful P5 members of the Security Council can find it expedient to ignore the legal provisions of the UN Charter, why should any of the 192 members of the UN feel obliged to respect this international institution? In the face of such actions the idea that the UN can foster global democracy is delusional. The UN itself has become an anachronism, a fossilized relic of World War II power

configurations that is on the precipice of a deeply entrenched irrele-
vancy, to paraphrase Ahlenius above.

There are two other significant global events that make the adherence
to the current configuration of an undemocratic UN a perilous path for
the international community to take. The first occurs in the so-called
geopolitical margins of international relations. Since the demise of the
Cold War the Balkans, Asia, the Middle East and Africa and select
regions of Latin America have witnessed the effervescence of violent
political unrest and the direct challenge to state formations in these
regions. This global occurrence was another indicator that the state-
centric configuration of post-colonial societies is also proving to be an
anachronism. The UN system is in effect a club of nation-states and is
singularly handicapped when it comes to resolving disputes between
illegitimate governments and the armed militia that seek to overthrow
them through violent means. This demonstrates that the UN is not an
adequate forum for sub-national groups to direct their grievances. This
escalation of sub-national contestations against the state should have
served as a clear signal that the UN had reached its systemic limits and
needed to transform itself in order to become more accessible to non-
state actors, but this has not happened (Polman 2003). Paradoxically, a
number of sub-national formations aspire to acquire their own states –
for example, Palestine and Kurdistan – in order to assure their positions
at the UN club of states. However, if they were to achieve statehood the
UN would still be tasked with how to manage the demands of the
minorities that will end up existing within prospective Palestinian and
Kurdish borders.

Another global event that poses a challenge to the UN is the escalation
of international terrorism. The UN has become incoherent in its approach
to defining and dealing with terrorism because some of its own members
could be accused of being 'terrorist' in nature. Terrorism is not the central
issue; the key problem is the absence of an international system that
can effectively provide would-be terrorists with a means to articulate
their grievances in non-violent ways. History is increasingly replete with
erstwhile so-called 'terrorists' who are now feted by the international
community as statesmen, including Nelson Mandela of South Africa,
Gerry Adams of Northern Ireland and the late Yasser Arafat who passed
away before he could witness the birth of an independent Palestine.
Incidentally, at the time of writing the issue of Palestine is being addressed
through an ad hoc mediation process with the tangential support of the
UN, but the UN is not an adequate forum to oversee these negotiations.

The key point is that if the international system had been configured
in a way that would pre-emptively flag the concerns and grievances of

these erstwhile terrorists and their sub-national constituencies then a considerable amount of bloodshed and suffering could have been avoided. The wider issue is that the international system, embodied by the UN and its specialized agencies, is in need of a more pronounced and radical overhaul than the proposed tinkering that is taking place under the guise of UN reform.

The fallacy of UN reform

The UN system still grants governments a monopoly on the representation of their societies, and so it should – this is precisely what its charter was designed to do when it was adopted over sixty years ago. In this regard, so long as efforts to bring about change continue to be pursued within the pre-established framework of UN reform then governments will remain the gatekeepers of any proposed institutional models. Similarly, when it comes to the specific issue of UN Security Council reform the P5 members of the body will continue to assert and exert a gatekeeper role through their vetoes, in terms of the degree and extent of change that will be permitted. In this regard, the notion of UN reform is a self-evident fallacy, which will be detrimental and inimical to the future well-being and security of middle-level and smaller countries. As discussed above, this was manifest in the dramatic tragedies experienced in genocides in Rwanda in 1994 and in Srebrenica in 1995 as well as the Iraq invasion of 2003.

States do not have a legitimate claim to be the sole representatives of their societies apart from the legitimacy which they have imbued themselves with. Similarly, the P5 members of the UN Security Council do not have any legitimate claim to retain their status apart from a twist of fate which saw them effectively 'muscle' their way into membership of this grouping by virtue of their historically perceived military might.

The suggestion that tinkering with the number of members of the UN Security Council and extending the veto provision to emerging regional economic power-houses, such as Germany, Japan, India and Brazil (G4), will increase the legitimacy of the body and allegedly 'democratize' the institution through regional representativity is another illusion. A key region such as Africa is completely external to this discourse of UN 'democratization'. Critiques of the Uniting for Consensus group (which questions the basis upon which the G4 have been selected) are therefore valid and illustrate the self-evident fallacy of UN reform on this premise.

The discourse of UN reform also ignores the issue of whether the wider UN system needs to be transformed. The issue of increasing the funding of the UN to adequately address the range of challenges facing societies around the world has also not been sufficiently addressed in the so-called reform processes. This masks the interest of the powerful members of the UN Security Council to maintain the status quo.

Commenting on UN reform, Ahlenius (2010, 2) observed that 'disintegrated and ill thought through "reforms" are launched without adequate analysis and with a lack of understanding'. She added that this 'translates into a weakening of the overall position of the United Nations, and a reduced relevance of the organization'. Amongst some of the negative consequences of this drift by the organization is its reduced 'capacity to protect the civilians in conflict and distress'.

The net result of the proposed convoluted system of compromises as far as UN reform is concerned has not, and probably will not, address the deep and structural crisis of international legitimacy that the decision-making structures of the universal body perpetuate. Ahlenius (2010) also concluded that as far as UN reform is concerned 'there is no transparency, there is a lack of accountability' and she was emphatic that she did 'not see any signs of reform in the organization' (1). What this suggests is that notions of participatory democracy need to be relocated at a global level (Archibugi 2000).

Contextualizing global democracy

Deliberation about the extension of democratic governance principles from the national to the global level has increased in the past few decades (Archibugi et al., this volume). The key issue is whether global democracy is desirable, and based on the critique developed above there is a prima facie case for exploring the strategies for a gradual transition towards such a dispensation (Tännsjö 2008, Murithi 2003).

The argument being advanced in this chapter is premised on the normative desirability of promoting global democracy. Specifically, with regards to the typology proposed by Archibugi et al. in this volume, the establishment of global democracy has to ensure that institutions of global governance are responsive to citizens across the world. The ideal type that would achieve this is a form of world federalism defined by 'several layers of state or state-like authority and citizens who have a direct relationship of democratic authorization and accountability with each of them' (8).

The fact that global democracy, if it is achieved, will necessarily be achieved through a widespread process of consultation means that the models that are developed do not need to rely exclusively on Western models of governance. Cultural models of governance drawn from other parts of the world could equally provide invaluable insights into how the consent of the governed can be infused into global institutions (Murithi, 2007).

Against global democracy

There is a growing body of literature that is wary of forms of global democracy. Increasing federalization is associated with a concomitant escalation of bureaucracy and a marginalization of individuals and the negation of their autonomy. Thomas Christiano (2010), for example, has argued that global legitimation can be achieved through the promotion of democracy within states and by ensuring fairness in negotiations among states. In other words, a fair system of voluntary association among highly representative states or a fair democratic association is sufficient to address the problems of the prevailing state-centric system and the existing lack of global democracy. However, this presupposes two things: that either democracy will inevitably emerge among all political communities across the world or that there will be an external agent which will exert sufficient pressure to ensure that democracy is promoted within states. The first assumption has been negated by the lessons of history, which have demonstrated that while democracy can flourish for a period of time, undemocratic forces are always inherent within human societies and can undermine democracy promotion periodically. Furthermore, Christiano's claim that 'the state and, more particularly, the modern democratic state is an extremely sophisticated system for the identification and the advancement of the interests of a very broad proportion of its population' (124) does not adequately address the issue of how states occasionally ignore and override the interests of minority cultural groups within their border, particularly when these groups seek to secede from the state. The assumption that it is in fact possible to foster democracy within states without the contribution of an external process of 'norm-promotion' could potentially enable exclusionary systems of government such as the former apartheid regime of South Africa, which reigned formally from 1948 to 1994, to utilize their monopoly over the means of violence to perpetuate their existence indefinitely. To ensure that democratic transition becomes entrenched within a nation-state, an overarching system of checks and balances has to be established to effectively monitor the consolidation of democratic principles and practices. The role played by the European Union (EU) in challenging attempts by its member states to contravene the rule of law or undermine democracy is a case in point that will be elaborated below.

The need for a system of norm-implementation suggests that simply promoting democracy within states is not a sufficient condition to achieve global legitimation. As discussed above, even if internal democracy was achieved and consequently utilized to forge a global democratic dispensation, it would not address the privileged position afforded to nation-states which is more an accident of history than an expression of the informed will of world citizens. Christiano argues that 'states should have the principal say in the making of international law' largely because 'the international system relies on their cooperation' (123–4). However, this is a tautological and circular argument which does not address the issue of whether this current state of affairs is normatively desirable. Even though 'state consent is the main source of international law' (122), it should not remain the only source for perpetuity. There is no convincing reason why a global assembly of parliamentarians elected through universal suffrage of world citizens cannot eventually become another countervailing source of international law. Such a transformation could provide a necessary checks-and-balances system against the excess of state collusion in decision making, particularly when it is inimical to the interests of world citizens or communal groups. For example, prior to the illegitimate US-led invasion of Iraq in 2003, world citizenry physically marched across the capitals of the world to protest against what subsequently became a travesty of justice and a direct infringement of the international rule of law embodied in the UN Charter and the Statute for the International Court of Justice. However, world citizenry could not legislate against the subsequent invasion, clearly illustrating a vacuum in the international system and the absence of a genuine global democratic architecture.

Christiano (2010) further argues that fairness in negotiations among states is also a potential path towards entrenching global democracy. However, this also presupposes that an equitable system of multilateral diplomacy and negotiation can be achieved without a fundamental transformation of the structural and power inequalities fostered by a system that privileges countries that have the resources to control, dominate and subvert these processes. The reality of negotiation processes in the UN Security Council is a case in point. More than 60 per cent of the issues discussed by the UN Security Council are focused on Africa, yet the continent does not have any representation among the P5 members of the Council. Given the fact that the P5 can veto all manner of decisions before the Council, it is a travesty of justice at its most basic level that African countries can only participate in key deliberations and decision-making processes as individual, non-permanent members of the Council. Furthermore, there is no guarantee that African non-permanent members of the Council will in fact articulate and advance positions that are in the interests of African citizens and vulnerable communities in countries that they do represent. UN Security Council negotiation and decision-making processes are in effect the highest manifestation of unfairness in the international system. If achieving fairness in negotiations among states is the preferred route to achieving global legitimation, as proposed by Christiano, then a fundamental transformation of the UN Security Council and the elimination of the veto provision are a necessary prerequisite action. The P5 are among the beneficiaries of the status quo within the international system, reproducing in reality a form of diplomatic apartheid. Given the fact that the asymmetrical distribution of global political, economic and military power has remained relatively unchanged since the end of the Cold War, the potential beneficiaries of global democratic transformation would remain the societies in the so-called developing regions of the world – Africa, Asia, the Middle East and Latin America.

In this regard, in March 2005 the African Union (AU) issued a declaration known as The Common African Position on the Proposed Reform of the United Nations: The Ezulwini Consensus (African Union 2005), which was a statement in response to the report of the High-Level Panel on Threats, Challenges and Change which had been issued in December 2004. The AU issued a position on UN reform and, in particular, on the reform of the Security Council by noting that 'in 1945, when the UN was formed, most of Africa was not represented and that in 1963, when the first reform took place, Africa was represented but was not in a particularly strong position' (9). The AU goes on to state that 'Africa is now in a position to influence the proposed UN reforms by maintaining her unity of purpose'; furthermore, it notes that 'Africa's goal is to be fully represented in all the decision-making organs of the UN, particularly in the Security Council' (9). The Common African Position enumerates what 'full representation' of Africa in the Security Council means by demanding 'not less than two permanent seats with all the prerogatives and privileges of permanent membership including the right to veto' and 'five non-permanent seats' (9). On 27 May 2010 the first-ever negotiating text on Security Council reform was issued by the chair of intergovernmental negotiations on Security Council reform, Ambassador Zahir Tanin of Afghanistan. In this document the AU, whose position was articulated by Sierra Leone, a current non-permanent member of the UN Security Council, retained its original position by stating that 'Africa seeks the abolition of the veto, but alternatively, so long as it continues to exist, its extension to all new permanent members in the Council as a matter of common justice'.

As noted above, the virtual impossibility of eliminating the veto provision from P5 members (due to their combined coercive power to subvert any such initiative) in the short- to medium-term weakens the argument that achieving fairness in negotiations among states is a potential route to global legitimation.

One argument suggests that attempting to address domestic issues through global forums would fundamentally undermine the core principles of democratic control and of addressing issues at the level where they are most pertinent. However, with the passage of time this argument has become a non sequitur as, increasingly, domestic issues are directly impacted upon by global forces or conditions. For example, the protection of a domestic environment and addressing the issue of depleting natural resources cannot be divorced from the impact of climate change or the trade practices of multinational resources. In fact, attempting to address environmental issues at an exclusively local level is to engage in an exercise of damage limitation rather than promoting sustainable change. Domestic concerns are now almost always impacted upon by global processes and there is a need for institutional frameworks for local actors to democratically participate in their regulation.

Regional models of multi-level governance

Carol Gould has compared and contrasted arguments pertaining to regional and global democracy. Regions have become 'important settings for increased transnational cooperation and regulation, particularly concerning economic and social justice matters' (this volume, 116). Gould argues 'that no forward-looking democratic theory can claim to be complete without considering these important new domains' (116). In particular, she has identified the relative benefits of regional coordination and cooperation as 'the retention or enabling of a certain level of cultural diversity around the world' (116).

There are important lessons that can be learned from the multi-level frameworks of governance currently being developed by the EU and the distribution of authority at the supranational, regional, national and local levels. As far as human political communities are concerned, the most established expression of the pooling of sovereignty is the creation of the European Union, cemented recently by the compromise decision by the Convention of Europe to agree to a set of terms which laid the foundation for closer integration (after the convention is ratified by governments and the constituent populations). The EU promotes norms of democracy and human rights protection that establish a standard which can offer the countries and regions in conflict within the European sphere of influence an incentive to subscribe to peaceful approaches of managing and regulating their own affairs. The EU through its Council of Europe and other institutions systematically intervenes diplomatically and has begun to intervene through policing action – in Macedonia, for example – to manage conflicts and bring about conditions for sustainable peace in the countries within its sphere of influence.

A similar process is under way on the African continent in the form of the newly created African Union. The overall objective is to create a transnational or supranational structure of governance that can bring pressure to bear on the behaviour of states and gradually transform attitudes and practices to build and promote sustainable peace and security. The international system has not developed a framework for incorporating these 'supranations' into the system of global governance. The concept of multi-level governance has begun to gain currency. In the EU, for example, 'supranational, national, regional and local governments are enmeshed in territorially overarching policy networks' (Hooghe and Marks 2001, 41) or what we can also conceptualize as 'overlapping sovereignty'. There is no reason why multi-level governance cannot be adopted to the global level even with the inclusion of non-state actors and transnational corporations as part of the framework of policy and decision making.

The utility of multi-level governance structures and institutions is that problems can best be solved at the level of competence of the actors. States can avoid getting entangled in peace-building at the grass-roots level beyond providing the security conditions which are conducive to encouraging sustainable peace-building and reconciliation. This therefore is a model that relies on less control from the centre and more power and autonomy devolved to the localities. The principle of subsidiarity according to which decision making should be kept as close to the people as possible should be emphasized as a central pillar in the evolution of global governance. Likewise, in a multi-level global governance framework governments would be held to account, through a higher supranational entity, for any actions that undermine peace and the general human and gender rights of their citizens. This would be a radical shift away from the notion that nations exist in a state of anarchy with no overarching authority.

Given the close proximity of regional institutions of cooperation to the nascent crisis in their member states they are more likely to take an active interest in managing potential issues so that they do not spill over into neighbouring states. This is certainly the impetus behind the AU's evolving African Peace and Security Architecture, for example. Furthermore, countries within regional groupings are coordinating their response to economic and environmental issues, particularly in the face of the increasingly manifest forces of globalization. For example, as noted above, the AU adopted a common position to negotiate on the issue of UN Security Council reform.

The AU has adopted a range of norms of governance articulated in its Constitutive Act, of 2000; its Charter on Democracy, Elections and Governance, of 2007; as well as the its Protocol Establishing the Peace and Security Council of the African Union, of 2002. It has also established a range of institutions such the Pan-African Parliament and the African Court of Justice and Human Rights to increase levels of participation and oversee the implementation of the rule of law. Since its formation, the AU has played a crucial role as a 'norm-promoter', particularly with regards to peacemaking and democratic governance. The AU has a range of human rights mechanisms such as the African Union Commission on Human and People's Rights based in Banjul, Gambia, which regularly adjudicates on issues pertaining to states. The institution regularly issues pronouncements on the internal behaviour of its member states (Murithi 2008b). The AU is, however, still a loose collectivity of independent nation-states and therefore does not have the democratic legitimacy to compel its member states to uphold the treaties, protocols and conventions that they have signed up to. In this regard, the AU is still beset by a democratic deficit.

The AU has for the most part not been able to exert influence on decisions made outside of Africa – for example, on the issue of improved funding of international development and human security institutions. This is largely due to the fact that even though the AU exists, it has not yet effectively unified African policy and decision making. However, in 2007, at the annual Assembly of Heads of State and Government, the AU initiated a continent-wide debate about the desirability of deepening continental political integration and the formation of a Union government of Africa premised on models that were first proposed during the era of decolonization in the early 1960s (Murithi 2008a). For the time being this debate has become mired in disagreement as to the precise nature and reach of the proposed Union government of Africa. Therefore, the AU is already grappling with the issue of regional democracy.

Even if regional democracy was to be achieved in Africa, given the current level of economic development within the continent this would not negate the need for the international system to play a proactive role in promoting peace and security on the continent. Specifically, Africa still depends on the ad hoc contributions to finance its own peace operations in Somalia through the AU Mission in Somalia (AMISOM) or its partnership in Darfur through the joint AU–UN Hybrid mission in Darfur (UNAMID). In this regard, regional democracy would be insufficient to address these challenges and would have to be complemented by a more representative and adequately funded system of global democracy. The important insight that these models of multi-level governance provide is that it is possible to replicate and gestate an embryonic form of global democratic governance.

The World Federation of Nations: towards a new global democratic architecture

The primary challenge of deepening global democracy is how to combine structures of international authority with mechanisms of citizen representation and participation. This chapter has sought to establish the principle that radical transformation is required to achieve global democracy (see also Marchetti, this volume). UN reform will not significantly alter the power imbalances; neither will it empower the citizens of the world to assert their right to hold global institutions accountable for their actions. Furthermore, radical transformation is also necessary to empower world citizens, through their own agency, to be in a position to actively reduce the socio-economic inequalities that plague the majority of humanity. The UN has become the anachronistic caterpillar which has ossified and is now ready to shed its depleted edifice through a process of metamorphosis which will allow a new global body politic to emerge.

World Federation of Nations

Based on ideas that have been promoted by the World Federalist Movement for close to half a century, perhaps the time has come to think about creating a new structure for global governance. This would require reactivating humanity's political imagination. It is evident that a new global democratic architecture (GDA) is required. The GDA would be premised on a fundamental shift away from privileging the nation-state in global affairs. *World Federation of Nations (WFN) would feasibly include the following organs: World Parliament, Council of Supranations, Assembly of Nation-states, Committee of Sub-national Groups, Global Forum of Non-governmental Organizations (NGOs), Global Committee of Unions and Transnational Corporations.* Any progress towards practical implementation will of course require much more deliberation about the purpose and functions of the various organs. The objective of setting out these organs here in this fashion is to provide food for thought and stimulate deeper reflection.

WFN Council of Supranations

This would be a grouping of existing and emerging supranational entities like the EU and the AU. This council would have a deliberative and decision-making capacity as well as the ability to sanction other actors for failing to uphold the implementation of international law developed by the Assembly of Nation-states, the Committee of Sub-national Groups and the World Parliament.

WFN Assembly of Nation-states

The grouping of nation-states would have the ability to continue to develop international law on any issues.

WFN Committee of Sub-national Groups

The grouping of sub-national groups would be representative and involved in having democratic oversight on international legislation being developed by the Assembly of Nation-states. This Committee of Sub-national Groups would also be empowered to petition either the WFN Parliament, the Assembly of Nation-states or the Council of Supranations. The criteria for being considered a sub-national group would have to be determined through a global consultation process. The modalities for representation would need to be determined through global consultation.

WFN World Parliament

As a practical objective the idea of a world parliament or some other democratically constituted global assembly is slowly gaining currency (Monbiot 2003). A WFN World Parliament would be able to formulate international law on a par with the Assembly of Nation-states. In addition, it would have an oversight function of the implementation or non-implementation of international law and the ability to sanction the non-compliant actors. The role of the World Parliament would be to make global decision making and the implementation of laws a more inclusive process. Members of the World Parliament would be elected through universal suffrage. The World Parliament would therefore require states to be more accountable to a global polity with regard to their actions and allocation of resources. This is one basis upon which humanity as a whole could begin to prevent unilateralism undermining collective and collaborative problem-solving. In terms of the potential routes to a global assembly Andrew Strauss (2005, 1) suggests 'a popularly elected representative body that will begin very modestly with largely advisory powers, and that following the trajectory of the European Parliament, would only gain powers slowly over time' (see below for a detailed discussion of the practical steps to such an evolution).

The normative proposal for a new GDA would have to be elaborated through a comprehensive and widespread process of global consultation.

WFN Global Forum of NGOs and civil society groups

This would be an institutional framework for the representation of NGOs, civil society groups, ecumenical groups and other associations. This group would have a largely consultative function with regards to the other branches of the GDA. The standards and criteria for membership, codes of conduct and ethics would be established through a global consultation process.

WFN Global Committee of Unions and Transnational Corporations

This would be an institutional framework for the incorporation of unions and transnational corporations as the inauguration of formal global union citizenship and global corporate citizenship. This group would have a largely consultative function with regards to the other branches of the GDA. The standards and criteria for membership, codes of conduct and ethics would be established through a global consultation process.

All these institutions would fall under the umbrella of a World Federation of Nations (WFN). Other programmes and specialized agencies, autonomous organizations, committees, ad hoc and related bodies within the current UN system would also need to adjust their statutes and mandates in order to correspond to the transformed WFN system.

Practical steps to the WFN through a UN Charter review conference

The founders of the UN recognized that the moment would arrive when it became imperative to transform the organization and included a practical mechanism to review the body's charter. Specifically, Article 109 of the UN Charter provides for a 'General Conference of the Members for the purpose of reviewing the present Charter'. This charter review conference could be convened at a specific date and place if it was approved by 'a two-thirds vote of the members of the General Assembly and by a vote of any nine members of the Security Council'

(United Nations 1945, Article 109, 1). Therefore, in practice there are no major obstacles to convening a charter review conference apart from securing the necessary percentages described above. In addition, the decision-making process at such a charter review conference would be relatively democratic in the sense that 'each member of the United Nations shall have one vote in the conference'. This conference could be initiated through a process of mobilizing the will of two-thirds of the General Assembly and nine members of the Security Council. The latter provision means that the P5 cannot veto any proposed UN Charter review conference. Such a conference could adopt a recommendation to substantially alter the UN Charter and introduce completely new provisions, including a change in the name of the institution to, for example, the World Federation of Nations. The adoption of these new recommendations could be on the basis of a two-thirds vote of the conference and each member of the UN would have one vote.

The major challenge will arise when it comes to ratifying any revised or new charter. Article 109 further stipulates that any alteration of the UN Charter can only take effect 'when ratified in accordance with their respective constitutional processes by two-thirds of the members of the United Nations including all the permanent members of the Security Council' (United Nations 1945, 1). In essence, if a UN Charter review conference makes recommendations then these have to be further ratified by the governments of member states, including all P5 members. Therefore, the final ratification of a new charter could potentially be held hostage by a veto from any of the P5, in what is in effect an undemocratic provision inserted by the founders of the UN, undoubtedly to serve their own interests of ensuring that any provisions meet with their approval.

There are precedents for charter review processes leading to the establishment of new international organizations, notably the Organization of African Unity's transformation into the African Union, initiated by a meeting of heads of state and government in 1999. Therefore, a UN Charter review conference could lead to the formation of the WFN through broad-based and inclusive consultations that encompass governments, civil society, business, trade unions and academics. Despite the potential veto of P5 members at the ratification stage, the General Assembly can nevertheless take the initiative and convene a UN Charter review conference. The recommendations adopted at a UN Charter review conference would be imbued with a degree of moral legitimacy and, therefore any efforts to sabotage the full adoption of such recommendations by the P5 would further expose the injustice entrenched in the international system.

In the absence of the political will within the UN to convene a charter review conference an alternative strategy would be to establish the WFN through the convening of a new and separate treaty which could be approved and adopted by 'which ever internationally progressive countries were willing to be pioneers' (Strauss 2005, 9). With reference to a global parliamentary assembly – or, as this proposal suggests, the WFN World Parliament – 'even twenty to thirty economically and geographically diverse countries would be enough to found the parliament' and 'the treaty agreed to by these countries would establish the legal structure for elections to be held within their territories including a voting system and electoral districts' (9). There is no reason why these pioneering countries would have to give up their membership of the UN whilst forming the WFN, since almost all countries belong to more than one international organization simultaneously. In fact, there could be an advantage to the pioneer members of the WFN to retain their membership of the UN and actively use their positions to advocate for the new GDA and convince an ever-increasing number of countries to join them in the new formation. The constitution of the WFN could be framed in such a way that any country could join the formation so long as it is willing to meet its obligations under the WFN treaty. If the WFN treaty begins to gain momentum then 'other less proactive countries would have an incentive to take part rather than be sidelined in the creation of an important new international organization' (Strauss 2005, 10). When membership of the WFN reaches an optimal number of countries then one could begin to see the gradual withering away of the relevance of the UN until it undergoes the same demise as the League of Nations. In fact, the UN itself was established by a pioneering group of countries so it has already provided an example of how to successfully achieve the establishment of the WFN. In terms of the way forward, what is required is for a group of progressive states to begin drafting a General Assembly resolution to put the UN Charter review conference on the agenda and also, in parallel, to begin financing the drafting of the treaty and constitutional framework of the WFN.

Conclusion

The Westphalian nation-state model is hindering the emergence of more democratic forms of global governance. Specifically, the UN system is unlikely to achieve a genuine transition to global democracy because of the nature of the nation-state and the persistence of realpolitik. It is unlikely that tinkering with the edges, in the form of so-called UN reform, will generate institutional models that lead to a deepening of global democracy. Yet the global challenges across regions and within states continue to mount without an adequate forum for those most affected by these challenges to voice their concerns.

The transition to global democracy cannot be left to its own devices. The current global system is defined by the selective respect for international law and a self-evident democratic deficit. If the status quo is permitted to persist, this model of elite global governance – for example, manifest through the P5 of the UN Security Council – will not reform itself but merely replicate and reproduce existing forms of exclusivity by co-opting a few more members.

There is therefore a need for global rules and standards to restrain the economic and political excesses that are currently undermining the fabric of societies worldwide. If one speaks of providing more opportunities for the global citizenry to participate in global affairs then it is logical that people should be represented at the global level by some kind of world people's assembly. The peace marches that took place in April and May 2003 around the world brought an estimated ten million people out into the streets to air their voices, but this did not really have a major impact on transforming the policies that were ultimately adopted. There was a revolution in global consciousness but not a parallel echoing of this transformation at the level of the institutions of global governance. It is therefore necessary to ensure that the next time an issue of global concern is voiced by the peoples of the world there will be an institution which can articulate these concerns and translate them into policy decisions which can contribute towards improving the democratic transparency and accountability of the global decision-making and implementation process.

The increase in issues of common concern to world citizens at the global level justifies the formation of new arenas for democratic decision making. There are of course important questions about the feasibility of global democratic institutions at this point in time. One school of thought maintains that there are ongoing democratic struggles in the national context which need to be allowed to play out before we can begin to talk about global democracy. There is also a viewpoint that maintains that democracy only functions well in relatively small communities.

The multi-level models of governance embodied by the EU and the AU suggest that supranational institutions can assist countries to make a transition to, and sustain, democratic institutions. A new GDA would be premised on the vertical disaggregation of the power of nation-states to a supranational grouping of regions and downwards to sub-national communal formations. This chapter proposed that a sufficient case can be made for the establishment of a World Federation of Nations to embody this new global democratic architecture. A UN Charter review conference can launch such a process; alternatively the WFN could be established by a separate and stand-alone treaty.

REFERENCES

African Union. 2005 (7–8 March). The Common African Position on the Proposed Reform of the United Nations: 'The Ezulwini Consensus', EXT/EX.CL/2 (VII). Addis Ababa: African Union.

Ahlenius, Inga-Britt. 2010. *End of Assignment Report.* New York: United Nations Office of Internal Oversight Services.

Archibugi, Daniele. 2000. 'Cosmopolitical Democracy', *New Left Review* 4, July/August: 137–50.

Christiano, Thomas. 2010. 'Democratic Legitimacy and International Institutions', in Samantha Besson and John Tasioulas (eds.), *The Philosophy of International Law* (pp. 119–38). Oxford University Press.

Hooghe, L., and G. Marks. 2001. *Multi-Level Governance and European Integration.* London: Rowman & Littlefield.

Monbiot, George. 2003. *The Age of Consent: A Manifesto for a New World Order.* London: Flamingo.

Murithi, Tim. 2003. 'Re-thinking the United Nations System: Prospects for a World Federation of Nations', *International Journal on World Peace* 20, 4, December: 3–28.

  2007. 'A Local Response to the Global Human Rights Standard: The Ubuntu Perspective on Human Dignity', *Globalisation, Societies and Education* 5, 3: 277–86.

  (ed.). 2008a. *Towards an African Union Government: Challenges and Opportunities.* Pretoria, South Africa: Institute for Security Studies.

  2008b. 'Developments under the African Charter on Human and Peoples' Rights Relevant to Minorities', in Kristin Henard and Ian Dunbar (eds.), *Synergies in Minority Protection: European and International Law Perspectives.* (pp. 385–400). Cambridge University Press.

Polman, Linda. 2003. *We Did Nothing: Why the Truth Doesn't Always Come Out When the UN Goes In.* London: Penguin.

Strauss, Andrew. 2005. *Taking Democracy Global: Assessing the Benefits and Challenges of a Global Parliamentary Assembly.* London: One World Trust.

Tännsjö, Torbjörn. 2008. *Global Democracy: The Case for a World Government.* Edinburgh University Press.

United Nations. 1945. Charter of the United Nations and Statute of the International Court of Justice. San Francisco: United Nations.

8   Flexible government for a globalized world

Bruno S. Frey

The quest for a world government

The fundamental conflict between globalization and democracy has often been discussed.[1] It has led to two quite different, and in many respects even opposite, reactions:

a) 'Idealists' resurrect the perennial dream of a *world government* committed to the rule of law, human rights and democratic procedures (see Archibugi et al. and Marchetti, both this volume). Many see the United Nations (UN) as the preliminary form of such a world government and are prepared to take its well-known limitations as a transitory phase that will be overcome with time.
b) 'Market believers' rely on the *global market* to essentially solve all problems, provided governments do not interfere. They generally admit the necessity of having some rules to the game (such as a guarantee of property rights) but they believe that such rules emerge endogenously as a result of international competition.

Both reactions are seriously lacking. The notion of a world government tries to superimpose a power structure on existing national government. It naively presumes that a world government would act out of global interest. However, even a representative democratic world government could not provide true democratic governance, but would exhibit pervasive government failure due to its large distance from the citizens and its monopoly power (see also the similar criticisms by Christiano, this volume). At best, such a 'world' government is the apex of the dominant world power (today the United States), which certainly does not meet the ideal of an institution fairly and equitably serving the interests of mankind.

The notion of a globalized world market setting its own efficient rules is equally naive. It disregards the classical problems of market failures

---

[1] For instance by Rodrik (1998), Weizsäcker (1999), Beck (2000), Bernholz (2000) and Frey (2002).

leading to monopolistic structures, wide-ranging negative external effects (particularly with respect to the natural environment) and insufficient supply of public goods, as well as an income distribution between regions and individuals which is not acceptable from most points of view. However, it is also unwarranted to expect that globalized economic markets induce governments to provide public goods effectively.

Fearing the consequences of globalization for the effectiveness of politics, citizens have lost trust in politics in general. They rightly feel that they have lost control over the decisions taken in the respective supranational and interjurisdictional bodies. In contrast, professional politicians, as well as public officials, aim at shifting decisions upwards to the international and cooperational arena. At this higher level, they are better able to pursue their own goals and what they believe to be in the interest of their countries, without always having to seek the citizens' approval.

The increased importance of 'technical' decisions induced by globalization has an important negative consequence: civic virtue, which mirrors the intrinsic motivation of the citizens and the politicians to contribute to public interest, is endangered. But it has by now been well established that civic virtue with both citizens and politicians is an indispensable factor for a successful democracy (see, e.g., Brennan and Hamlin 2000 or Putnam 2000). Traditional rational choice theory overlooks the systematic relationship between intrinsic and extrinsic motivation (see Frey 1997). *Citizens' civic virtue* depends on their involvement in politics. Having extensive participation rights in political decisions bolsters civic virtue. Frey and Stutzer (2002) empirically show that individuals derive substantial procedural utility from having political participation rights.

The decision-making process dealing with issues of globalization requires *more flexible democratic political institutions.*[2] They must be able to adjust to the 'geography of problems' instead of being constrained by traditional boundaries. Thus, globalization has to become symmetric: it has not only to increase the flexibility and effectiveness of economic units, but also of government institutions.

In the following, two proposals are advanced to change democratic structures in order to overcome the ossification of the present political system. The first one, *flexible political units*, refers to the supply side, and the second proposal, *flexible citizenship*, refers to the demand side of the political process.

---

[2] See, more extensively, Eichenberger and Frey (2001) and Frey (2003b).

Flexible political units

The political jurisdictions should extend according to the needs of the various government functions. These needs differ according to the particular function to be provided for. As a result, functional political units generally overlap; a particular geographical area is served by various political suppliers of governmental goods and services. In order to safeguard these units and ensure that they serve the interests of the citizens, they are to be democratically controlled, and the members (ideally small political units such as the communities or even parts of communities) must be able to enter and exit, thus establishing strong interjurisdictional competition. This concept has been called FOCJ, following the initials of its constitutive characteristics: functional, overlapping, competing jurisdictions.[3]

Based on the traditional analysis of (local) public goods and external effects, it could be argued that in FOCJ the members will resort to free riding. Thus, for example, communities with many childless inhabitants will give up membership in FOCJ devoted to the supply of school services, and so save the corresponding tax cost. They disregard the interests of the citizens with children, though they enjoy the positive external effects of a good school education. The competition between the jurisdictions is thus predicted to lead to a so-called 'race to the bottom', resulting in under-provision of public goods, and, in the extreme, to a complete breakdown of public supply.

This criticism assumes that individuals exploit any opportunity to free ride. But it is wrong to assume that individuals take full advantage of every opportunity to profit at the expense of others. In the majority of situations, most people do not behave in a purely egoistic way. This applies especially to situations in which moral or altruist behavior only implies low cost, as is the case in the collective democratic decisions at the level of communities.[4] As an individual only has negligible influence on the communal decision, he or she has no reason to vote in favour of collective free riding of the community.

Over the past few years, theoretical and empirical research has collected strong and cumulative evidence that shows that, in many situations, individuals are prepared to contribute substantially to what they consider the common good, even if the implied cost is much larger than

---

[3] See, more fully, Frey and Eichenberger (1999), and the critical discussion by Vanberg (2000) and Blatter and Ingram (2000).

[4] See, extensively, Brennan and Lomasky (1993) and Brennan and Hamlin (2000), and for experimental evidence see Eichenberger and Oberholzer-Gee (1998).

is the case in democratic decisions. Free riding in the presence of public goods (as analysed by Olson 1965) remains a serious problem, especially when people feel that others do not contribute their fair share, or when the situation is purely anonymous and the possible gain is all too large. But very extensive field studies (see, in particular, Ostrom 2000) confirm that these incentives to free ride need not dictate behaviour, especially when the persons know, and communicate with, each other. There is similar evidence from a large number of carefully controlled laboratory experiments. No less than 40–60 per cent of subjects in a one-shot public good situation contribute to the provision of a pure public good. The level of cooperation remains between 30 and 50 per cent of what would be socially optimal, even after many repetitions where the subjects could easily learn to take advantage of each other (e.g., Ledyard 1995, Bohnet and Frey 1999). Individuals do have a measure of intrinsic values and corresponding *intrinsic motivation*, which differs from extrinsic motivation induced by relative price variations (Frey 1997).

These insights link up with the rapidly growing research pointing out the importance of social capital for individuals' behaviour in the political and general social setting (Putnam 2000, Paldam 2000). There is now a wide consensus among social scientists that intrinsic motivation, loyalty or social capital is an indispensable resource for a well-functioning society.[5] When it is insufficiently developed, or scarcely exists at all, society threatens to break down altogether or at least functions at a low level of efficiency. Thus, care must be taken to protect it. It has indeed been shown in experimental (Deci and Ryan 1985, Deci, Koestner and Ryan 1999) as well as in field research (Frey and Jegen 2001) that external interventions, which are taken to be controlling by the persons affected, may crowd out intrinsic motivation. In contrast, external interventions, which are perceived to be supportive, tend to crowd in intrinsic motivation.

People's actions in the public sphere are well captured by the notion of 'quasi-voluntary' behaviour (Levi 1997). It has been empirically shown that the extent of tax compliance can only be explained in a satisfactory way by assuming that taxpayers do have some measure of civic virtue, or tax morale. But it would be naive to assume that people are just 'good' and are prepared to maximize the welfare of society. Rather, people are prepared to act in a non-selfish way only when they are explicitly or implicitly (i.e., via social norms) asked to do so, and when they see that relevant others also behave in that way.

[5] One might add that this also holds for relationships within firms (see Osterloh and Frey 2000).

In the public sphere, quasi-voluntary behaviour can only be counted on when the institutional conditions support such civic-minded action. A crucial task of institutions is thus to maintain and raise civic virtue. Institutions are therefore looked at in a fundamentally different way from traditional institutional economics (see e.g., Eggertsson 1990). Their task is no longer to exclusively establish efficiency with given individual preferences, but also to support intrinsic motivation.

FOCJ can be designed to meet these tasks. The term 'functional' should be interpreted in a broad, non-technocratic way. The functions, along which the jurisdictions should extend, should be designed in such a way that the citizens' involvement and commitment to specific public activities are strengthened. Thus, for example, citizens' intrinsic motivation to protect the natural environment should be reflected in jurisdictions catering for these preferences. Similarly, FOCJ should be designed to fulfil citizens' conceptions of fairness.

The flexible political institutions in the form of FOCJ are well capable of supporting directed civic virtue for two reasons. First, citizens are offered the possibility of getting democratically involved in, and becoming financially responsible for, political institutions catering for particular issues – for example, the natural environment or social work. They therewith experience a sense of belonging which is more difficult, if not impossible, to achieve in traditional democratic governmental institutions catering to the needs of many diverse functions, or in technocratic intergovernmental cooperation units without either democratic institutions or tax autonomy. Second, FOCJ are designed to extend over the geographic area in which the beneficiaries of the respective public supply live. Both positive and negative spillovers are thereby minimized, which means that the citizens contributing to its finance can be certain of not being exploited by others. The crucial requirement that free riding is prevented is better fulfilled in FOCJ than in traditional, all-purpose political units.

The concept of FOCJ can be applied to many different problems and issues. An example is decentralized multi-level systems of global democracy promoting worker empowerment and corporate accountability in global supply chains, as suggested by Kate Macdonald (this volume).

Flexible citizenship

Traditionally, citizenship is a relationship between an individual and a state, in which an individual owes allegiance to that state and is in turn entitled to its protection. Three aspects of this definition have to be noted.

First, the actors involved are the citizens and the *state*. Today, citizenship is a unique and monopolistic relationship between the individuals and a particular *nation*. It is strongly shaped geographically because most of the government services involved are only provided to residents – that is, citizens living within the boundaries of the respective state.

Second, the citizens have both *rights* and *obligations*. The rights refer to the *political* sphere (i.e., the citizens have the right to vote and to hold public office), to the *economic* sphere (i.e., the citizens have the right to become economically active as employees or employers), as well as to the *social* sphere (i.e., the citizens are protected against economic hardship within the welfare state).

Third, the *relationship* between an individual and the state goes well beyond an exchange of taxes for public services. Rather, the citizen 'owes allegiance' to the state. The citizens are expected to be public-spirited and to exhibit civic virtue. The relationship is thus partly non-functional and resorts to the intrinsic motivation of the citizens and to the community of people who share loyalty and identity. This aspect distinguishes the new type of citizenship proposed here from being purely a customer or member of an organization, as theoretically analysed in the well-established economic theory of clubs (Buchanan 1965).

The process of globalization with its decrease in communication and transportation costs undermines the geographically based concept of citizenship for two reasons: first, with increasing mobility of individuals, an increasing number of individuals are living in countries of which they are not citizens. Often, they live in a country only for a short period of time. Then they enjoy part of the rights of citizens, but do not have to carry the respective obligations. Second, the transaction costs for delivering government services to non-residents are decreasing dramatically. An example is education, which can be increasingly supplied via the Internet to non-residents. Thus, government institutions are becoming more and more virtual (see Colander 2000).

The existing concept of citizenship can be generalized, making it possible to uphold civic virtue and governmental institutions that provide for public goods.

Differentiating citizenship

There are various ways in which citizenship can be made more flexible (see more fully Frey 2003a). National citizenship may be extended, or a person may become a citizen of an organization other than the nation.

Extending national citizenship
Temporary citizenship An individual should be able to choose for a predetermined period to become a citizen of a particular political unit – for instance, because he or she is working and living in a country for a specific period of time.

Multiple citizenships For persons simultaneously working and living in various countries, a good solution might be to split up the citizenship into various parts. The rights going with the citizenship must be adjusted accordingly. In particular, the voting rights would reflect the fact that a person chooses to split up citizenship among several nations. In the computer age, there is no problem whatsoever in allowing for fractional votes.

Partial citizenship An individual might be a citizen of a political unit with respect to one particular function, while being a citizen of another political unit with respect to other functions. In referenda, the voting rights should accordingly only extend to issues referring to the respective function.

Citizenship in various types of organizations
The following possibilities are conceivable.

Levels of government Citizenship might refer to the national level – which is the rule – but also to a lower level, such as the region, province or commune (the latter being the case in Switzerland) or to a higher level, such as the European Union.

Governmental sub-organizations Individuals might choose to become a citizen of only part of a government, such as the diplomatic service, the military or the social security administration.

Quasi-governmental organizations There are many organizations close to the public sector in which individuals might become citizens. Universities are such an example. Indeed, the concept of the '*Universitätsbürger*' (university citizen) is well known in the German-speaking academic system. It obviously means much more than being an 'employee' of a university. Rather, it means that one is prepared to commit oneself to the academic life beyond considerations of short-term purely personal benefits and costs.

Non-governmental organizations (NGOs)   Citizenship may be of organizations such as churches, clubs (e.g., the Rotary Club, the Boy Scouts or even sport clubs such as Manchester United or FC Barcelona), action groups (e.g., the World Wildlife Fund [WWF], Médecins sans Frontières or the Red Cross) and functional organizations (e.g., the Internet Corporation for Assigned Names and Numbers [ICANN]). (On the role of NGOs, see Tallberg and Uhlin, this volume). Yet another organization in which citizenship may be considered are profit-oriented firms. Citizens of firms have a special relationship, which goes beyond just being a customer or employee or stakeholder. Shareholders have a decision weight according to the number of shares, while stakeholders have no formal voting right at all, but exert pressure outside of established channels – for example, via the media or demonstrations. In contrast, each citizen of a firm has a vote according to generally accepted democratic principles. While these principles differ, they are not necessarily incompatible with each other. Firm citizenship can exist quite well along with shareholder rights.

Citizenship in the broadest sense proposed here is based on *voluntary contracts* between the persons aspiring towards citizenship in a particular organization and the organization offering the possibility of citizenship. These contracts establish a special bond and are necessarily *incomplete* because it is impossible to state all the contingencies the future might hold.

An *essential* feature of citizenship is that an organization can expect a measure of allegiance and loyalty from its members. Citizens are prepared to abstain from exploiting all short-term advantages. 'Citizenship' means that the members exhibit an *intrinsically based motivation* to support 'their' organization over and above purely egoistic calculations. This also means that citizens are prepared to cooperate in the provision of public goods, even when pure egoists would try to free ride.

Conclusions

Globalization presents a great challenge to democracy. Under existing political institutions, globalization is likely to undermine democracy. If decisions are shifted to decision-making bodies at the world level, the citizens will increasingly lose influence over the course of politics.

This chapter argues that such a development need not occur if the institutions of democratic governance are made more flexible. Two proposals are advanced which serve to enable the citizens to maintain, or even to enlarge, their influence in the political process in a globalized society. On the supply side, individuals should have the authority to establish functional democratic units (FOCJ) adjusted to the geography of problems, and political markets should be opened to politicians coming from outside. On the demand side, individuals should be able to adjust their citizenship status to varying circumstances and may establish special bonds with organizations beyond the state. Putting these proposals for institutional flexibility into practice would reduce the extent to which globalization undermines democracy. In particular, they bolster civic virtue and reduce the temptation to free ride inherent in public goods supply.

REFERENCES

Beck, Ulrich. 2000. *What Is Globalisation?* Cambridge, UK: Polity Press.

Bernholz, Peter. 2000. *Globalisierung und Umstrukturierung der Wirtschaft: Sind sie neu?* University of St Gallen: Walter Adolf Jöhr-Vorlesung.

Blatter, Joachim, and Helen Ingram. 2000. 'States, Markets and Beyond: Governance of Transboundary Water Resources', *Natural Resources Journal* 40, 2: 439–73.

Bohnet, Iris, and Bruno S. Frey. 1999. 'The Sound of Silence in Prisoner's Dilemma and Dictator Games', *Journal of Economic Behavior and Organization* 38, 1: 43–57.

Brennan, Geoffrey, and Alan P. Hamlin. 2000. *Democratic Devices and Desires.* Cambridge University Press.

Brennan, Geoffrey, and Loren Lomasky. 1993, *Democracy and Decision.* Cambridge University Press.

Buchanan, James M. 1965. 'An Economic Theory of Clubs', *Economica* 32, 1: 1–14.

Colander, David. 2000. 'New Millennium Economics: How Did It Get this Way, and What Way Is It?', *Journal of Economic Perspectives* 14, 1: 121–32.

Deci, Edward L., Richard Koestner and Richard M. Ryan. 1999. 'A Meta-Analytic Review of Experiments Examining the Effects of Extrinsic Rewards on Intrinsic Motivation', *Psychological Bulletin* 125, 6: 627–68.

Deci, Edward L., and Richard M. Ryan. 1985. *Intrinsic Motivation and Self-Determination in Human Behavior.* New York: Plenum Press.

Eggertsson, Thrainn. 1990. *Economic Behaviour and Institutions: Principles of Neoinstitutional Economics.* Cambridge University Press.

Eichenberger, Reiner, and Bruno S. Frey. 2001. 'Democratic Governance for a Globalized World', *Kyklos* 55, 2: 265–88.

Eichenberger, Reiner, and Felix Oberholzer-Gee. 1998. 'Rational Moralists: The Role of Fairness in Democratic Economic Politics', *Public Choice* 94, 1–2: 191–210.

Frey, Bruno S. 1997. *Not Just for the Money: An Economic Theory of Personal Motivation.* Cheltenham, UK: Edward Elgar.

    2002. 'Liliput oder Leviathan? Der Staat in der globalisierten Gesellschaft', *Perspektiven der Wirtschaftspolitik* 3, 4: 363–75.

    2003a. 'Flexible Citizenship for a Global Society', *Politics, Philosophy and Economics* 2, 1: 93–114.

2003b. 'Globalisierung ohne Weltregierung', *Analyse und Kritik: Zeitschrift für Sozialtheorie* 25, 2: 121–34.

Frey, Bruno S., and Reiner Eichenberger. 1999. *The New Democratic Federalism for Europe: Functional Overlapping and Competing Jurisdictions*. Cheltenham, UK: Edward Elgar.

Frey, Bruno S., and Reto Jegen. 2001. 'Motivation Crowding Theory: A Survey of Empirical Evidence', *Journal of Economic Surveys* 15, 5: 589–611.

Frey, Bruno S., and Alois Stutzer. 2002. *Economics and Happiness*. Princeton University Press.

Ledyard, John O. 1995. 'Public Goods: A Survey of Experimental Research', in John Kagel and Alvin E. Roth (eds.), *Handbook of Experimental Economics* (pp. 111–94). Princeton University Press.

Levi, Margaret. 1997. *Consent, Dissent and Patriotism*. Cambridge University Press.

Olson, Mancur. 1965. *The Logic of Collective Action*. Cambridge, MA: Harvard University Press.

Osterloh, Margit, and Bruno S. Frey. 2000. 'Motivation, Knowledge Transfer and Organizational Forms', *Organization Science* 11, 5: 538–50.

Ostrom, Elinor. 2000. 'Crowding Out Citizenship', *Scandinavian Political Studies* 23, 1: 3–16.

Paldam, Martin. 2000. 'Social Capital: One or Many? Definition and Measurement', *Journal of Economic Surveys* 14, 5: 629–53.

Putnam, Robert D. 2000. *Bowling Alone: The Collapse and Revival of American Community*. New York: Simon & Schuster.

Rodrik, Dani. 1998. 'Symposium on Globalization in Perspective: An Introduction', *Journal of Economic Perspectives* 12, 4: 3–8.

Vanberg, Viktor J. 2000. 'Functional Federalism: Communal or Individual Rights?', *Kyklos* 53, 3: 363–86.

Weizsäcker, C. Christian von. 1999. *Logik der Globalisierung*. Goettingen, Germany: Vandenhoeck und Ruprecht.

9   Global democracy and domestic analogies

Mathias Koenig-Archibugi

Introduction

As shown in the introductory chapter of this volume (Archibugi et al.), for centuries intellectuals from Europe and other parts of the world have devised institutional blueprints aimed at 'domesticating' international politics – that is, at imbuing it with the alleged virtues of the domestic politics of well-functioning states, notably strictly controlled use of violence, rule of law and/or democratic methods of conflict resolution. Critiques of such projects have also been heard for centuries. Often the targets of criticism have been not the blueprints themselves but the perceived lack of a realistic explanation of how to get from here to there – that is, the features of possible transition paths towards the more peaceful and just world order envisaged by their authors. For instance, in his commentary on the 'project for settling an everlasting project in Europe' presented in 1713 by Charles-Irénée Castel, abbé de Saint-Pierre, Jean-Jacques Rousseau wrote in 1756 that 'though the scheme in itself was wise enough, the means proposed for its execution betray the simplicity of the author ... [T]his good man saw clearly enough how things would work, when once set going, but ... he judged like a child of the means for setting them in motion' (Rousseau 1756/ 2008, 126). Almost two and a half centuries later, Philippe Schmitter (1999) berated proponents of cosmopolitan democracy such as Daniele Archibugi and David Held in similar terms: 'What is even more discouraging than a credible idea of the end-product is the almost complete absence of any idea of the process whereby the world might get there' (940).

Militant cosmopolitan democrats may be tempted to respond in the spirit of Winston Churchill, who declared in 1946: 'We must build a

I am grateful to Daniele Archibugi, Robert Goodin and Raffaele Marchetti for their useful comments and suggestions, while remaining responsible for any shortcomings. I benefited from an Open Society Institute research grant while writing this chapter.

kind of United States of Europe ... The process is simple. All that is needed is the resolve of hundreds of millions of men and women to do right instead of wrong and to gain as their reward blessing instead of cursing' (Churchill 1946/1988, 664). Of course, such an answer would be unlikely to satisfy most political scientists, whose job often consists in accounting for outcomes that do not seem to be really wanted by anyone and that are variously explained with reference to structural constraints, collective action dilemmas, psychological biases and a range of other devices drawn from the analytical toolbox of the social sciences. If the case for global democratic blueprints such as those presented by Marchetti and Murithi (both this volume) is to be intellectually compelling, discussions about their feasibility should be firmly based on the knowledge of constraints on political choice that has been accumulated since Niccolò Machiavelli affirmed the importance of studying politics as it is and not just how we would like it to be.

But a careful examination of the conditions for, and pathways to, global democracy is equally necessary if the project is to be politically consequential, as sympathetic political actors need to be persuaded that it is worth pursuing. To provide a simple but pertinent concrete illustration of this point: a sample of the participants in the 2005 World Social Forum (WSF) was asked whether it was a good or bad idea to have a democratic world government. For 32 per cent it was a bad idea, for 39 per cent it was a good idea but not plausible and 29 per cent responded that it was a good idea and plausible (Chase-Dunn et al. 2008). It would not be too far-fetched to infer that, at present, a majority of WSF activists would be unwilling to campaign for democratic world government, but also that such a campaign would have a chance to gather majority support among them if the sympathetic but sceptical participants became persuaded of its feasibility.[1]

What can empirical social science contribute to such debates? Among the various directions of analysis that appear to be fruitful, this chapter considers two. It should be stressed that the focus here is on the transition to global democracy, rather than its consolidation and survival,

---

[1] Among the general public, support for global democratic institutions seems to be weaker but still sizeable. A 2007 international opinion poll commissioned by the BBC asked the following question to approximately 12,000 respondents in 15 countries: 'How likely would you be to support a Global Parliament, where votes are based on country population sizes, and the global parliament is able to make binding policies?' The results were: 14.4% responded 'Very likely – it is a good idea'; 23.1% responded 'Quite likely – but with reservations'; 14.9% responded 'Quite unlikely – but it might work'; and 19.1% responded 'Very unlikely – it is a bad idea'. Cross-national differences are very significant: an overwhelming majority of Indian respondents supported a global parliament, while US and Danish respondents were the most opposed (BBC 2007).

although the latter are also very important questions. First, analysts can try to determine the *necessary conditions* for a transition to global democracy. Second, they can try to determine the various *paths* that could lead to global democracy. For instance, Kate Macdonald (this volume) offers a thorough analysis of one possible pathway to global democracy, which is based on the progressive democratization of non-state structures of transnational governance.

One way of thinking about transition paths is in terms of *sufficient* conditions. Whereas the necessity of a condition does not depend on the presence or absence of other conditions, conditions can be – and usually are – sufficient only in combination with other conditions; in other words, analysts should expect that (a) particular *combinations* of conditions, rather than individual conditions, are sufficient to produce an outcome ('conjunctural causation'), and that (b) *several different* combinations of conditions may be sufficient for the outcome to occur ('equifinality'). The identification of different *paths* to global democracy may be conceptualized as the search for particular combinations of favourable conditions that can be seen as reliably associated with the outcome. Conjunctural causation and equifinality make the study of potentially sufficient conditions significantly more complex than the study of potentially necessary conditions. This chapter does not aim to perform this more demanding task, and instead focuses on necessary condition hypotheses. The next section discusses their role in the context of global democratization and the third section draws some lessons from experiences of domestic democratization, which are analysed through a systematic method called 'fuzzy-set qualitative comparative analysis'. A tentative research agenda on the identification of viable paths to global democracy is sketched in the final section.

Thinking about necessary conditions for global democratization

Robert Dahl expressed a widely held opinion when he stated that 'the conditions required for the function of democratic institutions simply do not exist at the international level and are unlikely to develop within any foreseeable time' (Dahl 1999a, 927). Hence, he concluded, 'even if the threshold is pretty hazy ... international systems will lie below any reasonable threshold of democracy' (Dahl 1999b, 21). Statements such as these raise at least two important questions. First, and more generally, how can we *know* if a given condition is necessary for democracy or not? Second, and more specifically, *which* conditions should be regarded as necessary for democracy?

With regard to the first question, scepticism about the possibility of global democracy can be based on the belief that countries experiencing successful transitions to democracy did so because of the presence of certain prerequisites, and that these prerequisites are lacking at the international level, now and in the foreseeable future. The comparison between democratic and non-democratic countries is thought to provide insights into the possibility of democratizing global politics. In other words, not only optimists but also sceptics about global democracy may rely, implicitly or explicitly, on a 'domestic analogy', which in its broader definition is 'presumptive reasoning ... about international relations based on the assumption that since domestic and international phenomena are similar in a number of respects, a given proposition which holds true domestically, but whose validity is as yet uncertain internationally, will also hold true internationally' (Suganami 1989, 24).

Diagnostic (as opposed to prescriptive) domestic analogies have been used to affirm as well as to deny the possibility of global democracy.[2] An important recent example of the 'possibilist' use is Robert Goodin's (2010) argument that '[s]imilar things seem to be happening in today's international order as happened centuries ago in the domestic sphere to curtail the arbitrary exercise of power and to make it accountable' (181). 'Absence-of-conditions' arguments against the possibility of global democracy often use the same logic in reverse, for they draw on what is known about the successful democratization of states to deny the possibility of democratization at the global level.

It is beyond the scope of this chapter to examine the validity of this domestic analogy. It is sufficient that it is plausible enough to warrant an examination of its premises.[3] Despite their numerous differences, both international systems and domestic political systems consist of a multitude of collective actors who engage in a variety of modes of interaction – from coercion and competition to negotiation and co-operation – on the basis of complex power relations, conflicting and compatible interests, and norms of appropriate behaviour. A rigid analytical separation is therefore unwarranted (Milner 1991). As those interactions can be considered more or less democratic within the context of individual states, it is legitimate to apply similar criteria to analyse political structures beyond that level (Moravcsik 2005). By extension, the

---

[2] See Suganami (1989, 136) for the distinction between the diagnostic and the prescriptive use of the domestic analogy.

[3] The domestic analogy could be expressed: '*If* x is necessary for domestic democracy, *then* x is necessary for global democracy' (to which sceptics add 'x is absent at the global level'). This chapter focuses on the '*if*' part of the argument, not the '*then*' part.

question 'under what conditions can a political system be democratized?' can be legitimately asked with regard to international as well as intranational interactions.

I thus accept that insights garnered from the study of domestic political processes may be relevant to arguments about potential international processes. But do sceptical conclusions follow from this premise? To provide an answer, we need to examine the experience of democratic countries in order to test claims that certain conditions were necessary for their democratization. If any condition is identified as necessary in the domestic context, we need to ask whether it can be found at the international level. If any necessary condition is identified that is not present and cannot be replicated at the international level, we would be left with strong reasons to believe global democracy – or at least forms of global democracy that resemble those realized within states (see Marchetti, this volume)[4] – to be impossible. But such a conclusion hinges on the basic question: are there any such conditions?

The second question posed at the beginning of this section is exactly which conditions can plausibly be regarded as necessary for democratic transitions and thus deserve closer examination. Clearly, a large number of conditions are necessary for any interesting social process to occur, but most of them are trivial – for instance, air is a necessary condition for freedom of speech.[5] A first step is thus to discriminate among conditions and to select non-trivial conditions for closer analysis. A useful second step is to divide such conditions into two broad categories: those related to structures and those related to agency. The question of the relationship between agency and structure is at the core of many ontological debates in the social and political sciences, and cannot be addressed in any depth here.[6] For the limited purposes of this chapter it suffices to say that approaches to the study of democratization are commonly

---

[4] Polycentric forms of global democracy, such as those advocated by Kate Macdonald, Terry Macdonald and Bruno Frey in this volume, are less vulnerable to this kind of argument.

[5] A necessary condition can be considered trivial when it is present across all cases in the relevant universe of analysis. An in-depth discussion of the trivialness of necessary conditions is provided by Goertz (2006).

[6] All action is ultimately determined by some kind of structure, but the reverse is not necessarily true. While this general point would support a 'structuralist' worldview, it is of little relevance for actual empirical research. Since no research agenda can capture all structures that may determine action, it is perfectly legitimate for research programmes to focus on some structures and neglect others, and the former may well 'only' constrain the behaviour of actors without determining or even affecting their desires and beliefs. This means that an agency-oriented research programme is legitimate even in the context of an ultimately structuralist worldview.

distinguished on the basis of whether they emphasize structural 'background' conditions or rather the goals and strategic interactions of political actors.

A key forerunner of the 'structuralist' approach was Seymour Martin Lipset (1959), whose conjectures on economic development as requisite of democratization had a decisive impact on subsequent scholarship. The agency-oriented or voluntarist approach was propelled by Guillermo O'Donnell and Philippe Schmitter's (1986) path-breaking volumes on 'transitions from authoritarian rule'. Despite several attempts at integrating the two perspectives,[7] the debate shows little sign of abating. A scholar who emphasizes structural factors has lamented that for actor-oriented scholars 'democratization is ultimately a matter of political crafting. It seems that democracy can be crafted and promoted in all sorts of places, even in culturally and structurally unfavorable circumstances' (Doorenspleet 2004, 310). On the other side, Larry Diamond (2003) has insisted that '[c]learly, most states can become democratic, because most states already are. Moreover . . . the overwhelming bulk of the states that have become democratic during the third wave [of democratization] have remained so, even in countries lacking virtually all of the supposed "conditions" for democracy' (5).

In sum, the search for necessary conditions in the context of domestic democratization provides a good starting point for reflecting about plausible necessary conditions for global democratization. This search should involve conditions highlighted by structuralist approaches as well as those stressed by voluntarist approaches, and this distinction can provide a useful framework for analysing democratic processes beyond the state as well. The next section singles out a number of conditions that are especially relevant in controversies about global democratization, and investigates whether they can be regarded as necessary in the domestic context.

Searching for necessary conditions for domestic democratization

In this section I look for necessary conditions for the transition of democracy within states by comparing systematically the experiences of a large number of countries with the aid of a method called 'fuzzy-set qualitative comparative analysis'. Large-scale comparisons are easier with regard to structural conditions than with regard to agential and strategic conditions. This is mainly because the former are captured by a

---

[7] For a thorough examination of such attempts see Mahoney and Snyder (1999).

number of existing datasets, whereas to the best of my knowledge there is
no dataset that provides a standardized description of the political strategies and interactions in all or most countries that have experienced a
democratic transition. For this reason, only structural conditions are
subject to systematic scrutiny in this section, while the necessity of
agential conditions is addressed more cursorily at the end.

Which structural conditions should be included in the assessment of
necessity? Some conditions are trivial, in the sense described above.
Others, while not trivial, are not directly relevant to a discussion of
global democracy. The analysis should include those conditions whose
alleged weakness or absence at the global level has been invoked as
reasons to be sceptical about the possibility of global democracy.[8]
Among those reasons are: (a) cultural heterogeneity in the world is an
insurmountable obstacle to democracy; (b) most of the world is too poor
to allow the emergence of democratic institutions; (c) democracy at the
global level could not work because of huge differences in the economic
conditions of the world's inhabitants; (d) the world is too large to allow
the establishment of democratic institutions; and (e) democracy can
only emerge in the context of established statehood – that is, within a
polity where the monopoly of legitimate force by a central institution
has deep historical roots and is taken for granted by the population. The
question thus is whether any of the following conditions can be considered as necessary for democratic transitions in the domestic context:
(a) cultural and ethnic homogeneity; (b) economic development;
(c) relatively high levels of economic equality; (d) a small or moderate polity
size; or (e) established statehood.

Condition (e) requires some elaboration. There are authors who
maintain that '[d]emocracy is a form of governance of a modern state.
Thus, without a state, no modern democracy is possible' (Linz and
Stepan 1996, 17). As I argue elsewhere (Koenig-Archibugi 2010), there
are reasons to believe that a degree of political centralization is a necessary condition for democracy, but it is debatable whether this requires a
monopoly over legitimate violence.[9] According to Chris Brown (2002),

---

[8] For instance, Dahl (1999a, 1999b), Doyle (2000), Nye (2002), Keohane (2003) and
Christiano (this volume). See also Offe (2006).

[9] Democracy requires ability to enforce collective decisions. But legal rules produced
by a political unit are not enforced *only* when the unit possesses the key attributes
of statehood, notably a monopoly of the legitimate use of force and
bureaucratic control over a territorial jurisdiction. The most notable example of
this disjunction is the European Union (EU). For instance, J.H.H. Weiler (2003)
interprets the EU as a combination of a 'confederal' institutional arrangement and a
'federal' legal arrangement. On the one hand, EU law is accepted as having direct effect

'Contemporary liberal democracies emerged from pre-democratic state-structures; by analogy, global democracy would require the existence of a global state-structure that could be democratized'(246).[10] But how can we test the hypothesis that democracy can only emerge after a relatively long experience and generalized acceptance of statehood? One way to do so is to ask whether democratic governance emerged after periods in which the key element of statehood – the monopoly over legitimate violence – was challenged by significant sectors of the population – more specifically, after civil wars. While 'domestic anarchy' and 'international anarchy' differ in significant ways, examining the former can provide insights into the context of global democratization.

A useful tool for answering the kinds of questions stated above is qualitative comparative analysis (QCA), which is a configurational method that has been developed by Charles Ragin and other scholars over the past 25 years.[11] This method is particularly useful for the problem at hand because of three reasons. The first reason is that QCA is specifically aimed at testing hypotheses about necessary and sufficient conditions, rather than hypotheses about correlation among variables. QCA interprets statements about necessary conditions in logical and set-theoretic terms. To say that a condition is necessary for an outcome is equivalent to saying that cases where the outcome is present are a subset of the cases where the condition is present. This means that, if researchers find instances of the outcome that are not within the set of instances of the condition, then they can interpret this finding as contradicting the necessary condition hypothesis.

The second advantage is that QCA is specifically designed to test verbal hypotheses whose terms are not 'given' but require careful interpretation. For instance, the hypothesis that cultural homogeneity is a necessary condition for democratic transitions is inherently vague and makes little sense without a careful definition of thresholds between homogeneous and non-homogeneous countries and between democratic transitions and other instances of regime change or stability. Over the

---

in the jurisdictions of member states and supremacy over national law, without significant problems of compliance. On the other hand, EU institutions lack both the means of coercion and the bureaucratic apparatus to enforce EU law. 'There is a hierarchy of norms: Community norms trump conflicting Member State norms. But this hierarchy is not rooted in a hierarchy of normative authority or in a hierarchy of real power. Indeed, European federalism is constructed with a top-to-bottom hierarchy of norms, but with a bottom-to-top hierarchy of authority and real power' (9). Zürn and Joerges (2005) show systematically that the experience of the EU disproves the thesis that a central monopoly of force is *necessary* to ensure high levels of compliance with the law.

[10] See Nagel (2005) for a similar argument.
[11] For descriptions of the method see Ragin (2000, 2008) and Rihoux and Ragin (2009).

past ten years, QCA has incorporated sophisticated procedures for the systematic analysis of 'fuzzy' concepts such as 'democratic transition'. QCA now exists in two versions. In the 'crisp-set' version, conditions and outcomes are recorded as being either present or absent. In the 'fuzzy-set' version, cases can be recorded as being either 'fully in' the set of cases displaying a certain condition or outcome, or 'fully out' of that set, or 'partly in' the set, with various degrees of membership. In other words, fuzzy-set QCA (fsQCA) allows researchers to code cases as having not only full membership and full non-membership, but also degrees of membership.

The third advantage is that the notion of necessity and sufficiency embodied in fsQCA is compatible with a 'probabilistic' approach to social science data, which does not force researchers to discard necessary conditions hypotheses because of the presence of a relatively small number of deviant cases (Goertz 2005). Statements about necessary conditions for democracy are rarely phrased in absolute terms with no allowance for exceptions.[12] FsQCA takes this into account by providing ways to measure the strength of the set-theoretic relationship between conditions and outcomes. The key measure for the purpose of this chapter is 'consistency', which varies between 0 and 1 and measures the degree to which a set relation has been approximated –that is, the degree to which the evidence is consistent with the argument that a set relation exists. If all cases where the outcome is present are found to be a subset of the cases where the condition is present, the consistency of that condition is 1, and that provides researchers with a strong reason to believe that the condition is necessary for the outcome. Perfectly consistent set relationships are rarely found in social research, and thus researchers may conclude that a condition is necessary even if its consistency is lower than 1. The lower the consistency score, however, the weaker are claims that a condition is necessary (Ragin 2006).[13]

---

[12] The following statement by John Stuart Mill is typical: 'Free institutions are *next to* impossible in a country made up of different nationalities' (Mill 1861/1991, 428, emphasis added).

[13] FsQCA calculates the consistency of hypothesized necessary conditions according to the following formula:

$$\text{Consistency } (Y_i \leq X_i) = \Sigma \,(\min(X_i, Y_i)) / \Sigma \,(Y_i),$$

where X are the fuzzy-set values of the condition, Y are the fuzzy-set values of the outcome, and 'min' indicates the selection of the lower of the two values.

It should be noted that in the fsQCA literature there are no established conventions on the minimum level of consistency that is needed to support a necessary condition hypothesis, or even on the criteria for determining what level is most appropriate given the features of the research problem. Schneider and Wagemann (2007, 213) make a rare attempt to identify such a threshold by suggesting that only scores of 'at least' 0.9 should be accepted in the case of *necessary* conditions.

The rest of this section describes the data sources and assignment of fuzzy-set scores before presenting the findings – that is, the consistency of cultural and ethnic homogeneity, economic development, economic equality, and small size as necessary conditions for transitions to democracy.

The outcome is membership in the 'set of countries experiencing a major democratic transition' and it is based on Polity IV values.[14] The Polity IV project defines a 'major democratic transition' as a six points or greater increase in Polity value over a period of 3 years or less, including a shift from an autocratic Polity value (-10 to 0) to a partial democratic Polity value (+1 to +6) or full democratic Polity value (+7 to +10) or a shift from a partial democratic value to a full democratic value. The Polity project defines a 'minor democratic transition' as a 3–5 point increase in Polity values over a period of 3 years or less, which includes a shift from autocratic to partial democratic or from partial to full democratic value (Marshall and Jaggers 2009). I assign to countries experiencing a major democratic transition a fuzzy-set score of 1 in the set of countries experiencing a major democratic transition, whereas countries experiencing a minor democratic transition are assigned a fuzzy-set score of 0.5 in that set.

I assign to each case of a country experiencing a democratic transition one of four degrees of membership in the five causal conditions: 'fully in' (fuzzy-set score of 1), 'more in than out' (0.66), 'more out than in' (0.33), and 'fully out' (0).

Membership in the 'set of ethnically homogeneous countries' is based on the database compiled by James Fearon (2003). The database includes an ethnic fractionalization index for most countries in the world, which measures the probability that two individuals selected at random from a country will be from different ethnic groups. The index ranges from 0 to 1 and depends on the number of ethnic groups as well as their share of the total population. I consider countries with an ethnic fractionalization index between 0 and 0.249999 to be fully in the 'set of ethnically homogeneous countries'; countries with an ethnic fractionalization index between 0.25 and 0.49999 are considered more in than out of that set; countries with an ethnic fractionalization between 0.50 and 0.749999 are considered more out of than in the set; and countries whose ethnic fractionalization ranges between 0.75 and 1 are considered fully out of the set.

---

[14] Polity IV scores suffer from a number of problems (see, e.g., Munck and Verkuilen 2002, Treier and Jackman 2008), but they are probably more suitable than any other democracy measurement with comparable coverage of years and countries.

Fearon (2003) argues that measures of ethnic diversity are not always adequate to capture the political effects of cultural differences. For that reason, he also provides an index of *cultural* fractionalization that uses the distance between the 'tree branches' of two languages as a proxy of the cultural distance between groups that speak them as a first language. Fractionalization is lower when groups speak a related language (e.g., Byelorussians and Russians in Belarus) and higher when the languages are structurally unrelated (e.g., Greeks and Turks in Cyprus). I consider countries with a cultural fractionalization index between 0 and 0.249999 to be fully in the 'set of culturally homogeneous countries'; countries with an cultural fractionalization index between 0.25 and 0.49999 are considered to be more in than out of that set; countries with a cultural fractionalization between 0.50 and 0.749999 are considered more out of than in the set; and countries whose cultural fractionalization ranges between 0.75 and 1 are considered fully out of the set.

Membership in the 'set of economically developed countries' is based on World Bank classification, which in turn is based on the gross national income per capita of countries. I use the thresholds adopted by the World Bank in 1989, when it introduced the four-fold classification on the basis of 1987 data (World Bank 2010a). Countries that, in the first year of the democratic transition, had a gross domestic product (GDP) per capita that exceeds the threshold used by the World Bank to identify 'high-income' countries (over $6,000), are considered fully in the 'set of economically developed countries'; countries that would have qualified as higher-middle-income countries according to the 1987 World Bank criteria ($1,941–6,000) are considered more in than out of the set; countries that would have qualified as lower-middle-income countries ($481–1,940) are considered 'more out of than in' the set; and countries that would have qualified as low income (less than $480) are considered 'fully out'.[15] GDP per capita data come from the World Bank (2010b).

Membership in the 'set of economically equal countries' is based on the Standardized World Income Inequality Database (SWIID) compiled by Frederik Solt (2009), which in turn is based mainly on the World Income Inequality Database created by the World Institute for Development Economics Research of the United Nations University. The

[15] The country data I use are based on GDP per capita, whereas the World Bank thresholds refer to GNI per capita, but with a few exceptions (e.g., Ireland) the two indicators are similar.

SWIID provides Gini indices of gross and net income inequality for 153 countries between 1960 and the present. I consider countries with a net (i.e., after tax and transfers) Gini index below 0.20 in the year of the democratic transition to be fully in the set of economically equal countries; countries with a net Gini index between 0.20 and 0.34999 are more in than out of that set; countries with a net Gini index between 0.35 and 0.49999 are more out of than in that set; and countries with a net Gini index over 0.50 are fully out.

Membership in the 'set of small countries' is based on population data collected by Angus Maddison (2008). Countries with a population of 10 million or less in the first year of their democratic transition are fully in the set of small countries; countries with a population between 10 and 50 million are more in than out of that set; countries with a population between 50 and 100 million are more out than in; and countries with a population of over 100 million are fully out of the set of small countries.

Membership in the 'set of countries with established statehood' is based on whether a country experienced a civil war at any time during the 10 years preceding the democratic transition. A score of 0 is assigned if this is the case, otherwise 1. The data on civil wars are from Sambanis (2004). As noted above, a civil war in recent history is an indication that a significant share of the population does not take a monopoly of legitimate violence for granted.

The dataset on which the following analysis is based only includes countries that experienced either a major or minor democratic transition to democracy, as defined above. This is consistent with the general principle that cases not displaying the outcome of interest are not relevant for testing necessary condition hypotheses (as opposed to sufficient condition hypotheses) (Ragin 2000).[16] The Polity IV database includes 151 cases of major democratic transition and 34 cases of minor transition between 1800 and 2009.[17] Because of issues of data availability, only a subset of these cases is included in the following analysis. First, only democratic transitions that occurred between 1945 and 2009 are considered. Second, a few cases from this period are excluded because of lack of data on one or more causal conditions. Another two limitations should be noted. First, since Fearon's ethnic and cultural fractionalization index is not available for multiple years, the analysis is based on the assumption that the index approximates a country's

---

[16] This principle is not entirely uncontroversial: see, for instance, the debate between Seawright (2002), Braumoeller and Goertz (2002) and Clarke (2002).

[17] Counting only the first year of a multiyear democratic transition, and counting democratic transitions in non-contiguous years in the same country as separate cases.

Table 9.1 *Summary of outcome, conditions, measurements and sources*

Outcome	Measure	Source
Major and minor democratic transition	Change in Polity value (see text for details)	Marshall and Jaggers (2009)

Conditions	Measure	Source
Ethnic homogeneity	Ethnic fractionalization index	Fearon (2003)
Cultural homogeneity	Cultural fractionalization index	Fearon (2003)
Economic development	GDP per capita	World Bank (2010b)
Economic equality	Net Gini index	Solt (2009)
Small size	Population	Maddison (2008)
Established statehood	No civil war in previous 10 years	Sambanis (2004)

situation at the time of the transition, given the relatively slow changes in the ethnic composition of most countries and the low likelihood that such changes are substantial enough to shift countries across the four categories used here. Second, when data on per capita income and income inequality are not available for the year of transition, figures for the nearest available year are used.

Table 9.1 summarizes which outcome and conditions are analysed, how they are measured and which sources are used.

I conducted the analysis on 126 cases of democratic transition. Applying the procedures implemented in the fsQCA 2.0 software (Ragin et al. 2006) yields the following consistency scores for the five causal conditions of interest:

Ethnic homogeneity:	0.500427
Cultural homogeneity:	0.716667
Economic development:	0.262735
Economic equality:	0.354274
Small size:	0.762393
Established statehood:	0.653846

The consistency values for all six conditions are well below 1, which suggests that none of these conditions can be regarded as necessary for democratic transitions. Size is somewhat more consistent than the others, but this is likely to be due to skewed membership scores (see Ragin 2006, 298), and in any case the consistency score is too low to support the conclusion that it is a necessary condition. The low consistency of established statehood (i.e., no civil war in the preceding 10 years) is especially notable, and the implication that democracy can emerge from 'anarchy' is consistent with Wantchekon's (2004) finding that nearly 40 per cent of all civil wars that took place from 1945 to 1993 resulted in an improvement in the level of democracy.[18]

In sum, the 'structural' conditions included in this analysis may perhaps increase the likelihood of a democratic transition, but the evidence does not support the contention that they are necessary, even taking into account the possibility of exceptions to the general pattern.

However, one further possibility should be considered: even if none of the conditions examined can be considered necessary for democratic transition, the presence of at least one of them – *any* of them – may be necessary for it. In other words, it could be that, in order to experience a democratic transition, a country needs to be ethnically/culturally homogeneous *or* economically developed *or* economically equal *or* small *or* with established statehood; the simultaneous lack of *all* these conditions may prevent a democratic transition. Elsewhere (Koenig-Archibugi 2010) I argue that India contradicts such a 'conditional necessity' conjecture: India is a heterogeneous, poor, unequal and large country and yet it possesses stable democratic institutions. However, fsQCA allows us to test the conditional necessity conjecture more systematically.[19] If we treat 'cultural homogeneity *or* economic development *or* economic equality *or* small size' as a possible necessary condition, then its consistency score is 0.881368, which appears still too low to support the conclusion that it is a necessary condition. On the other hand, an expression that includes established statehood achieves a higher score: 'established statehood *or* cultural homogeneity *or* economic equality *or* small size' has a consistency of 0.939231. Given that some authors suggest that the threshold for consistency scores should be 'at least' 0.90 in the case of necessary condition hypotheses,[20] that disjunctive condition may be seen as passing (just) the threshold required for an affirmative verdict. However, it should be noted that the disjunctive condition has a very high *average* membership score (since the score of

---

[18] Since organized groups fighting each other in civil wars are often not internally democratic, this finding can also shed some light on an important question addressed by Archibugi (2008) and others: can a global democratic polity emerge only from the union of political units that are already democratic themselves? By using a domestic analogy, the fact that democracy can emerge from a condition of anarchy (and even war) among organized groups that are not necessarily democratic provides some reasons to answer that question in the negative. I am grateful to Daniele Archibugi for highlighting the importance of the question.

[19] I am grateful to Robert Goodin for suggesting this 'disjunctive' analysis.

[20] See Schneider and Wagemann (2007) referred to in footnote 14.

each case consists in the *maximum* among the membership scores in each of the four conditions), and thus the finding should be treated with caution (see Ragin 2006, 298).

The preceding analysis only considered 'structural' conditions, neglecting the agency-based and strategic conditions that are emphasized by a sizeable part of the democratization literature. As noted above, ascertaining the necessity of such agential conditions is difficult because of the absence (to the best of my knowledge) of a dataset that provides a standardized description of the political constellation of all or most countries that have experienced a democratic transition in their history. However, political scientists have accumulated a substantial amount of knowledge on the political processes and strategies that resulted in democratic transitions. Do any necessary conditions emerge from this literature? While this chapter cannot provide a comprehensive answer, there are reasons to believe that agential theories are no better than structural theories in uncovering *necessary* conditions across a large number of countries. Barbara Geddes (1999) notes that the initially proposed generalization that divisions within the authoritarian regime were an essential condition of transitions was disproved by later developments in the Soviet bloc. Conversely, popular mobilization was unimportant as a cause of democratization in early studies focusing on Latin America, but then appeared to be crucial in Eastern Europe. Studies of Latin America and Europe stressed the importance of pacts among elites, but there is little evidence of pacts in African cases of democratization. Geddes notes that '[v]irtually every suggested generalization to arise from this literature ... has been challenged' (119). We can conclude that the agency-oriented research tradition has not found conditions that can be regarded as unambiguously necessary rather than merely supportive.

Thinking about paths to global democracy

The findings of the previous section appear to support the commonly held view that 'there is no single path to democracy, and, therefore, no generalization is to be had about the conditions that give rise to it' (Shapiro 2003, 80).[21] While Shapiro's inference that no generalization can be made is questionable, the claim that there are multiple paths to democracy is now widely accepted. One of the challenges for analysts

---

[21] Shapiro continues: 'Democracy can result from decades of gradual evolution (Britain and the United States), imitation (India), cascades (most of Eastern Europe in 1989), collapse (Russia after 1991), imposition from above (Chile), revolutions (Portugal), negotiated settlements (Poland, Nicaragua, and South Africa), or external imposition (Japan and West Germany) ... Perhaps there are other possibilities' (Shapiro 2003, 80).

of domestic democratization has been to identify those paths theoretically and empirically, and to develop hypotheses on the causes and consequences of different paths. One of the challenges for analysts of global democratization is to extract the most relevant insights from this literature and apply them to actual instances of change in particular international institutional contexts (Uhlin 2010) or to stylized accounts of future large-scale transformations (Goodin 2010).

One way in which the literature on domestic democratization has tried to make the idea of multiple paths more specific is by developing typologies of 'modes of transition'. Huntington (1991), for instance, distinguished between 'transformations', where the elites in power lead the transition, 'replacements', where opposition groups lead the transition, and 'transplacements', where elites in power and opposition groups cooperate in the transition. Karl (1990) distinguished between possible modes of transition to democracy on the basis of two criteria: first, whether democratic transitions result from strategies based primarily on overt force or rather from compromise; second, whether incumbent ruling elites or mass actors have predominant power. Intersecting these distinctions produces four ideal types of democratic transition: reform, revolution, imposition and pact. Similarly, Munck and Leff (1997) classified modes of transition by asking two questions: whether the agent of change is the incumbent elite or a counterelite or a combination of the two; and whether the strategy of the agent of change is confrontation or accommodation or a combination of the two. Various combinations of these criteria generate several modes of transition, notably four 'pure' modes – revolution from above, social revolution, conservative reform and reform from below – and three 'mixed' modes – reform through rupture, reform through extrication and reform through transaction.

Mutatis mutandis, these typological exercises can provide useful building blocks for theorizing pathways to *global* democracy. But it should be noted that they do not (aim to) identify the conditions under which the actors' strategies will actually result in democratic transitions. This is partly a consequence of the high level of generality of the categories on which such typologies are based. Notably, the distinction between ruling elite and counterelite, or between ruling elite and mass actors, offers little information on the relative amounts of power resources that those groups can mobilize in pursuit of their goals and on the likelihood that actors' strategies will succeed.

Analyses in the tradition of macrohistorical comparative sociology tend to display lower levels of indeterminacy. They usually start from structuralist premises about historically developing class structures and political structures and ascribe broadly defined (material and ideational) interests to members of particular classes and state elites. According to one of the most significant contributions to this tradition, Barrington Moore's (1966) *The Social Origins of Dictatorship and Democracy*, countries reach one or the other of three political outcomes – parliamentary democracy, fascist dictatorship and communist dictatorship – depending on the relative strength of states, land-owning classes, peasants and bourgeois classes. Moore argued that a strong bourgeoisie was a necessary component of all paths to democracy: 'No bourgeoisie, no democracy' (418). However, a strong bourgeoisie was not described as sufficient to produce democracy, and the paths to democracy of the three main cases studied by Moore – Britain, France and the United States – displayed significant differences. Adopting a similar macrohistorical comparative approach, Rueschemeyer et al. (1992) reached a different conclusion: the 'crucial' explanatory variable in the development of democracy is the relative size and density of the industrial working class, which had most to gain from, and was most favourable to, democracy. (Their case studies reveal several exceptions to the general pattern, notably the 'agrarian democracies' of the early United States, Switzerland and Norway). They conclude that 'significant working-class strength was a necessary condition for the installation and consolidation of full democracy, but it was not a sufficient condition' (Rueschemeyer et al. 1992, 282). Among the other relevant factors are the ideologies of the groups leading working-class mobilization, and strong allies among the urban and rural middle classes.

For a number of reasons, these and other macrohistorical theories to domestic democratization cannot be applied directly to the analysis of actual and potential trends in the democratization of global politics.[22] One of those reasons is that the traditional class divisions highlighted by these theories are reflected only very weakly in a dimension that is arguably very important for the prospects of global democracy: the distinction between those holding 'cosmopolitan' identities and values and those who do not. Opinion surveys across a large number of developed and developing countries show that the degree of 'moral cosmopolitanism' and 'political cosmopolitanism' of individuals bears a very weak relationship to their income and education (Furia 2005).

---

[22] For an insightful discussion in the context of European Union democratization see Schimmelfennig (2010).

Furia notes that 'knowing a person's educational attainment and income provides only a tiny hint about whether she will be favourably disposed towards ideals of global citizenship' (348). Nor are cosmopolitan political orientations more common in richer countries than in poor countries, as the BBC poll cited above shows. A straightforward 'class analysis' of potential transition paths to global democracy is thus likely to miss important drivers of support for, and resistance to, global democratic projects.

However, macrosociological studies on domestic transitions can inspire analyses on global transitions with regard to two important elements. First, different transition paths to democracy are feasible depending on which social groups play a leadership role. Second, the success of those transition paths depends crucially on the ability of the leading group to build a broad coalition in support of the transition.[23] In other words, analysts may speculate on the various 'minimum winning coalitions'. The identification of the various relevant groups is of course crucial to such an exercise. Some of them are predominantly based in individual states, whereas others have significant transnational dimensions. Among the former, 'segmented', groups are of course governments, but also sectoral bureaucracies, parliamentarians, political parties, domestic pressure groups such as trade unions and employers' organizations and – with less capacity for collective action – various groups of voters (defined on the basis of age cohorts, economic class, education, minority status or degree of involvement in international economic or social networks). Among the transnational, 'interlinked', groups are transnational capitalists, networks of activists and NGOs, officials of international organizations, and a range of 'epistemic communities'.

On the basis of a mapping of leading groups and their allies, as well as their opponents, it could be possible to identify several paths to global democracy, as well as the shifts in material, ideational and institutional resources that could allow reformist coalitions to prevail over conservative coalitions. The following is a tentative and incomplete list of such paths.

> An *intergovernmental path*, possibly based on a government-driven reform and strengthening of the UN system, which would generate a need for democratic legitimacy that could be met by the establishment of a global parliamentary assembly and eventually the popular election of its members.

---

[23] A further important 'lesson' of domestic democratization has been stressed by Goodin (2010): *how* expansions of democratic accountability come about may be less important for the long-term prospects of democracy than the fact that, once it is expanded, accountability almost never contracts.

This path would essentially replicate what happened in the European Union (EU) (Rittberger 2005, Schimmelfennig 2010).

- A *social movement path*, where global networks of activists and civil society organizations create non-state democratic institutions (see K. Macdonald, this volume) and/or campaign successfully for the democratization of primarily intergovernmental institutions (see Tallberg and Uhlin, this volume, Uhlin 2010, Scholte 2011).
- A *labourist path*, where international labour unions lead a progressive coalition for the democratization of world governance (Boswell and Chase-Dunn 2000, 239–46; Stevis and Boswell 2008). The role of the organized working classes would parallel their historic role in promoting domestic democratization (Rueschemeyer et al. 1992).
- A *capitalist path*, where transnational business demands and obtains strengthened global governance institutions, which could then function as a focal point for democratization efforts (Boswell and Chase-Dunn 2000, 214–15).[24]
- A *functionalist path*, where democratization follows the establishment of sectoral but increasingly dense governance networks among specialized bureaucracies (Slaughter 2005).
- Even an *imperialist path*, where a dominant power institutionalizes its dominance over the rest of the world and then eventually accedes to demands for democratic representation.

Some of these paths appear incompatible with others, while others may be complementary and converging. Arguably, different paths may lead to different outcomes, although such varied outcomes may all pass the kind of 'democratic threshold' envisaged by Dahl. It could turn out to be impossible to estimate the likelihood that they will lead to successful global democratization, but researchers may well be able to assess their relative plausibility by extrapolating trends on the global distribution of various forms of power among state and non-state actors.

This is an extremely ambitious research agenda, but it would constitute a worthwhile – perhaps necessary – complement to the

---

[24] Two prominent proponents of a global parliamentary assembly note that 'many of the leading figures in world business seem to find congenial the idea that some sort of democratizing improvisation along the lines we are suggesting is necessary to make globalization politically acceptable to more of the peoples of the world' (Falk and Strauss 2003, 224). Marxist analysts such as Chimni (Chapter 12) are of course sceptical that global capitalism and genuine global democracy can be reconciled.

more prescriptively oriented approaches to global democracy that have been prevalent so far and that underpin several chapters in this volume.

REFERENCES

Archibugi, Daniele. 2008. *The Global Commonwealth of Citizens: Toward Cosmopolitan Democracy.* Princeton University Press.
BBC. 2007. 'Why Democracy? Poll commissioned by BBC'. Retrieved 8 July 2009 from: http://news.bbc.co.uk/1/shared/bsp/hi/pdfs/08_10_07_democracy.pdf
Boswell, Terry, and Christopher K. Chase-Dunn. 2000. *The Spiral of Capitalism and Socialism: Toward Global Democracy.* Boulder, CO: Lynne Rienner.
Braumoeller, Bear F., and Gary Goertz. 2002. 'Watching Your Posterior: Comment on Seawright', *Political Analysis* 10, 2: 198–203.
Brown, Chris. 2002. *Sovereignty, Rights, and Justice: International Political Theory Today.* Cambridge, UK: Polity Press.
Chase-Dunn, Christopher, Ellen Reese, Mark Herkenrath, Rebecca Giem, Erika Gutierrez, Linda Kim and Christine Petit. 2008. 'North–South Contradictions and Bridges at the World Social Forum', in Rafael Reuveny and William R. Thompson (eds.), *North and South in the World Political Economy* (pp. 341–66). Oxford, UK: Blackwell.
Churchill, Winston. 1946/1988. 'Zurich Speech, 19 September 1946', in Walter Lipgens and Wilfried Loth (eds.), *Documents on the History of European Integration: The Struggle for European Union by Political Parties and Pressure Groups in Western European Countries, 1945–1950* (pp. 662–5). Berlin, Germany: Walter de Gruyter.
Clarke, Kevin A. 2002. 'The Reverend and the Ravens: Comment on Seawright', *Political Analysis* 10, 2: 194–7.
Dahl, Robert A. 1999a. 'The Shifting Boundaries of Democratic Governments', *Social Research* 66, 3: 915–31.
    1999b. 'Can International Organizations Be Democratic? A Skeptic's View', in Ian Shapiro and Casiano Hacker-Cordón (eds.), *Democracy's Edges* (pp. 19–36). Cambridge University Press.
Diamond, Larry. 2003. '*Can the Whole World Become Democratic? Democracy, Development, and International Policies*', Paper 03–05. Irvine: Center for the Study of Democracy, University of California.
Doorenspleet, Renske. 2004. 'The Structural Context of Recent Transitions to Democracy', *European Journal of Political Research* 43, 3: 309–35.
Doyle, Michael W. 2000. 'A More Perfect Union? The Liberal Peace and the Challenge of Globalization', *Review of International Studies* 26, 5: 81–94.
Falk, Richard, and Andrew Strauss. 2003. 'The Deeper Challenges of Global Terrorism: A Democratizing Response', in Daniele Archibugi (ed.), *Debating Cosmopolitics* (pp. 203–31). London: Verso.
Fearon, James D. 2003. 'Ethnic and Cultural Diversity by Country', *Journal of Economic Growth* 8, 2: 195–222.
Furia, Peter A. 2005. 'Global Citizenship, Anyone? Cosmopolitanism, Privilege and Public Opinion', *Global Society* 19, 4: 331–60.

Geddes, Barbara. 1999. 'What Do We Know about Democratization after Twenty Years?', *Annual Review of Political Science* 2: 115–44.

Goertz, Gary. 2005. 'Necessary Condition Hypotheses as Deterministic or Probabilistic: Does it Matter?' *Qualitative Methods* 3, 1: 22–7.

2006. 'Assessing the Trivialness, Relevance, and Relative Importance of Necessary or Sufficient Conditions in Social Science', *Studies in Comparative International Development* 41, 2: 88–109.

Goodin, Robert E. 2010. 'Global Democracy: In the Beginning', *International Theory* 2, 2: 175–209.

Huntington, Samuel P. 1991. *The Third Wave: Democratization in the Late Twentieth Century.* Norman: University of Oklahoma Press.

Karl, Terry Lynn. 1990. 'Dilemmas of Democratization in Latin America', *Comparative Politics* 23, 1: 1–21.

Keohane, Robert O. 2003. 'Global Governance and Democratic Accountability', in David Held and Mathias Koenig-Archibugi (eds.), *Taming Globalization: Frontiers of Governance* (pp. 130–59). Cambridge, UK: Polity Press.

Koenig-Archibugi, Mathias. 2010. 'Is Global Democracy Possible?' *European Journal of International Relations.* Published online before print, 16 June 2010: doi: 10.1177/1354066110366056.

Linz, Juan J., and Alfred C. Stepan. 1996. *Problems of Democratic Transition and Consolidation: Southern Europe, South America, and Post-Communist Europe.* Baltimore, MD: Johns Hopkins University Press.

Lipset, Seymour Martin. 1959. 'Some Social Requisites of Democracy: Economic Development and Political Legitimacy', *American Political Science Review* 53, 1: 69–105.

Maddison, Angus. 2008. *'Historical Statistics of the World Economy: 1–2008 AD'.* Retrieved 10 October 2010 from: www.ggdc.net/MADDISON/oriindex.htm

Mahoney, James, and Richard Snyder. 1999. 'Rethinking Agency and Structure in the Study of Regime Change', *Studies in Comparative International Development* 34, 2: 3–32.

Marshall, Monty G., and Keith Jaggers. 2009 (14 February). *Polity IV Project: Political Regime Characteristics and Transitions, 1800–2007.* Dataset Users' Manual, Colorado State University.

Mill, John Stuart. 1861/1991. 'Considerations on Representative Government', in *On Liberty and Other Essays* (ed. John Gray) (pp. 203–467). Oxford University Press.

Milner, Helen. 1991. 'The Assumption of Anarchy in International Relations Theory: A Critique', *Review of International Studies* 17, 1: 67–85.

Moore, Barrington. 1966. *The Social Origins of Dictatorship and Democracy: Lord and Peasant in the Making of the Modern World.* Boston, MA: Beacon Press.

Moravcsik, Andrew. 2005. 'Is There a "Democratic Deficit" in World Politics? A Framework for Analysis', in David Held and Mathias Koenig-Archibugi (eds.), *Global Governance and Public Accountability* (pp. 219–39). Oxford, UK: Blackwell.

Munck, Gerardo L., and Carol Skalnik Leff. 1997. 'Modes of Transition and Democratization: South America and Eastern Europe in Comparative Perspective', *Comparative Politics* 29, 3: 343–62.

Munck, Gerardo L., and Jan Verkuilen. 2002. 'Conceptualizing and Measuring Democracy: Evaluating Alternative Indices', *Comparative Political Studies* 35, 1: 5–34.

Nagel, Thomas. 2005. 'The Problem of Global Justice', *Philosophy and Public Affairs* 33, 2: 113–47.

Nye, Joseph S., Jr. 2002. 'Parliament of Dreams', *WorldLink* March/April: 15–17.

O'Donnell, Guillermo, and Philippe C. Schmitter (eds.). 1986. *Transitions from Authoritarian Rule: Tentative Conclusions about Uncertain Democracies.* Baltimore, MD: Johns Hopkins University Press.

Offe, Claus. 2006. 'Is There, or Can There Be, a "European Society"?' In John Keane (ed.), *Civil Society: Berlin Perspectives* (pp. 169–88). Oxford, UK: Berghahn Books.

Ragin, Charles C. 2000. *Fuzzy-Set Social Science.* University of Chicago Press.
  2006. 'Set Relations in Social Research: Evaluating Their Consistency and Coverage', *Political Analysis* 14, 3: 291–310.
  2008. *Redesigning Social Inquiry: Fuzzy Sets and Beyond.* University of Chicago Press.

Ragin, Charles C., Kriss A. Drass and Sean Davey. 2006. *Fuzzy-Set/Qualitative Comparative Analysis 2.0.* Tucson: Department of Sociology, University of Arizona.

Rihoux, Benoît, and Charles C. Ragin (eds.). 2009. *Configurational Comparative Methods: Qualitative Comparative Analysis (QCA) and Related Techniques.* London: Sage.

Rittberger, Berthold. 2005. *Building Europe's Parliament: Democratic Representation Beyond the Nation-state.* Oxford University Press.

Rousseau, Jean-Jacques. 1756/2008. '"Abstract" and "Judgement" of the Abbé De Saint-Pierre's Project for Perpetual Peace', in Eşref Aksu (ed.), *Early Notions of Global Governance: Selected Eighteenth-Century Proposals for 'Perpetual Peace'* (pp. 95–131). Cardiff: University of Wales Press.

Rueschemeyer, Dietrich, Evelyne Huber Stephens and John D. Stephens. 1992. *Capitalist Development and Democracy.* Cambridge, UK: Polity Press.

Sambanis, Nicholas. 2004. 'What Is Civil War? Conceptual and Empirical Complexities of an Operational Definition', *Journal of Conflict Resolution* 48, 6: 814–58.

Schimmelfennig, Frank. 2010. 'The Normative Origins of Democracy in the European Union: Toward a Transformationalist Theory of Democratization', *European Political Science Review* 2, 2: 211–33.

Schmitter, Philippe C. 1999. 'The Future of Democracy: Could It Be a Matter of Scale?' *Social Research* 66, 3: 933–58.

Schneider, Carten Q., and Claudius Wagemann. 2007. *Qualitative Comparative Analysis (QCA) und Fuzzy Sets.* Opladen, Germany: Verlag Barbara Budrich.

Scholte, Jan Aart (ed.). 2011. *Building Global Democracy? Civil Society and Accountable Global Governance.* Cambridge University Press.

Seawright, Jason. 2002. 'Testing for Necessary and/or Sufficient Causation: Which Cases Are Relevant?', *Political Analysis* 10, 2: 178–93.

Shapiro, Ian. 2003. *The State of Democratic Theory*. Princeton University Press.

Slaughter, Anne-Marie. 2005. 'Disaggregated Sovereignty: Towards the Public Accountability of Global Government Networks', in David Held and Mathias Koenig-Archibugi (eds.), *Global Governance and Public Accountability* (pp. 35–66). Oxford, UK: Blackwell.

Solt, Frederik. 2009. 'Standardizing the World Income Inequality Database', *Social Science Quarterly* 90, 2: 231–42.

Stevis, Dimitris, and Terry Boswell. 2008. *Globalization and Labor: Democratizing Global Governance*. Lanham, MD: Rowman & Littlefield.

Suganami, Hidemi. 1989. *The Domestic Analogy and World Order Proposals*. Cambridge University Press.

Treier, Shawn, and Simon Jackman. 2008. 'Democracy as a Latent Variable', *American Journal of Political Science* 52, 1: 201–17.

Uhlin, Anders. 2010. 'National Democratization Theory and Global Governance: Understanding Processes of Liberalization in the Asian Development Bank'. Paper prepared for presentation at the International Studies Association Annual Convention, 16–20 February 2010, New Orleans, LA.

Wantchekon, Leonard. 2004. 'The Paradox of "Warlord" Democracy: A Theoretical Investigation', *American Political Science Review* 98, 1: 17–33.

Weiler, J.H.H. 2003. 'In Defence of the Status Quo: Europe's Constitutional Sonderweg', in J.H.H. Weiler and Marlene Wind (eds.), *European Constitutionalism Beyond the State* (pp. 7–23). Cambridge University Press.

World Bank. 2010a. 'How We Classify Countries: A Short History'. Retrieved 10 October 2010 from: http://data.worldbank.org/about/country-classifications/a-short-history

2010b. 'World Development Indicators (WDI)'. Retrieved 10 October 2010 from: http://data.worldbank.org/indicator

Zürn, Michael, and Christian Joerges (eds.). 2005. *Law and Governance in Postnational Europe: Compliance Beyond the Nation-State*. Cambridge University Press.

10 Global democracy for a partially joined-up world

Toward a multi-level system of public power and democratic governance?

Kate Macdonald

Introduction

For many people throughout the world, the ideal of democracy is now accepted – at least in principle – as the pre-eminent source of political authority and legitimacy. Accordingly, as global-level systems of power, interconnection and organized political governance have expanded in recent years, the challenge of holding the exercise of power in global politics to democratic account has attracted increasing attention. Most commentators concur that increasing the democratic accountability of those wielding power in the global domain is in principle a desirable goal, and agree with proponents of 'global democracy' that the exercise of power at a global level – beyond the jurisdictional boundaries of democratic states – frequently suffers from significant and problematic 'democratic deficits'.

Despite this widespread recognition of the need for further strengthening of democratic governance in global politics, the paucity of workable 'blueprints' for instituting democratic arrangements within the existing global order remains a key obstacle. History demonstrates that such 'blueprints' have often played a key role in interpreting, justifying and, in some cases, steering processes of institutional and ideational evolution. However, such abstractly devised reform programmes have often emerged in response to institutional developments driven in the first instance by the pragmatic experiments of 'practical men', searching for solutions to local problems of immediate importance to them.

To a significant extent, democracy in its currently recognized form has evolved in precisely this evolutionary, path-dependent manner. The much celebrated 'birth' of democratic institutions and ideals emerged as a response to an intensely local and contingent set of problems, as described by Dunn (1992):

Two thousand five hundred years ago the small Greek city state of Athens made a series of adjustments to its domestic political arrangements. The reforms of Kleisthenes were a severely local response to protracted local difficulties, not an attempt to implement a coherently thought-out general conception of the political and social good for human beings (or even just for Greeks). No contemporary of Kleisthenes could possibly have imagined that his reforms might pioneer a form of regime that would come to serve as a virtually unchallenged standard for political legitimacy for all the peoples of the world. (v)

In this chapter I review some of the normative and empirical challenges confronting contemporary pathways to global democracy, conceiving them as part of an ongoing process of historical and path-dependent institutional evolution. Accordingly, the central purpose of the chapter is to describe and interpret the democratic practices emerging in response to the rise of unaccountable corporate power within a globalizing economy, which is a contemporary problem of concentrated power and weakened accountability.

Specifically, my analysis focuses on the emergence within the global garment industry of democratic practices in the form of agendas of corporate accountability and worker empowerment. This industry provides an ideal case study for elucidating the dynamics of global democratization, since it is extensively 'globalized' through supply chains connecting some of the world's poorest and most politically marginalized workers with affluent and powerful consumer markets and corporate entities in the global north. The disparities of power within the institutions connecting these groups generate significant accountability deficits, since the workers have few channels for exercising democratic control over the corporate actors wielding decision-making power over important dimensions of their lives. The resulting imperative to achieve democratic accountability within this industry has been asserted in recent years by political coalitions of non-state actors, who have promoted 'stakeholder empowerment' and 'corporate accountability' as means of placing democratic constraints on the exercise of corporate power. My empirical analysis of this case draws on field research conducted in 2003–5, including around 150 interviews with key stakeholders and decision makers within garment supply chains reaching from Nicaraguan factories to consumer markets in the US and to investors and civil society activists in the US, Europe and east Asia.[1]

---

[1] The Nicaragua-based garment supply chain is characterized by factories that are predominantly financed and controlled by Taiwanese, US and Korean capital, and export almost exclusively to US consumer markets (Centro de Exportaciones e

Drawing on evidence from this empirical case study, I track the evolution of these emerging global democratic practices, and interpret and assess their implications in relation to two central questions, the first of which is descriptive and interpretive: what kinds of global democracy models do these pragmatic and iterative responses to this problem appear to be leading towards (see also Archibugi et al. and Marchetti, both this volume)? The second question is evaluative: how institutionally effective and normatively justified are the emerging democratic practices, as judged by their capacity to promote core democratic functions and goals (see also T. Macdonald, this volume)? My responses to these questions are intended to provide clearer understanding of existing trends towards global democratization, in terms of both their demonstrated achievements and limits, and their ongoing feasibility and justification.

I work throughout with a 'non-institutionally specific' understanding of democracy (Macdonald and Macdonald 2006). On this definition, democracy is not defined with reference to specific institutional forms or practices such as regular elections, but rather in relation to core *democratic purposes and functions*. From this perspective, the legitimacy conferred by democratic institutions is derived from their capacity to promote these purposes and perform these functions, rather than from any intrinsic value embodied in particular institutional mechanisms. Working with such a definition requires specification of the central normative function of democracy. I take *autonomy* and *equality* to be the core values that democratic institutions should promote. Democracy can therefore be substantively defined as a system that gives institutional expression to the fundamental democratic values of individual autonomy and equality (Held 1998, T. Macdonald 2008 and this volume).

Working with this understanding of democracy, I argue that the progressive democratization of power within certain sectors of the global economy is already producing significant forms of democratic institution-building. Such democratization is shown to be emerging from the creation of systems of direct democratic accountability which 'track' existing transnational systems of organized power. These are helping to restore democratic principles within transnational economic systems, despite both their important functional weaknesses and the tendency for a pluralist system of global democracy to generate problematic patterns of political (in)equality between different groups of democratic stakeholders.

Inversiones de Nicaragua 2001). This case study is presented here for illustrative purposes only; similar arguments could be made with respect to many other production sites in the global garment industry.

I develop this overarching argument in four stages. First, I document the ways in which democratic deficits are emerging within global production systems as transnational systems of power extend beyond the boundaries of territorially delimited institutions of democratic governance. Second, I show that pluralist mechanisms of democratic accountability are already being constructed, and identify some of the most significant implications for democratic control and equality. Third, I highlight some functional limitations that currently constrain these emerging democratic institutions, but argue that most such weaknesses could, at least theoretically, be rectified within the terms of a pluralist institutional model. Fourth, I explore some of the challenges to political equality presented by pluralist processes of institution-building, since significant discrepancies in democratic empowerment appear to be emerging between stakeholder groups.

Despite the identified challenges to a pluralist model of global democracy, I conclude by defending the potential for such a model to develop in ways that are both institutionally feasible and normatively defensible, and address the concerns of sceptics such as Thomas Christiano (this volume). Moreover, at least judging by current trajectories of institutional and normative transformation, such a model appears considerably less utopian than many non-pluralist democratic blueprints, such as the one defended by Marchetti (this volume).

Transnational power and an emerging democratic deficit

The emerging democratic practices on which this chapter focuses need to be understood against the backdrop of an emerging democratic deficit. Many observers of contemporary global governance and democracy have suggested that such deficits result from a disjuncture between territorially bounded systems of democratic governance on the one hand, and transnational systems of power and interconnection on the other (Held 1995, Rodrik 2000, Scholte 2000). Such a disjuncture is clearly evident within the transnational institutions through which production in the global garment industry is organized and governed.

Decision-making power within this industry's production structures is currently distributed through 'buyer-driven production chains', in which power to control production processes is skewed towards those brands and retailers that control marketing and design activities. Within these buyer-driven chains, the control of northern brands and retailers over strategic marketing and design activities enables them to wield extensive power over decision making throughout the global chain

(Gereffi et al. 2005). We can therefore characterize the power exercised by these northern corporate entities over poor and relatively powerless workers in the global south as 'public power', in the sense that the impacts of corporate decisions often have significant implications for workers' living conditions and available life choices.

While these forms of transnational power can easily be traced to particular agents, in some important respects the control of identifiable decision makers over the core well-being of others is *structurally constrained or diffused*. Control is diffused 'vertically' between actors within supply chains, although the extent of such diffusion varies between individual chains depending on the relative power of particular buyers, intermediaries and producers. Control is also diffused 'horizontally' across a broad range of decision makers beyond the supply chain, including some actors participating in global markets and some integrated within social, labour and market relations at production sites. Such structurally diffused patterns of transnational power and interconnection exert important influence over dimensions of core well-being related to issues such as 'poverty wages' and wider patterns of unemployment and exclusion, all of which are structurally reproduced via complex dynamics, both local and transnational in origin.

Taken as a whole, this industry's transnational configurations of autonomy-limiting power and interconnection can be characterized as multi-level or 'pluralist' in structure, in the sense that control over important dimensions of worker autonomy is diffused among a heterogenous and decentralized range of actors and institutional forms.

Simply the existence of autonomy-limiting relations of power and interconnection over transnational scope would not in itself be sufficient to establish the existence of a democratic deficit, since territorially bounded democratic governance should in theory be able to constrain and govern such external sources of power. In practice, however, the way in which the Nicaraguan economy is integrated within a global production system substantially constrains the capacity of the Nicaraguan government to discharge its designated responsibilities for governing such corporate power via national-level democratic processes.

Nicaragua's constitution and labour laws codify extensive safeguards of working conditions and other entitlements of workers (CENIDH 2003), but the Nicaraguan government's performance in monitoring and enforcing these rules has demonstrated significant weaknesses. The main proximate cause of such ineffectiveness is inadequate resources and penalties available to inspectors within the Ministry of Labour. According to the ministry's own records, they carried out only 75 inspections in the country's 62 free-trade-zone factories over a period of 4 years, despite rules requiring periodic visits (CENIDH 2003). The penalties themselves are also very weak, with the maximum fine payable by companies violating the labour laws being only 10,000 cordobas (approximately US$630 in 2004). This absence of strong coercive mechanisms dilutes the impact of the enforcement regime, even in cases where penalties are imposed.

However, the weakness of such regulatory regimes is in turn attributable to direct pressures placed on governments by investors, who enjoy considerable mobility with respect to production locations due to the labour-intensive nature of assembly production, and who openly express their preference for investing in countries where labour legislation will not cause them 'problems'.[2] Such pressure from investors is exerted upon host governments not only in relation to the overall legislative framework of the labour law, but also in the context of specific labour disputes. While many of the smaller single-enterprise investors operating in Nicaragua's free trade zones engage only rarely in direct forms of political engagement with the Nicaraguan government, there are many examples of larger firms explicitly wielding such forms of power.[3]

As a result, while the Nicaraguan government is almost exclusively assigned public responsibility to govern and regulate the impact of transnational corporate decision making on workers, effectively it is unable to govern such transnational decision-making systems. Consequently, there is a significant disjuncture between territorially bounded systems of national democratic governance and transnational systems of corporate power.

Consequences for democratic autonomy and equality: identifying democratic deficits and democratic stakeholders

The autonomy-limiting impacts of these transnational systems of corporate power are experienced most directly and intensively by workers, whose 'vital interests' as well as broader 'life chances' (Held 2004) are affected in multiple ways.

A key complaint of workers is that their wages fail to cover the basic cost of living – a claim that is unambiguously supported by official estimates for a basic basket of goods. With regard to health and safety,

---

[2] Interview by the author at Nien Hsing head office, Taipei, 10 March 2004.
[3] The role of Lucas Wong from the Nien Hsing group is referred to repeatedly by many observers, but there are also examples of US (and to a lesser extent Korean) firms engaging in such forms of dialogue and pressure.

common problems described by workers relate not only to immediately obvious dangers, but also to both poorly designed work environments (in interaction with long working hours) and poor hygiene, particularly in the bathrooms and eating areas. Other problems and deprivations commonly reported by workers relate to a broad range of variables affecting their personal and political agency within the workplace. These problems include discrimination in hiring and firing, denial of access to personal and medical leave, denial of sufficient time to go to the bathroom and to eat, compulsory overtime, excessive pressure regarding levels of work intensity, and general mistreatment by company managers and supervisors, most commonly in the form of verbal abuse, but also in some cases involving physical or sexual abuse.

From this viewpoint, corporate decision makers may be identified as primary agents of public power within the global garment industry, while the workers within these production structures may be identified as key democratic stakeholders with entitlements to hold these corporate 'principals' to account within democratic accountability relationships. And to the extent that those exercising autonomy-limiting forms of power are able systematically to escape democratic accountability, a global democratic deficit can be identified.

At least in theory, workers are not the only category of democratic stakeholder in these transnational systems of power. Throughout the supply chains (in both production facilities and brands and retailers), firm managers and shareholders have a stake in these systems of power and interconnection of kinds argued to have what Held (2004) classifies as a 'medium' impact on their autonomy (affecting the quality of their 'life chances'). The autonomy of consumers may be similarly classified as affected 'weakly' (affecting their lifestyle choices).[4] Taking into account all these possible channels and dimensions of effects, hundreds of millions of people across the globe may be affected to varying degrees by these transnational systems of corporate decision making.

Nevertheless, democratic obligations to these broader categories of stakeholders have not so far been recognized, and corresponding institutional mechanisms of democratic accountability have not been created.[5] This could be interpreted to suggest that the threshold for

[4] To this extent such actors could be regarded as both stakeholders and agents of public power.
[5] This is not to deny that other stakeholder groups frequently have legitimate claims to other (non-democratic) forms of accountability, many of which are already institutionalized via conventional structures of corporate governance and underlying systems of corporate law.

identifying democratic stakeholders is currently being drawn at the level of 'strong' forms of autonomy limitation, with implications only for 'vital interests and needs'. Within this threshold, workers remain the only category of stakeholder to whom democratic entitlements have been recognized and at least partially extended. I discuss some of the problematic features of existing patterns of stakeholder identification below; in the following sections, I simply take workers to be the only recognized class of democratic stakeholder, and examine those mechanisms of democratic accountability that emerge on this basis.

The democratic response: a plural system of democratic accountability

The plural, decentralized configurations of democratically unaccountable transnational power described above support better understanding of correspondingly plural systems of democratic institution-building. As Nagel (2005) reminds us:

> In thinking about the future, we should keep in mind that political power is rarely created as a result of demands for legitimacy, and that there is little reason to think that things will be different in this [contemporary, global] case ... First there is the concentration of power; then, gradually, there grows a demand for consideration of the interests of the governed, and for giving them a greater voice in the exercise of power. (145)

Viewed from this perspective, processes of democratic institution-building within global supply chains can be seen as *responses* to the transnational systems of corporate power identified above. The creation of new non-state systems of *democratic accountability* therefore operates *directly* to democratize pluralist configurations of transnational corporate power.

Such direct mechanisms of democratic accountability are emerging from sustained activist campaigns designed to promote 'corporate accountability' in the global garment sector. Major initiatives driving such changes have included 'anti-sweatshop' campaigns targeting high-profile brands and retailers; factory-based 'international solidarity campaigns' in support of local worker struggles; and retailer and brand-based 'codes of conduct', with the latter emerging largely in response to persistent campaigning. Taken together, these various initiatives have promoted the construction of stronger mechanisms of corporate accountability within this industry, through which stakeholders can exert new forms of control over corporate decision makers. As described below, such mechanisms are increasing the exercise of democratic control over public decision-making processes within transnational supply chains. To the extent that these mechanisms resulted from campaigns organized by transnational activists, they illustrate a contribution to global democratization that parallels and complements the impact of civil society actors on global governance institutions described by Tallberg and Uhlin (this volume).

Before further detailing this empirical case, I briefly elucidate the term 'democratic accountability'. In general terms, 'accountability' can be defined as a property of an institutionalized relationship in which the exercise of power by one set of actors is constrained subject to some requirement of *responsiveness* to those over whom their power is exercised (Keohane 2003, Newell and Bellour 2002). While accountability relationships can exist within any institutionalized relationship between the bearers and objects of power, the meaning of *democratic accountability* is more specific, relating to the ability of subjects of public power to exercise control over public decision makers in ways that are consistent with principles of political equality. Thus, democratic accountability represents a particular institutional means of regulating *power relationships* between rulers and ruled, so as to ensure that power exercised by public political agents remains *subordinate, in some significant respects*, to power wielded collectively by the 'publics' subject to it. In short, the key purpose of democratic accountability is to ensure a reasonable degree of *public control over public decision making*.

Democratic accountability can be characterized as having three distinct functional elements: transparency in the exercise of public power, collective preference formation and signalling among affected 'publics', and public enforcement. Achieving *transparency in the exercise of public power* requires transparency at two levels: in the identification of public agency and with respect to the actions and outcomes resulting from the exercise of such agency. *Collective preference formation and signalling* functions require some capacity for collective choice between stakeholders, and a means of communicating these preferences to decision makers. *Public enforcement* requires an effective sanctioning or enforcement mechanism to compel compliance with these preferences (or, ultimately, some means of disempowering public decision makers from continuing to exercise public power).

In the remainder of this section, I analyse emerging practices of democratic accountability in the global garment industry by examining the embryonic mechanisms contributing to each of the above three constitutive functions: public transparency, collective preference formation and signalling, and public enforcement.

Transparency in the exercise of public power

To enable rigorous public evaluation of the performance of those wielding public decision-making power – which is the central purpose of transparency mechanisms – it is first necessary for publics to have some knowledge of what powers are wielded, and by whom, to provide some basis on which to allocate *responsibility* for decisions. Public evaluation of public power also requires transparent disclosure of both the *outcomes* of decision-making processes (i.e., the substance of the decisions taken), and the *means* employed to enact them.

One of the most important democratic achievements of corporate accountability campaigns in the garment industry has been their promotion of transparency in the first of the above ways: identification of what powers are wielded by whom. This has been achieved by identification of the significant autonomy-limiting power wielded by major retailers and brands over workers in developing countries, and a corresponding acknowledgement of the public responsibility of corporate power-holders.

In the early 1990s, when the anti-sweatshop campaigns began to emerge, public awareness of the direct power wielded by brands and retailers over workers in the global south was very limited (Spar and Burns 2000). Activists persistently pressed the message that 'the current international economic order of trade liberalisation and economic globalisation ... places [multinational corporations] in positions of extraordinary power and equally extraordinary lack of accountability' (IRENE 2000, 1).[6] As companies initially resisted this characterization of their role – pointing to long chains of subcontracting as evidence that violations of human rights in individual factories were 'beyond their control' – activists worked through the construction of transnational networks to explicitly and publicly expose the ways in which corporations in the north exert autonomy-limiting power over workers in the south via their control of buyer-driven supply chains.[7]

One of a number of high-profile public campaigns targeting familiar consumer brands and major retailers was launched by the US-based National Labor Committee (NLC) in late 1997. The campaign targeted Walmart, K-Mart and JC Penny, and featured an 'exposé' of conditions

---

[6] Even more specifically, it was claimed that 'sweatshops are the result of corporate abuse, greed, excessive power and the lack of accountability' (National Labor Committee, 'No More Sweatshops: Campaign for the Abolition of Sweatshops and Child Labor'. Retrieved June 2004 from: www.abolishsweatshops.org).

[7] Such control of garment supply chains by large northern buyers has been documented elsewhere. See, for instance, K. Macdonald (2007).

within Nicaraguan factories that was screened on the US *Hard Copy* television programme (Elliott and Freeman 2000).[8] The NLC and its allies spent months gathering documentation: finding labels and company documents in local garbage dumps and collecting customs and shipping documents, payslips and worker testimonies (Ricker 2003, Spar and Burns 2000). Having assembled this evidence, it was then communicated to a broad 'public' in the US and Nicaragua via three episodes of *Hard Copy*, in which both the existence of corporate power and its impact on core human rights of workers were starkly illustrated (see Rosen 2004).

Communication of such images was designed to demonstrate the direct responsibility of these northern corporate actors for the public, autonomy-limiting power they wielded over Nicaraguan workers. By the end of the 1990s, companies throughout the industry had begun, at least nominally, to accept such responsibilities. Prominent reversals of public positions came from a series of high-profile brands, including both Nike and Kathy Lee Gifford – a US TV personality with her own line of clothing in Walmart (see States News Service 1996). The effects of these high-profile media exposés spread quickly throughout the garment and footwear industries, leading to public admissions of responsibility from high-ranking corporate decision makers such as the chief executive officer of Reebok, who acknowledged in 1999 that 'it is time to confront and accept responsibility for correcting the sometimes abusive conditions in [our] factories overseas'.[9]

Even more importantly for the democratic function of transparency in the exercise of public power, this recognition has been formally expressed via corporate 'codes of conduct', the establishment of which rapidly became an industry norm among major US brands and retailers during the second half of the 1990s. By adopting codes of conduct, firms have institutionalized their acknowledgement of the power and corresponding responsibility that they wield within transnational supply chains. Such codes have therefore provided a formalized framework that is capable of delineating the roles, identities and responsibilities of specific public political actors, thus enabling stakeholders to evaluate more effectively the way in which these companies exercise their public power.

---

[8] See www.sweatshopwatch.org/swatch/headlines/1997/nica_dec97.html (accessed July 2004).

[9] Paul Fireman, Reebok's chairman and chief executive officer, speaking on 18 October 1999, quoted in 'Life, Liberty and the Pursuit of Fairness', *Footwear News*, 6 March 2000.

Collective preference formation and signalling

In addition to identifying public decision makers, building an effective system of democratic accountability requires some institutional means by which democratic stakeholders can formulate 'collective' preferences regarding how public power should be wielded and then signal such preferences to relevant decision makers.

The first step requires the creation of what are generally characterized as mechanisms of 'public choice' (or 'social choice').[10] This step is particularly important given that individual workers frequently differ in their views regarding relevant decisions (such as optimal trade-offs between the maintenance of employment security versus a desire to push for higher wages and conditions), so that frequently there are conflicts *between* members of this single category of stakeholder.[11]

To the extent that workers are *equally* affected by the exercise of corporate power, conflicting preferences between workers can be legitimately resolved via familiar *aggregative* institutional mechanisms, such as the election of worker representatives together with appropriate deliberative processes. Collective choice mechanisms have operated on this basis via existing worker organizations, although the weakness and fragmentation of worker organization has often undermined the effectiveness and representative capabilities of such mechanisms. Usually, aggregative processes of decision making are complemented by deliberative processes that cut across worker organizations of different kinds.

In addition to horizontal mechanisms through which the collective preferences of relevant stakeholders can be negotiated and defined, mechanisms are required through which these preferences can be signalled to relevant power-holders. The most direct kind of signalling mechanism would *directly* link stakeholders to power wielders; codes of conduct and factory-based monitoring and remediation systems are frequently claimed to provide a mechanism whereby stakeholders can communicate directly with decision makers. However, for the majority of workers these systems are inadequate:

There is no mechanism to communicate the problems – for us the problems go through the administration, and there is no way for us to communicate with the

---

[10] Within conventional, state-bound democratic frameworks, institutions for 'public choice' usually involve some combination of mechanisms of public deliberation (through democratic 'civil society' institutions as well as through more formalized deliberative processes of various kinds) and mechanisms for aggregation of individual preferences (achieved via electoral processes of various kinds).

[11] For instance, in the case of Nicaraguan factory disputes such as that in Chentex (described below), there have been very pronounced conflicts between the two opposing union confederations, and between the unions and the influential women's organization Maria Elena Cuadra (K. Macdonald 2007).

buyers. They don't give the contact information of the brands to the workers ...
In firms where they don't comply with the standards often there is no union, so
there is no way for people to communicate their problems. (Focus group with
workers from Chentex, CTNa union, November 2004, Managua)

This failing is compounded by the tendency of the private sector
auditors monitoring code compliance in Nicaraguan factories to devote
little time to speaking directly with workers, and, even when they do this,
to conduct such interviews inside the factories where workers are afraid
to speak openly and honestly.

Given the absence of adequate means of direct communication,
signalling of worker preferences has tended to take place (if at all) via
northern *intermediaries* – for example, by 'international solidarity
campaigns'. This is a strategy in which international 'solidarity'
networks comprised of non-state actors such as labour unions and
non-governmental organizations (NGOs) are formed to support the
demands of local unions in specific factories; it offers a means by which
complaints from workers at the factory level can be communicated, via
networks of activists, to the diverse decision-making sites within global
supply chains. A good example of such a strategy is provided by the
campaign launched in 2001 in support of workers at the Taiwanese-
owned Chentex factory in Nicaragua's Las Mercedes Free Trade Zone,
with the support of both local unions and a range of labour and human
rights NGOs (K. Macdonald 2007). In Taiwan, the participating coalition of labour activists, Taiwan Solidarity for Nicaraguan Workers,
exerted pressure on the Taiwanese owner of the Chentex factory (the
Nien Hsing consortium) by protesting outside the stockmarket and at
the company's annual meeting. In Nicaragua, the Sandinista-based
Chentex union placed direct pressure on local management via widespread protests and strikes. In the US, labour campaigners organized
consumer boycotts and protests at retail outlets across the country,
directed against major clients of the Chentex factory. Coordinated,
delegitimizing signals were therefore sent directly to each major point
of decision making within the global production chain, communicating
the preferences of workers for changes in supply chain decision making
that would more adequately protect relevant elements of their autonomy.

Enforcement of collective preferences

Such signalling mechanisms are of little use unless sanctions can be
imposed on decision makers in ways that enforce responsiveness of
decision makers to collectively determined and communicated

preferences. In addition to mechanisms for public signalling of stakeholder preferences, the effective operation of democratic accountability mechanisms also requires enforcement mechanisms (either centralized or decentralized).

The anti-sweatshop campaigns undertaken by activists within this industry have deployed the communicative and coordinating capabilities of their transnational networks to construct complex webs of influence, exerting pressure at strategic nodes of decision-making power. In the short term, greater consumer awareness and concern regarding working conditions in offshore factories facilitates the strategic mobilization of consumer action as an independent coercive weapon able to be wielded in support of campaigners' demands. Such sanctioning mechanisms operate through both direct consumer boycotts and deeper processes of socialization manifested as broader reputational damage to company brands. Although these strategies can offer effective means of sanctioning corporate decision makers, the effectiveness of such strategies varies significantly between companies.

By gradually constructing institutional mechanisms that contribute to the three functional elements of democratic accountability – that is, public transparency, formulation and communication of public preferences, and public enforcement – the non-state accountability systems outlined above have contributed importantly to strengthening the democratic accountability of decision making within global garment supply chains.

Functional weaknesses within existing global democratic practices

Despite these significant achievements in building global democratic institutions, the accountability mechanisms described above have remained underdeveloped in a number of ways. A range of *functional weaknesses* undermine their capacity to strengthen the democratic control of public power within the global economy. These weaknesses undermine the extent to which emerging democratic practices can promote each of the three functional dimensions of democratic accountability identified above; such weaknesses have therefore limited the contribution of these emerging systems to the protection of democratic control and equality.

Transparency in the exercise of public power

The public power wielded by major corporate brands occupying lead positions within global supply chains is becoming increasingly transparent at the level of general role delineation, as described above. However, progress towards greater transparency regarding specific actions and impacts of corporate decision makers has been much weaker.

Workers in any given factory are often not aware of the *specific* identity of the brands for which they are producing. Even in cases where workers are able to access such information and understand its significance, the labour and human rights groups who commonly act as intermediaries in such communications do not have systematic access to information regarding factory locations, since most brands regard this information as 'proprietary' and refuse to disclose it publicly. In the conduct of particular campaigns, activists typically depend on evidence (such as clothing labels) gathered by workers at the expense of significant time and effort, and often also substantial risk to their own job security. Such means of collecting information therefore fail to fulfil the democratic requirement that information be systematically and routinely available so that it can be accessed at affordable cost.

Additionally, most workers have very limited knowledge of the content of codes or, in many cases, even the fact that they exist.[12] They also typically lack information about auditing methodologies, as well as outcomes of audits in specific factories. This makes it extremely difficult for individual workers, or organizations seeking to represent their interests, to independently verify the accuracy of reported audit findings within individual factories.

Current failings in the transparency of public political action are even more serious in relation to the *internal* decisions of relevant companies. Workers are typically given information regarding internal rules and regulations they are expected to follow (and sometimes even reasons for these), but receive little information or reason-giving in relation to other forms of 'internal' decision making. This is true even in cases where such decisions have direct implications for the realization or denial of workers' core entitlements, such as determination of the terms of contracts with buyers which have direct implications for the imposition of extended and often obligatory overtime. In cases where workers solicit such information (something that usually occurs only in rare cases where a union is present), firms tend to vigorously reject such requests, deeming the information to be 'confidential' or 'proprietary'.[13]

---

[12] Focus group with workers participating in the *Mesa Laboral* (a grouping of Sandinista affiliated unions), September 2004, Managua.

[13] This view was advanced, for example, by representatives of the Taiwanese garment sector during author interviews in Managua in November 2004.

In resisting demands for increased transparency of corporate decision making, companies explicitly invoke discourses of 'private' entitlements to label such information 'proprietary', confidential and privileged. This occurs despite the fact that such decision making impacts upon workers directly, in autonomy-limiting ways, and should therefore be considered to constitute the exercise of *public power*, as explained above. In framing such decision making within the protected realm of 'the private sphere', firms seek to defend the absence of democratic transparency with respect to the power they exercise over workers. To this extent, strengthening transparency in the exercise of public power in these private sites of decision making would entail a direct conflict with principles of proprietary rights from which discourses of 'privileged and confidential' business information are derived, and the existing liberal public–private dividing line in which these are grounded.

Collective preference formation and signalling mechanisms

Functional failings in existing non-state systems that facilitate collective choice and signalling of collective preferences are also weakening the extent to which such systems are able to promote principles of political control and political equality. Weaknesses can be observed at several levels.

First, such weaknesses are manifested 'horizontally', at the level of collective choice systems for democratic stakeholders. The primary problem here has been the weaknesses of local organization noted above, together with the absence of centralized or other systems to both incentivize and facilitate such organization. While in theory these weaknesses could be at least partly compensated via provision of centralized mechanisms corresponding with the boundaries of relevant stakeholder publics, no such initiatives have been forthcoming.

Second, weaknesses arise due to the asymmetric power relations between workers (democratic stakeholders) and the northern intermediaries who currently enable communication of workers' collective preferences. In particular, such asymmetries undermine principles of democratic equality, to the extent that power is distributed disproportionately to stakeholders with *weaker* autonomy-limiting stakes in the outcomes of public decision-making processes. Although solidarity campaigns are nominally driven from the factory level, campaign structures tend to reflect the structure of global production chains. Accordingly, the 'transnational advocacy networks' through which many of these campaigns are conducted tend themselves to embody asymmetric power relations in which it is often northern participants rather than workers themselves who play the dominant decision-making roles.[14] As a result, while the 'de-masking' and delegitimization of certain expressions of corporate power has been one of the big achievements of the sweatshop movement, such signalling has not always taken place in direct response to stakeholders, as democratic criteria require. Because networks lack a centralized or hierarchical decision-making structure, they are poorly equipped to facilitate deliberation and conflict resolution. Such forms of inequality have therefore been particularly problematic in those cases where substantively conflicting preferences between workers and network intermediaries have emerged (K. Macdonald 2007).

Third, existing collective choice mechanisms provide few means by which democratic stakeholders can exercise *control over trade-offs* between potentially competing goals (such as working conditions and employment opportunities). In a descriptive sense, this reflects the absence of any democratic process at the transnational level able to resolve trade-offs between competing goals in relation to both different constituencies and different issue areas. At a more theoretical level, this weakness of appropriately constituted coordinating capabilities can be understood as a product of the underlying absence of a constitutional structure able to articulate between different issues and governance objectives on a global scale.

States are able to perform such coordination functions by utilizing hierarchical and centralized administrative and legal structures within their territorial jurisdiction. The capacity of the state system to perform this function depends not only on centralized administrative capacities, but also on the *boundedness of state jurisdiction* and thus the containment of all relevant actors and issues within a single, articulated decision-making system.[15] Non-state supply chain accountability systems in their current form have neither of these features, and are therefore ill-equipped to perform such coordination functions. Consequently, such rule- or procedure-based coordination functions are not being effectively performed by either state or non-state actors within current supply chain governance and accountability systems. Instead, interactions among non-state initiatives (such as activist campaigns and corporate codes of conduct) and between non-state and wider

---

[14] This concentration of power in the hands of US members of the network results both from their greater ease of access to corporate headquarters and from their disproportionate access to financial resources and communication technology.

[15] By a single, articulated decision-making system I mean that it is centralized and/or constitutionalized.

state-based systems occur via decentralized, non-hierarchical dynamics, in which neither processes of deliberation nor any other norm-governed or procedure-governed mechanisms are used to determine outcomes or resolve conflict.

Enforcement mechanisms

Despite the construction of non-state systems of enforcement as described above, current forms of these have significant functional weaknesses. Whereas states are able to use legal mechanisms backed by certain coercive powers to create strong, consistent and durable enforcement mechanisms, institutions within transnational non-state governance systems typically lack these qualities. This is problematic not only from the perspective of democratic control; it also undermines principles of political equality in the limited, formal sense of a common, consistently applied set of rules, as weak enforcement mechanisms generate uneven and morally arbitrary patterns of standards enforcement.

Because non-state enforcement systems depend on market-based sanctions, their effectiveness varies substantially between companies with different organizational structures, business strategies and target consumer markets. For example, companies such as Walmart, which dominates production volumes in Nicaraguan factories, base their commercial success more on high volumes, low margins and 'everyday low prices' than on carefully constructed brand image, and are therefore much less vulnerable to such sanctioning mechanisms than are firms such as Nike. These differences limit the extent to which market-based sanctioning mechanisms can be effectively deployed to promote democratic accountability.

The excessive costs for workers of non-state enforcement mechanisms in targeted factories are also problematic, as strategies of 'naming and shaming' have frequently led to firings and even factory closures. In addition, activists do not have the resources to run these kinds of campaigns every time a problem arises in a factory. In Chentex, for instance, the campaign involved mobilization and involvement of thousands of actors over a 2 year period. To a significant extent, such mechanisms operate in practice more as implicit threats than routinized sanctioning mechanisms, making it even easier for 'laggard' firms to resist demands of stakeholders and those claiming to speak on their behalf.

Some activists have sought to redress such problems by seeking to harness or reshape existing legal instruments: some have mobilized mechanisms to enable extra-territorial litigation (e.g., the Alien Tort Law), while others have pursued mechanisms to hold 'private' actors directly accountable for 'public' implications of their activities (e.g., attempts to draw on Californian contract and business practices law to sue companies for human rights and code of conduct violations) (Cutler 1997, McBarnet et al. 2007). In this way they seek to *reconstitute* the legal obligations and entitlements of corporate actors in ways that would strengthen the ability of emerging accountability systems to promote democratic principles. In general, however, the ongoing provision of indemnities from public obligations for 'private' actors, and persistent resistance to the development of extra-territorial jurisdiction that might enable corporate decision makers to be effectively pursued across territorial dividing lines, have tended to work against such transformative efforts.[16]

Consequently, while current enforcement mechanisms have been highly effective in a number of specific and highly publicized cases, overall they fall considerably short of the requirements of democratic principles.

Functional weaknesses reflecting incomplete pathways to a pluralist model

Despite current problems, I suggest that these functional weaknesses are primarily due to the incomplete ways in which global democratic principles have been institutionalized, rather than being an intrinsic, insurmountable weakness of the evolving pluralist model of democracy itself.

Many of the weaknesses identified above have resulted from the excessive reliance of existing systems of transnational democratic accountability on *non-state mechanisms* (primarily networks and markets), which are poorly equipped to perform coordination and enforcement functions, compared with state-based alternatives. Such weaknesses have been compounded by the absence of an overarching 'constitutional' structure through which distinct systems of decision making and interaction can be coordinated; this undermines workers' capacity to *control trade-offs between different goals*. Moreover, the maintenance in most legal jurisdictions of strong confidentiality protections for corporate actors compounds the weakness of non-state accountability systems as means of facilitating transparency of public power.

---

[16] Chentex could only be sued under the Alien Tort Law because it happened to have business operations based in the United States; activists have been unable to utilize such legal instruments in their engagements with most non-US companies.

Although each of these weaknesses presents significant obstacles, each could potentially be remedied to a significant degree *within the terms* of existing pluralist institutions of democratic accountability. This could take place via the appropriate harnessing of state as well as non-state mechanisms. For illustrative purposes, several potential means of remedying such weaknesses are suggested below, though these suggestions are by no means exhaustive.

First, such weaknesses could be addressed via transnational *juridification* of redefined corporate responsibilities within emerging global democratic systems – a change that would require legal reconstitution of the public–private dividing line in some significant ways.[17] The application of (democratic) principles of public law to institutional spaces of private transactions, and to the body of private law through which they are facilitated and legitimized, would represent a shift of enormous significance; democrats would need to espouse and entrench it at multiple levels – political discourse, law and the wider social understandings in which these are grounded. Furthermore, such changes would need to be reconstituted over appropriate transnational scope; at a minimum this would mean addressing existing limits to the standing of marginalized groups within those extra-territorial jurisdictions where decision makers wielding direct forms of influence over their well-being are located. If instituted, however, such changes could significantly strengthen the capacity of these pluralist systems of democratic accountability to promote both transparency and enforcement.

Public transparency could be improved in this way via the introduction of legal obligations for companies to comply with certain mandated reporting requirements. Of particular importance would be enhanced information about factory locations and supply chain identity (together with more effective communication of this information directly to workers), to help raise workers' awareness of the specific brands and retailers exercising power over their factory working conditions. In relation to the design and administration of codes of conduct and associated programmes of monitoring and enforcement, information should be available to workers regarding the content of codes of conduct, the processes via which monitoring and audit visits occur and the outcomes of these audits. Additionally, we could, for example, imagine certain principles of public law being applied directly to contract law, via some requirement that contractual arrangements between clients and factories

---

[17] This point has much in common with arguments elsewhere advocating 'constitutionalisation' (Black 1996) or 'juridification' (McBarnet et al. 2007) of non-state governance initiatives.

with direct implications for overtime and workload demands placed subsequently upon workers be subject to similar freedom of information provisions as are currently applied in many traditional public sector sites of *administrative* decision making.[18] Transparency at all these levels would be required to enable workers to scrutinize and evaluate the appropriateness of these rules and the effectiveness of the monitoring and remediation processes designed to enforce them.

Public enforcement mechanisms could also be substantially strengthened via appropriate modification of legal mechanisms, enabling affected workers to hold retail clients *directly* accountable in law for damages suffered in the conduct of their corporate sourcing policies. In this context, changes to a range of legal instruments may be appropriate; company law, labour law, tort law, contract law and laws regarding unfair or restrictive business practices are all obvious areas in which change would probably be required (McBarnet et al. 2007).

The development of such mechanisms would require significant legal innovation across a range of jurisdictions. Reforms would need to be adopted by countries in which companies were incorporated, and/or in which they conducted retail operations. In the case of Nicaraguan workers, this would require adoption of legal reforms by governments and/or courts in the US, and potentially also in South Korea and Taiwan.

Contemplation of such forms of extra-territorial judicial authority raises important questions about the boundaries of democratic or constitutional systems in which judicial authority is legitimated. These questions are particularly challenging for pluralist institutional models in which a unified constitutional framework is absent, meaning that the kind of 'standing' authorization enabled (at least potentially) by the constitutional embedding of judicial authority is not possible. Instead, judicial authorization within a pluralist model would require some kind of more decentralized mechanism, sufficiently flexible in scope as to enable alignment with relevant transnational constituencies in any given case.

Functional weaknesses within a pluralist model could be further remedied via appropriate forms of institutional strengthening at the local level to facilitate stronger mechanisms of *public choice*. Workers' capacity to participate directly in signalling processes could be substantially improved via the adoption of monitoring procedures through which workers could

---

[18] According to such provisions, companies can be required to release to relevant public bodies 'privileged and confidential' business information with implications for public decision making, while information remains protected from wider public release subject to some kind of public interest test. See, for example, Committee on Government Reform (2003).

communicate their views to trusted organizations, in locations perceived as safe from management scrutiny. Such forms of local capacity building could also support goals of *transparency* – for example, via increased involvement of local groups in processes of monitoring and remediation, provision of ongoing worker training and relevant information within workplaces and public reporting of audit findings for *specific* factories.

Moreover, establishment of some organized means of communicating and coordinating between distinct, decentralized decision-making sites would facilitate choices about *trade-offs* between different goals via more transparent and purposively chosen processes. This would not necessarily require the creation of centralized or hierarchical institutions, but it would need some degree of 'constitutionalization' of the pluralist system, at least in the minimalist sense of formally identifying the constituent elements of the system and their normative and institutional modes of interaction (McGrew 1999, Teubner 1983, 1996, 2000).

The uneven dynamics of pluralist institution-building: a challenge to political equality?

Further challenges to a pluralist project of global democratization result from the significant *unevenness* of the processes through which pluralist institution-building appears to be unfolding. As discussed above, a concern for political equality requires democratic control over public decisions to be distributed *proportionately* to the scope or intensity of different individuals' or groups' autonomy-limiting stake in any given decision. This requires reasonably close mapping of processes through which new transnational democratic entitlements are recognized and institutionalized onto configurations of autonomy-limiting affectedness. In practice, however, there appear to be significant inconsistencies in the extent to which pluralist institution-building addresses the democratic deficits of different groups of democratic stakeholders, generating troubling patterns of political inequality between different stakeholder groups.

First, global democratic entitlements associated with the exercise of corporate power have tended to be recognized only in relation to a narrow group of stakeholders: that is, *workers participating very directly in existing relationships of transnational production*. Defining democratic stakeholders on the basis of criteria of autonomy-limiting affectedness requires complex empirical analysis of material interconnection as well as normative judgements regarding relevant thresholds of autonomy limitation at which democratic obligations are invoked. For workers in this situation, there is sufficient ambiguity to make it plausible to suggest that they constitute the only category of stakeholder whose autonomy is sufficiently affected by the exercise of corporate power to create normative obligations of democratic accountability. Nevertheless, the vital interests of groups such as those with the *potential* to be employed in this situation (some of those employed in other low-skill sectors, or currently unemployed) are also significantly affected by decision-making patterns within garment supply chains, despite (or, in some respects, because of) their lack of proximate integration into these transnational chains.

Norms of political equality demand that such groups should also be empowered to exercise appropriate shares of political control over relevant forms of corporate decision making. Yet pluralist processes of institution-building have tended to neglect such groups – neither recognizing their status as democratic stakeholders, nor building institutional mechanisms through which their democratic entitlements could be exercised. This failure of pluralist institutions to democratically empower those stakeholders who are affected in more *indirect* ways by corporate power contributes to problematic patterns of political inequality between different stakeholder groups.

This appears to reflect a broader weakness in the capacity of pluralist processes of institution-building to identify and respond to forms of corporate power that are exercised via relatively diffuse and indirect processes. Because structurally diffuse patterns of corporate power are *not* experienced 'primarily in small-scale interactions, with clearly demarcated lines of causation, among independent individual agents' (Scheffler 2001, 39; see also Young 2006), activists have often struggled to identify responsible corporate agents to whom democratic obligations can be assigned. It has therefore proved much more difficult to place effective democratic constraints on structurally diffused forms of corporate power, compared with more direct and easily traceable forms of corporate 'harm'. This has implications for determining not only which democratic stakeholders receive recognition, but also the range of corporate decisions identified as being the legitimate target of democratic accountability processes. For example, it has proven easier to assert constraints on corporate power in relation to the physical abuse of workers or directly observable health and safety violations than in relation to the more diffuse exercise of corporate power over issues such as wage-setting. As a result, workers affected by such neglected forms of corporate power are usually unable to exercise a proportionate share of control over that corporate power.

Political inequality between different groups of democratic stakeholders also appears to result from disparities in the scope and strength of democratic accountability mechanisms that are created in relation to different economic sectors and firms. To a significant extent, the success of pluralist institution-building depends on a range of factors unrelated to relevant normative criteria of autonomy-limiting affectedness. Rather, the effectiveness of institution-building in any given case is typically determined by factors such as relative market share and purchasing volumes of different companies, relative strength of the marketing mechanisms of different companies and relative strength of civil society organizations and their communicative and advocacy strategies in different industries and different territorial locations. Such factors lead political control to be distributed via morally arbitrary processes that cannot consistently promote the democratic goal of political equality.

How harshly we should judge the current processes of pluralist institution-building depends on whether we consider these problems to be primarily contingent and realistically surmountable, or as intrinsic characteristics of a pluralist model. This judgement in turn depends on the degree to which pluralist institution-building processes tend over time to cluster in path-dependent and cumulative ways (gradually/progressively reinforcing inequalities), or whether they tend to promote *diffusion* of transnational democratic institution-building to a broader range of issues and individuals. This is clearly a complex empirical question whose resolution is beyond the scope of this chapter. Nevertheless, to the extent that the diffusion of institution-building processes might outweigh path-dependent clustering effects, those who remain deeply uneasy in the face of the political inequality patterns documented above may nonetheless wish to support pluralist *pathways* of institutional transformation on the basis that such pathways represent the best of currently feasible options, and are potentially also the first step along a pathway towards increasingly progressive and cosmopolitan democratic transformation.

Conclusion: a pluralist model of global democracy for a partially joined-up world?

Taken as a whole, the above analysis outlines a pluralist institutional pathway to the widely embraced normative goal of strengthening the democratic basis on which power is exercised within global politics, which differs in a number of significant ways from other conceivable paths to global democracy mentioned by Koenig-Archibugi (this volume). The pathways towards global democratization along which we are currently advancing appear to be unfolding in accord with plural, decentred configurations of established corporate power in the global economy. Plural distributions of power in the global economy are then giving rise to a pluralist democratic response, in which paradigmatically 'private' institutional systems are being directly democratized.

Importantly, some notable advances towards development of transnational institutions of democratic accountability described above *have already been achieved*. This analysis departs from the democratic scepticism voiced by liberal scholars such as Robert Dahl (1999), Robert Keohane (2003) and Thomas Christiano (this volume). This analysis suggests instead that there are some firm grounds for optimism about prospects for establishing effective democratic governance and accountability in the global domain.

Nevertheless, this chapter has also highlighted some of the significant conceptual and institutional challenges that continue to confront those aiming to establish democratic systems of decision making within the global garment industry, and within global institutions more broadly. Emerging mechanisms of global democratic accountability remain incomplete and non-constitutionalized, undermining their current functional efficacy in spite of the potential for such weaknesses to be remedied in important ways by entrenching democratic principles within a reconfigured system of pluralist, transnational law. An even more significant challenge confronting pluralist models of global democratization is presented by the unequalizing dynamics through which pluralist democratic entitlements are being recognized and democratic accountability mechanisms created.

Those who doubt the feasibility of overcoming some of the current limitations of pluralist democracy might still be willing to endorse the current pluralist *pathway*, on the basis that it represents the least-worst solution of those currently feasible, given the lack of normative consensus around more expansive cosmopolitan obligations such as those envisaged by Marchetti (this volume), and the associated obstacles to utilizing nation-states as vehicles to enact more ambitious agendas of global democratic reform. Based on such a view, this emerging democratic system – while profoundly imperfect in many ways – at least represents a practicable means of overcoming some part of the democratic deficit that persists at the global level.

Certainly, the challenges confronting present efforts to promote pluralist processes of global democratic institution-building do not warrant abandoning the project of global democracy, as some democratic sceptics appear willing to countenance. By harnessing the democratic potentials within these emerging accountability institutions, and creatively seeking further directions for institutional innovation, it appears possible to achieve real progress along a pluralist pathway to global democracy that is both democratically legitimate and institutionally feasible.

REFERENCES

Black, Julia. 1996. 'Constitutionalising Self-Regulation', *The Modern Law Review* 59, 1: 24–55.

CENIDH. 2003. *Maquila en Nicaragua. . . ¿Una esperanza? Conflictividad laboral en la maquila: Un análisis desde la práctica de los derechos humanos.* Managua: Centro Nicaraguense de Derechos Humanos.

Centro de Exportaciones e Inversiones de Nicaragua. 2001. *Nicaragua: Situación Laboral de Zonas Francas.* Managua: Centro de Exportaciones e Inversiones Nicaragua.

Committee on Government Reform. 2003. *A Citizen's Guide on Using the Freedom of Information Act and the Privacy Act of 1974 to Request Government Records*, House of Representatives, 108th Congress, 1st Session, Report 108–72.

Cutler, Claire. 1997. 'Artifice, Ideology and Paradox: The Public/Private Distinction in International Law', *Review of International Political Economy* 4, 2: 261–85.

Dahl, Robert. 1999. 'Can International Organizations Be Democratic? A Skeptic's View', in Ian Shapiro and Casiano Hacker-Cordón (eds.), *Democracy's Edges* (pp. 19–36). Cambridge University Press.

Dunn, John. 1992. *Democracy: The Unfinished Journey, 508 BC to AD 1993.* Oxford University Press.

Elliott, Kimberly Ann, and Richard B. Freeman. 2000. 'White Hats or Don Quixotes? Human Rights Vigilantes in the Global Economy'. NBER Working Paper 8102. Available at: http://papers.nber.org/papers/W8102

Gereffi, Gary, John Humphrey and Timothy Sturgeon. 2005. 'The Governance of Global Value Chains', *Review of International Political Economy* 12, 1: 78–104.

Held, David. 1995. *Democracy and the Global Order: From the Modern State to Cosmopolitan Governance.* Cambridge, UK: Polity Press.
  1998. *Models of Democracy.* Cambridge, UK: Polity Press.
  2004. 'Democratic Accountability and Political Effectiveness from a Cosmopolitan Perspective', *Government and Opposition* 39, 2: 364–91.

IRENE. 2000. 'Controlling Corporate Wrongs: The Liability of Multinational Corporations. Legal Possibilities, Initiatives and Strategies for Civil Society'. Report of the international IRENE seminar held at the University of Warwick, UK, 20–1 March.

Keohane, Robert O. 2003. 'Global Governance and Democratic Accountability', in David Held and Mathias Koenig-Archibugi (eds.), *Taming Globalization: Frontiers of Governance* (pp. 130–59). Cambridge, UK: Polity Press.

Macdonald, Kate. 2007. 'Public Accountability within Transnational Supply Chains: A Global Agenda for Empowering Southern Workers?', in Alnoor Ebrahim and Edward Weisband (eds.), *Forging Global Accountabilities: Participation, Pluralism and Public Ethics* (pp. 252–79). Cambridge University Press.

Macdonald, Terry. 2008. *Global Stakeholder Democracy: Power and Representation Beyond Liberal States.* Oxford University Press.

Macdonald, Terry, and Kate Macdonald. 2006. 'Non-Electoral Accountability in Global Politics: Strengthening Democratic Control within the Global Garment Industry', *European Journal of International Law* 17, 1: 89–119.

McBarnet, Doreen, A. Voiculescu and Tom Campbell (eds.). 2007. *The New Corporate Accountability: Corporate Social Responsibility and the Law.* Cambridge University Press.

McGrew, Anthony G. 2000. 'Democracy Beyond Borders?', in David Held and Anthony G. McGrew (eds.), *The Global Transformations Reader: An Introduction to the Globalization Debate* (pp. 405–19). Cambridge, UK: Polity Press.

Nagel, Thomas. 2005. 'The Problem of Global Justice', *Philosophy and Public Affairs* 33, 2: 113–47.

Newell, Peter, and Shaula Bellour. 2002. 'Mapping Accountability: Origins, Contexts and Implications for Development'. IDS Working Paper 168.

Ricker, Tom. 2003. 'Network Mobilisation'. Unpublished paper.

Rodrik, Dani. 2000. 'Governance of Economic Globalisation', in Joseph S. Nye and John D. Donahue (eds.), *Governance in a Globalising World* (pp. 347–66). Washington, DC: Brookings Institution Press.

Rosen, G. 2004. 'Neediest, Greediest Sweatshop Companies Listed by National Labor Committee'. Retrieved July 2004 from: www.houstonprogressive.org/hpn/nlc-swsh.html

Scheffler, Samuel. 2001. *Boundaries and Allegiances: Problems of Justice and Responsibility in Liberal Thought.* Oxford University Press.

Scholte, Jan Aart. 2000. 'Global Civil Society', in Ngaire Woods (ed.), *The Political Economy of Globalisation* (pp. 173–201). London: Macmillan Press.

Spar, Debora, and Jennifer Burns. 2000. *Hitting the Wall: Nike and International Labor Practices.* Boston, MA: Harvard Business School.

States News Service. 1996, 2 August. 'Rep. George Miller Joins President in Effort to Stop Child Labor'.

Teubner, Gunther. 1983. 'Substantive and Reflexive Elements in Modern Law', *Law and Society Review* 17, 2: 239–86.

(ed.). 1996. *Global Law without a State.* Aldershot, UK: Dartmouth.

2000. 'Hybrid Laws: Constitutionalising Private Governance Networks', in Robert Kagan and Kenneth Winston (eds.), *Legality and Community* (pp. 311–31). California University Press.

Young, Iris Marion. 2006. 'Ideals of Democracy and Justice Extended to Transnational Interaction'. Paper presented at the conference on 'Normative and Empirical Evaluation of Global Governance', Princeton University, USA, February 16–18.

11 Civil society and global democracy
An assessment

Jonas Tallberg and Anders Uhlin

Introduction

Civil society actors are increasingly seen as holding the promise of a democratization of global governance. Rejecting confederal and federal blueprints for global democracy, such as the federal model defended by Marchetti (this volume), a number of theorists in recent years have advanced models for how to democratize existing institutional arrangements through the involvement of civil society actors. Terry Macdonald (2008) argues that 'we should embrace the prospect of a "pluralist" liberal democratic order in global politics, composed of multiple agents of public power held to account by their overlapping "stakeholder" communities' (13) (see also T. Macdonald and K. Macdonald, both this volume). In the same vein, Jan Aart Scholte (2005) submits that 'civil society associations ... offer significant possibilities to increase democratic accountability in global regulatory arrangements' (88–9), while Jens Steffek and Patrizia Nanz (2008) suggest that 'organized civil society ... has the potential to function as a "transmission belt" between a global citizenry and the institutions of global governance' (3). Other authors, such as Thomas Christiano (this volume), are more sceptical about the ability of non-governmental organizations (NGOs) to perform this role at the international level.

In this chapter, we assess the empirical viability of this normative vision, variously referred to as 'global stakeholder democracy', 'transnational democracy' and 'democratic polycentrism' (see Archibugi et al., this volume). This chapter thereby seeks to advance a new agenda on research in global democracy, informed by the ambition to explore the empirical preconditions of alternative theoretical models. We share this

This chapter draws on research conducted within the Transdemos/Transaccess group at Lund University and Stockholm University, generously funded by Riksbankens Jubileumsfond, the European Research Council and Formas. For detailed comments on an earlier version of this chapter, we thank Hans Agné, Eva Erman, Catia Gregoratti, Christer Jönsson and the editors of this volume.

ambition with recent contributions that evaluate the extent to which the conditions that once facilitated democratization at the domestic level also are present at the global level (Goodin 2010, Koenig-Archibugi 2010 and this volume). Yet we choose to proceed in an alternative way, focusing instead on *existing patterns of participation and accountability*, and their implications for the normative vision of democratic polycentrism. This is a normative vision that features relatively short-term and specific proposals for how to democratize global governance, and therefore is suitable for the kind of empirical assessment we undertake (cf. Macdonald and Marchetti 2010, 14). Drawing on primary empirical observations and secondary sources, we map the actual patterns of civil society involvement in global governance. This chapter follows up on an earlier article, outlining in principal terms the promises and pitfalls of transnational actors in the democratization of global governance (Bexell et al. 2010).

We focus our assessment on the democratic values of *participation* and *accountability*. While normative theory presents us with a range of democratic values against which empirical practices could be evaluated – including equality, rule of law and transparency – participation and accountability feature prominently both in the vision of democratic polycentrism in global governance and in traditional models of democracy, such as competitive, participatory and deliberative democracy. The participatory ideal, following the all-affected principle, is that all people significantly affected by a decision should have equal possibility to participate in its making (Dahl 1970). Hence, the more inclusive the deliberation and decision making in global governance, the more democratic it is. Accountability as an ideal entails that some actors have the right to hold other actors to a set of standards, to assess whether they have fulfilled their responsibilities in the light of these standards, and to impose sanctions if they find that these responsibilities have not been met (see also K. Macdonald, this volume). Accountability may be *internal*, in relation to the principals who have delegated authority to power-wielders, or *external*, in relation to those affected by the decisions and activities of power-wielders (Grant and Keohane 2005).

Substantively, our assessment proceeds in two steps. We begin by mapping the involvement of civil society organizations (CSOs) in global governance, exploring patterns of participation in international institutions as well as mechanisms whereby CSOs may hold states and international institutions accountable for their decisions. Yet, when assessing the potential of civil society actors to contribute to a democratization of global governance, it is essential to examine the democratic credentials of these actors as well. Hence, we proceed in a second step to examine whether civil society actors themselves live up to standards of inclusive participation and adequate accountability.

We conclude that existing procedures and practices in global governance fall short of fulfilling the normative proposals in the vision of democratic polycentrism, but may qualify as a step in a long-term process of democratization toward this vision.

Civil society and democratic polycentrism: the normative vision

In recent years, a particular vision of global democracy has become increasingly prominent in the academic debate. The starting point of this model is the observation that global governance is characterized by the involvement of a diversity of state and non-state actors in policy making. This polycentric form of global governance is not per definition more democratic than a more centralized system, but polycentrism can be democratized through the establishment of mechanisms of authorization and accountability. If powerful actors in global governance are authorized by, and become accountable to, significantly affected stakeholders, a distinct form of global democracy develops. This type of global democracy – which we along with the editors of this volume call *democratic polycentrism* – does not draw on traditional state power and avoids the global concentration of power characterizing federalist visions of global democracy.

Civil society actors, in particular, are typically believed to have the potential to contribute to the development of democratic polycentrism. NGOs, social movements and activist networks operating beyond state borders may give voice to otherwise marginalized groups and serve as transmission belts between local stakeholders and global rule-makers. Through formal and informal participation in international institutions and other global governance arrangements, civil society actors may not only contribute to a broadened participation in global policy making, but also improve the accountability of powerful global actors. CSOs may also have a more indirect democratizing effect as norm entrepreneurs spreading a norm that global policy making should be more inclusive and accountable to affected stakeholders. Moreover, the deliberative qualities of global civil society actors may contribute to the emergence of a global public sphere. In short, civil society actors play a key role in the vision of democratic polycentrism (cf. Gould 2009, Scholte 2005, 2007, 2011, Steffek and Nanz 2008).

A distinct form of democratic polycentrism, focusing on the democratic qualities of civil society and other non-state actors, is 'global stakeholder democracy' as outlined by Karin Bäckstrand (2006) and Terry MacDonald (2008 and this volume), among others. Departing from the all-affected principle, this model suggests that we need to conceptualize the people in global governance as consisting of different political communities, *demoi*, for different issues, and that individuals consequently can be members of multiple overlapping stakeholder communities. When direct stakeholder participation is not practical, authority might be transferred from stakeholders to representatives through various non-electoral mechanisms for democratic social choice and political control. Deliberation rather than voting is central to global stakeholder democracy. It is a form of democracy appropriate for various public–private partnerships including civil society and business actors as well as representatives of states and international institutions.

The promise of civil society to contribute to democratic polycentrism is not a vision limited to the academic debate. Legitimizing the expanding participation of transnational actors in international institutions in terms of democracy is common among practitioners. For instance, former United Nations (UN) Secretary-General Boutros Boutros-Ghali characterized NGOs as 'a basic form of popular representation in the present-day world', arguing that 'their participation in international organizations is, in a way, a guarantee of the political legitimacy of those international organizations' (quoted in Götz 2008, 244). The Cardoso Report, the most recent document outlining the relationship between civil society and the UN, stated categorically that 'the growing participation and influence of nonstate actors is enhancing democracy and reshaping multilateralism' (quoted in Wapner 2007, 257).

We assess this vision, focusing on issues of participation and accountability, as outlined in the introduction. While citizens may participate in local and national decision making, either indirectly through the election of representatives or directly through petitions and citizen initiatives, such mechanisms are typically absent at the global level. According to the vision of democratic polycentrism, involving CSOs in international institutions may help to reduce the resultant democratic deficit in global governance, by expanding the range of participation and offering a complementary channel for citizen influence. CSOs may help bring citizen concerns into the debate and onto the agenda. Conversely, CSOs may help raise the public's awareness of the decisions and actions of international institutions. In addition, civil society participation can open up means of influence for societal groups that often are marginalized in representative bodies. Moreover, CSOs themselves are often believed to be more inclusive than states and international institutions, providing avenues for participation of otherwise marginalized groups. Broader and more direct forms of participation are hence part of the normative vision whose empirical viability we set out to examine.

Strengthened accountability is also part of the vision of democratic polycentrism. CSOs can offer stakeholders opportunities to evaluate and sanction global decision makers. In the traditional model of international institutions, accountability is a product of member states (principals) holding international officials (agents) accountable through control mechanisms. However, this model offers no means for citizens affected by the decisions and actions of international institutions to express support or discontent. The vision of democratic polycentrism suggests that opening up international institutions to civil society actors could remedy this situation, by granting stakeholders a role in the process of securing accountability. This would entail supplementing existing forms of internal accountability with new mechanisms of external accountability. The accountability of CSOs themselves could in turn be secured through electoral mechanisms, such as elections for leadership positions within membership CSOs, and non-electoral mechanisms, such as more unconventional forms of authorization and control.

Having outlined the normative vision of how civil society can contribute to a democratization of polycentric global governance, we now turn to an assessment of the extent to which emergent patterns and practices in global governance suggest that this vision is being, or could become, realized. Our focus on international institutions can be seen as complementary to Kate Macdonald's discussion of the democratizing effect of CSOs on non-state 'institutions' such as global supply chains (this volume).

Civil society and the democratization of international institutions

Over the past two decades, international institutions to an increasing extent have created mechanisms for participation by, and accountability through, civil society actors. Yet significant variation remains in the availability, use and importance of these mechanisms, highlighting the real world challenges involved in democratizing global governance through expanded civil society involvement.

Civil society participation in international institutions

The growth in civil society participation over time effectively spans all areas of global governance. International institutions with a historical record of no or limited access have slowly and gradually opened up to civil society actors, while institutions that already had a tradition of interaction have become even more open. An absolute absence of civil society access to international institutions is today exceedingly rare, which testifies to the breadth of this transnational turn in global governance.

The UN was among the earliest post-war institutions to offer NGOs access to select bodies, notably the Economic and Social Committee (ECOSOC). Over the years, the number of NGOs with consultative status has increased dramatically, from 41 in 1948 to some 2,870 today (Wapner 2007, 258). In addition, the initial openness of ECOSOC toward civil society actors has subsequently spread to other parts of the UN system, generating a pattern where few or no UN bodies remain entirely closed to NGOs (Weiss and Gordenker 1996, Willetts 2000, 2006). Environmental treaties and negotiations constitute another area where civil society involvement has been both extensive historically and accelerating in recent years (Raustiala 1997, Betsill and Corell 2008). Summarizing data on delegation to private actors in more than 150 environmental treaties over the past century, one recent study found that the proportion of policy functions delegated to non-state actors has grown dramatically over the past 25 years (Green 2010).

Institutions that illustrate how once-closed organizations gradually have come to open up include the multilateral economic institutions. The World Bank has undergone significant change in this respect under the credo of participatory development (O'Brien et al. 2000, Pincus and Winters 2002). Whereas only 21 per cent of all World Bank funded projects involved civil society participation in 1990, this figure had risen to 72 per cent in 2006 (World Bank 2009). The World Trade Organization (WTO), traditionally hesitant to engage directly with civil society actors, nowadays invites NGOs as observers at ministerial meetings and grants private actors the right to submit legal briefs on trade disputes (Charnovitz 2000, Steffek and Ehling 2008). Its ministerial conference in 2005 was attended by more than 700 NGOs, among them faith-based organizations; business, labour and farmer associations; and human rights, environmental and development groups (WTO 2009). Even the International Monetary Fund (IMF), by far the most closed of the three economic institutions, has opened up on the margins, consulting with civil society in association with IMF summits (O'Brien et al. 2000, Scholte and Schnabel 2002).

By testifying to increasing CSO participation in global policy making, existing research offers empirical support for the notion of civil society involvement as a mechanism of democratization in global governance.

The opening up of international institutions to CSOs expands participation, establishes a complementary channel of representation of citizen concerns and ultimately improves the prospects of those being affected by global decisions to also have a stake in their formulation and implementation.

Against this positive verdict speaks a set of enduring imbalances and limitations in global governance as regards the participation of civil society. To the extent that we demand participatory opportunities, like voting in domestic political systems, to be equally distributed, applicable to most or all policy domains and potentially consequential for political outcomes, then existing empirical patterns in global governance give cause for concern.

The first concern pertains to the question of *who* gets to participate. Empirical research suggests that the participation of civil society actors is far from evenly balanced (Risse 2002, Steffek et al. 2008, Scholte 2011). In the broader category of transnational actors, economically powerful transnational corporations tend to have most access points and resources for influence. Among civil society actors, well-organized and well-funded NGOs tend to be overrepresented, whereas marginalized groups from developing countries tend to be highly underrepresented. These are patterns that appear to hold true irrespective of policy domain. Even where the conditions for formal civil society participation are particularly favourable, as in the UN process on Internet governance, over- and underrepresentation are an issue (Dany 2008). Accreditation procedures that screen and select civil society actors partly on the basis of their usefulness for the international institution in question further contribute to these patterns. But biases may also arise when accreditation procedures are not used, when the lack of transparency may hide privileged access for those civil society actors whose input is most useful to an international institution. While these patterns are most likely well known to national and international officials, it is very rare that international institutions explicitly attempt to address such biases through mechanisms or strategies designed to include more peripheral groups and actors (Kissling and Steffek 2008, 214; Scholte 2011, 317).

A second concern pertains to *where* in global governance CSOs get to participate. Broad comparisons of NGO participation in multiple policy domains point to a variegated pattern, with some domains of great political magnitude still closed off from civil society (Steffek et al. 2008, Jönsson and Tallberg 2010). One recent project, engaged in cross-policy comparison of civil society participation in more than thirty international institutions, documented significant variation across issue areas (for a summary, see Steffek 2010). This research confirmed a high level of CSO participation in environmental policy institutions and processes, such as the United Nations Environmental Programme (UNEP) and the United Nations Framework Convention on Climate Change (UNFCCC), both of which offer particularly good access for CSOs to official negotiation and decision meetings. Another policy area with extensive CSO participation is human rights, where institutions such as the Council of Europe and the Human Rights Council of the UN operate well-developed consultative arrangements and rely on civil society actors to monitor state compliance. A policy area at the other end of the spectrum is security, where the North Atlantic Treaty Organization remains closed to civil society actors in most respects, while the Organization for Security and Cooperation in Europe couples exclusion from the decision-making process with involvement in post-conflict activities. Similarly, in the field of finance, the International Monetary Fund and the Bank of International Settlements have been very reluctant to open up to transnational actors.

A third concern pertains to *when* CSOs get to participate in global governance. Existing research indicates that CSO participation is considerably more extensive in the formulation and implementation of policy, than in decision making, the politically most consequential stage of international cooperation (Steffek et al. 2008, Green 2010). Consultation at the stage of policy formulation probably constitutes the most common form of CSO participation. Most international institutions have created civil society advisory bodies, arrange civil society forums in association with summits or major conferences or have established civil society liaison officers and departments. Indeed, it appears that 'a degree of consultation with civil society has become a *sine qua non* of contemporary global governance', to quote the conclusions of a recent project, involving thirteen case studies from varying policy domains (Scholte 2011, 315). However, once we get to the stage of decision making, participation by civil society actors is exceedingly rare. While accreditation to international institutions and conferences may allow NGOs to follow negotiations, circulate papers and sometimes even address the parties, they almost never take part in formal decision making. Exceptions in this regard are the European Union (EU), where transnational parties compete for power in the European Parliament, and the International Labour Organization (ILO), where representatives of governments, employers and workers serve together on the Governing Council. Finally, civil society engagement once again becomes more frequent at the stage of policy implementation. Reliance on service NGOs for implementation tasks is particularly common in the fields of development, humanitarian relief and post-conflict management. The

UN, the World Bank and the Asian Development Bank are all examples of institutions that work extensively with CSOs as subcontractors in development projects.

A fourth and final concern pertains to *how* CSOs get to participate in global policy making. Participation at any given stage of the policy cycle may be varyingly deep or far-reaching, ranging from *passive participation* (receive policy information, observe decision making, consult on implementation) to *active participation* (invitation to present information, right to make statement in decision body and partnership in implementation) and finally *full participation* (formal agenda-setting power, right to vote and implementation of independent project). Preliminary empirical observations suggest that deep and potentially influential forms of participation are rare, while more shallow and less consequential forms of civil society involvement are more common. One recent project concluded that the approach of international institutions toward civil society actors often remains ad hoc, ritualistic and one-way (Scholte 2011, 316–18), while another project found that governments and international institutions often react to the demands of CSO involvement by only opening up at the margins (Kissling and Steffek 2008, 211). These patterns may help to explain why CSOs in some international institutions, such as the WTO, have made *decreasing* use in recent years of existing institutional possibilities for participation and influence; these shallow forms of participation are simply less effective than other strategies for the achievement of CSO goals (Casula Vifell 2010).

Civil society and accountability in global governance

Beyond participation in global policy-making processes, CSOs may help to render international institutions more democratic by strengthening accountability, supplementing existing forms of internal accountability with new mechanisms of external accountability toward stakeholders. Civil society actors may hold international institutions accountable through a number of non-electoral mechanisms, including legal redress, monitoring of commitments and policy evaluation. Empirical research suggests that these forms of external accountability mechanisms have become more common over the past two decades.

Judicial access for private parties has grown from being a central feature of a limited set of important international courts (European Court of Justice, European Court of Human Rights) to becoming a defining feature of the new generation of international courts. Nearly all new courts and tribunals created since 1990 offer direct access for individuals, NGOs or firms (Alter 2006). Examples include courts in the area of trade, such as the European Court of First Instance, the Andean Court of Justice and NAFTA arbitration panels. Where civil society actors do not enjoy the right to initiate formal complaints themselves, they sometimes enjoy the right to submit observations on cases initiated by state or supranational actors. A prominent example is WTO dispute settlement, where CSOs may submit amicus curiae briefs on cases being heard by panels and the Appellate Body.

'Fire-alarm' procedures whereby civil society actors help to *monitor state commitments* constitute an additional form of accountability mechanism. International secretariats frequently operate complaints procedures that allow private parties and organizations to bring to their attention potential infringements of regime rules. In the EU, for instance, the European Commission operates an informal procedure through which it records and examines complaints lodged by citizens, firms and NGOs (Tallberg 2002). In practice, this complaints procedure has developed into the primary source of infringement cases initiated by the Commission against non-complying states. In a similar way, the citizen submission process of the North American Agreement on Environmental Cooperation (NAAEC) permits individuals and NGOs to lodge complaints with the Secretariat against parties failing to enforce environmental law (Raustiala 2004). The area of human rights offers multiple examples of civil society monitoring as well, as individuals and NGOs typically enjoy the right to lodge complaints with the commissions associated with human rights courts, such as the Inter-American Court of Human Rights.

Civil society involvement in *policy evaluation* constitutes a third form of accountability mechanism. It is very common that CSOs on their own initiative issue reports on the performance of institutions, regimes and parties in delivering policies and meeting policy commitments. Often, such policy feedback is a central component of the advocacy work of NGOs. But, in addition, there are instances where civil society actors explicitly and formally are granted a role in policy evaluation. The Convention on the Rights of the Child is sometimes regarded as a breakthrough in this respect, embodying for the first time in a treaty a role for NGOs in providing expert advice on the implementation of the convention (Willetts 2000, 204). Yet the policy domain where this is probably most common is the environmental field, where NGOs often play an extensive role in gathering and analysing information on implementation and effects on the ground, especially in conservation regimes, such as the Convention on Trade in Endangered Species (Raustiala 1997, Green 2010).

These mechanisms suggest that external accountability to civil society actors may constructively supplement chains of internal accountability within international institutions. Yet, if we move from presence to practice, and assess the actual exercise of accountability, two concerns come to the fore. First, these mechanisms are not necessarily used by civil society actors to the extent we could expect. Second, when they are used, privileged societal interests tend to be overrepresented.

The mechanisms of judicial access, monitoring and policy evaluation are largely subject to the same problems of underutilization and unbalanced utilization. While hailed by legal and political scholars as important participatory innovations, neither the citizen submission process in the NAAEC, nor the amicus curiae procedure in the WTO, is frequently used in practice. Since it is highly time- and resource-consuming to pursue legal cases in international courts, collect information on compliance and evaluate policy effectiveness, only the best equipped CSOs can engage in such activities. Even in the EU, with homogenously high levels of socio-economic development in global comparison, variation in legal resources shapes the pattern of private litigation in the organization's courts (Conant 2002). In more heterogeneous global governance institutions, this pattern becomes even more pronounced, with an overrepresentation of well-funded and well-organized northern CSOs in the use of accountability mechanisms. As Jan Aart Scholte (2011) concludes, when summarizing the results of an ambitious comparative assessment of non-electoral accountability: 'civil society monitoring and evaluation of global governance has to date been undertaken disproportionately by actors from more advantaged countries and social circles, thus again raising the crucial democratic question of "accountability for whom?"' (319).

In sum, the empirical record to date offers both encouraging and discouraging news for advocates of democratic polycentrism. On the positive side, it is clear that one of the most profound trends in global governance in recent decades is the expansion of opportunities for civil society actors to participate and hold decision makers accountable. On the negative side, civil society involvement often remains unbalanced and circumscribed, which compromises the potential of its expansion as a democratizing process in global governance.

Democratic credentials of civil society actors

If civil society actors are increasingly important players in global governance, as demonstrated in the previous section, then questions about the democratic credentials of these actors must also be raised. CSOs which participate directly in global policy making need to have democratic legitimacy if the policy making should be deemed more democratic as a result of their involvement. Relatively few CSOs, however, have direct access to global policy making. Much more common is more diffuse civil society influence on global governance through agenda-setting and norm diffusion. Also, in those cases it is reasonable to demand some democratic credentials of the CSOs themselves. NGOs and social movements claiming to be a force for global democracy naturally have to answer questions about their own democratic qualities.

For a long time the democratic credentials of civil society actors were taken for granted or at least poorly problematized in the literature on global civil society, transnational advocacy networks and transnational social movements. However, representatives of private companies, international institutions and governments, as well as many scholars, have asked with what legitimacy CSOs claim to speak on behalf of marginalized groups. A frequently quoted example of this kind of argument is an article from *The Economist* (2000):

The increasing clout of NGOs, respectable and not so respectable, raises an important question: who elected Oxfam, or, for that matter, the League for a Revolutionary Communist International? Bodies such as these are, to varying degrees, extorting admissions of fault from law-abiding companies and changes in policy from democratically elected governments. They may claim to be acting in the interests of the people – but then so do the objects of their criticism: governments and the despised international institutions. In the West, governments and their agencies are, in the end, accountable to voters. Who holds the activists accountable? (129)

By contrast, proponents of civil society engagement in global governance still tend to portray CSOs as more or less inherently democratic. The coordinator of the EU Civil Society Contact Group 2006–9, for example, argues:

NGOs and NGO networks pay a lot of attention to making decisions in an inclusive, participatory and democratic way. European NGO networks have elected boards, working groups in which members jointly develop positions, and general assemblies where members decide on strategy, approve work programmes and elect representatives. As most European NGO networks consist of either other European networks with national and regional affiliation or themselves have members in most EU member states, the opinion and decision making process is a relatively long one in order to ensure inclusiveness and ownership of positions and decisions by members. Democracy and responsibility is at the heart of NGOs' raison d'être. (Heggli 2010, 246)

In between the very critical position reflected in the first citation and the very positive evaluation of transnational NGOs in the second, there is a growing scholarly debate on democratic legitimacy issues in a global civil society context (e.g., Van Rooy 2004, Jordan and van Tuijl 2006, Ebrahim and Weisband 2007, Brown 2008, T. MacDonald 2008, Erman and Uhlin 2010, Piewitt, Rodekamp and Steffek 2010, Raggo and Schmitz 2010, Steffek and Hahn 2010). Drawing on this literature, we examine to what extent empirical observations support the assumptions about democratic civil society actors found in much of the literature on global civil society and transnational activism, and in the vision of democratic polycentrism in particular. As in the previous section, we focus on the democratic values of participation and accountability.

Participation in civil society organizations and movements

A first question to ask is *who* participates in civil society organizations and movements. From a normative vision of participatory democracy we might wish that all *significantly affected stakeholders* – that is, people significantly affected by the activities of the civil society actor – should have an opportunity to participate in deliberation and/or decision making within the civil society actor. More specifically, it seems reasonable that the *beneficiaries* of the civil society actor – that is, people on whose behalf the civil society group claims to speak – should have a say within the organization or movement. In membership organizations we expect *members* to participate in deliberation and decision making.

Civil society actors are often believed to have less elitist features than states, international institutions and companies. They may ideally offer avenues for popular political participation by significantly affected stakeholders that are not available in other forms of organizations and institutions. It is not difficult to find examples of relatively inclusive CSOs with broad participation that may strengthen otherwise marginalized groups in society. However, an empirical assessment must also conclude that while transnational CSOs play an important role in giving voice to some marginalized groups, they do not ensure equal voice for all relevant stakeholders (Halpin and McLaverty 2010). The dominance of Western interests within many transnational CSOs has been frequently noted (e.g., Brühl 2010, Scholte 2011). Transnationally active NGOs are typically run by economically relatively well-off, Western-educated, white, heterosexual men, whereas participation by more marginalized groups is limited. Likewise, when examining participation in transnational social movements – which are generally believed to be more grassroots-oriented and less elitist than most NGOs – we often find that social hierarchies and inequalities are reproduced rather than countered (Beauzamy 2010).

Not only do many CSOs fail to provide avenues for direct participation by the people they claim to represent; in some cases they may even have a disempowering impact on their beneficiaries. If CSOs claiming to represent marginalized and disadvantaged groups describe these people as 'victims' in need of help, this might result in a further disempowerment of these groups as their own agency is not acknowledged. One example might be anti-trafficking NGOs describing prostitutes/sex workers as helpless and speechless victims. Such NGOs sometimes take fundamentally different positions on key issues compared to self-organized associations of sex workers (Hahn 2010).

Membership CSOs are typically less vulnerable to criticism against poor participation and lack of representativeness. A study of sixty transnational CSOs (Piewitt, Rodekamp and Steffek 2010) concluded that there are typically opportunities for members to participate.[1] The *forms* of participation, however, vary considerably. Members and other stakeholders can participate through some kind of electoral or other form of authorization of representatives. They can also participate in a more direct way in deliberation and decision making.

While many membership CSOs have regular elections to decision-making bodies, electoral representation is not applicable to all civil society groups. Instead of representing a well-defined constituency, many CSOs represent ideas and values (e.g., human rights, global justice) or the interests of actors that are unable to form their own interest groups (e.g., future generations, animals). In such cases, representative and participatory demands are misplaced (cf. Peruzzotti 2010). Some civil society organizations and movements which reject representative forms of democracy, have instead practised new deliberative-participatory methods, including deliberative polling, focus groups, citizen juries, science shops and electronic participation (Steffek and Ferretti 2009, 39). Development CSOs tend to facilitate stakeholder participation though methods like participatory rural appraisal and participatory learning and action (T. Macdonald 2008, 196). The large transnational NGO Oxfam allows stakeholders to participate in deliberation and decision making concerning key policy issues through stakeholder assemblies and surveys (T. Macdonald 2008, 197). The so-called global justice movement practises a number of new forms of direct and deliberative democracy. The 'social forum' is a space for political deliberation that does not aim at decision making or the development of

---

[1] The researchers interviewed representatives of sixty transnational advocacy CSOs targeting the EU, the UN and the WTO respectively. The selection included a variety of issue areas (Piewitt, Rodekamp and Steffek 2010, 12–13).

a common programme. Rather the goal is to clarify opposing positions and improve the general content of the debate. In this sense it might be seen as a pure form of deliberative democracy (Beauzamy 2010, 119).

Membership NGOs may combine mechanisms for representation with forms of direct participation. Members can participate in strategic decision making in a number of different ways, including at annual meetings, through participation in issue-specific committees and through member surveys etc. (Piewitt, Rodekamp and Steffek 2010, 23). Hence, there are many forms of direct and indirect participation practised within civil society organizations and movements. However, this does not mean equal participation of all stakeholders.

Accountability of civil society actors

It is far from clear *to whom* civil society actors should be accountable. Referring to external accountability, the all-affected principle demands that civil society actors, like other politically influential actors, should be accountable to all *significantly affected stakeholders*. In practice it is often difficult to establish exactly who is significantly affected by the activities of a certain CSO. One way of treating the accountability problem is to argue that a civil society actor should be accountable to its *beneficiaries* – that is, the people on whose behalf the civil society organization or movement claims to speak. Internal accountability may apply if the CSO is based on formal membership, in which case it is natural to demand accountability to the *members*. Finally, most civil society actors rely on funding from different public and private sources, which makes accountability to the *funders* a significant issue too.

Perceptions about accountability among CSOs themselves point in somewhat different directions. Data from interviews with representatives of transnational CSOs indicate that accountability to funders is perceived to be important, whereas accountability to beneficiaries and broader stakeholder categories seems to be much more neglected. The findings on accountability to members, however, are less conclusive. A research group at Syracuse University has interviewed leaders of 152 transnational NGOs registered in the United States (Raggo and Schmitz 2010). A majority of respondents (64%) defined accountability in financial terms and 78% declared that their organization was accountable to donors. Only 9% mentioned accountability to members. Slightly less than half of the respondents (48%) claimed to be accountable to the beneficiaries of the organization (Raggo and Schmitz 2010,16–17). The importance of transnational CSO accountability to funders and the relative lack of accountability to beneficiaries are confirmed in another large comparative study. About 70% of the sixty transnational CSOs examined by Piewitt, Rodekamp and Steffek (2010) claimed that they were accountable to their members. Donors were the second most important accountability holder. Only eighteen out of the sixty CSOs mentioned beneficiaries as a category of accountability holders, indicating a common lack of transnational CSO accountability to the people these organizations claim to represent or give voice to.

Some transnational CSOs are heavily dependent on public funding (Piewitt, Rodekamp and Steffek 2010). Dependence on funding agencies may influence policy decisions within the CSOs, as demonstrated by Pallas (2010) concerning advocacy NGOs involved in the campaign focusing on the tenth replenishment of funds for the World Bank's International Development Association (IDA) between 1992 and 1995. US-based environmental advocacy NGOs forced cuts in IDA funding against the will of many development-oriented NGOs, of which several were southern-based. According to Pallas's analysis, priorities of the main funders together with the pre-existing missions of the organizations determined the policy positions espoused by the NGOs. This finding puts the accountability of these advocacy NGOs to their beneficiaries into question.

One type of transnational CSO that appears to be particularly problematic from an accountability perspective is transnational standard-setting NGOs. Examples include the International Organization for Standardization (ISO), the Worldwide Responsible Accredited Production and the Forest Stewardship Council (Bendell et al. 2010). These CSOs – or rather public–private partnerships – are business dominated and southern stakeholders are typically marginalized. ISO brings together national standards institutes that often are membership-based, consisting of companies, trade associations, specialist assessment firms and government agencies. This is a form of private rule-making through which a large number of technical standards have been established (the best-known is probably on photographic film). Nowadays, ISO also develops standards on human rights, labour rights and environmental governance. Social and environmental CSOs have directed extensive criticism against ISO, challenging its democratic credentials (Bendell et al. 2010).

Accountability can work through different mechanisms, many of which may not be related to democracy. Several conventional forms of accountability are rather technocratic and include some kind of supervision by a principal. Financial accountability, in particular, is highly formalized and includes financial reports, evaluations and audits. This is a form of accountability to which many NGOs have to devote a lot of time and resources. Electoral accountability is the main form of account-ability associated with representative democracy. Some CSOs with regu-lar election to leadership positions have this kind of democratic accountability, but, as argued above, the logic of representation through elections is hardly applicable to a majority of civil society actors.

Many CSOs create their own accountability systems (Jordan and van Tuijl 2006, Brown 2008). Examples from the global or transnational sphere include the Global Accountability Project (GAP) run by the One World Trust (http://oneworldtrust.org/), which publishes annual assess-ments of the accountability of selected international non-governmental organizations (INGOs) (as well as international organizations and trans-national corporations), and codes of conduct like the INGO Account-ability Charter, and the Code of Ethics Project initiated by the World Association of NGOs. Such voluntary arrangements may be instruments for stakeholders to hold a CSO accountable if the organization acts in a way that contradicts the principles it has committed to. Humanitarian NGOs, for instance, have developed a number of such codes and proto-cols. However, these standards are quite vague and have been drafted by the NGOs themselves in cooperation with governments and UN agen-cies, with no or little participation of other stakeholders (T. Macdonald 2008, 195). Most scholars tend to agree that self-regulation is seldom effective (Kovach 2006, 197; Heinrich et al. 2008, 334–5; Havrda and Kutílek 2010, 167–8).

Moreover, while codes of conduct are often highlighted in the litera-ture, these types of accountability mechanisms do not seem to be par-ticularly important for many transnational CSOs themselves (Piewitt, Rodekamp and Steffek 2010). When asked about accountability mech-anisms, most leaders of transnational CSOs interviewed for one of the studies referred to above mentioned audits (Raggo and Schmitz 2010, 18). In general, empirical findings indicate that traditional under-standings of accountability in terms of financial accountability are more prominent than innovative forms of stakeholder accountability high-lighted in visions of democratic polycentrism. Accountability mechan-isms in (transnational) NGOs tend to privilege powerful stakeholders, as accountability is often understood as technocratic supervision and con-trol (Kovach 2006, 197).

On balance, this evaluation of the democratic credentials of civil society actors operating in global governance generates mixed results. On the one hand, many CSOs are more inclusive and less elitist than most governments, international institutions and corporations. They feature avenues for participation and new forms of accountability mech-anisms seldom found within other types of organizations and institutions. On the other hand, most civil society actors suffer from severe democratic deficits, including non-existent, poor or unequal participation and weak accountability mechanisms, especially when it comes to empowering the weakest stakeholders and beneficiaries of the actors. Moreover, innovative forms of accountability highlighted in the theoretical literature on stakeholder democracy and NGO accountability, according to empirical observations, tend to be rather insignificant in practice.

Conclusion

In this chapter, we have sought to advance the interaction between normative and empirical approaches to the study of democracy in global governance, by assessing the empirical viability of a particular normative vision – democratic polycentrism. Starting from the theoretical premise that civil society involvement can further global democracy by expanding participation and strengthening accountability, we have explored the extent to which the empirical patterns and practices in present-day global governance lend support to this vision.

The conclusion from this assessment, we suggest, depends on whether we relate our results to global democracy as a *condition* or democratization of global governance as a long-term *process*. Clearly, existing patterns of civil society involvement in global governance fall far short of the threshold requirements that would have to be fulfilled for global democracy to be present. Participation by CSOs in global policy making is unequal, select, circumscribed and shallow, as only some civil society actors can participate, in specific issue areas, in particular policy functions and at less consequential levels of engagement. Likewise, mechanisms for external accountability toward stakeholders are typically underutilized or unequally utilized. Moreover, the actors on which we pin these hopes, CSOs, frequently have weak democratic credentials themselves, either in the shape of unequal participation by citizens or vague and insufficient mechanisms of internal accountability. The all-affected principle, which is a key component of the vision of democratic polycentrism, is very far from being realized.

Yet, if we put these patterns in the perspective of democratization in global governance as a long-term process, and focus on institutions for participation and accountability, there is some scope for cautious optimism. Some current developments in global governance are in line with what proponents of democratic polycentrism emphasize as important aspects of their normative vision. Compared to the situation three decades ago, the involvement of CSOs in global governance has undergone a profound transformation, with more citizen activism on a global scale and more venues of access to international institutions. Expanded participation and strengthened accountability can thus be seen as steps in a process of democratization, even if the current condition of global governance is far below the threshold of global democracy, according to visions of democratic polycentrism or any other theory of global democracy.

REFERENCES

Alter, Karen J. 2006. 'Private Litigants and the New International Courts', *Comparative Political Studies* 39, 1: 1–27.

Bäckstrand, Karin. 2006. 'Democratising Global Environmental Governance: Stakeholder Democracy after the World Summit on Sustainable Development', *European Journal of International Relations* 12, 4: 467–98.

Beauzamy, Brigitte. 2010. 'Transnational Social Movements and Democratic Legitimacy', in Eva Erman and Anders Uhlin (eds.), *Legitimacy Beyond the State? Re-examining the Democratic Credentials of Transnational Actors* (pp. 110–29). Basingstoke, UK: Palgrave.

Bendell, Jem, Phyllida Jay and Mark Bendell. 2010. 'These Pages Have Been Regulated for You: Issues Arising from the Governance of Markets by NGOs', in Jens Steffek and Kristina Hahn (eds.), *Evaluating Transnational NGOs: Legitimacy, Accountability, Representation* (pp. 129–56). Basingstoke, UK: Palgrave.

Betsill, Michele M., and Elisabeth Corell. 2008. *NGO Diplomacy: The Influence of Nongovernmental Organizations in International Environmental Negotiations.* Cambridge, MA: MIT Press.

Bexell, Magdalena, Jonas Tallberg and Anders Uhlin. 2010. 'Democracy in Global Governance: The Promises and Pitfalls of Transnational Actors', *Global Governance* 16, 1: 81–101.

Brown, L. David. 2008. *Creating Credibility: Legitimacy and Accountability for Transnational Civil Society.* Sterling, VA: Kumarian Press.

Brühl, Tanja. 2010. 'Representing the People? NGOs in International Negotiations', in Jens Steffek and Kristina Hahn (eds.), *Evaluating Transnational NGOs: Legitimacy, Accountability, Representation* (pp. 181–99). Basingstoke, UK: Palgrave.

Casula Vifell, Åsa. 2010. 'WTO and the Environmental Movement: On the Path to Participatory Governance?', in Christer Jönsson and Jonas Tallberg (eds.), *Transnational Actors in Global Governance: Patterns, Explanations, and Implications* (pp. 110–35). Basingstoke, UK: Palgrave.

Charnovitz, Steve. 2000. 'Opening the WTO to Nongovernmental Interests', *Fordham International Law Journal* 24: 173–216.

Conant, Lisa. 2002. *Justice Contained: Law and Politics in the European Union.* Ithaca, NY: Cornell University Press.

Dahl, Robert. 1970. *After the Revolution: Authority in Good Society.* New Haven, CT: Yale University Press.

Dany, Charlotte. 2008. 'Civil Society Participation under Most Favourable
    Conditions: Assessing the Deliberative Quality of the WSIS', in Jens Steffek,
    Claudia Kissling and Patrizia Nanz (eds.), *Civil Society Participation
    in European and Global Governance: A Cure for the Democratic Deficit?*
    (pp. 53–70). Basingstoke, UK: Palgrave.
Ebrahim, Alnoor, and Edward Weisband (eds.). 2007. *Global Accountabilities:
    Participation, Pluralism, and Public Ethics.* Cambridge University Press.
The Economist. 2000 (23 September). 'Anti-Capitalist Protests: Angry and Effective'.
Erman, Eva, and Anders Uhlin (eds.). 2010. *Legitimacy Beyond the State?
    Re-examining the Democratic Credentials of Transnational Actors.* Basingstoke,
    UK: Palgrave.
Goodin, Robert E. 2010. 'Global Democracy: In the Beginning', *International
    Theory* 2, 2: 175–209.
Götz, Norbert. 2008. 'Reframing NGOs: The Identity of an International
    Relations Non-Starter', *European Journal of International Relations* 14,
    2: 231–58.
Gould, Carol C. 2009. 'Structuring Global Democracy: Political Communities,
    Universal Human Rights, and Transnational Representation',
    Metaphilosophy 40, 1: 24–41.
Grant, Ruth W., and Robert O. Keohane. 2005. 'Accountability and Abuses of
    Power in World Politics', *American Political Science Review*, 99, 1: 29–43.
Green, Jessica F. 2010. 'Private Authority on the Rise: A Century of Delegation
    in Multilateral Environmental Agreements', in Christer Jönsson and Jonas
    Tallberg (eds.), *Transnational Actors in Global Governance: Patterns,
    Explanations, and Implications* (pp. 155–76). Basingstoke, UK: Palgrave.
Hahn, Kristina. 2010. 'NGOs' Power of Advocacy: The Construction of
    Identities in UN Counter-Human Trafficking Policies', in Jens Steffek and
    Kristina Hahn (eds.), *Evaluating Transnational NGOs: Legitimacy,
    Accountability, Representation* (pp. 220–42). Basingstoke, UK: Palgrave.
Halpin, Darren, and Peter McLaverty. 2010. 'Legitimating INGO Advocacy:
    The Case of Internal Democracies', in Jens Steffek and Kristina Hahn
    (eds.), *Evaluating Transnational NGOs: Legitimacy, Accountability,
    Representation* (pp. 55–73). Basingstoke, UK: Palgrave.
Havrda, Marek, and Petr Kutílek. 2010. 'Accountability 2.0: In Search for a
    New Approach to International Non-Governmental Organisations'
    Accountability', in Jens Steffek and Kristina Hahn (eds.), *Evaluating
    Transnational NGOs: Legitimacy, Accountability, Representation* (pp. 157–78).
    Basingstoke, UK: Palgrave.
Heggli, Regula. 2010. 'Evaluating NGOs: A Practitioner's Perspective', in Jens
    Steffek and Kristina Hahn (eds.), *Evaluating Transnational NGOs:
    Legitimacy, Accountability, Representation* (pp. 245–56). Basingstoke,
    UK: Palgrave.
Heinrich, V. Finn, Jacob M. Mati and L. David Brown. 2008. 'The Varying
    Contexts for Civil Society Accountability: Insights from a Global Analysis of
    Country-level Assessments', in V. Finn Heinrich and L. Fioramonti (eds.),
    *CIVICUS Global Survey of the State of Civil Society, Volume 2: Comparative
    Perspectives* (pp. 325–40). Bloomfield, CT: Kumarian Press.

Jönsson, Christer, and Jonas Tallberg (eds.). 2010. *Transnational Actors in Global Governance: Patterns, Explanations, and Implications*. Basingstoke, UK: Palgrave.

Jordan, Lisa, and Peter van Tuijl (eds.). 2006. *NGO Accountability. Politics, Principles and Innovations*. London: Earthscan.

Kissling, Claudia, and Jens Steffek. 2008. 'CSOs and the Democratization of International Governance: Prospects and Problems', in Jens Steffek, Claudia Kissling, and Patrizia Nanz (eds.), *Civil Society Participation in European and Global Governance: A Cure for the Democratic Deficit?* (pp. 208–18). Basingstoke, UK: Palgrave.

Koenig-Archibugi, Mathias. 2010. 'Is Global Democracy Possible?', *European Journal of International Relations*. Published online before print, 16 June 2010.

Kovach, Hetty. 2006. 'Addressing Accountability at the Global Level: The Challenges Facing International NGOs', in Lisa Jordan and Peter van Tuijl (eds.), *NGO Accountability: Politics, Principles and Innovations* (pp. 195–210). London: Earthscan.

Macdonald, Terry. 2008. *Global Stakeholder Democracy: Power and Representation Beyond Liberal States*. Oxford University Press.

Macdonald, Terry, and Raffaele Marchetti. 2010. 'Symposium on Global Democracy: Introduction', *Ethics and International Affairs* 24, 1: 13–18.

O'Brien, Robert, Anne Marie Goetz, Jan Aart Scholte and Michael Williams. 2000. *Contesting Global Governance: Multilateral Economic Institutions and Global Social Movements*. Cambridge University Press.

Pallas, Christopher L. 2010. 'Good Morals or Good Business? NGO Advocacy and the World Bank's 10th IDA', in Eva Erman and Anders Uhlin (eds.), *Legitimacy Beyond the State? Re-examining the Democratic Credentials of Transnational Actors* (pp. 85–109). Basingstoke, UK: Palgrave.

Peruzzotti, Enrique. 2010. 'Democratic Credentials or Bridging Mechanisms? Constituents, Representatives, and the Dual Politics of Democratic Representation', in Eva Erman and Anders Uhlin (eds.), *Legitimacy Beyond the State? Re-examining the Democratic Credentials of Transnational Actors* (pp. 153–72). Basingstoke, UK: Palgrave.

Piewitt, Martina, Meike Rodekamp and Jens Steffek. 2010. 'Civil Society in World Politics: How Accountable Are Transnational CSOs?'. Paper presented at the ECPR Standing Group on International Relations 7th Pan-European Conference, Stockholm.

Pincus, Jonathan R., and Jeffrey A. Winters (eds.). 2002. *Reinventing the World Bank*. Ithaca, NY: Cornell University Press.

Raggo, Paloma, and Hans Peter Schmitz. 2010. 'Governance Challenges of Transnational NGOs'. Paper presented at the Annual Meeting of the International Studies Association, New Orleans, LA, 17–21 February.

Raustiala, Kal. 1997. 'States, NGOs, and International Environmental Institutions', *International Studies Quarterly* 41, 4: 719–40.

2004. 'Police Patrols and Fire Alarms in the NAAEC', *Loyola of Los Angeles International and Comparative Law Review* 26, 3: 389–413.

Risse, Thomas. 2002. 'Transnational Actors and World Politics', in Walter Carlsnaes, Thomas Risse and Beth A. Simmons (eds.), *Handbook of International Relations* (pp. 255–74). London: Sage.

Scholte, Jan Aart. 2005. 'Civil Society and Democratically Accountable Global Governance', in David Held and Mathias Koenig-Archibugi (eds.), *Global Governance and Public Accountability* (pp. 87–109). Oxford, UK: Blackwell.

2007. 'Civil Society and the Legitimation of Global Governance'. CSGR Working Paper 223/07.

2011. 'Conclusion', in Jan Aart Scholte (ed.), *Building Global Democracy? Civil Society and Accountable Global Governance* (pp. 306–42). Cambridge University Press.

Scholte, Jan Aart, and Albrecht Schnabel (eds.). 2002. *Civil Society and Global Finance*. London: Routledge.

Steffek, Jens. 2010. 'Explaining Patterns of Transnational Participation: The Role of Policy Fields', in Christer Jönsson and Jonas Tallberg (eds.), *Transnational Actors in Global Governance: Patterns, Explanations, and Implications* (pp. 67–87). Basingstoke, UK: Palgrave.

Steffek, Jens, and Ulrike Ehling. 2008. 'Civil Society Participation at the Margins: The Case of the WTO', in Jens Steffek, Claudia Kissling and Patrizia Nanz (eds.), *Civil Society Participation in European and Global Governance: A Cure for the Democratic Deficit?* (pp. 95–115). Basingstoke, UK: Palgrave.

Steffek, Jens, and Maria Paola Ferretti. 2009. 'Accountability or "Good Decisions"? The Competing Goals of Civil Society Participation in International Governance', *Global Society* 23, 1: 37–57.

Steffek, Jens, and Kristina Hahn (eds.). 2010. *Evaluating Transnational NGOs: Legitimacy, Accountability, Representation*. Basingstoke, UK: Palgrave.

Steffek, Jens, Claudia Kissling and Patrizia Nanz (eds.). 2008. *Civil Society Participation in European and Global Governance: A Cure for the Democratic Deficit?* Basingstoke, UK: Palgrave.

Steffek, Jens, and Patrizia Nanz. 2008. 'Emergent Patterns of Civil Society Participation in Global and European Governance', in Jens Steffek, Claudia Kissling and Patrizia Nanz (eds.), *Civil Society Participation in European and Global Governance: A Cure for the Democratic Deficit?* (pp. 1–29). Basingstoke, UK: Palgrave.

Tallberg, Jonas. 2002. 'Paths to Compliance: Enforcement, Management, and the European Union', *International Organization* 56, 3: 609–43.

Van Rooy, Alison. 2004. *The Global Legitimacy Game: Civil Society, Globalization, and Protest*. Basingstoke, UK: Palgrave.

Wapner, Paul. 2007. 'Civil Society', in Thomas G. Weiss and Sam Daws (eds.), *The Oxford Handbook on the United Nations* (pp. 254–63). Oxford University Press.

Weiss, Thomas G., and Leon Gordenker (eds.). 1996. *NGOs, the UN, and Global Governance*. Boulder, CO: Lynne Rienner.

Willetts, Peter. 2000. 'From "Consultative Arrangements" to "Partnership": The Changing Status of NGOs in Diplomacy at the UN', *Global Governance* 6, 2: 191–212.

2006. 'The Cardoso Report on the UN and Civil Society: Functionalism, Global Corporatism, or Global Democracy?', *Global Governance* 3, 12: 305–24.

World Bank. 2009. 'Civil Society – Background.' Retrieved 11 November 2009 from: http://web.worldbank.org/WBSITE/EXTERNAL/TOPICS/CSO/0,contentMDK:20093161~menuPK:220423~pagePK:220503~piPK:220476~theSitePK:228717,00.html

WTO. 2009. 'NGOs Attendance to the WTO Sixth Ministerial Conference, Hong Kong, China, 13–18 December, 2005.' Retrieved 11 November 2009 from: www.wto.org/english/thewto_e/minist_e/min05_e/ngo_info_e.htm

12 Global capitalism and global democracy
Subverting the other?

B.S. Chimni

The setting: liberal versus insurgent cosmopolitanism

Marxists have long argued that bourgeois democracy is the best political shell for capitalism. The question it raises is whether an embryonic form of bourgeois democracy at the global level is more likely to facilitate global capitalism.[1] The fact that capitalism and imperialism have historically proceeded hand in hand would suggest that the creation of institutional mechanisms that take the global democracy project forward is either not possible or will assume a shape and content that only goes to legitimize imperialist globalization. The experience of the intricate and stable European Parliament (EP) shows that democracy beyond the nation-state, even if rooted in the relatively high cohesion of common values of European Union (EU) states, has a minimal welfare-bearing impact on the lives of ordinary citizens. More to the point, the creation of an EP has not transformed the external relations of Europe – that is, its approach towards the developing world; this relationship is still best defined in the language of exploitation and domination. Its consequences are manifested within the EU in the lack of a cosmopolitan outlook towards asylum seekers and migrant populations from the poor world. A principal reason for these outcomes is that the political aggregation in Europe has taken place under the guidance and influence of a transnational capitalist class (TCC) that is less concerned with configuring it for the benefit of peoples in the developing world and more towards enhancing its global influence and profits (Bourdieu 2002, Appeldoorn 2003, Stevenson 2007, Manners 2007).[2] To put it differently, bourgeois democracy in

---

[1] A crucial element of bourgeois democracy is already embodied in the international law principle of sovereign equality of states.

[2] The EU is important because 'the first international model which begins to resemble the cosmopolitan model is the European Union' (Archibugi 1998, 219). On the concept of a TCC see Robinson and Harris (2000) and Chimni (2004, 2010).

the imperial world has always tolerated exploitation and domination abroad and inhospitality to aliens within.

It can yet be argued that the creation of bourgeois democratic institutional forms on EU lines (e.g., a global people's assembly) with all its limitations will represent a step forward as the voices of the transnational oppressed classes (TOC) will have a better chance of being heard and influencing global policy making (Falk and Strauss 2001, Marchetti and Murithi, both this volume).[3] The value of the accompanying idea of reducing democracy deficit in key international institutions (such as the International Monetary Fund [IMF], World Bank and World Trade Organization [WTO]) should also not be underestimated. This has been the demand of subaltern states and groups for a long time and was initially embodied in the idea of establishing a new international economic order and more generally in the long-held demand for the democratization of international relations and institutions. It is also the goal of many initiatives coming from the 'global civil society' today, as can be seen from the claims emerging from the World Social Forum (WSF). To put it differently, the fact that a fragmented global state constituted by proliferating and powerful international institutions is already in the process of emerging makes its democratization an unavoidable practical task (Chimni 2004).

The central thesis of this chapter is that a model of insurgent cosmopolitanism, that seeks substantial changes in the economic and political structures of global capitalism, is more conducive to the promotion of global democracy. It contends that in assessing different views and proposals advanced to further global democracy five *overlapping* factors need to be foregrounded. These factors help distinguish liberal from insurgent cosmopolitanism.

First, the complex relationship between global democracy and global justice should not be neglected.[4] Global democracy will not, even in the medium term, assume the form of direct elections to a world government and/or possess powers of intervention of the EP. Incipient institutions of global democracy cannot therefore seriously address the goals of global justice, understood as constituted by the principles of recognition, redistributive justice and representation (Fraser 2009). While even a small step in strengthening the principle of representation at the global level is welcome, including in the decision-making

---

[3] For a more specific understanding of TOC see Section III, subheading 'Taking class seriously'.

[4] There are a variety of cosmopolitanisms and 'they do not all advocate forms of global citizenship or global justice' (Rumford 2007, 2).

structures of international institutions, these can become modes of legitimizing domination unless the principles of recognition and redistributive justice (on which more presently) are sought to be simultaneously realized. For each of the principles of global justice is in synergic relationship with the others (Honneth 2002, 52ff.).[5] Liberal cosmopolitanism is unfortunately more focused on the principle of representation, ignoring the principles of recognition and redistributive justice, and therefore works with a truncated notion of global democracy.

Second, pursuant to the principle of recognition it is crucial to take cognizance of 'the epistemological diversity of the world' in shaping the future of global order (Santos et al. 2007, xix). The radical heterogeneity of discourse on global futures must, in other words, be given its due (Fraser 2009, 2). Thus, for instance, non-Western visions of the future of global order will have to be given a serious hearing; an example is the writings of Sri Aurobindo on the future of humanity and the emergence of a world state (Chimni 2006). This move is not to be interpreted as suggesting the exclusion of Western emancipatory visions and strategies. On the contrary, the carp of critics is that the extant diversity in progressive thinking on global futures in Western civilization is neglected by liberal cosmopolitanism.[6] As Žižek observes, '. . . it is not enough to find new terms with which to define oneself outside of the dominant white tradition – one should go a step further and deprive the whites of the monopoly on defining their own tradition' (Žižek 2010, 120). Thus, for instance, Marxist visions of global democracy are permanently excluded as these are seen as tainted by 'actually existing socialism'. In short, there is an absence of 'global cognitive justice' in the liberal cosmopolitan tradition for it seriously engages only a singular Western tradition to the exclusion of non-Western visions of cosmopolitanism.

Third, the proposals for taking the global democracy project must consider serious changes in the global production and financial systems if it is not to represent a form of political determinism paralleling the problem of economic determinism in Marxism. Only such changes can make possible the realization of the principle of global redistributive justice. While in this respect some proponents of liberal cosmopolitanism are sceptical about the fashionable idea of corporate social

---

[5] Thus, for instance, '. . . struggles over distribution, contrary to Nancy Fraser's assumption, are themselves locked into a struggle for recognition' (Honneth 2002, 54).
[6] Likewise it has been said that '. . . even within Eurocentric normative frameworks, there is still scope for the right to difference to be affirmed, through conceptions of normality, nature, and morality that are alternative to the dominant ones' (Santos et al. 2007, xxi).

responsibility (CSR), a discourse that is not promising in terms of either globalizing democracy or democratizing globalization (Archibugi 2004, 438), they do not seriously challenge the tenets of global capitalism. While it is certainly irresponsible to argue that some fundamental transformation in the capitalist world economy should be awaited before proposing changes that advance global democracy, it is equally problematic to suggest, especially after the experience of the global financial crisis, that the cause of global democracy can be served without seeking changes in the structure of global capitalism. If we are not to be satisfied with a pale version of low intensity democracy at the global level changes must be envisaged in the workings of global capitalism.[7]

Fourth, if global democracy has to have a real chance, there must be an attempt to rethink and democratize global governance at multiple levels (global, regional, national and local). Thus, for instance, the relationship of the imperial world with the developing regions (e.g., the US with Latin America and the EU with former colonies) needs to be reimagined and redefined. Likewise, local governance – in particular, urban governance in cities (the basic spatial unit of capitalist globalization) – should invite concerted attention, as the city is where the most marginalized and oppressed sections are struggling with the adverse consequences of globalization (especially as a result of its impact on land relations and agriculture). However, liberal cosmopolitanism most often ignores inter-regional relations and has little to say on the democratic governance of cities in its discourse on global democracy.

Fifth, the discourse on global democracy should pay heed to voices of opposition and resistance to the ongoing neo-liberal capitalist globalization, especially in the global south. The resistance assumes multiple languages, forms and practices. The struggles of peoples range from the local to the global and are being waged by both old and new social movements. Local struggles often tie in with national and global networks and movements, in many instances using the Internet, to generate active debates around the idea of global democracy. However, liberal cosmopolitanism inadequately concerns itself with the growing resistance in the global south to the political economy of neo-liberal globalization, and when it does it tends to valorize new social movements

---

[7] As Santos (2002), for instance, notes: 'discussions about counter-hegemonic globalization tend to focus on social, political, and cultural initiatives, only rarely focusing on the economic ones, that is, on local/global initiatives consisting of non-capitalist production and distribution of goods and services, whether in rural or urban settings: cooperatives, mutualities, credit systems, farming of invaded land by landless peasants, sustainable water systems and fishing communities, ecological logging, etc' (210).

as against the traditional labour and peasant movements. More generally, there is a neglect of resistance movements as a result of a formal conception of global democracy.

These factors indicate certain epistemological and ontological features that contrast the model of liberal cosmopolitanism with that of insurgent cosmopolitanism (Santos 2007, 9). On the epistemological plane, insurgent cosmopolitanism embraces the idea of cognitive reciprocity which requires that the experiences of non-Western civilizations and states – in particular, the path of alternative modernity that is shaping their destiny in the post-colonial era in the matrix of global capitalism – be part of the accumulated knowledge and practices of humankind that inform social and political theories that are used to flesh out the idea of cosmopolitanism. In ontological terms, insurgent cosmopolitanism, in contrast to its liberal counterpart, takes resistance more seriously and seeks manifold changes in the structures of global capitalism, including the reframing and reconfiguration of global property rights and emphasizes that multiple democratic transformations must accompany distinct levels of global governance. In sum, the essence of insurgent cosmopolitanism is the emphasis on simultaneously creating local, regional and global democratic political structures while seeking material changes in structures of global capitalism to realize the goals of global justice arrived at on the basis of the principle of cognitive reciprocity.

This chapter proceeds to elaborate a vision of insurgent cosmopolitanism by at first offering a more systematic critique of liberal cosmopolitanism to reveal the limits of its vision to deepen global democracy and promote global justice. Second, in this backdrop, it attempts to identify and elaborate key elements of the model of insurgent cosmopolitanism. The last section of the chapter contains some final remarks.

More on liberal cosmopolitanism and its limits

Elements of bourgeois global democracy

Many Western intellectuals, including Archibugi, Falk, Habermas and Held, rightly rejecting what Beck terms 'methodological nationalism', have articulated a vision of liberal cosmopolitanism that can help strengthen the structures of democracy in the global system. Their writings embody the belief that embedding democracy (in a variety of ways) in the international system is possible without being preceded by substantive changes in the capitalist global economy and the policies and practices of international institutions that facilitate its expansion and functioning.

The proposals mooted for deepening global democracy include the following: adherence to the principle of democratic governance (or principle of free and fair elections) at the level of the nation-state; the creation of a people's assembly at the global level; the acceptance of CSR at the level of the firm; greater transparency and regulation of financial markets and institutions at the national and global levels; the implementation of an understanding of development as freedom; adherence to deliberative democracy in framing global laws; reducing the democratic deficit in international institutions, including applying the principles of 'global administrative law' to the functioning of international bodies; greater civil society engagement with national, regional and global institutions; the universal membership and effective functioning of the International Criminal Court (ICC); a more sensitive approach to the man–nature relationship to respond to the ecological crisis; a liberal migration regime, in particular for forced migrants; and adherence to the rule of law in international relations in general and acceptance of the compulsory jurisdiction of the International Court of Justice (ICJ) in particular. The realization of these goals would, in the view of the advocates of liberal cosmopolitanism, usher in a more democratic world order.

Nature and character of global capitalism

Most of these proposals are of unimpeachable integrity. But liberal cosmopolitans do not adequately acknowledge the extent to which the reform of global political structures is constrained by the economics of global imperialism. This lapse can in turn be attributed to the failure to admit the centrality of colonialism and neo-colonialism to the evolution of global capitalism and the shaping of the global political order since the sixteenth century (Anghie 2004, Mignolo 2000, 723). An essential feature of global capitalism is its inherent tendency to spatial expansion.[8] This tendency was not fully integrated into even Marx's understanding of capitalism. His analysis was 'concerned essentially with a "closed" capitalist economy' (Patnaik 1999, 77). The role of colonies was

---

[8] In a bid to show how globalization has transformed the Westphalian states system and made possible the construction of a democratic global order, liberal cosmopolitans elide over the fact that the Westphalian system always had an essential non-territorial (imperial) dimension (Rosenberg 2000, 30ff.). It is no accident that the discipline of international relations 'had its real beginnings in studies of imperialism' (Olson and Groom 1991, 47). The theme of imperialism was co-present with that of internationalism from the very beginning as it was realized that the question of global democracy could not be addressed outside the relationship of the two opposites (Long and Schmidt 2005, 1).

therefore not an integral part of the Marx's theory of capitalism (77). This fact continues to inhibit, despite the work of Rosa Luxemburg, the full appreciation of contemporary forms of imperialism (77). While Marx and Engels later condemned the destructive nature of colonialism in no uncertain terms (especially in their writings on India) this did not impact their (or for that matter Lenin's) analysis of the capitalist mode of production as a closed system (77).

It led to the neglect of the fact that capitalism and imperialism have an *internal* and not merely a contingent relationship; capitalism has therefore been from the very beginning imperialist (Patnaik 1997, 183).[9] Of course, the ensemble of economic, social and political practices that constitute imperialism experience transformation over time. What is being witnessed today is the emergence of *global imperialism*. Its distinct characteristic is that the classes that primarily profit from it are the transnational fractions of the national capitalist classes, constituting globally the TCC with *international finance capital as the central driving force* (as against a combination of industrial and finance capital in the period of high colonialism). The benefits accruing to the TCC are used to secure the support of the managerial and middle classes in the first and the third worlds (Resnick and Wolff 2006). On the other hand, as the recent global financial crisis has shown, finance-driven imperialist globalization is incompatible with the values of even embryonic forms of global democracy as there is little control of ordinary citizens, or for that matter even democratically elected governments, over the workings of international finance capital. The TOC, in particular, suffers at its hands. In fact, in recent times '... international capital has used money as one of its primary weapons against the working class; indeed ... money has become the ultimate and most sophisticated instrument for world capitalist restructuring today' (Marazzi 1995, 70).

Financial imperialism is accompanied by other forms of imperialism that involve industrial exploitation, including benefiting from the privatization of public services – in particular, water, health and education services – and the misappropriation of the natural resources of the global south. Even as the concept of development as freedom has gained momentum in recent years, most essential to the articulation of the ends of global democracy, it has run up against new and expanding structures

---

[9] This is a truth neglected even by eminent Marxist and critical writers, with grave theoretical and political consequences. Petras (2003), for instance, notes that 'reading the Miliband–Poulantzas debates [in the 1970s] on the capitalist state, one would never know that the major ideological/economic resources and institutions of the US "capitalist state" were engaged in a major imperialist war' (154).

of global capitalism (Sen 2000, Chimni 2008). Thus, the privatization and commodification of core public services like the provision of water, education and health under the influence of the TCC has meant reduced access to these services for the poor and marginal sections in the developing world. Harvey has aptly called the phenomenon 'accumulation by dispossession' as it takes place at the expense of core rights of peoples (Harvey 2003, 2005). A further example of 'accumulation by dispossession' is bio-imperialism, which involves the exploitation of the biodiversity of the global south by biotechnology multinationals (Escobar and Pardo 2007, 288). Indeed, a colonial vision of development for the global south, that is all about development 'of resources and, not of people', is in the process of displacing the idea of 'development as freedom' (Arndt 1981, 463).

The prospect of global democracy is weak also because of the impact of the changing nature of global capitalism on the world of work in the industrialized world. Negri (2006) argues that in the last decade of the twentieth century industrial labour lost its hegemony and in its place 'immaterial labor' emerged: 'there is an emergent hegemony of immaterial production compared with other forms of production', replacing 'the previous hegemony of industrial production' (127). In other words, 'labor that creates immaterial products: knowledge, information, communications, linguistic and emotional relations' is dominating the global economy (128). The hegemony is not quantitative but qualitative – that is, 'in the extent to which it has the power to transform the others' (127). While Negri is perhaps hasty in inaugurating a new global mode of production, as the size of the industrial working class continually expands in the global south, he does help explain the absence of unity among the working classes in the centres of imperialism. The interests of the new service class tend to diverge from the traditional working class. Its relatively dispersed condition also makes it more difficult to organize. This factor allows the TCC to divide the working classes and thereby curb the demand for the reform of global capitalism. Besides, both the traditional working class and the new class are potential beneficiaries of the policies of global imperialism: it leads to the creation of what Lenin called 'labour aristocracy'. The imperial state is also used to protect the working and service classes in the centres of imperialism from the adverse consequences of expanding capitalism through, among other things, instituting protectionist policies.

Finally, the discourse of social justice in global capitalism is increasingly coming to be subsumed under the idea of CSR, an idea liberal cosmopolitanism does not seriously challenge. This is troubling because CSR does not impact the fundamental values of the capitalist enterprise that 'include the right to make a profit, the universal good of free trade, the freedom of capital, the supremacy of private property, the commoditization of things including labor, the superiority of markets in determining price and value, and the privileging of companies as citizens and moral entities' (Blowfield 2005, 520). On the other hand, the idea of CSR patronizes and denies agency to the TOC; resistance to the corporatist discourse is even said to be counterproductive. What CSR implies in terms of a vision of global democracy can be seen from the attempt in the nineties by the TCC to adopt a multilateral agreement on investment that bordered on legislating the global rule by corporations (Sklair 2002, 164–8). The recent emergence of third world TNCs has resulted in key third world states (Brazil, China, India and South Africa) no longer talking about the global regulation of TNCs. This is what TCC-led globalization is all about and liberal cosmopolitans need to contest the corresponding vision encapsulated in the idea of CSR.

Emerging imperial global state and law

Such a challenge is crucial today as the global rule of corporations is also coming to be facilitated by a network of international institutions in all areas of international life – economic, social and political. An emerging global capitalist social formation, the outcome of the rapid expansion of capitalism in the era of accelerated globalization, is presided over by a nascent global state constituted by a range of international institutions that prescribe, supervise and enforce rules in the international system to further the interests of global capitalism (Chimni 2004). While the embryonic global state will be co-present with sovereign states in a long period of transition to a fully evolved global state, the nation-state has already ceded core elements of its sovereign powers to international institutions (such as the IMF, World Bank and WTO). This has meant a *loss of critical policy space* for third world countries, disabling them from adopting a range of measures that further the welfare of their people (Chimni 2004). It has led to the institutionalization of low intensity democracies in the international system as sovereign states are deprived of powers to shape independent social and economic policies. The fundamental point is that if the substantive norms that are enforced by international institutions have adverse consequences for global democracy and global justice some modest reform of institutional structures, as proposed by liberal cosmopolitans, may not help address the problem; indeed it may only go to legitimize an unequal world order. The advocates of insurgent cosmopolitanism are therefore understandably sceptical about the possibility of democratizing international institutions without transforming the policies and practices that these institutions prescribe and enforce.

Human rights and global democracy

There is much weight placed in liberal cosmopolitanism on the rapid development of international human rights law in promoting global democracy. This enthusiasm is not necessarily misplaced. The discourse of rights has helped the TOC in the global south to have their demands heard and has facilitated the mobilization of world public opinion through approaching national and international institutions concerned with the promotion and protection of human rights. But can human rights discourse 'fill the void left by socialist politics'? (Santos 2007, 3). According to Santos, it can do so 'only if a politics of human rights radically different from the hegemonic liberal one is adopted and only if such a politics is conceived as part of a broader constellation of struggles and discourses of resistance and emancipation rather than as the sole politics of resistance against oppression' (3). Santos goes on to talk of what he calls 'intercultural post-imperial human rights' that will be based on the right to knowledge ('a new epistemology from the South'), the right to bring historical capitalism to trial in a world tribunal, the right to a solidarity-oriented transformation of the right to property, the right to grant rights to entities incapable of bearing duties – namely nature and future generations – and the right to democratic self-determination (28ff.). Liberal cosmopolitanism has, however, failed to advance such an agenda.

Liberal cosmopolitans have also not paid adequate attention to the fact that the idea of new humanitarianism, or the responsibility to protect, that accompanies the rise of the language of rights was in its earlier incarnation used to legitimize colonialism (Mehta 1999, Dirks 2006). It is today being manipulated to justify unlawful armed humanitarian intervention in the global south. The idea of humanitarianism thus returns as a discursive commodity to legitimize global imperialism. The support for unilateral armed humanitarian interventions by many liberal cosmopolitans (e.g., Habermas 1999) is not acceptable to peoples of the third world. In 2000 the G-77 (constituted of 131 states) unanimously passed a resolution opposing humanitarian intervention outside the UN Charter (Chimni 2010). In short, while the developments in international human rights law, including the creation of the ICC, are welcome developments these do not always serve as instruments of global democracy. The celebrated ICC, for instance, can hardly be expected to deal with first world violations of international humanitarian laws (Anghie and Chimni 2003).

Insurgent cosmopolitanism: key elements

The alienation of structures and institutions of global governance from the lives of ordinary peoples, especially the TOC, is the dark side of the project of unification of the world by global capital (Chimni 2007). The unification process is itself an inevitable historical process. It also holds out the potential of realizing global democracy and justice. However, the ideologues of global capitalism have chosen an expedient moment in the history of global society – that is, the collapse of 'actually existing socialism' – to embrace 'endism' with the hope of preventing global social transformation (Bhaskar 2002, 57). They have relied on the mystical shell in Hegel where 'he absents the very crucial notion of absence itself' to sustain the myth of endism, for without absence there can be no social tensions and contradictions (57). The dialectical movement of history, however, does not pause or halt. Among those who believe that the end of 'actually existing socialism' opens up opportunities for furthering global democracy and justice there are a plurality of voices. Liberal cosmopolitanism is one of them. Insurgent cosmopolitanism that relies on Marxist insights is the other. It insists that the answer lies in reconfiguring the deep economic and political structures of global capitalism. This understanding can be given practical shape by accepting at least four analytical claims: (1) that the nation-state remains the primary site for undertaking progressive reforms; (2) that the project of global democracy must have a decentralized face that involves the creation of democratic urban and regional spaces; (3) that the category of class and the wider interests of TOC need to be taken seriously in institutionalizing global democracy; and (4) that the reframing of global property rights is a precondition for deepening global democracy.

Taking nation-state seriously

The nation-state retains its importance in the global democracy project as a counterpoint to the loss of policy space, especially of developing countries, to international institutions or the emerging global state. The following reasons, among others, sustain this view.

First, it is no accident that protests against global imperialism assume the form of anti-imperialist nationalism.[10] The problem today is not

---

[10] 'We need not embrace nationalism uncritically to see that nation-states still provide the context of everyday solidarities and most people's life projects; they still are the primary arenas for democratic public life; and they are focal points for resistance to imperialism' (Calhoun 2009, 227).

necessarily too much state sovereignty, as it is often made out to be, but rather its erosion (Chimni 2004). Thus, the tortuous road to global democracy and the realization of the goals of global justice lies in the retrieval of lost (especially economic) sovereignty to forces of global imperialism. In short, 'we need to be global in part through how we are national' (Calhoun 2009, 238).

Second, the absence of a thick global political culture at present means that territorial citizenship cannot be set aside and readily reconstituted at the global level (Chandler 2009, 62ff.; Erskine 2008). For, as Chandler points out, 'without a formal focal point of accountability – of government – there can be no political community; no framework binding and subordinating individuals as political subjects' (64). It will take a long time for institutions of bourgeois democracy to be sufficiently embedded at the global level to replace it at the level of the nation-state.

Third, an emerging global civil society can only play a limited role in taking the global democracy project forward. Scholte (2004) has identified four ways in which non-state actors can contribute to the democratization of global governance: 'by increasing the public transparency of global governance operations; by monitoring and reviewing global policies; by seeking redress for mistakes and harms attributable to global regulatory bodies; and by advancing the creation of formal accountability mechanisms for global governance' (217). However, empirical studies of decision-making processes in international institutions show that '... even when institutional conditions are favorable, input from civil society actors is often marginalized' (Steffek 2007, 110).[11] The civil society cannot therefore bear the burden of bringing about fundamental changes in the workings of key international institutions like the IMF, World Bank and the WTO. What will make a difference are local political struggles that coalesce at the national level, through aggregating left and democratic social forces, and compel those who represent them in the external world to undermine the growing influence of the TCC, retrieve policy space from international institutions and demand the democratization of global relations.

Democratizing cities and relations between regions

The global democracy project cannot also be taken forward without thinking about the role of its other building block – that is, cities in global governance. By the year 2030 nearly 5 billion people are expected

---

[11] Steffek reports a study of civil society participation in thirty-two international organizations and informal regimes (110).

to live in cities. Cities are thus becoming a world unto themselves and the centres from which global capitalism is reproduced. In the words of Negri (2006), the 'urban territory is the factory of postmodern accumulation, the laboratory of immaterial valorization . . .' (150). Cities are also sites of neo-liberal globalization. It is therefore in cities that alienation festers. Of course, cities also teach us how to live with strangers. But liberal cosmopolitanism does not address questions related to the governance of the city to advance the global democratic project. For example, what kind of legal and policy structures need to be put in place to make urban spaces inclusive and hospitable to all? This question is important as corporate cosmopolitanism is coming to dominate global cities. It has divided cities along class lines, introducing forms of apartheid. The answer perhaps lies in institutionalizing new forms of participatory democracy that help limit the influence of global capital on decisions that bear on the welfare of ordinary citizens. An instance is the role of participatory budgeting in promoting democratic practices in cities like Porto Allegre (Leubolt et al. 2008, 435). New forms of participatory urban democracy can be the decentralized face of global democracy.

The relationship between different regions of the world also does not gain the sustained attention of liberal cosmopolitanism. This is troubling, for if global democracy has to be advanced, inter-regional cooperation must be 'rooted in equality, social justice, and solidarity', especially vis-à-vis regions subjected to centuries of domination or colonial rule (De la Barra and Dello Buono 2009, 274). Thus, 'the reconfiguration of regional relations' remains a prerequisite for genuine progress on the global democratic front (274). The idea is the same: the need for inter-regional cooperation that 'responds better to the interests of the popular sectors within the structures of globalized capitalism' (277). Instead, today instruments like the Regional or Free Trade Agreement (FTA) are being used by the advanced capitalist world to advance the cause of global capital to the detriment of the welfare of peoples in weaker regions. The FTA is used as a vehicle for notching up standards in crucial areas like foreign investment and intellectual property rights with negative consequences for the poor and marginalized.[12] In short, the global democratic project needs to address the range of global spaces and different levels of global governance (see, on this issue, Gould, this volume).

---

[12] There are thus ongoing protests in India, organized by different segments of the civil society, against the EU–India FTA that is in the final stages of negotiations.

Taking class seriously

A problem with the socialist imaginary that informs insurgent cosmopolitanism, as liberal cosmopolitans contend, is the 'death of class'. This is not the occasion to undertake a full critique of that position but reference may be made to Archibugi's reliance on Beck to sustain the end-of-class thesis. Archibugi (2004) writes that the aim of liberal cosmopolitanism 'is not to overcome social classes, but an objective more modest but equally ambitious – offering channels of direct representation to all people at the global level, regardless of their social status. This implies basing decision-making on global issues on the preferences of a majority, rather than on those of a single class. In this vein, Ulrich Beck invoked, "Citizens of the world, unite!"' (457).

The Beck clarion call follows from his assessment that at least in the case of advanced capitalist societies, the creation of the welfare state has meant the dissolution of 'the culture of classes' (Beck 2007, 682). It has led to the 'demise of collective identities' and the emergence of individualization and thereby to what Beck terms 'capitalism without classes' (cited by Atkinson 2007, 354). As Beck puts it, 'for the first time in history, the individual rather than the class is becoming the basic unit of social reproduction' (Beck and Willms 2004, 101). But critics contend that Beck's theory and observations are not empirically grounded – that is, it is 'data free' (Atkinson 2007, 355) and that he does not appreciate the distinction between situations of individual discrimination and class subordination.[13] The latter perhaps explains why there is 'ambivalence and contradiction' in his conceptualization of 'individualization', for at times he does not think that class is being entirely effaced (Atkinson 2007, 356–7). The Beck formulation suffers from Eurocentrism as well, in as much it does not consider the fate of 'class' in the third world or in transitional economies and its implications for the culture of classes in the Western world. The underlying assumption that class can only be located in the national frame is also problematic for there is no reason why classes cannot be constituted at the global level and indeed have been. For someone who lays stress on post-national forms of inegalitarianism this omission is difficult to comprehend.

On the other hand, the model of insurgent cosmopolitanism does not have to be confined to the working class alone but would extend to the TOC. As Santos (2007) clarifies, '[i]nsurgent cosmopolitanism includes vast populations in the world that are not sufficiently useful or skilled enough to "have chains", that is, to be directly exploited by capital.

---

[13] The observations rely on Chimni (2010b).

It aims at uniting social groups on both a class and non-class basis, the victims of exploitation as well as the victims of social exclusion, of sexual, ethnic, racist and religious discrimination' (10). It gives equal weight 'to the principle of equality and to the principle of recognition of difference' (10). But this inclusive understanding still does not equal 'citizens of the world unite'. An idea of cosmopolitanism that rests on a theory of shared humanity *alone* is problematic. It crucially disregards class, race and gender fractures.

Here, a key question presents itself: how are classes, if it is treated as a category that is in a central way constitutive of the race and gender divides, to be given political representation in global politics? Looking at international institutions, the one that comes closest to offering class representation is the International Labour Organization (ILO) model with its tripartite structure. It gives representation to trade unions besides states and employers. The ILO model could be complemented to ensure the representation of women in the global parliament. An electoral model that is being actively debated in India, and on which there is a consensus among the principal national parties, is to reserve a certain percentage of constituencies for women in the general elections. Some such policy of reservation can inform the election of the global people's assembly.

Reframing and reconfiguring property rights

A final element that constitutes insurgent cosmopolitanism is the need to reframe and reconfigure property rights as a way of restructuring global capitalism. Harvey thus calls for the construction of 'an alternative mode of production, exchange, and consumption that is risk reducing and environmentally as well as socially just and sensitive . . .' (Harvey 2000, 223). But how is this vision to be realized in a world in which gigantic private global corporations in alliance with sovereign states wield enormous power? One possibility is to revisit the idea of socialist property. The experience of 'actually existing socialism', however, showed that a system founded on state-owned property produces its own forms of inequalities and modes of domination. Moreover, as Kagarlitsky (2000) notes, 'the existence of state property on its own does not yet constitute socialism. It does not automatically ensure either a more just distribution of national income or a more harmonious development' (55). On the other hand, as he goes on to observe, 'without a strong state sector, resolving . . . [social] problems is impossible in principle' (55). Consequently, at the global level 'the internationalization of the public sector' is society's only real answer to transnational corporations

(TNCs). For it will potentially permit democratic control over the operations of TNCs and ensure that state-owned TNCs work for the benefit of global society, especially the subaltern classes. As is well known, decision making in a TNC is not devolved to the subsidiaries but vests in the headquarters, which plans its global operations to maximize profits for its shareholders.[14] In contrast, a state-owned international public company will actively respond to the goals of host state and peoples. To be sure, this will not happen simply because it is an international public corporation (thus state-owned international corporations from China are as interested in profits as their capitalist counterparts),[15] but is financed by a state that has global welfare as its vision. It will therefore have to be established and supervised by a democratic post-capitalist state committed to internationalism – that is, global democracy and global justice.

The post-capitalist state, it is important to clarify, will not entirely reject the role of the private sector. It will seek to balance the public and private sector in ways that help maximize global welfare. The act of balancing anticipates, among other things, the need to find alternatives to the extant global property regimes without eliminating space for private property rights. In the words of Santos (2007), 'beyond the state and the market, a third social domain must be reinvented: a collective, but not state-centered, private but not profit-oriented, a social domain in which the right to a solidarity-oriented transformation of property rights will be socially and politically anchored' (31). The idea will be to see what bundle or combination of property rights serves the global community better, especially when it comes to meeting the most fundamental needs of people. To consider this issue a good starting point is the world of intellectual property rights (IPRs), the first set of truly global property rights. Can we think of rewarding scientists and technologists and addressing the concerns of private firms in ways that do not inhibit the realization of the right of health of global peoples? Boldrin and Levine (2008) have shown how the case for increased IPRs (embodied in the WTO Agreement on Intellectual Property Rights) cannot be made on the basis of a study of the poster boy of the global IPR regime, namely the global pharmaceutical sector.[16] A large number of useful

---

[14] The interests of host states and peoples that need to be safeguarded are inter alia codified in the United Nations Draft Code of Conduct on Transnational Corporations, 1990. The code was never adopted.

[15] Indeed it has been argued that 'statist globalizers are part of the transnational capitalist class integrated at the levels of production and finance' (Harris 2009, 6, 15–21).

[16] They note: '... the case for patents in pharmaceuticals is a lot weaker than most people think – and so, apparently, even under the most favorable circumstances, patents are not

drugs come from university and not private labs; for instance, as Boldrin and Levine point out, 'it is wise to remember that the modern drug cocktail that is used to treat HIV was not invented by a large pharmaceutical company. It was invented by an academic researcher, Dr. David Ho' (227). In the circumstances, strengthening state-funded research and development is not altogether irrational. This move can be coupled with an appropriate IPR regime that retains incentives for the private sector even as it is encouraged to respond to public interests. At present the Western private pharmaceutical sector has designed a global patent system that allows it to make monopoly profits, stifles innovation in the pharmaceutical industry and denies the state effective measures to meet the health needs of its population.

Conclusion

This essay has argued that the global democracy project can seriously move forward only if it is elaborated around the idea of insurgent cosmopolitanism encompassing a number of propositions.

First, insurgent cosmopolitanism contends that cognitive reciprocity must inform all attempts to determine the meaning and content of the global democracy and global justice projects. In this view all Western discourse in which European civilization lays claims to all that is worthy in human inheritance, even if it is willing to concede the ravages of 'actually existing modernity', is suspect. Insurgent cosmopolitanism instead privileges the idea of multiple and alternative modernities. It calls for the diverse and rich experience of non-Western civilizations, many of them amongst the most ancient, to be taken cognizance of in mapping alternative global futures.

Second, insurgent cosmopolitanism anticipates serious changes in the global production and financial systems if the goals of global democracy and justice are to be realized. In this regard, the evolution, working and consequences of the global capitalist system – in particular, its internal relationship to global imperialism – need to be assessed to consider the nature of reforms that will advance global social welfare. From this perspective there is a need to reconfigure the idea of global property rights and prevent corporatist discourse from monopolizing the discourse on democracy and development.

Third, insurgent cosmopolitanism believes that the nation-state today remains the primary site for carrying out reforms that further the cause

necessarily good for society, for consumers, or in this case, for sick people. Patents are good for monopolists, but that much we knew already' (214).

of global democracy and justice. It calls for the recovery of policy space from an emerging global state constituted by a network of international institutions that are today implementing policies prescribed by an influential TCC.

Fourth, insurgent cosmopolitanism contends that the global democratic project must have a decentralized dimension. There must be democracy at all levels – that is, at local, national, regional and global levels. In this direction an inclusive politics of urban and regional spaces is to be shaped. The possibility of inclusive politics rests on taking the category 'class' seriously and creating democratic structures in which the TOC are able to voice their concerns and anxieties.

In the absence of these moves the idea of a people's assembly, mild democratization of international institutions and such like suggestions tend to lose their edge. To be sure, insurgent cosmopolitanism does not reject these moves. But without more fundamental transformations in the workings of global capitalism it believes that these changes will contribute little to improving global welfare, especially of the TOC.

REFERENCES

Anghie, Anthony. 2004. *Imperialism, Sovereignty and the Making of International Law.* Cambridge University Press.

Antony Anghie, and B.S. Chimni. 2003. 'Third World Approaches to International Law and Individual Responsibility in Internal Conflicts', *Chinese Journal of International Law* 2, 1: 77–105.

Appeldoorn, Bastiaan van. 2003. 'The Struggle over European Order: Transnational Class Agency in the Making of "Embedded Neo-Liberalism"', in Neil Brenner, Bob Jessop, Martin Jones and Gordon MacLeod (eds.), *State/Space: A Reader* (pp. 147–65). Oxford, UK: Blackwell.

Archibugi, Daniele. 1998. 'Principles of Cosmopolitan Democracy', in Daniele Archibugi, David Held and Martin Köhler (eds.), *Reimagining Political Community: Studies in Cosmopolitan Democracy* (pp. 198–228). Cambridge, UK: Polity Press.

2004. 'Cosmopolitan Democracy and Its Critics', *European Journal of International Relations* 10, 3: 437–73.

Arndt, H.W. 1981. 'Economic Development: A Semantic History', *Economic Development and Cultural Change* 29, 3: 457–66.

Atkinson, Will. 2007. 'Beck, Individualization and the Death of Class: A Critique', *The British Journal of Sociology* 58: 349–66.

Beck, Ulrich. 2007. 'Beyond Class and Nation: Reframing Social Inequalities in a Globalizing World', *The British Journal of Sociology* 58, 4: 679–705.

Beck, Ulrich, and Johannes Willms. 2004. *Conversations with Ulrich Beck.* Cambridge, UK: Polity Press.

Bhaskar, Roy. 2002. *From Science to Emancipation: Alienation and the Actuality of Enlightenment*. New Delhi: Sage.

Blowfield, Michael. 2005. 'Corporate Social Responsibility: Reinventing the Meaning of Development?', *International Affairs* 81, 3: 515–24.

Boldrin, Michele, and David K. Levine. 2008. *Against Intellectual Monopoly*. Cambridge University Press.

Bourdieu, Pierre. 2002. 'Unifying to Better Dominate', in *Firing Back: Against the Tyranny of the Market* (trans. Loïc Wacquant). New York: New Press.

Calhoun, Craig. 2009. 'Cosmopolitanism and Nationalism', in William Schinkel (ed.), *Globalization and the State: Sociological Perspectives on the State of the State* (pp. 209–43). New York: Palgrave Macmillan.

Chandler, David. 2009. 'Critiquing Liberal Cosmopolitanism? The Limits of the Biopolitical Approach', *International Political Sociology* 3, 1: 53–70.

Chimni, B.S. 2004. 'International Institutions Today: An Imperial Global State in the Making', *European Journal of International Law* 15, 1: 1–39.

  2006. 'Retrieving "Other" Visions of the Future: Sri Aurobindo and the Ideal of Human Unity', in Branwen Gruffyd Jones (ed.), *Decolonizing International Relations* (pp. 197–219). Lanham, MD: Rowman & Littlefield.

  2007. 'The Past, Present and Future of International Law: A Critical Third World Approach', *Melbourne Journal of International Law* 8: 499–515.

  2008. 'The Sen Conception of Development and Contemporary International Law Discourse: Some Parallels', *The Law and Development Review* 1: 1–22.

  2010a. 'Sovereignty, Rights and Armed Intervention: A Dialectical Perspective', in Hilary Charlesworth and Jean-Marc Coicaud (eds.), *Fault Lines of International Legitimacy* (pp. 303–27). Cambridge University Press.

  2010b. 'Prolegomena to a Class Approach to International Law', *European Journal of International Law* 21, 1: 57–82.

De la Barra, Ximena, and Richard Dello Buono. 2009. *Latin America after the Neoliberal Debacle: Another Region is Possible*. Lanham, MD: Rowman & Littlefield.

Dirks, Nicholas B. 2006. *The Scandal of Empire: India and the Creation of Imperial Britain*. New Delhi: Permanent Black.

Erskine, Toni. 2008. *Embedded Cosmopolitanism: Duties to Strangers and Enemies in a World of 'Dislocated Communities'*. Oxford University Press.

Escobar, Arturo, and Mauricio Pardo. 2007. 'Social Movements and Biodiversity on the Pacific Coast of Colombia', in Boaventurade Sousa Santos (ed.), *Another Knowledge is Possible: Beyond Northern Epistemologies* (pp. 288–314). London: Verso.

Falk, Richard, and Andrew L. Strauss. 2001. 'Toward Global Parliament', *Foreign Affairs* 80, 1: 212–20.

Fraser, Nancy. 2009. *Scales of Justice: Reimagining Political Space in a Globalizing World*. New York: Columbia University Press.

Habermas, Jürgen. 1999. 'The War in Kosovo: Bestiality and Humanity: A War on the Border between Legality and Morality', *Constellations* 6, 3: 263–72.

Harris, Jerry. 2009. 'Statist Globalization in China, Russia and the Gulf States', *Science and Society* 73, 1: 6–33.

Harvey, David. 2000. *Spaces of Hope*. Edinburgh University Press.
  2003. *The New Imperialism*. Oxford University Press.
  2005. *A Brief History of Neo-Liberalism*. Oxford University Press.
Honneth, Axel. 2002. 'Recognition or Redistribution? Changing Perspectives on
  the Moral Order of Society', in Scott Lash and Mike Featherstone (eds.),
  Recognition and Difference: Politics, Identity, Multiculture (pp. 43–57).
  London: Sage.
Kagarlitsky, Boris. 2000. *The Twilight of Globalization: Property, State and
  Capitalism*. London: Pluto Press.
Leubolt, Bernhardt, Andreas Novy and Joachim Becker. 2008. 'Changing
  Patterns of Participation in Porto Alegre', *International Social Science Journal*
  193/4: 435–48.
Long, David, and Brian Schmidt. 2005. *Imperialism and Internationalism in the
  Discipline of International Relations*. Albany: State University of New York
  Press.
Manners, Ian. 2007. 'Another Europe is Possible: Critical Perspectives on European
  Union Politics', in Knud Erik Jørgensen, Mark Pollack and Ben Rosamond
  (eds.), *Handbook of European Union Politics* (pp. 77–95). London: Sage.
Marazzi, Christian. 1995. 'Money in the World Crisis: The New Basis of
  Capitalist Power', in Werner Bonefeld and John Holloway (eds.), *Global
  Capital, National State and the Politics of Money* (pp. 69–91). New York:
  St Martin's Press.
Mehta, Uday S. 1999. *Liberalism and Empire: India in British Liberal Thought*.
  Oxford University Press.
Mignolo, Walter D. 2000. 'The Many Faces of Cosmo-polis: Border Thinking
  and Critical Cosmopolitanism', *Public Culture* 12, 3: 721–48.
Negri, Antonio. 2006. *Empire and Beyond* (trans. Ed Emery). Cambridge, UK:
  Polity Press.
Olson, William C., and A.J.R. Groom. 1991. *International Relations Then and
  Now: Origins and Trends in Interpretation*. London: HarperCollins.
Patnaik, Prabhat. 1997. *Accumulation and Stability*. Oxford, UK: Clarendon
  Press.
  1999. 'The Communist Manifesto after 150 years', in Prakash Karat (ed.),
  A World to Win: Essays on The Communist Manifesto (pp. 68–86). New Delhi:
  Leftword Books.
Petras, James. 2003. *The New Development Politics: The Age of Empire Building and
  New Social Movements*. Aldershot, UK: Ashgate.
Resnick, Stephen A., and Wolff, Richard D. 2006. *New Departures in Marxist
  Theory*. New York: Routledge.
Robinson, William I., and Jeffry Harris. 2000. 'Towards a Global Ruling Class?
  Globalization and the Transnational Capitalist Class', *Science and Society*
  64, 1: 11–54.
Rosenberg, Justin. 2000. *The Follies of Globalization Theory: Polemical Essays*.
  London: Verso.
Rumford, Chris. 2007. 'Introduction: Cosmopolitanism and Europe', in
  C. Rumford (ed.), *Cosmopolitanism and Europe* (pp. 1–19). Liverpool
  University Press.

Santos, Boaventura de Sousa. 2002. 'Nuestra America: Reinventing a Subaltern Paradigm of Recognition and Redistribution', in Scott Lash and Mike Featherstone (eds.), *Recognition and Difference: Politics, Identity, Multiculture* (pp. 185–219). London: Sage.

2007. 'Human Rights as an Emancipatory Script? Cultural and Political Conditions', in Boaventura de Sousa Santos (ed.), *Another Knowledge Is Possible: Beyond Northern Epistemologies* (pp. 3–41). London: Verso.

Santos, Boaventura de Sousa, Joao Arriscado Nunes and Maria Paula Meneses. 2007. 'Opening Up the Cannon of Knowledge and Recognition of Difference', in Boaventura de Sousa Santos (ed.), *Another Knowledge Is Possible* (pp. xix–lxii). London: Verso.

Scholte, Jan Aart. 2004. 'Civil Society and Democratically Accountable Global Governance', *Government and Opposition* 39, 2: 211–33.

Sen, Amartya. 2000. *Development as Freedom*. New Delhi: Oxford University Press.

Sklair, Leslie. 2002. 'The Transnational Capitalist Class and Global Politics: Deconstructing the Corporate-State Connection', *International Political Science Review* 23, 2: 159–74.

Steffek, Jen. 2007. 'Breaking the Nation State Shell: Prospects for Democratic Legitimacy in the International Domain', in Achim Hurrelmann, Stephan Leibfried, Kerstin Martens and Peter Mayer (eds.), *Transforming the Golden-Age Nation State* (pp. 109–30). Basingstoke, UK: Palgrave Macmillan.

Stevenson, Nick. 2007. 'Cosmopolitan Europe, Post-colonialism and the Politics of Imperialism', in C. Rumford (ed.), *Cosmopolitanism and Europe* (pp. 51–72). Liverpool University Press.

Žižek, S. 2010. *First as Tragedy, Then as Farce*. New Delhi: Navayana Publishers.

13 From peace between democracies to global democracy

Daniele Archibugi

In memory of Francesco and Alessandro Archibugi
who died in defence of the Roman Republic (1849)

The Roman Republic 1848–9

The revolutions of 1848, which led to the Second French Republic, also elicited emulators in the Papal States. On 9 February 1849, the Constituent Assembly, elected after free elections, established by decree that 'the form of government of the Roman state, will be pure democracy and will take the glorious name of Roman Republic' (Tommasini 2008, 246). The new republic was soon under fire from the old powers of Europe: Austrian troops from the north and troops from the Kingdom of the Two Sicilies and Spain from the south were eager to restore the temporal power of the pope and to suppress the revolutionary movement. But the first regiment to arrive at the gates of Rome was neither from the reactionary Austrians nor from the anachronistic Bourbons. Landing at Civitavecchia, a port less than 45 miles from Rome, was instead a contingent of 7,000 soldiers of republican France, led by General Nicolas-Charles Oudinot.

In Rome, they wondered whether these soldiers were sent to defend or to attack the republic. With the sole purpose of landing at the port of Civitavecchia without striking as much as a blow, the French sent a reassuring message: 'The Government of the French republic, moved by liberal intentions, declares that it will respect the vote of the majority of the Roman population, and that it does as a friend, aiming at maintaining its legitimate influence: it is determined not to impose any form of Government on these people that is not desired by them' (Tommasini 2008, 316). This was certainly sweet music to the Italian patriots, who

Parts of this chapter draw on previous writings co-authored with Mathias Koenig-Archibugi. I also wish to thank Luigi Caranti, Raffaele Marchetti and Tiziana Torresi for comments on previous versions.

perceived the Austro-Hungarian Empire as the principal enemy. It already occupied the Romagna region of the old Church state, with the consent of the pope, but against the will of the Constituent Assembly.

After heated debate, the Constitution of the Second French Republic was finally adopted on 4 November 1848, less than six months before the landing at Civitavecchia. That constitution had given inspiration to the patriots in Rome as in the whole of Europe and Article V contained a statement in its preamble that the Romans reread continuously in those uncertain days: 'France respects foreign nationalities, just as it intends to enforce respect for its own, it does not undertake any war for conquest, and never employs its forces against the freedom of any people.' Some citizens had even gone to the trouble of attaching those words, on posters in French, to the pines that adorn the Via Aurelia, the ancient Roman consular road that connects Rome to Civitavecchia.

But when the French troops showed up ready for battle on 30 April 1849 by the San Pancrazio and Cavalleggeri gates, the Romans had already ceased for some time to trust that lofty statement. Giuseppe Garibaldi, called to lead the Roman army, trusted more in the guns than the constitutional right and managed to repel the enemy. The battalion of volunteers of the University 'La Sapienza' distinguished itself for its zeal in fighting. Francesco and Alessandro Archibugi, students of philosophy and mathematics, and medicine respectively, joined this very battalion and had their baptism of fire that day (Silvagni 1893, 61). The French troops were forced to flee, suffering heavy losses, and the losses to the foreign army would have been heavier, had it not been for the fact that the Romans did not want to humiliate the European power that was still their most valuable ally in achieving the unification of Italy.

On hearing of that first defeat, Louis-Napoléon Bonaparte decided not to give up pursuing what he believed to be a 'legitimate influence' in Italian affairs, also because he could gain an advantage in domestic politics through it – Catholics in his country certainly did not appreciate the forced expulsion of the pope. Louis-Napoléon then sent a diplomat to Rome, Ferdinand de Lesseps, with instructions to negotiate with the Roman Republic. Giuseppe Mazzini, one of the promoters of the republic, hoped that the two regimes, based on similar ideologies, could reach an agreement and was very happy to have a partner, especially one well-disposed towards the Roman Republic, to deal with. In reality, the French diplomatic mission had the aim of stalling in order to prepare a more substantial and better-armed expedition. When the reinforcements arrived in Civitavecchia, and France could count on a contingent of more than 30,000 soldiers, Louis-Napoléon recalled the ambassador, Lesseps, and put everything in the hands of General Oudinot.

On the morning of 3 June, the French troops attacked the city again. That same day, the most important democratic theorist of the nineteenth century, Alexis de Tocqueville, became Foreign Minister of the French Republic. Despite the young Roman Republic being so much inspired by the French model, Tocqueville did not then, or at any time later, have a favourable attitude towards it, claiming in his memoirs that 'Rome, after repelling our first attack, was calling all the demagogues of Italy to its assistance and exciting all of Europe with its clamour' (Toqueville 1850–1/1896, 333). As neo-Minister of Foreign Affairs Tocqueville did not intend to take a position: 'I disapproved entirely of the manner in which the Roman expedition had been undertaken and conducted. Before joining the Cabinet, I had solemnly declared to Barrot [the chief of Louis-Napoléon's cabinet] that I declined to take any responsibility, except for the future, and that he must himself be prepared to defend what had up to that time been done in Italy. I had only accepted office on this condition' (Toqueville 1850–1/1893, 293).

Against an enemy far more numerous, with greater expertise and better armed, the Roman Republic defended itself as best it could, but the French troops broke through the defences at Gianicolo Hill and began to bombard the city. On 11 June the French soldiers tried to circumvent the defence by entering also via the Ponte Milvio. On the slopes of the Monti Parioli, there was another clash with the University Battalion, which vainly tried to stop the entry of the invaders. Among the first hit there were the Archibugi brothers. The French troops picked up the two wounded and took them prisoners. One French soldier called the arrested Roman volunteers 'bandits', and they replied by calling the French 'soldiers of the pope', an epithet perhaps even more offensive to the soldiers of the French Republic (Silvagni 1893, 92). The Archibugis both died, Francesco near the site of battle, Alessandro 11 days later, carried by the attackers, along with other wounded, to the Fate Bene Fratelli hospital in Civitavecchia. They would never know that '[t]he closest thing we have to a law in international politics' (Levy 1988, 653) is that democracies do not fight each other.

Peace between democracies and global democracy

The hypothesis that democracies do not fight each other[1] is one of the most studied themes of the past two decades in international relations,

---

[1] It is now common to refer to this hypothesis as 'democratic peace'. But this may seem to indicate that the countries in a condition of peace also have democratic agreements for government and administration. As this is not implied even by the supporters of the hypothesis, I prefer the expression 'peace between democracies'.

an interest that grew at the end of the Cold War and the associated wave of democratization. Proponents of this hypothesis believe that the case of the Roman Republic is an exception that proves the rule: for the rule to be valid it is necessary that democratic regimes be consolidated by at least a few years, and this condition was not satisfied either by the Roman Republic or the French Republic. Perhaps due to being Roman, or perhaps as a relative of Francesco and Alessandro, I continue to be sceptical of that theory and, even more so, of the conjectures implied by it.

What is the link between the idea of peace between democracies and the hope of a global democracy, the theme which this book is dedicated to? The idea of global democracy[2] is essentially *normative* and refers to *prospect* while the theory that democracies do not fight each other is instead behavioural and based on observations of past experience. Not only that, but the former involves the creation of procedures and institutions above the state, while the latter deals exclusively with the connection between a particular internal regime (democracy) and an event of foreign policy (war). It would almost appear as though there was no tension between the two themes. Still, both issues have in common the key word *democracy* and this makes them contiguous on the map of knowledge. A global democracy that is not based on domination of one party over the other (in which case it would be a global *empire*) requires that the political communities that make it up subordinate the use of force to the rule of law and that they are able to solve their contentions with peaceful means. The condition of *bellum omnium contra omnes* does not allow for the generation of any global democracy, making peace an essential precondition. If it was proven that achieving democracy in all countries of the world is a way to ensure peace – some even say the only way to ensure peace (Moravcsik 1996) – we would already see the delineation of some priorities for advocates of global democracy. The first stage should be concerned with achieving internal democracy in all countries of the world and this, aside from being a desirable goal in itself, would also ensure peace throughout the planet. After reaching this state of peace it would be possible to plan the second stage, namely the creation of democratic interactions among states. The entire programme of global democracy would be premature until democracy had been achieved within states. What remains unconvincing about this perspective?

---

[2] David Held and I have presented the idea of cosmopolitan democracy in Held (1995), Archibugi and Held (1995) and Archibugi (2008). I have discussed the meanings of the terms 'global' and 'cosmopolitan' applied to democracy in Archibugi (2008, 88–97 and 125).

From the behavioural standpoint, the theory of peace between democracies is less well founded than its most ardent supporters claim. From a normative standpoint, it doesn't appear that we can draw a clear line to say: let us first deal with democracy within states, and then think about building a global democracy. An international system inspired by certain values and norms of democracy may in fact contribute not only to reducing war and strengthening peace, but also to strengthening democracy within states. The next two sections trace the intellectual path that leads to the idea of peace between democracies. The subsequent section distinguishes between strong and weak versions of the hypothesis. I then explain what appear to me to be the critical points, and highlight the possible implications for foreign policy. The last section explores the importance of the programme of global democracy for democratization within states.

The hope of liberalism: democracy as a vehicle for peace

The idea that democracies could be peaceful states arose in the late eighteenth century, when the countries that had a parliamentary system were no more than a handful. Liberal philosophers are the bearers of that hope. Jeremy Bentham (1786–9/1927) argued that in order to limit war, it was necessary to remove the secrecy from the work of the Ministry of Foreign Affairs. This would allow citizens to ensure that foreign policy is in accordance with their interests rather than those of small elites. Some of the basic requirements of a democratic system, namely the principle of transparency and parliamentary control over the executive, would have been the main antidotes to indiscriminate recourse to war. James Madison (1792/1981) believed that to decrease the incidence of wars it was necessary to impose the will of the people on the government. Madison was aware that a government expressing the will of the public would not have been sufficient to eliminate all wars. If the wars, he noted, were supported by popular fervour, there was little opportunity to avoid them other than by forcing every generation responsible for causing them to pay the cost. Immanuel Kant (1795/1991) argued that if each state had a republican constitution, war would be diminished because 'if the consent of citizens is required to decide whether or not war is to be declared, it is very natural that they will have greater hesitation in embarking on so dangerous an enterprise' (100).

The arguments of Bentham, Madison and Kant are essentially utilitarian, since it is generally not in the interests of the public to enter a war, and because the consequences tend to be paid by the people rather than the elites in government. These authors state that making the executive accountable to the will of the public would give precedence to the general interests of the public. The historical analysis and statistics available, unfortunately, deny the hopes of the founding fathers of liberal thought: the incidence of wars fought by democracies is similar to that of autocracies (see, e.g., Rasler and Thompson 2003). It seems, then, that the non-aggression pact between political parties, which is the hallmark of democracies, doesn't lead to a non-aggression pact between sovereign states. It may be true that democracies are, in proportion, slightly less involved in conflicts than autocracies (Benoit 1996), and that the wars they have fought in are a little less bloody than the others (Rummel 1995). Democracies have, in fact, an understandable resistance to endangering the lives of their soldiers and, even more so, of their civilian population. In recent years, some democracies, even in war, have tended increasingly to minimize casualties among the civilian population of enemy countries. Yet it is remarkable how one of the founding principles of democracy, non-violence, is still so little and so poorly extended beyond borders.

We need, then, to explain why democracy – a political system based on non-violence internally – has had so little success in eliminating external conflicts. Perhaps it is because a war is not necessarily contrary to the interests of the citizens of a state – for example, when the damage is limited and more than compensated for by the benefits, not only distributed to elites, but also to the population (Caranti 2006a, 207). Any benefits can be quantified only at the end of a conflict, but a government eager to fight could have us believe that there are significant benefits to be gained, and the public might not have enough information to contradict it. On these occasions, the moderating influence of public opinion in favour of peace may fail for the simple reason that an alliance of interests is created between government elites and the people, as evidenced by the colonialism of Great Britain, France and Holland. To decrease wars it would, then, be necessary to find ways to extend the peace pact of democracy beyond borders.

And if it was the fault of bad company?

The decision to fight a war is not unilateral, but rather depends on an external environment that can facilitate diplomatic and peaceful solutions to disputes, or may make them difficult to achieve. For there to be a war, there must be at least two contenders, and, if one is aggressive, even the meekest of states is forced to defend itself. It is this hypothesis that opened the line of investigation on peace between democracies: in an international system composed of democratic and autocratic states and, above all, with autocratic states that until a decade ago quantitatively dominated the planet, democratic countries would not have the option of extending the principle of non-violence beyond their borders due to lack of reciprocity. This, it is suggested, could explain their involvement in so many wars. This is an hypothesis charitable to democracy, suggesting as it does that democracies are dragged into conflicts against their will, and attributing the existence of war to the bad companies found in the international system. Proof, then, must be sought in a sub-hypothesis: do democracies fight each other? This hypothesis, first suggested by Dean Babst (1964/1972) and then articulated by Michael Doyle (1983), has had the spectacular success I have described. The so-called monadic hypothesis (i.e, how much a democracy fights in absolute terms) has been obscured by the so-called dyadic hypothesis (i.e., how much a democracy fights another democracy). If, from an empirical point of view, the studies on the monadic hypothesis show that democracies fight as much as any other regime, studies on the dyadic hypothesis, to the contrary, tend to empirically prove that democracies do not fight each other. A vast array of sophisticated statistical tools has been employed to support this thesis.

The more astute advocates of peace between democracies are well aware of its limitations (Russett 1993, Russett and Oneal 2001). Nobody denies that democracies fight wars, that they may be the initiators, nor that they can ally with autocratic regimes, even when the autocratic regimes are fighting against democracies. Nor is it denied that democracies may engage in more or less covert hostile actions against other democratic governments. The hypothesis merely asserts that democratic states do not wage war directly. The hypothesis is not even disproven by the turmoil that is often associated with the transition from an authoritarian regime to a democracy. Mansfield and Snyder (2005) have pointed out that a nascent democracy can, in fact, be even more aggressive than an autocracy. The transition involves a change in the elites who control the country and, at the same time, a unity of purpose of the people, which may often be associated with new or renewed nationalist demands that may be expressed outside.

In the evergreen debate between realists and idealists in international relations, it has finally been shown that not all states are equal, and that at least in some aspects the nature of the internal political system is able to influence foreign policy. This shows that democracies are able to extend outward the practice of non-violence, even if only with states which are also democratic: a sort of separate peace that only applies between the like-minded. 'Dogs don't eat dogs', you could say, but the same rule does not apply to other races: the wars between authoritarian regimes are as frequent as those between democratic and authoritarian regimes. The wolf bites not only the dog but also the wolf. Taking this idea to its logical conclusion, you can argue that the phenomenon of war would be eliminated if all states of the world were democratic: democracy of individual countries delivers peace internationally.

Determinists and probabilists

Proponents of the theory of peace between democracies support it with varying degrees of conviction. The strong version is actually deterministic, and it was already formulated by the precursor of democratic peace, Dean Babst (1964/1972), who stated that 'no wars have been fought between independent nations with elective governments between 1789 and 1941' (55). The common democratic character of two countries is a sufficient (but not necessary) condition for the absence of war. The historian Spencer Weart (1998) provides the most ambitious story in support of the deterministic thesis. Examining the relationships between democratic regimes and republics from Ancient Greece to today, through the towns of medieval Italy, the Swiss republics and the vicissitudes of the twentieth century, Weart induced two 'rules': first, well-established democracies have never been to war and, second, well-established oligarchic republics have hardly ever gone to war.

The interpretation of historical events and classification of political systems, however, is highly debatable, and cases of potential wars between democracies are rejected with excessive ease, sometimes with irritation, by those who espouse the idea of peace between democracies. For example, most of these studies exclude the case of the American Civil War, on the basis that it is an internal conflict rather than between states, although the high degree of autonomy held by each member of the Union before 1864 might lead it to be considered an interstate war. With regard to World War I, France, Britain and Italy are classified as democratic countries, while Germany isn't. This classification may seem arbitrary since the differential in the democratic quality between these states was too small to justify classification of their political systems at opposing ends of a dichotomy. Most empirical studies also exclude the conflict between the young French and Roman republics in 1849, the recent war between Serbia and Croatia between 1991 and 1995 and the war waged by the North Atlantic Treaty Organization (NATO) in 1999, whose members are all democratic, against Serbia. The reason for exclusion of these cases is the fact that the democratic regimes of at least one of the parties were not sufficiently consolidated. As mentioned above, the hypothesis follows only after a country has consolidated its democracy for at least a few years. In short, there are exceptions, and to affirm the thesis rigidly it is often necessary to use specific means to catalogue historical cases.

In a more thoughtful view, other studies have focused on a weak version, which merely states that it is less likely that two democratic states will wage war. The probabilistic version of the dyadic thesis argues that the probability that pairs of democratic states fight each other is significantly lower than the probability of war between two states of which at least one is not a democracy (Russett and Oneal 2001). Compared to the deterministic theory, the probabilistic variant, more modestly, argues that the common democratic nature reduces, but does not completely eliminate, the risk of armed conflict between two states. Wars, fortunately, are few compared to the number of pairs of states. States may be too far apart or have no pending disputes giving reason to fight. Only 2.69 dyads of states in 10,000 have actually been involved in wars (Ray 1995). If the odds are so low, and if we consider that democratic states had been until recently very few, only a few cases of war between democracies are sufficient to remove any statistical value from the hypothesis. The few cases mentioned suffice to make the probability of war among democracies equal to the probability of war between any states. Classifying differently the regime of a country or an event similar to war may lead to opposite results.

Finally, there are indirect actions to be taken into account, which do not qualify as war, but bear witness to hostility between democratic states. Sometimes the government of a democratic state intending to strike another democratic state prefers, in fact, to act without the knowledge of the general public rather than publicly justifying actions by denying the democratic nature of the opponent.[3] Russett (1993) referred to covert operations carried out by the United States against other democracies as an 'anomaly' for the theory of peace between democracies (120). However, he has taken care to point out that governments that have been subject to such covert hostile actions had ideologies very different from that predominating in the United States – for example, the government headed by Salvador Allende was 'openly Marxist' (121). According to Russett, in these cases, rules and institutions of the American political system proved sufficiently binding as to prevent direct and open military action, but not strong enough to

---

[3] On hostile actions by the United States against the elected governments in Iran (1953), Guatemala (1954), Indonesia (1955), Brazil (1960s), Chile (1973) and Nicaragua (1980s), see Forsythe (1992).

prevent covert actions to support the internal enemies of the democratically elected politicians. This is an important admission because it indicates that, even in the presence of pairs of democratic states, the common values can be secondary when other interests – strategic or economic – are at stake. And, most importantly, it shows that to ensure a state of peace it is not enough that both states are democratic; they must also have non-conflicting ideologies.

Democracy in time and space

One of the most controversial points of the theory of peace between democracies concerns the definition of democracy. In recent years, a certain consensus has developed in the classification of countries based on their political system, but this becomes more arbitrary when establishing which regimes of the past were democratic. The Periclean Athens was more democratic than the Spartan, but in the twentieth century it would have been considered a system of apartheid, at least as bad as, and perhaps even worse than, South Africa. In what time frame and cultural climate should we test the theory of non-belligerence between democracies? One of the main supporters of the theory of peace between democracies, Bruce Russett (1993, chapters 3 and 5), has studied the phenomenon in societies very different from modern democracies, such as the Greek city-state and pre-industrial societies. With the help of historians and anthropologists, Russett has tried to see if indigenous pre-industrial populations in which power was shared, and in which there were the first seeds of what we call democracy today, were less inclined to fight wars, and especially if they were less inclined to fight amongst themselves. The space for applying the theory has expanded considerably, even to societies of smaller scale than the modern state, to more primitive social systems and rather remote times. The empirical data seem to confirm that non-authoritarian pre-industrial societies were less inclined to fight each other. But cases that make the thesis uncomfortable tend to disappear: for example, it excludes the conflicts between the Western colonizers, who often lived in very cohesive and participatory communities, and aboriginal tribes. The same Russett (1993, 34) admits that the European and American colonizers did not consider it possible that the indigenous inhabitants of colonized territories could have institutions of self-government. Can we infer that if the settlers of the Far West had realized that the native Americans were governed by a council of old tribal chiefs which functioned according to majoritarian vote they would have refrained from annihilating them? If this hypothesis seems hardly credible, one must look for other explanations to understand why democracies, despite internal tolerance, have so many difficulties in living peacefully with very different societies.

From an analytical standpoint, it's also worth asking what sense there is in comparing conflicts as diverse as those among the settlers of the Far West and the Apache with those among Andean populations and between modern states. It is precisely the heterogeneity of the historical material studied that demonstrates the least convincing aspect of the hypothesis of peace between democracies, namely the fact that it takes into account political systems that are very different without considering those differences and their historical evolution. From the time of Athens to today, democracies have evolved and there are still equally significant differences between pairs of countries with elected governments such as Sweden and Iran. The problem is not only historical: democracies are political systems in evolution which have progressed in the past and will do so also in the future. Democratic states today may evolve in the same direction or may take different paths: it is likely that in a few years some countries will consider that democracy is incompatible with the death penalty or even eating animals, while others continue to believe these practices are completely legitimate. We cannot know, therefore, whether states which recognize each other as democratic today will still see each other as democracies in the future. We can only say that some groups of countries that are recognized as democratic in certain specified periods lived in a state of peace. From 1945 to 1989 there was a fairly homogenous group of democratic countries that did not engage in conflict with each other. This may depend not only on the rivalry with the block dominated by the Soviet Union,[4] but also on the fact that, perhaps because of this threat, those countries were allies, having similar ideologies and being mutually recognized as democratic.

The hypothesis should therefore be rephrased: similar democratic systems, which identify each other as such, have a low probability of fighting each other. It's a less ambitious hypothesis, and also much more acceptable. This is also directly linked to one of the main explanations of peace between democracies: that based on the type of political culture of a democratic regime, which 'extends to the international arena the cultural norms of live-and-let-live and peaceful conflict resolution that operate within democracies' (Russett 1993, 119). The supporters of peace between democracies argue, in fact, that those who govern democratic states tend to assume that their counterparts at the head of other

---

[4] At the conclusion of a pondered empirical analysis Joanne Gowa (1999) argues: 'The most unambiguous and important message of this book is that the democratic peace is a Cold War phenomenon' (198).

democracies behave in accordance with the same standards that guide their behaviour. This approach could also implicitly explain why democracies become involved in wars against authoritarian states. Those who act on the international arena on behalf of democratic states tend to think that those who are in charge of non-democratic states follow rules of behaviour that are in fundamental contrast with those of democracies. In particular, democratic governments would maintain that the governments of authoritarian states have a greater propensity to use coercion and violence to achieve their foreign policy objectives, because this is the way they behave towards their own citizens. Democracies not only presume that other democracies project their internal principles towards the outside, but that autocracies project their unjust and oppressive behaviour outwardly: they can find agreement with democracies but not with oligarchies. In short, democracies do not trust autocratic states and do not respect them (Doyle 1997). One consequence of this is that a democratic state that finds itself in a dispute with a non-democratic state is not likely to externalize its internal rules, since 'it may feel obliged to adapt to the harsher norms of international conduct of the latter (the non-democratic state), lest it be exploited or eliminated by the non-democratic state that takes advantage of the inherent moderation of democracies' (Russett 1993, 33).

This kind of explanation is not entirely convincing for several reasons. First, cases where democratic states have failed to apply certain democratic principles are certainly not limited to situations in which they found themselves in fear for their security. Democracies decide to use violence and coercion, not only when they are forced to do so. The history of European colonialism and of American imperialism widely demonstrates that economic and strategic advantages can easily have more weight than any inclination to manage external relationships in harmony by the principles of internal order (Losurdo 2005). The European powers had no reason to consider themselves endangered by the communities which they were preparing to colonize and to feel justified in ignoring their general rules against violence. This form of aggressiveness of liberal political systems is what Mann (2005) has called 'the dark side of democracy', which often turns violence outwardly while keeping it under control internally. The result is to impose a forced assimilation onto different populations; then, in case of failure to assimilate, to engage in ethnic cleansing or even genocide. It doesn't only depend on how intrinsically democratic a country is, but also how democratic it is deemed to be by the state next door, which considers itself in any case more democratic. While the neighbour's grass is always greener, the neighbour's democracy is always less satisfactory.

The governments of democratic states have often used arbitrary criteria, fickle and inconsistent in defining the political regimes of their potential adversaries. In some cases this depended on the insurmountable difference between civilizations, which prompted Western countries to opt for clashes between civilizations. But in other cases, the perception of a state can change according to what is convenient and can even be manipulated. Perceptions of Imperial Germany toward the United States, for example, changed with the deterioration of political relations between the two states in the years preceding World War I (Oren 1995). The perception of India as a democracy changed in the United States in 1971 so much that the two countries risked an armed conflict (Widmeier 2005). The US interest in the consolidation of democracy in Serbia was gained only after Slobodan Milosevic was removed from power (Presnall 2009). These cases show that the foreign policy of state A towards state B is not determined by the nature of the political system of B, but, on the contrary, it is the foreign policy of A, according to its conveniences, which leads to the system of B being perceived as more or less democratic. Changes in perception may occur for different reasons: 1) it may be the result of a misunderstanding; 2) it may be the result of unintentional processes that lead to developing a negative image of the nature of an actor with whom they come into conflict; 3) it may be a deliberate manipulation of public opinion orchestrated by the political elites of a country. Western states have always led the dance of democracy, through the media, through their foreign policy experts and even through sources also used by academia, such as Freedom House and Polity IV, which determine whether, and to what extent, other countries are democratic. The perception of a political system of a non-Western country could often be the result, rather than the cause, of the Western policies toward that state.

The political implications

A behavioural theory so heavily loaded with ideological implications, such as peace between democracies, inevitably has consequences of a political nature. This was explicitly recognized, even espoused, by Russett (1993, 136): it could become a self-fulfilling prophecy. Arguing that democracies do not fight each other could be used to induce democracies to not feel threatened by other democracies, and hence make them better disposed to find peaceful means to resolve their disputes. The theory was not known either to Louis Bonaparte or to Tocqueville at the time of the French attack against the Roman Republic, but it was well known in the NATO headquarters during the war against Serbia in 1999; nevertheless knowledge of the theory was not sufficient to induce NATO countries to find peaceful means to resolve the dispute.

On the other hand, there is also the danger that the argument may have the opposite effect and lead democracies to believe that it is sufficient to force enemy states to become democratic, in order to achieve a peaceful international community (Caranti 2006b). The causal connection from democracy to peace can bring forth the policy of war, with democracy as the goal. The self-fulfilling prophecy which has, in fact, entered into the heart of political debate, is not, as hoped, to avert wars between democracies, but rather to promote the wars of democracies against autocracies. At least two US presidents have referred to the peace between democracies in their speeches. Bill Clinton argued that the best strategy to ensure national security is the advancement of democracy. George Bush Jr. was more direct still: in the middle of the invasion of Iraq, he recalled that after their defeat in World War II, Japan and Germany were transformed into democracies, and this had had the effect of reinforcing the security of the United States, because these countries had become their political and commercial partners and were no longer a source of threat.[5] Following the same reasoning, Bush defended the invasion of Iraq, arguing that a democratic Iraq would cease to pose a threat to the United States. If democratic states promote democracy in authoritarian states, this would not only have the effect of realizing the aspirations of the peoples of those states, but also increase their own security. It would appear that the President of the United States has been inspired by the theorists of international relations of his country. But if one takes into account that, in 1988, Ronald Reagan had already argued that '[t]he Greater the freedoms in other countries the more secure both our own freedoms and peace' (cited by Russett 1993, 127), one would think that perhaps the doctrine of US foreign policy and the theory of international relations have influenced each other.

Yet, the theorists of peace between democracies had already warned of the danger of an instrumental use of their thesis: already in 1993, Russett had explicitly warned against too simplistic a practical translation of these principles: 'the model of "fight them, beat them, and then make them democratic" is irrevocably flawed as a basis for contemporary action. It probably would not work anyway, and no one is prepared to make the kind of effort that would be required. A crusade for democracy

---

[5] See, respectively, President Bill Clinton's State of the Union speech, 25 January 1994; and President George Bush Jr.'s speech on 6 November 2003 at the National Endowment for Democracy, dedicated to democratization in the Middle East.

is not in order' (Russett 1993, 136). But, as perhaps might be expected, politicians take from the social sciences that which suits them, and they were certainly not paying attention to these academic 'cautions' when they prepared public justifications for their choices, including the war in Iraq. Not surprising, therefore, are the concerns of the same Russett: 'Many advocates of the democratic peace may now feel rather like many atomic scientists did in 1945. They created something intended to prevent conquest by Nazi Germany, but only after Germany was defeated was the bomb tested and then used – against Japanese civilians whose government was already near defeat. Our creation too has been perverted!' (Russett 2005, 396).

Return ticket: from peace between democracies to global democracy

The idea of peace between democracies emerges historically less robust than thought; it does not rule out covert hostile behaviour from democracies against other democracies which are not aligned ideologically. It lends itself to an arbitrary definition of who is and who is not democratic, and is likely to induce governments of some democracies to export their own political system, even through waging of war. It seems, therefore, that you cannot hope to attain perpetual peace solely through internal democratization. Faced with these objections, it seems not to make sense to postpone the construction of a global democracy at a time when all states of the world are (according to criteria that are not yet clearly definable and are probably indefinable) considered democratic.

We return, then, to the project of a global democracy, since it can help to strengthen not only international peace but also democracy within its member states. The idea of a global democracy is based on the assumption that there is a causal link, opposite to that predicted by the hypothesis of peace between democracies, namely that a democratic transformation of the international system can contribute not only to peace, but also to democratization within states. I examine below three areas where the project of global democracy may help overcome some of the limitations encountered in the theory of peace between democracies.

The definition of democracy

Common institutions between states also have the ability to critically evaluate political systems of member states. If this assessment is carried out multilaterally, and with due attention to cultural differences between countries, it can reduce one of the problems faced in the theory of peace between democracies, namely that some democratic communities define the friendly communities as 'democratic', and hostile ones as undemocratic, giving ideological grounds to justify a perception which is rather dictated by economic or political interests. The Conquistadores were genuinely horrified by human sacrifice and cannibalism practised by the Aztecs, but none of them ever questioned whether the traditional practice in their native Spain of burning witches in the square was equally brutal. In the sixteenth century there were no conditions for establishing multilateral councils to discuss the permissibility of cannibalism and the fires, while today there are organizations such as the United Nations (UN) Human Rights Council, and regional councils, such as the Council of Europe, who perform regular reviews of domestic political systems in order to provide advice to member countries. Strengthening mutual evaluation of political systems can therefore help us to understand better the different political systems, to prevent manipulation and to limit wars of democracies against countries they do not recognize as equally democratic.

The role of international organizations in promoting democratization

The democratization process can be facilitated or hindered also by the international dimension (Whitehead 2001). The international and regional organizations provide the opportunity for states to come into contact with each other and guide elites of countries in transition to democracy or in unstable democracies. As indicated by an important new line of research, international organizations and, even more so, regional organizations (Pevehouse 2002, 2005) help the national elites to get to know each other, reducing the risk of conflicts associated with misunderstanding and spreading the practice of democracy. Some of these regional organizations, most notably the European Union, are open to countries with similar political systems, but the very process of integration requires countries to know their own system better, and, at the same time, to introduce the necessary reforms into their country to enable integration. Regional organizations made up of states which are all democratic also seem to have a stronger role in ensuring peace (Pevehouse and Russett, 2006).

International organizations not only allow exchanges among elites, but also facilitate trade and transnational connections. In addition to the activities of specific groups (from student exchanges to cultural ones), the international and regional organizations are often associated with free trade zones, foreign investment and technology collaborations.

These are connections that allow different types of associations to know each other directly, creating transnational connections that counterbalance the distorted perceptions that elites in power may have an interest in presenting. These distribution channels contribute to stabilizing and consolidating the international system, but also to providing new learning occasions to national groups. The behavioural component remains to be explored, as regards the extent to which citizens' participation can be broadened in international organizations (as suggested by the idea of global democracy) and whether it may, in turn, help to strengthen peace and consolidate internal democracy.

Is global democracy possible even with undemocratic states?

Is it possible to imagine a global democracy when many countries worldwide are still not democratic? That question is implicit in the whole debate on peace and democracy. If there is not only one causal link from internal democracy to international peace, but also the opposite link, which leads from international peace to internal democracy, one wonders to what extent opening up at least some international organizations to autocratic governments may, in the medium to long term, help these to make the transition. The UN has accepted governments on the basis of their effectiveness, rather than their legitimacy, but it has also managed, albeit with excessive caution and timidity, to offer a channel for the peaceful resolution of disputes and, at times, to put on notice the authoritarian regimes of some member states. If international organizations increase the channels of participation, becoming themselves more democratic, they may also succeed in facilitating democratization in member states. The question is then to find the right balance, in the same international organizations, between inclusion and exclusion. This means working to include, even in the international sphere, citizens and opposition movements that do not enjoy political rights in tyrannical regimes and exclude, where possible, despotic governments.

If there are pragmatic reasons to also include non-democratic states in intergovernmental organizations, it can be maintained that the institutions that represent citizens directly, such as the proposed World Parliamentary Assembly, should be open only if the members are selected on the basis of a competitive electoral process, free and fair. Authoritarian regimes would thus have two options: allow a free election campaign for the election of members of a World Parliamentary Assembly (such free elections as they themselves do not allow at the national level), or hinder the participation, extending their international exclusion. The same country may well be represented by opposing political forces: the General Assembly may be represented by autocratic forces (governmental ones), while the World Parliamentary Assembly may also be represented by members of the internal opposition or not be represented at all.

Other channels, such as the stakeholder democracy (see T. Macdonald and K. Macdonald, both this volume), or those accessible through the global civil society, allow individuals to have a form of political discussion, even if some of them are living under autocratic government rule. The project of global democracy can operate in the gaps that exist in a world which is still composed of democratic and authoritarian states, and which will probably continue to be so for many years. But arguing that global democracy should wait for a world where all states are democratic seems to be the surest way to sink it even before birth.

Designing a global democracy presupposes that there are many democratic states around the world, that they have sufficient political, economic and cultural resources, that they have a solid network of common interests and of political cooperation, and that these states are willing to extend the core principles of their internal system to the outside world. Many of these conditions exist today: 1) democracies have increased considerably since the fall of the Berlin Wall; 2) they are no longer isolated as they were in the 1930s, nor do they still have to fight a large and formidable opponent block as they had to in the 1950s and 1960s; 3) the major established democracies tend, at least on essential issues, to give priority to cooperation rather than competition; and 4) above all, democratic states today have an enormous concentrated power. But one condition doesn't seem to have been met yet: the willingness of democracies to extend their own principles beyond their borders (Archibugi 1997, 2008). This goal requires not only that established democracies encourage other countries of the world to adopt a political system similar to their own, which is the consequence of the assumptions held within the theory of peace between democracies, but also that they are willing to submit their foreign policies to the values they apply at home.

REFERENCES

Archibugi, Daniele. 1997. 'So What if Democracies Don't Fight Each Other?' *Peace Review* 9, 3: 379–84.
  2008. *The Global Commonwealth of Citizens: Toward Cosmopolitan Democracy.* Princeton University Press.
Archibugi, Daniele, and David Held (eds.). 1995. *Cosmopolitan Democracy.* Cambridge, UK: Polity Press.
Babst, Dean V. 1964/1972. 'Elective Governments: A Force for Peace', *Industrial Research* 14, 4: 55–8.

272   *Daniele Archibugi*

Benoit, Kenneth. 1996. 'Democracies Really Are More Pacific (In General): Reexamining Regime Type and War Involvement', *Journal of Conflict Resolution* 40, 4: 636–57.

Bentham, Jeremy. 1786–9/1927. *Plan for a Universal and Perpetual Peace.* London: Sweet & Maxwell.

Caranti, Luigi. 2006a. 'One More Time Back to Kant: From the Democratic Peace to the Kantian Peace', in Luigi Caranti (ed.), *Kant's Perpetual Peace: New Interpretative Essays* (pp. 197–223). Rome: Luiss University Press.

2006b. 'Perpetual War for Perpetual Peace? Reflections on the Realist Critique of Kant's Project', *Journal of Human Rights* 18, 3: 23–45.

Doyle, Michael. 1983a. 'Kant, Liberal Legacies, and Foreign Affairs', *Philosophy and Public Affairs* 12, 3 and 4: 205–35 and 323–54.

1997. *Ways of War and Peace: Realism, Liberalism, and Socialism.* New York: W.W. Norton.

Forsythe, David P. 1992. 'Democracy, War, and Covert Action', *Journal of Peace Research* 29, 4: 385–95.

Gowa, Joanne. 1999. *Ballots and Bullets: The Elusive Democratic Peace.* Princeton University Press.

Held, David. 1995. *Democracy and the Global Order.* Cambridge, UK: Polity Press.

Kant, Immanuel. 1795/1991. 'Toward Perpetual Peace', in *Kant: Political Writings* (ed. Hans Reiss). Cambridge University Press.

Levy, Jack S. 1988. 'Domestic Politics and War', *Journal of Interdisciplinary History* 18, 4: 653–73.

Losurdo, Domenico. 2005. *Controstoria del liberalismo.* Roma-Bari: Laterza.

Madison, James. 1792/1981. 'Universal Peace', in *The Mind of the Founder: Sources of Political Thought of James Madison* (ed. Marvin Meyers). Hannover, Germany: Brandeis University Press.

Mann, Michael. 2005. *The Dark Side of Democracy: Explaining Ethnic Cleansing.* Cambridge University Press.

Mansfied, Edward, and Jack Snyder. 2005. *Electing to Fight: Why Emerging Democracies Go to War.* Cambridge, MA: MIT Press.

Moravcsik, Andrew. 1996. 'Federalism and Peace: A Structural Liberal Perspective', *Zeitschrift für Internationale Beziehungen* 3, 1: 123–32.

Oren, Ido. 1995. 'The Subjectivity of the "Democratic" Peace: Changing U.S. Perceptions of Imperial Germany', *International Security* 20, 2: 147–84.

Pevehouse, Jon. 2002. 'Democracy from Outside-In? International Organizations and Democratization', *International Organization* 56, 3: 515–49.

2005. *Democracy from the Above? Regional Organizations and Democratization.* New York: Cambridge University Press.

Pevehouse, Jon, and Bruce Russett. 2006. 'Democratic International Governmental Organizations Promote Peace', *International Organization* 60, 3: 969–1000.

Presnall, Aroon. 2009. 'Which Way the Wind Blows: Democracy Promotion and International Actors in Serbia', *Democratization* 16, 4: 661–81.

Rasler, Karen, and William Thompson. 2003. 'The Monadic Democratic Puzzle and an "End of History" Partial Solution?', *International Politics* 40, 1: 5–27.

Ray, James Lee. 1995. *Democracy and International Conflict: An Evaluation of the Democratic Peace Proposition.* Columbia: University of South Carolina Press.

Rummel, Rudolph J. 1995. 'Democracies ARE Less Warlike than Other
    Regimes', *European Journal of International Relations* 1, 4: 457–79.
Russett, Bruce. 1993. *Grasping the Democratic Peace*. Princeton University Press.
    2005. 'Bushwacking the Democratic Peace', *International Studies Perspectives* 6,
    4: 395–408.
Russett, Bruce, and John Oneal. 2001. *Triangulating Peace: Democracy,
    Interdependence, and International Organizations*. New York: W.W. Norton.
Silvagni, David. 1893. *Eroi Sconosciuti (Fratelli Archibugi), 1848–49*. Città di
    Castello, Italy: S. Lapi Tipografo-Editore.
Tocqueville, Alexis de. 1850–1/1896. *The Recollections of Alexis de Tocqueville*
    (ed. Alexander Teixeira de Mattos). New York: Macmillan.
Tommasini, Stefano. 2008. *Storia avventurosa della Repubblica Romana:
    Repubblicani, liberali e papalini nella Roma del'48*. Milan, Italy: Il Saggiatore.
Weart, Spencer. 1998. *Never at War: Why Democracies Will Not Fight One
    Another*. New Haven, CT: Yale University Press.
Whitehead, Lawrence (ed.). 2001. *The International Dimension of Democratization*.
    Oxford University Press.
Widmaier, Wesley W. 2005. 'The Democratic Peace Is What States Make of
    It: A Constructivist Analysis of the US– Indian "Near-miss" in the
    1971 South Asian Crisis', *European Journal of International Relations* 11,
    3: 431–55.

14   The promise and perils of global democracy

Richard A. Falk

Why global democracy now?

Reading the chapters comprising this volume filled me with admiration for the conceptual and social science rigour, conceptual clarity and sophistication of the individual undertakings, for the illuminating depictions of several ways to frame global democracy as goal, process and vision, and, finally, for the attention given to transition pathways seeking to bridge the gap between global governance as of 2011 and some realization of global democracy at an undetermined, and undeterminable, future date. As such, these authors have delivered a superb intellectual tool with which to study present and future international relations from a normative standpoint specified by their shared preoccupations with global democracy. This is a notable pedagogic achievement as it lays claim to an alternative paradigm for study and research that is not completely state-centric, and yet at the same time cannot be dismissed as utopian or mere advocacy. In this respect, the orientation of this global democracy scholarly gathering can be described as proceeding from a post-Westphalian consensus that is fully sensitive to the resilience of sovereign states, and to their continuing prominence in almost any achievable global democratic polity.

As reader and sympathizer I believe there is a significant, and likely illuminating, issue present that does not seem to be raised: why has this interest in global democracy flourished now in the early twenty-first century, and rarely earlier except in the marginal literature of utopian critics of a politically fragmented world order that built security and national interests on the foundations of an ever more menacing and expensive war system. World federalists, dreamers and proponents of world government, were the most notable antecedents to the sort of less structurally and constitutionally driven models of global democracy found in the various chapters. Unlike these authors, world federalists were typically amateurs with regard to social science, and almost totally Western in outlook and prescription. Quite often world federalists were unabashedly seeking a world order that generalized the American experience with domestic federalism, relying for persuasion on an argumentative logic that was unduly confident about the mobilizing potential of common sense and rationality. It seems only slightly unfair to characterize such advocacy as a legacy of the Enlightenment, culturally provincial and lacking in mass appeal *even in the West*, and indifferent to the political obstacles that beset any path from the 'here' of war and sovereign states to the promised land of 'there'.

Let me venture a hypothesis: earlier surges of global reformism were essentially post-war phenomena in relation to the two great wars of the twentieth century. World War I struck many as the death knell of a balance-of-power world, causing many million deaths for no discernible worthwhile human end, prompting Woodrow Wilson and others to insist on finding an institutional arrangement that would put an end to war. The League of Nations was posited as the means to such an end. It turned out to be too much for a state-centric world that was unwilling to participate in such a scheme, with even the United States awkwardly refusing to join the organization that its wartime president had so ardently promoted as the best way to overcome the curse of war and militarism. Contrariwise, the League blueprint was too little for those that believed only a genuine world government could tame the militarist tendencies of sovereign states and a subculture of arms merchants. As we know, the League failed miserably when it came to coping with the re-emergence of war and conquest, and the world drifted into a disastrous second world war.

Unlike World War I, World War II seemed to most as if both necessary and desirable, defeating Fascism and aggression, and even holding the surviving leaders of defeated Germany and Japan accountable as war criminals. Yet future war avoidance was nevertheless very much part of the political consciousness after 1945, especially catalyzed by the atomic attacks on Hiroshima and Nagasaki, and the resulting widespread belief that a third world war would destroy civilization, perhaps permanently. Major warfare had to be prevented for the sake of the powerful as much as for the benefit of the weak. Two elements of this outcome are relevant to the normative narrative of global democracy that gives coherence to this volume. The first is the renewal of the impulse to institutionalize peace and security, giving rise to the United Nations (UN), which also was constituted in such a way as to be related to sustaining economic stability through the establishment of the so-called Bretton Woods institutions (World Bank, International Monetary Fund, with a much later extension to trade, World Trade Organization). Second, and most relevant, implanting constitutional democracy in each of the defeated countries with the objective of building stable, moderate and economically robust political actors on the ashes of Nazi Germany, Fascist Italy and Imperial Japan. In most respects, the UN failed, at least if envisioned as the transformative force implied by the Preamble to the Charter, which grandiosely promised 'to save succeeding generations from the scourge of war'. To the extent that a third world war was avoided, this was mainly a result of an old-fashioned geopolitics combining prudence and some luck. That geopolitics was given the new name of 'mutual deterrence' so as to seem responsive to the radical impact on world politics of nuclear weaponry.

Here again the post-war efforts at global reform had a complex relationship to a state-centric world order. The UN was in many respects a child of the Westphalian understanding of global society as constituted by sovereign states, and managed by those states that were dominant in 1945. The importance of granting the victorious powers in World War II a right of veto in the Security Council was a dramatic recognition that the repudiation of aggressive force, the core commitment embedded in the charter, was not meant to override or do away with the discretionary authority of geopolitical actors to use force and wage wars. In this sense, the primacy of geopolitics was reasserted in the charter itself, and the danger of nuclear war was either repressed or supposedly managed via the rationality of deterrence, and, in this respect, a militarist component of the Enlightenment legacy. These five states with a veto power (and their friends) were given a constitutional exemption from the discipline supposedly being imposed on the system as a whole. In the lead up to the Iraq War George Bush Jr. pushed this geopolitical logic so far as to claim that the UN would itself lose relevance if it withheld support from the United States in its unshakeable resolve to wage aggressive war against Iraq. As we know, the US government went ahead, with its flimsy coalition of the willing, and the UN failed to condemn the attack, much less organize collective action in support of Iraq's right of self-defence, and even seemed ready to pick up the pieces afterwards by cooperating with the occupation of the country.

But the other reformist undertaking, implanting democracy to achieve a *restorative* peace, had a much more enduring effect that seems also relevant to the growing interest in, and support for, global democracy.[1] The extraordinarily impressive economic recovery of Germany and

---

[1] In contrast, after World War I Germany was subjected to a punitive peace by way of obligations to pay reparations to the victorious powers and to renounce any option to rebuild its military capabilities. This approach was widely believed to have contributed significantly to the rise of Hitler in Germany. Also, the related view was that authoritarian governments are more inclined toward war. Significantly, in the ceasefire imposed on a devastated Iraq after the First Gulf War (1991), a regime of harsh sanctions maintained for 12 years seemed to represent a punitive peace, an approach thought to have been discredited on the basis of the Versailles Peace Treaty in 1919.

Japan fostered the belief that there was a correlation between democracy and sovereignty. Also relevant was the idea that fostering a tradition of *international* human rights was important to discourage the sort of failure by the liberal democracies to do more than they did to oppose the genocidal policies of Nazi Germany. A consensus gradually took shape throughout the world with respect to governance on the domestic level that presupposed both adherence to democracy and respect for human rights. Governments felt obliged to give lip service, at least, to these twin normative pillars, regardless of the often anti-democratic and oppressive patterns of existential governance that persist to varying degrees in all parts of the world. I would argue that 'democracy' became the only legitimate form of governance toward the end of the twentieth century, especially after the fall of the Berlin Wall in 1989, which was quickly followed by the collapse of the Soviet Union. It is also significant that all the successor states to the Soviet Union opted for constitutional democracy, nominally at least, and for the free market, although here, too, there were regressions and deviations in practice. What emerged from the Cold War outcome was this fusion of democracy and capitalism, openly espoused by such phrases as 'market-oriented constitutionalism' used to identify the only acceptable form of governance.[2] Arguably, as the experience of China during recent decades dramatically underscores, if capitalist economic policies are adopted with respect to trade and investment, the constitutional demands for human rights either disappear altogether or are mostly muted. Another quite different example of this dynamic is Saudi Arabia, which makes no pretensions of democracy, and yet finds its legitimacy as a governing process rarely drawn into question. That is, democracy is rhetorically to be preferred, even demanded, but what alone seems indispensable for political acceptability on the global stage is adherence to neo-liberal policies and behaviour.[3] It is this economistic tone given to world politics after the Cold War that casts something of a shadow across the ideological triumphalism associated with the privileging of democracy as the only legitimate governing process for a sovereign state. Some scholarly attention was paid to 'democratic peace' theorizing which crudely informed American foreign policy after the 9/11 attacks, underpinning the claim that enlarging the

---

[2] Undoubtedly, the high point in this ideological trope came during the Bush presidency, clearly set forth in a kind of manifesto: 'The National Security Policy of the United States of America', US Government, Washington, DC, 2002. The first sentence of the covering letter signed by the president was particularly revealing in this regard.

[3] Such a position was explicitly advocated in several influential books by Thomas P.M. Barnett. See especially Barnett 2004 and 2005.

sphere of democratic governance at the level of the state would correspondingly and automatically extend the domain of peace (see Archibugi, this volume, p. 267).

Despite this enthusiasm for democracy as the basis for economic and political viability of states, there was surprisingly little spillover with respect to world politics. The most liberal of democracies were quite comfortable with the lack of popular participation, transparency, accountability and even the rule of law when it came to the procedures and decisions of international institutions. In this regard, operative diplomacy never extended democratic values to global arenas of policy making and contestation. When civil society actors began to attend global policy conferences under UN auspices in large numbers during the 1990s it generally alarmed most democratic states, and especially the important ones. In recent years, such events either have not been held, or, if organized, have been sharply criticized or boycotted, as was the fate of the UN conferences on racism held in South Africa. If democracy globally means, in part, participation from below, more inclusive forms of representation of social forces, greater accountability by those that carry out policy, and increased transparency for the operation of international institutions, then most 'democratic states' are not behaviourally sympathetic to the claims of 'global democracy' no matter what their leaders might say on ritual occasions.

Yet, such an assessment does not answer the question posed at the outset: namely, why is there now emerging a serious social science interest in global democracy as a desirable future for world politics? I believe there are three kinds of explanation each of which could be explored at length, but will only be briefly mentioned here. The first line of explanation has to do with an effort to rediscover a coherent and historically relevant framework for progressive politics, here conceived as dedication to human betterment by actual design rather than by reliance on the automaticity of market forces ('the invisible hand' and the like).[4] Global democracy presents itself as an attractive normative project in the form of a post-Marxist engagement with the classless achievement of a more just social and political order. The second line of explanation overlaps with the first, but it involves an insistence on *political* agency, and a repudiation of a purely economistic approach to change, reform and revolution. A central, rarely expressed motive seems to disentangle politics from its Marxist and neo-liberal immersions that always depict political economy scenarios as the inevitable wave of the future. More vocationally, the motive may also be to reclaim some of the policy-relevant ground from

[4] My own effort to think through this puzzle from an angle different to, although congenial with, global democracy is presented in Falk 2010.

economists who have been so influential in the formation of national policy for the past half century. The third, and possibly decisive, line of explanation is the political recognition that globalization is generating a need for global authority structures and norms to facilitate effective responses to global-scale challenges such as weaponry of mass destruction, global warming and world poverty. If these structures are not democratically constituted, then either hegemonic or imperial solutions will be forthcoming, doing severe damage to overall human well-being, or a dysfunctional chaos will ensue, also causing devastation and massive suffering. In effect, such reasoning insists that global steering mechanisms are increasingly needed, and it seems preferable that these should be shaped by democratic values and procedures.

My intention is not to be reductive with respect to the contributors in this volume. There are many diversities in style, substance and methods, which overall is a strength, in presenting global democracy as a rich body of evolving thought that is becoming more nuanced through reliance on empirical observation and a willingness to construct abstract models of global governance.

Should we privilege global democracy?

In conceiving of a just world order should we presuppose that some form of global democracy must be realized, or do other modes of political belief deserve serious attention? I would have liked to have read a chapter that was devoted to such an inquiry, a discussion evincing more sensitivity to civilizational and ethical diversity, and either championing the exclusive consideration of global democracy or opting for a wider range of normatively desirable world order solutions.

I appreciate that several authors represented here are sensitive to the perils of global political centralization, even if constitutionally based on separation of powers and maximal decentralization of authority and capabilities. But sensitive or not, there seem to be serious dangers that any realization of global democracy in the near future would fall captive to either world capitalist machinations or to schemes for global empire once power and authority are centralized so as to achieve globally beneficial results. In effect, even if global democracy might be accepted as the most desirable basis of world order, it could still be too vulnerable to appropriation by anti-democratic and exploitative forces to be favoured due to the risk averse. The same concern arises with respect to regionalism, but less insistently, as it is not based on the organization of the whole. A regional form of world order remains pluralist even if the parts are larger, and likely stronger, and probably provides greater opportunity for political embodiments of 'regional democracy' to give more expression to distinctive regional values, traditions and priorities.[5]

It is important not to introduce the difficulties associated with democratic states into the consideration of global democracy. At the same time, it seems likely that any foreseeable pathway to global democracy would involve the passive or active participation of leading states, especially the United States. There are claims that US global leadership is already a nascent form of global government that provides other governments and the peoples of the world with many global public goods.[6] I find this sort of political agency for global democracy disquieting within the current configuration of world social forces, introducing an excessively militarist version of security and predatory capitalist outlook into global policy forums.

In this respect, might it not be important to explore whether, for very large political groupings, some other form of political organization might not work better even if its actualization seems remote: let's say a Council of Nobel Peace Prize winners providing a kind of global policy oversight within a political framework that could be regarded as a form of 'moral hegemony' or 'normative oligarchy'?[7] And might it not be worth considering a radical localization of power and authority that, in effect, repudiated the assumptions that central guidance in some form was an unavoidable effect of modern technologies and the apparent ineluctable momentum of ever greater fragility, complexity and interdependence?

There seems to me to be a need to draw into critical question the normative horizoning of global democracy from a variety of perspectives: effectiveness, achievability, acceptability, sustainability, community, citizenship, justice and non-violence. I realize that such explorations exceed the scope of what is being undertaken here, but it colours any assessment of global democracy as purportedly the only desirable political future and amounts to a proposal for future inquiry and research.

In search of history and context: the loneliness of the social scientist

As someone trained in law but teaching for decades in a social science environment of a liberal arts college, I appreciate the prodigious efforts

---

[5] For a well-developed argument along these lines see Paupp (2009). See also Gould (this volume).

[6] This position has been most elaborately, albeit rather uncritically, espoused by Michael Mandelbaum (2005, 2010).

[7] Although it is important to take account of the significant argument of Fredrik Heffermehl who argues that many recent Nobel Peace Prize awardees do not reflect the values of peace or the vision of Alfred Nobel. See Heffermehl (2010).

in recent years to establish an empirically grounded and conceptually sophisticated epistemology for the study of issues of global scope. The contributions to this volume confirm the importance of this enterprise, but they also generate some concerns that touch on what sorts of knowledge are useful to achieve the best possible understanding of world order policy options. There are three sets of issues responsive to these concerns that I wish to raise in the spirit of constructive dialogue.

When talking about 'global democracy' the speculative nexus is embedded in analogic reasoning because such a political set of circumstances has never existed. As such, the normative advocacy is inherently speculative – that is, without any experience that we can learn from, either positively or negatively. Derrida often spoke about 'democracy to come' as a way of expressing the unrealized but realizable potential of democratic political arrangements within sovereign states. Of course, he also implied, without using the terminology of 'global democracy', that aspects of benevolent future democracies would show great respect for international law, and particularly for the stigmatization of crimes against humanity, in carrying further the ideas of accountability launched at Nuremberg.[8] It seems to me that when, if ever, the leadership of major states are socialized to the extent of submitting their foreign policy to the discipline of international law and the procedures of the UN, a major precondition for transition to global democracy will have been satisfied. In effect, since we cannot speak about the future with experiential authority, it is important to be attentive to antagonist behavioural patterns on the part of the dominant actors that inform international relations practice, particularly geopolitical actors who continue to insist on relying upon unrestricted self-help as the foundation of their security, including even extending to claiming a unilateral and unregulated option to wage preventive wars.[9] We can have an important discourse on the geopolitics to come, but unless we are sensitive to the geopolitics that persists, there will be a utopian disconnect between advocacy of global democracy and the actuality of global militarism.[10]

A second concern in my view insufficiently addressed in this volume has to do with the particularity of global challenges associated with the presently emergent historical moment. The shape of problems such as climate change, proliferation, possession and possible use of weaponry of mass destruction, and pandemics involving deadly disease are substantive contingencies of such a magnitude as to condition the kind of

[8] See Borradori (2003, 110–24).
[9] For perceptive exploration of these issues, see Doyle (2008).
[10] For one attempt to depict a geopolitics to come, see Falk (2006).

political futures that seem likely and desirable under an array of quite conceivable happenings. In other words, one plausible array of scenarios for a dramatic political rupture from state centrism would involve a response to a condition of global emergency generated by perceptions of an imminent or existing catastrophe that cannot be dealt with by traditional mechanisms of crisis management. Would a move toward some variant of global democracy be more or less plausible under such circumstances?

A third concern relates to agency, and the unlikelihood that entrenched national elites would voluntarily cede participatory rights and accept accountability procedures implied by the establishment of global democracy on a foundation of global law and constitutionalism. If this concern is particularized to take into account the role of geopolitical actors, insistent on their rights of veto at the UN and resting security on a logic of non-accountable self-help, the prospect of moving toward global democracy, unless possibly in the altered atmosphere of a post-catastrophe global setting, seems currently inconceivable. The prevailing political consciousness of the publics in major states is still infused with such a deep attachment to what continues misleadingly to be called 'realism', but is much better understood as dysfunctional 'militarism'. This background condition makes any mobilization of civil society on behalf of global democracy difficult to envision at this stage of global history.

The main contention here is that theorizing about global democracy needs also to be rooted in the historical experience of change during the past several centuries and to be explicitly attuned to contextual variables that might provoke ruptures or, put differently, the advent of the unexpected.

In essence, social science research on global democracy needs to become more substantive, as well as being attentive to empirical testing, normative hopes and conceptual alternatives.

A concluding thought

Theorizing at the global level is in its infancy. Until very recently, serious political theory in the West almost always was state-centric, and was predominantly preoccupied with internal state–society relations. The global realities surrounding the state were regarded as a realm of acute chaos (Hobbes, Machiavelli) or relative anarchy (Bull and 'the English School'), and not viewed as being of great intrinsic interest or relevance. Theorizing about global democracy remains ambiguous as to whether it is postulating a rupture with the Westphalian framework (as embodied, for instance, in the UN Charter) or some kind of normative extension by way of institutional innovations (world parliament, global taxing system, compulsory participation in the International Criminal Court and International Court of Justice). That is, global democracy, in theory, could come about incrementally, with a cumulative effect that is dramatic, or it could be the consequence of a constitutional leap of faith at a given moment in time, unlikely as a rational coming to terms with globalization but possibly as a trauma-induced adjustment to an emergency or unmanageable crisis.

No matter how the reflections on the global future are situated, the *idea* of global democracy is rapidly becoming more than a manifestation of utopian imaginaries. This volume demonstrates that global democracy is staking serious claims as to its relevance for political theorizing about the future. Whether global democracy becomes a *project* to be realized in addition to an *idea* to be delimited is essentially unknowable at present. Whether global democracy should occupy the *entire* horizon of desire for humanity deserves debate and further exploration. And whether the horizon of desire can or should be separated completely from horizons of feasibility (what seems politically attainable at present) and horizons of necessity (what seems necessary to address severe global challenges to security, sustainability and stability) requires both conceptual clarification and ethical judgement. What can be said with confidence is that as citizens in the troubled early period of the twenty-first century we need to act, think and feel globally and normatively, whatever we decide to do locally and personally.

REFERENCES

Barnett, Thomas P.M. 2004. *The Pentagon's New War Map: War and Peace in the Twenty-first Century.* New York: G.P. Putnam.
    2005. *Blueprint for Action: A Future Worth Creating.* New York: G.P. Putnam.
Borradori, Giovanna. 2003. *Philosophy in a Time of Terror: Dialogues with Jürgen Habermas and Jacques Derrida.* University of Chicago Press.
Doyle, Michael W. 2008. *Striking First: Preemption and Preventive War in International Conflict.* Princeton University Press.
Falk, Richard A. 2006. 'Renouncing Wars of Choice: Toward a Geopolitics of Nonviolence', in David Ray Griffin, John B. Cobb Jr., Richard A. Falk and Catherine Keller (eds.), *The American Empire and the Commonwealth of God: A Political, Economic, Religious, Statement* (pp. 69–85). Louisville, KY: Westminster John Knox Press.
    2010. 'Anarchism without "Anarchism": The Search for Progressive Politics in the Early Twenty-first Century', *Millennium* 39, 2: 381–98.
Heffermehl, Fredrik. 2010. *The Nobel Peace Prize: What Nobel Really Wanted.* Santa Barbara, CA: Praeger.

Mandelbaum, Michael. 2005. *The Case for Goliath: How America Acts as the World's Government in the Twenty-First Century.* New York: Public Affairs.
   2010. *Frugal Superpower: America's Global Leadership in a Cash-Strapped Era.* New York: Public Affairs.
Paupp, Terrence Edward. 2009. *The Future of Global Relations: Crumbling Walls, Rising Regions.* New York: Palgrave Macmillan.

Index

9/11, 277

Abizadeh, Arash, 106
accountability, 8–9, 11, 13, 17–18, 22, 28,
    30–1, 34–5, 42, 70, 72, 94, 97–9,
    102–3, 110–11, 116, 136, 148, 154,
    177, 183–6, 189–92, 194, 196,
    199–202, 205, 207, 210–14, 218–20,
    222, 224–7, 244, 278, 281–2
  corporate, 184, 190
  democratic, 190–1
accreditation, 216–17
activists, 10, 12, 14, 161, 177–8, 184, 191–2,
    195–7, 200–1, 205, 221
Adams, Gerry, 134
advisory bodies, 217
advocacy, 1, 19, 198, 206, 219, 221, 223,
    225, 274–5, 281
Afghanistan, 139
Africa, 134–5, 138–9, 142
African Court of Justice and Human
    Rights, 142
African Peace and Security Architecture, 141
African Union (AU), 16, 139, 141–2, 144,
    146, 148
African Union Commission on Human and
    People's Rights, 142
agency, 15, 23, 49, 59, 88, 123, 125, 143,
    164–5, 174, 189, 191, 223, 241, 278,
    280, 282
agenda-setting, 54, 218, 221
Agné, Hans, 27, 210
Ahlenius, Inga-Britt, 132, 134, 136
Aksu, Esref, 6
Albin, Cecilia, 85
Alien Tort Law, 201
alienation, 243, 245
all-affected principle, 15, 32, 34, 39, 47,
    50, 73, 90, 110–11, 117, 123, 126,
    211, 213, 224, 227
  affectedness, 47, 50–1, 55, 119, 126,
    204, 206

Allende, Salvador, 262
all-inclusive principle, 54
Alter, Karen, 218
American Civil War, 261
anarchy, 141, 167, 173, 282
Andean Court of Justice, 219
Anderson, Elizabeth, 51
Anheier, Helmut, 28
apartheid, 137, 139, 245, 263
Appeldoorn, Bastiaan, 233
Arafat, Yasser, 134
Archibugi, Alessandro, 254–7
Archibugi, Daniele, 3, 23, 26, 97–8, 136,
    150, 160, 173, 185, 210, 233, 236–7,
    246, 254
Archibugi, Francesco, 254–7
Arndt, H.W., 240
Asia, 134, 139, 184
Asian Development Bank, 218
Association of Southeast Asian Nations
    (ASEAN), 119
associative democracy, 27–9
Athens, 184, 263–4
Atkinson, Will, 246
AU, see African Union
Aurobindo, Sri, 235, 251
Austro-Hungarian Empire, 255
authoritarianism, 128, 165, 174, 260, 263,
    265, 267, 270–1, 276
authorization, 8–10, 136, 203, 212,
    214, 223
autonomy, 4, 17, 23, 27, 29, 40, 47, 49, 51,
    55, 62, 76–7, 100, 118, 124, 137, 141,
    154, 185, 187–90, 192–3, 195, 198,
    204, 206, 261
Aztecs, 269

Babst, Dean, 260–1
Bäckstrand, Karin, 213
Balkans, 134
Bank of International Settlements, 217
Baratta, Joseph, 40

285